Ten Years of CLA*rity*

A compilation of articles from issues of the CLA*rity* newsletter published between Spring 2007 and Holiday 2016

Ten Years of CL*Arity*

All articles, artwork, poems, and cartoons in this book originally appeared in issues of CL*Arity*, the Clutterers Anonymous newsletter, from the Spring 2007 issue through the Holiday 2016 issue.

CL*Arity* Team

The CL*Arity* Team makes all decisions regarding the CL*Arity* newsletter, includng when and where to print articles, need for and composition of Editor's Notes, and final proofreading of the newsletter. All edits are done with at least two people. The members of the CL*Arity* Committee have changed through the years. This list comprises all those who were on the team between 2007 and 2016.

Alison B., New Jersey
Andrew S., Maryland
Betsey K., New Jersey
Gloria S., New York
Jan G., California
Kathy H., California
Parker, Nevada
Ruthe S., Pennsylvania
Wendy L., Illinois

Contributors

Contributors are those who helped edit articles or wrote a series of articles over many issues.

Carol N., California
Dove, Washington
Karen, California
Lauren R., New Jersey
Marcia R., New Jersey
Marie M., New York
Nancy D., California
Rick M, Maryland
Tannette, Pennsylvania

CL*Arity*, 184 South Livingston Avenue, Suite 9-203, Livingston, New Jersey 07039
CLArity@CluttererersAnonymous.org
(866) 402-6685

Introduction

Welcome to CLA*rity*, the newsletter of Clutterers Anonymous. Whether you are a new reader or have been with us for some time, we hope that you will gain inspiration, knowledge, and solace from these pages.

This book consists of articles written during the first ten years of CLA*rity* production—from the Spring 2007 issue through the Holiday 2016 issue. We largely omitted "News Flash" articles and announcements, except for a couple of cases where we deemed the announcements were worthy of future notice.

For ease in finding certain subjects, we sorted the articles by topic, rather than publication order. Within each section (or subsection), the articles are laid out in chronological order.

CLA*rity* is produced entirely by CLA volunteers; all entries are written by members, and all editing, proofreading, typesetting, and layout is performed by members. If you are interested in writing an article, CLA*rity* would love to hear from you.

At CLA*rity*, we welcome feedback, so please let us know what you think. Also, we are interested in hearing about groups that use CLA*rity* in their meetings. How is that working out for you?

Happy reading!
The CLA*rity* Team

Notes

Several articles refer to CLA telephone meetings. Since the writing of these articles, meetings may have changed focus, meeting dates and times, phone numbers, and access codes. For current information, check the "CLA Meeting Directory" at ClutterersAnonymous.org; send a letter to CLA WSO, PO Box 91413, Los Angeles, CA 90009, requesting the latest Meeting Directory; or call (866) 402-6685 and leave a message.

Some articles list duties and requirements of officers of the CLA World Service Organization (WSO). These requirements, duties, and positions may change from time to time. For an up-to-date listing of officers, along with the requirements for and the duties entailed in these positions, go to ClutterersAnonymous.org>Members>WSO Officers.

Be aware that other information may have changed since articles were written; check for up-to-date information using one of the contact methods listed above. This information includes, but is not limited to: price of literature and CLA*rity* and WSO committees (whether they are active, as well as meeting times and phone access information).

Interested in writing an article for CLA*rity*? Send it via email to CLArity@ClutterersAnonymous.org or via postal mail to CLA*rity*, 184 South Livingston Ave., Suite 9-203, Livingston, NJ 07039. For a listing of article columns and further information, see the section on "Guidelines for Submission of Articles" on page 305.

CLA*rity* is produced entirely by members for the CLA Fellowship, upholding all 12 Traditions. Names on articles submitted will be withheld upon request, and only first names and last initials or pseudonyms are ever used.

MD denotes the state of Maryland, not medical doctor.

Table of Contents

Twelve Steps of Clutterers Anonymous

The Twelve Steps of Clutterers Anonymous are based upon the Steps of Alcoholics Anonymous. They are the basis for the spiritual program of recovery of Clutterers Anonymous. Some of these articles contain an intellectual discussion of the Steps; others are written from the personal experience of the author.

Step 1

Twelve and Twelve—Step 1

Spring 2007
Rick M., MD

Some Thoughts on the 12 Steps…

Step 1. *We admitted we were powerless over clutter—that our lives had become unmanageable.*

Many people in our society have heard of the 12-Step program of Alcoholics Anonymous. Since the 12 Steps can effectively be used to deal with so many problem behaviors, other 12-Step Fellowships that have sprung out of this movement have applied them. Happily, we of Clutterers Anonymous have found that we can apply these principles to our cluttering problems.

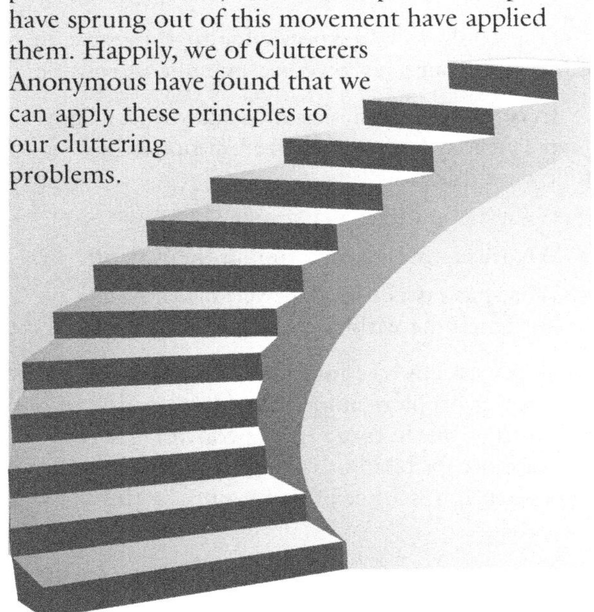

But what exactly is the 12-Step program? In this, and upcoming issues, I will share some thoughts on each of the 12 Steps. In this issue, I will focus on Step 1 of the 12-Step program. What does it mean when we say, "Our lives had become unmanageable"? A person suffers negative consequences from the addictive behavior in many areas of his or her life. Some of the areas where life becomes unmanageable to one extent or another may include physical, spiritual, mental, emotional, financial, legal, family, and social problems.

CLA literature addresses the physical and emotional nature of our cluttering problems in this way:

Physical: This is the behavior that results in the stacks, the piles, and the objects that fill our home, our car, our workplace, and our world. Whether organized or strewn about, it is all so overwhelming. We find ourselves drowning in a sea of clutter. We have become owned by our possessions.

Emotional: "This is the fog we create in our heads—resentments, unfinished thoughts, emotional baggage, daydreams, worries about the future, regrets about the past. Our mind is a contstant spin; we lose today because our time is spent living in yesterday and tomorrow." (from the CLA "Welcome"[18] leaflet)

The first Step is not just intellectual in nature. It is also the emotional acceptance that one is unable to remain in control of oneself when under the influence of alcohol, drugs, or other addictive behaviors. Step 1 is a **surrender** step. We might ask ourselves, "Why does the 1st Step start with the word "We"? Why doesn't it say, "I admitted...'?"

The wording suggests that none of us can handle this problem by ourselves. We already tried, to no avail. But **we** can do together what we cannot do alone.

Spiritual: Twelve-Step philosophy suggests that people participate in addictive behaviors to fill a spiritual emptiness. Our literature puts it this way:

"This is the deep emptiness we feel inside—the emptiness we compulsively try to fill by clinging to useless objects, nonproductive ideas, meaningless activities, and unsatisfying relationships." (from the CLA "Welcome"[18] leaflet)

A spiritual problem requires a spiritual solution. We will address this in our upcoming discussion of Step 2.

Working Step 1

Spring 2007

Alison B., NJ

When I swallowed my shame and stepped into my first meeting of CLA at the end of 2002, I had 18 months of urgent paperwork on my kitchen table and 3 months of mail that I was scared to open. I learned to admit every day that I was completely powerless over my mail and that my life had become unmanageable. Papers were piled in bottoms of closets: "memorabilia" from when I was young and photos I'd been meaning to sort.

The dishes were always piled high in the sink; I hated washing them. I was so defeated over my dishes. I had, maybe, 20 loads of laundry, and the "junk" room had clothes covering the floor. I admitted I was powerless over my laundry and my excess clothing. I was 40 pounds heavier. Well, I could admit I had no power over food, I had done that before! I was in debt, with creditors calling, and I was terrified to answer the phone. I hit bottom over money. What a dilemma! I was addicted to cigarettes but hated them. I found out I was really powerless. I needed help there!

I am variously addicted to: not enough/too much sleep, singing, reading, acting, TV, computer (another clutter area!), relationships (big one!). I have the potential to be an alcoholic, drug addict, gambler, compulsive spender, and perfectionist. I have time management clutter, mind clutter, and—like the 12 Steps say—physical, emotional, and spiritual clutter. Is it any wonder I have too much stuff?!

I remember from many 12-Step programs I've attended over 20 years, all require "abstinence"; so the more I strive for abstinence in all areas, the easier it is to "abstain from new clutter." I commit every week at my meeting to opening mail and doing dishes daily, among a variety of decluttering tasks, in both my life and home. I use a timer to break chores down. That in itself is a huge improvement! But now I'm going beyond Step 1, the only non-action Step.

For today, I follow the Steps and Traditions and Tools[19] to the best of my ability. Today I am a beginner again.

Step 1

Spring 2007

Joyce S., MD

Step 1 asks us to acknowledge that, because of our clutter, our lives have become uncontrollable.

In order to determine our readiness to take Step 1, it may be helpful to reflect upon the following questions:

- What has cluttering cost me?
- What has my clutter gotten in the way of?
- What has my clutter deprived me of or burdened me with?

Step 1 asks us to admit that we cannot solve our clutter problem alone. Also that because of our clutter, our lives are out of control. We can get support for taking this Step from the group or a sponsor, but neither of them can take this Step for us!

Are you ready to take Step 1? The long journey through recovery begins with that first Step.

Steps 2 and 3

Twelve and Twelve–Steps 2 and 3

Summer 2007
Rick M., MD

In the last issue, we discussed our powerlessness over clutter and how our life became unmanageable as a result. We will now explore the role spirituality plays in our recovery towards clarity.

Step 2: *Came to believe that a Power greater than ourselves could restore us to sanity.*

What is the insane thinking that keeps us stuck in our clutter, or returns us back to cluttering behaviors even after we've supposedly cleaned up our act? Our literature addresses this in a passage from "What Is Clutter?†"[22]

"No matter how we deal with our clutter, it can be a source of pain and shame to ourselves and to those we live with...." (This is the unmanageability we experience as a result of our clutter.)

"Despite this pain, we fear throwing things out. We think we might need it, fix it, or wear it again. We don't want to be wasteful or ungrateful. We don't know what to keep and what to discard. We don't know how much is enough."

If our own thinking is insane in regard to clutter, then what will restore us back to sanity? This is where a Power greater than ourselves comes in.

For a long time, our addiction was our Higher Power. Whatever our Higher Power is, it must be bigger than us, and powerful enough to help us in our recovery. It could be the God that we learned about from our religious institutions. Or, it could be *higher ideals and principles—honesty, purity, love*, etc. It could be the CLA Fellowship, or the 12-Step program as a whole. We could define our Higher Power as GOD (= Good Orderly Direction). What we really need to know about God is that there is one and we are not it!

If we believe, or are even *willing* to believe, that there is something bigger than us that can restore us to more sane ideals and actions, then we have successfully taken Step 2.

Step 3: *Made a decision to turn our will and our lives over to the care of God as we understood Him.*

What does it mean to turn our will and our lives over to this Power? Another way to understand this idea is to equate "will" with our thoughts, and "lives" with our actions. When we turn over our *will* and our *lives* to our Higher Power, we are turning over our *thoughts* and our *actions.*

Turning over our will and our lives (our *thoughts* and *actions*) is an act of humility. Humility is not the same as humiliation, although it may feel like humiliation to our inflated egos. Humility is putting our Higher Power's will before our own. Though we make decisions about the actions of our lives, we must leave the results to God. The burden of our having to run the world is lifted.

When we are ready, we say a prayer. You may use any words you find personally meaningful to you. Many people like to use the Serenity Prayer—

God, grant me the serenity to accept the
things I cannot change,
Courage to change the things I can,
And wisdom to know the difference.

We have now completed Step 3. We must continually remake the decision to turn it over on a daily basis. How do we follow through with our decision? First we have to clear away the clutter that gets in the way of our relationship with our Higher Power. We accomplish this by doing a thorough housecleaning. We do this by taking Steps 4 through 9, which we will discuss in future issues.

Working Steps 2 and 3

Summer 2007
Alison B.,NJ

My Experience, Strength and Hope (ESH)

I originally started going to 12-Step groups 23 years ago. It took two years before I noticed I was spiritually aware. At first I considered myself agnostic, not to mention "terminally unique" mentally. In my religious background were many differing sects, and my family barely followed any doctrine, so I always felt like a hypocrite as far as God was concerned. Growing up, I embarked on a religious quest that seemed to raise more questions than answers. I was forever looking for something that appeared to be beyond my reach.

My spirituality is ever-evolving. At this point I have decided that I am fully integrated with the intelligent entity that shapes all molecules. It may be above my total comprehension, but I feel it, always. I call it the Universal Power. It works for me. I can call UP any time because I am always connected. I feel it expects me to become my highest self, but knows I make mistakes along the way, and stays with me, despite that.

The Universal Power speaks to me through people and all sentient beings. Though I often seek opinions and affirmations from others because of my low self-esteem, which is gradually healing, I have learned that when I trust my instincts I have an innate wisdom which could only come from that Universal Power. All of this speaks to Step 2.

Step 3 teaches me that I am "responsible for the input and not the outcome," so on a daily basis, I do the best I can and then pray to "give it UP!" It is stress-releasing and frees me from much anxiety and guilt. I have discovered that I seek permission even to go ahead and do my best. This must be a clutterer's trait! Well, I know one thing: there's only one way for me and that's UP..."with a little help from my friends!"

Step 4

Twelve and Twelve–Step 4

Fall 2007
Rick M., MD

Housecleaning Steps (Part 1)

Before we move on to Step 4, let's take another look at Step 3.

Step 3—*"Made a decision to turn our will and our lives over to the care of God as we understood Him."*

There is a riddle that is often heard in 12-Step meetings when discussing Step 3 or the 12-Step program. Three frogs are sitting on a log that sits over the surface of a stream. The frog sitting on the left-hand side of the log decides to jump into the water. How many frogs are left sitting on the log? The answer is three. If your answer was "two," you probably know how to add and subtract. What you may not have considered is that "Lefty" only made a *decision* to jump. He didn't actually do it!

Step 3 doesn't require us to turn our will and our lives over to the care of a Higher Power. All it asks us to do is make a decision. How do we follow through on that decision? By taking the rest of the Steps.

Even though we may try to turn things over to our Higher Power, we find that we keep taking our will back. In order to "let go and let God" more effectively, we need to find out what's getting in the way and get it out of our lives. That's where Steps 4 through 9 come in. We call these the "housecleaning Steps."

Step 4—*Made a searching and fearless moral inventory of ourselves.*

When I was younger, I used to work at the local minimart. One of my responsibilities was to go in the back and take stock of our milk. Any milk dated past three or four days had to be thrown out, and new milk had to be ordered. If we sold bad milk, we'd go out of business!

In the same way, we are being asked to take a look at our personal assets and liabilities. We want to find out what personal strengths we have that will help us in the recovery process. Even more importantly, we want to look at the thoughts, actions, and beliefs that are getting in the way of our having a more sober, sane and serene relationship with ourselves, our fellows, and our Higher Power.

The "Big Book"[4] of Alcoholics Anonymous, and other 12-Step texts, suggests that we get down to causes and conditions. It gives us a method to look at conflicts we have had with ourselves, our family and friends, institutions, and ideas. We look at our resentments and fears. What caused them? Low self-esteem? Lack of safety? Financial insecurity? Emotional insecurity? How about our personal relationships? Our ambition level?

Usually when there is a conflict, it takes two to tango. So we look at *our* part in these problems. In what ways were *we* dishonest? Selfish? Self-centered? Inconsiderate? What role did fear play in all this?

It is suggested that we put this all down on paper, so we can see it in black and white. Once we can identify what we need to clean up in our lives we can move closer to the spiritual attributes of honesty, purity, unselfishness, and love.

My Step Four: Grounded in 1, 2, 3

Fall 2007 and Spring 2010

Anonymous

Doing my current 4th Step is one of the most exciting things I've ever done. How does that happen? How does a spoiled, envious, controlling girl get the humility and guts to look at her wrongs? In a word: grace. Another: HP. And, for me, Step 4 is not possible without 1, 2, and 3.

This journey began in an unlikely place: a steamy NYC subway, August 2006. My life was not going well. As I surveyed my fellow commuters—people I knew not at all, mind you—each was found lacking. I recoiled. The problem, of course, was mine. My mind was a cesspool of negativity, judgment, and ceaseless discontent posing as thoughts. Ruin—or insanity—lay ahead if I continued and, as I climbed the dingy, crowded stairs, I thought: "I've got to get a sponsor and do Step 4." How appropriate. On those steps, that day, Step 1.

Though I looked and listened and called, a sponsor didn't appear until February, when crisis prompted a reinvigorated search. (Funny how tragedies bring us to our knees, to willingness, to HP.) And we didn't start the Steps until late April. But the delay only made me more eager.

The cornerstone of this journey, for me, is Step 2 and finding a "good" HP. How did that happen? Short answer: by reading "We Agnostics" (the AA Big Book's[4] first 164 pages is our lodestar) and willingly following every single suggestion from my sponsor.

Next came the 3rd Step prayer.* Though I had memorized it in 1990 and loved its promise, the surrender it required terrified me. Finding a "good" HP in Step 2, however, dissolved resistance. Kneeling on my sponsor's living room carpet, I was amazed as each word tumbled easily from my lips, no reservations, and I experienced a trust never felt before that moment.

Even though inventorying my wrongs seems a small price for the glorious promises of the program, this sinner is lucky that Step 4, the Big Book way, starts with listing our resentments, the juicy part of the task. Before we've recovered, reveling in how "they done me wrong" is such fun. Of course the book also says that if we stay there, we go back to "hell." But, at the start of Step 4, one gets to wallow!

Today, about halfway through Step 4, a curious thing is happening. I am seeing—without regrets—how often I resent people for merely being themselves, how my extreme anxiety leads me to feel I literally cannot survive unless everything happens as I think it "should," and how I get angry with people for doing the very things I do myself. And each admission that spontaneously springs from my defogging brain brings a sense of calm, like it may be possible to live a fabulous life. What magic.

Nowhere near finished, not knowing where I'll be at journey's end, I do know three things: For an arrogant addict to begin to see her part in so many situations is nothing short of miraculous. Had I not come to believe in a fabulous Higher Power, none of this would be possible. The fleeting glimpses of the tranquility available to those who fearlessly and thoroughly do this work are glorious.

My final words: "Come on in; the water's more than fine."

For another article on this topic, see the Literature section, pages 85 and 86).

Step 5

Twelve and Twelve–Step 5

Holiday 2007

Rick M., MD

Step 5—*Admitted to God, to ourselves, and to another human being the exact nature of our wrongs.*

As we write out our searching and fearless moral inventories of ourselves during our 4th Step, we are already admitting to ourselves and God the exact nature of our wrongs. But why is it important to share it with another person? The principal reason is that if we neglect to take this major Step, we may not be able to overcome our cluttering behavior.

The "Big Book"[4] of Alcoholics Anonymous (Fourth Edition) puts it this way:

> ...*Time after time, newcomers have tried to keep to themselves certain facts about their lives. Trying to avoid this humbling experience, they have turned to easier methods. Almost invariably they got drunk. Having persevered with the rest of the program, they wondered why they fell. We think the reason is that they never completed their housecleaning. They took inventory, all right, but hung on to some of the worst items in stock. They only thought they had lost their egoism and fear; they only thought they had humbled themselves. But they had not learned enough of humility, fearlessness and honesty, in the sense we find it necessary, until they told someone all their life story.* (A.A., p.72, para. 2, lines 9-13; p.73, lines 1–10)

To be totally honest with sanother person about the flaws in our makeup can be very scary. So, we must choose carefully who we are going to ask to listen to our 5th Step. Ideally, our sponsor would be the person we would share our story with openly. We can also choose a therapist, clergy member, or trusted friend. Anyone chosen to listen to our story has to be closemouthed, trustworthy, and supportive. He or she must agree to never discuss our inventory with anyone else.

Another aspect of 5th-Step work that is specific to our clutter is sharing with another person the extent of our clutter. This means trusting someone enough to allow that person into our home and personal space, no matter how bad it might seem. When we get our secrets out, they lose their power over us.

Sharing our 5th Step with another person serves three functions—confession, clarification, and connection.

Confession—We're only as sick as our secrets. The longer we hold on to these secrets, the more they eat us up. Getting these things off our chest can provide us with a release from the inner turmoil that we have been prisoner to.

Clarification—As honest and thorough as we may try to be, we're only human. It is helpful to share our inventory with another person. That person can give us feedback on things we may not have noticed about ourselves. Another person may help us see our faulty thinking more clearly. We may also learn more about strengths we didn't even know we had. As we tell our story, certain patterns begin to emerge. What character defects keep showing up? These are the things we want to move away from. What strengths keep showing up? These are the things we want to move toward.

Connection—This is the Step that makes us feel connected with the human race. Once we have finished sharing our inventory with another person, we find that the person actually still likes us! What a relief! Often the person we have shared our inventory with may share some of his or her own experiences. We find out that we are just "not that good at being bad." We are just imperfect people who did what we knew how to do best in order to survive in the world. Now we have a chance to stop doing the things that are no longer working for us, and practice doing things that will benefit ourselves and others.

We will continue with our housecleaning in our next issue, when we discuss Steps 6 and 7.

Reflections on the 5th Step

Holiday 2007

Carol N., CA

The first time I did a 5th Step (in another 12-Step program), I expected there to be some sense of turning a corner, as if the act of "confessing" what I had written in my 4th Step would magically make things different. I expected my happiness quotient to increase dramatically.

I was torn, conflicted—not wanting anyone to really know about me, because if they did, they might want to "make me shape up." I was comfortable. I wanted a new life, but I didn't know how much I was willing to change to get it. But I did go through the motions, because that's what the 12 Steps say to do. I vaguely remember my then-sponsor reading the passage from the A.A. Big Book[4] that comes just after Step 5.

After the initial boost of well-being, I was vaguely disappointed to find it didn't last. I wanted permanent peace. And I wanted to feel it now. Years later, I understand more about the process of it all, the surrender, the beginning of faith, the transfer of trust to a Higher Power, the need "to clean house"...and the need to tell someone else. It says in the Big Book[4] that until this is done, the program is largely theoretical. That is so true.

This time around, the 5th Step I did was a combination of Steps 4 and 5. I answered questions provided for me from an inventory guide, one a day, and gave my sponsor the answers every day instead of waiting to dump them on him. I rather like that way of doing it; I feel it is less brutal. I also received immediate feedback while it was fresh in my mind. My happiness quotient has been raised slowly, but more solidly.

Steps 6 and 7

Twelve and Twelve–Steps 6 and 7

Spring 2008
Rick M., MD

In Steps 4 and 5 we began cleaning house by taking inventory—what we wanted to get rid of and what we wanted to keep—in order to lead a more orderly life. After discussing this with another person, it is time to let go of the things that are no longer serving our recovery from addiction to clutter. Steps 6 and 7 are about willingness and change.

Step 6—*Were entirely ready to have God remove all these defects of character.*

During the 4th Step, we identified our assets and liabilities; then we shared them with another and God in the 5th Step. In the 6th Step, we make the preparations necessary to turn these shortcomings over to God.

What are character defects? They are all traits that keep us from the "sunlight of the spirit." The problem in working Step 6 has to do with willingness. Are we ready to let go of those things that keep us from the "sunlight of the spirit"? After all, these are the things with which we are most familiar. Some of them were actually fun! More importantly, we have attached our identities to these character traits. Our unwillingness to change has to do with fear. Fear of change is what keeps us clutter addicts holding on to so many useless relics from the past. As long as we hold on to these old familiars, nothing will change, and we will continue to be robbed of the rewards of recovery.

On page 76 of the "Big Book"[4] of Alcoholics Anonymous, Fourth Edition, it says: "Are we now ready to let God remove from us all the things which we have admitted are objectionable? Can he now take them all—every one? If we still cling to something we will not let go, we ask God to help us to be willing."

If we are not *entirely* ready and don't feel *entirely* humble, that's okay. This is a program of spiritual progress, not spiritual perfection. In the meantime, we can at least start practicing the virtues.

Step 7—*Humbly asked God to remove our shortcomings.*

Step 7 is where we actually begin to make the changes. It is a straightforward Step, consisting of a prayer where we ask God to remove our liabilities and strengthen our assets so we can be of maximum service to all.

This prayer is found in the second paragraph of the "Big Book" on page 76. It reads:

My Creator, I am now willing that you should

have all of me, good and bad. I pray that you now remove from me every single defect of character which stands in the way of my usefulness to you and my fellows. Grant me strength as I go out from here to do your bidding. Amen.

What we are trying to do here is to declutter ourselves of self-centeredness, that we may allow spiritual centeredness into our lives. We are letting go of dishonest motives and behaviors, so that we have room to live honestly with ourselves and others. We release our resentments to have room for forgiveness and love in our lives. We do not allow fear to control our thoughts and actions. We begin to move toward the actions of faith, courage, hope, and love. In this way, we let go of the inner turmoil, so that we may experience peace, love, and serenity in our lives. Once these changes have been made from the inside, we will have an easier time decluttering our outside environment.

Still, in order to have a fully clean house, we must get rid of the wreckage from our past. We do this in Steps 8 and 9, the "Amends" Steps.

My Process: Working Steps 6 and 7

Spring 2008

Jan S., ME

I was asked to write something to explain my "process" of working Steps 6 and 7 and thought, "How do I explain that to anyone?"

I guess by, first, saying it is just that—a process—and it continues to be a process to move up and down the Steps.

The first time I took Step 6, I was in major denial: Why should I have to be ready to have God remove "defects of character"? I had written things in my 4th Step inventory and talked about them in the 5th Step. But, when I am being honest with myself and everyone else, I really was only talking the talk and not walking the walk.

I was totally in my head, and I didn't like the idea I had to be willing; moreover, that I had to "humbly" *ask*? Hel-lo… I was the way I was because of "them," not me.

I was still in the blame game, and I didn't want to take any responsibility for my life. I did a lot of soul-searching and talking with other 12-Steppers in various programs and finally decided that I could be "willing to be willing." And that was where I stalled for a long time. I was willing to be willing, but I wasn't sure what willingness looked like!

Higher Power finally got through and helped me realize that pointing fingers at the infamous "they" was not helping.

I got serious about prayer and meditation and really listening to *God* in my heart. Then, miracle of miracles, I moved out of my head and into my heart, and I really took my Step 6 and Step 7.

It was simple, but it certainly was not easy. I cried, blamed, and railed against it all. I also held on to the Serenity Prayer like a mantra. Then, gradually, glimpses of serenity and recovery appeared.

I have had major recovery moments—and big backslides—over my time in the program; but, when I work my program and listen to my Higher Power, I find I am always moving forward—even in what appears to be abject failure.

I pull out my pictures of what it was like and realize that, yes, I may have been backsliding, but I am not back to where I was. And I, again, get willing and ask God.

As the saying goes, "It works if you work it!" So, Godspeed to all of you, and trust the process.

Steps 8 and 9

Twelve and Twelve: Steps 8 and 9

Summer 2008

Rick M., MD

We began the 12-Step process by surrendering to the fact that we were powerless over our ability to manage our clutter by ourselves. We came to believe that a Higher Power of our understanding could help us solve our problem. Once we decided to allow that power to work in our lives, we had to clean our house, so to speak, in order to make room for a spiritual way of life. First, we had to take inventory of the various manifestations of self-centered fear that were cluttering up our hearts and minds. We shared these findings with someone else and became willing to change. The final part of our housecleaning process is to fix, to the best of our ability, what we have damaged. This is where Steps 8 and 9 come in.

Step 8—*Made a list of all persons we had harmed and became willing to make amends to them all.*

Step 9—*Made direct amends to such people wherever possible, except when to do so would injure them or others.*

The final part of the spiritual housecleaning is to clear away the wreckage of the past. We already made a list of people we had harmed by our actions. We made it in our 4th-Step inventory. Now we must become willing to mend any wrongs we have done to others. This includes families, friends, partners, business associates, creditors, etc.

Some of the people on our list may have done more harm to us than we did to them. But we can't change them; we can only change ourselves. We clean up our side of the street. Making amends can take many forms. Amends, in some cases, may be as simple as making an apology or confession. We may owe money to some people, so we pay off our financial debts. Whatever we do, we don't want to harm the other person in the process.

We should go over our list and discuss it with a sponsor before we take any action. Once we have taken Steps 4 through 9, we will find ourselves in a much cleaner spiritual house. There will be more space to be who we were meant to be. We will have much healthier relationships with others, our Higher Power, and ourselves. Now that our house is in order, all we have to do is maintain it. We do this by practicing Steps 10 through 12, which we will begin to discuss in our next issue.

Working Steps 8 and 9

Summer 2008 and Summer 2011

Gloria S., NY

The 8th and 9th Steps are the culmination of the work done in Steps 4 through 7.

After getting rid of the physical clutter in my life seven years ago when I joined CLA, I turned to the leaflet "Decluttering Resentment: Steps 4–10."[8] It's possibly the best material I had ever seen on the subject.

Step 8: I proceeded to do just that—I took a pad and pencil and listed my resentments. I named names and wrote what happened. When and why and by whom, and then the hard part: identify my part in it. Steps 5 through 7 came next. I was ready to make a list, which was all my sponsor requested of me at that stage. Step 8 is the forgiveness step. I became willing to let go of the anger that was cluttering my heart and soul—to see that others, like me, were not perfect and that although some things would never go away, I could at last let the past go. I was also encouraged to put myself first on this Step list, as I would never be able to forgive others if I was not able to forgive myself.

Step 9: There are many ways to approach Step 9, depending on the situations, and I have used almost all of them. I have gone in person to speak to individuals one on one. I have written notes. Where the person had passed, I wrote a note and burned it or tossed it into the ocean. This Step is about moving on. Sometimes a person wants nothing more than to be left alone. And, that's okay. Sometimes, even with the most heartfelt amends, a person wants nothing more to do with us, and that's okay. Sometimes we are welcomed with open arms, but we don't want to resume the relationship—and that's okay. It has more to do with acknowledging any hurt or harm we may have caused, while letting go of our ego-driven resentment toward them. Amends also means change, and Step 9 is about the change in our attitudes.

Sometimes we need to make amends for the resentment we have for another, while they might not even be aware of how we felt.

An example: I had been jealous of an acquaintance of mine for a long time. She was a beautiful, talented lady, highly regarded in her profession; well-liked by all who knew her. And I resented everything about her. So I asked my sponsor what to do. Should I go up to her and tell her how I feel and tell her I'm sorry? She said no; I have to go out of my way to be nice to her, compliment her, and be of help to her. So I did as she suggested: I amended my attitude and my actions toward her. That was a few years ago. Today, I see her as a genuine, warm, and funny person. I appreciate and respect her. Plus, I have come to treasure her friendship.

For me, Steps 8 and 9 have given me a new freedom and happiness. I have decluttered the burden of rage, anger, and resentments, which had been keeping me in isolation. It rid me of negativity, which was killing my spirit—and it set me free.

Wishing You All Happy Stepping.

Step 10

Twelve and Twelve–Step 10

Fall 2008

Rick M., MD

So far, we have surrendered to the fact that we are unable to manage our clutter on our own. No human can solve our problems. We must learn to rely on a power greater than ourselves. In order to allow this power to help us, we must stop trying to do things our way—it didn't work. We each must learn to get out of our own way. How? By decluttering and getting rid of the messes that we've made—not only of our physical spaces but of our minds, as well.

First, we must take inventory of what we must release. We must be honest and share it with someone else to reduce shame, gain clarity, and find out that we are not alone; we are only human and cannot do it by ourselves. Because of this, we ask God to remove our defects to the extent that we will be able to live happy, sober lives and be of maximum service to our fellows. We then repair any damages we have made so that we can bring harmony back into our lives and the lives of those we have harmed in some way. In other words, we fix what we broke.

Steps 1 through 3 are the "surrender" Steps. Steps 4 through 9 are the "housecleaning" Steps. After we have completed our spring cleaning, it will benefit us to maintain the order we have achieved; therefore, we maintain our "houses" by taking Steps 10 through 12. Let's begin with Step 10.

Step 10—*Continued to take personal inventory and when we were wrong, promptly admitted it.*

Step 10 is essentially working Steps 4 through 9, as well as part of Step 12, on a daily basis. *Alcoholics Anonymous* (The "Big Book"[4]), Fourth Edition, p. 84, gives us the following directions for taking Step 10:

> *Continue to watch for selfishness, dishonesty, resentment, and fear (Step 4). When these crop up, we ask God at once to remove them (Steps 6 and 7). We discuss them with someone immediately (Step 5) and make amends quickly if we have harmed anyone (Steps 8 and 9). Then we resolutely turn our thoughts to someone we can help (Step 12). Love and tolerance of others is our code.*

Basically, we are sentries who must keep watchful eyes over our houses. We must do this if we want to keep our houses in order. If we do not remain vigilant, guess what will likely sneak back in?—our dysfunctional thoughts and behaviors. If we allow this, we could lose everything for which we worked so hard.

We also need to keep our eyes on how we are working the program in general. Are we attending meetings regularly? Are we taking daily actions to keep our physical clutter from taking over? Are we keeping in touch with our sponsors? How are we giving back to the Fellowship?

What methods are we using to minimize physical clutter? Are we using these methods consistently? How are they working for us?

When we are having trouble in any of these areas, we cannot change them by ourselves. That is not the job of a sentry. We need to ask for backup. For us, our backup is our Higher Power and the Fellowship.

The "Big Book,"[4] p. 85, has this to say:

It is easy to let up on the spiritual program of action and rest on our laurels. We are headed for trouble if we do, for alcohol [clutter] is a subtle foe. We are not cured of alcoholism [our clutter addiction]. What we really have is a daily reprieve contingent on the maintenance of our spiritual condition. Every day is a day when we must carry the vision of God's will into all of our activities. "How can I best serve Thee—Thy will (not mine) be done." These are thoughts which must go with us constantly. We can exercise our willpower along this line all we wish. It is the proper use of the will.

In the next issue, we will cover Step 11. Through studying it, we will continue to learn to deepen our own relationship with God.

How I Work Step 10

Fall 2008 and Summer 2011

Gloria S., NY

"Continued to take personal inventory and when we were wrong promptly admitted it."—Step 10

In continuing to work the Steps of the program and making progress on a daily basis, I have found that holding on to anger and resentments clutters me mentally, spiritually, and emotionally. So, I have found it useful to regularly make a short list of my attitudes and actions towards people. I also make note of the way I have spoken to people I have been in contact with. This I do in order to gauge my progress and to make right any possible wrong I might have done in the course of my day. I also do this to see the areas in which I am doing so much better and to build on those accomplishments.

By this time in my recovery, I have found that I can own my part in any discourse, and I want to clean up my side of the track so that I can feel better about myself. This Step has also taught me restraint of pen and tongue, big time. I am more willing to let things go these days, choosing to think, perhaps, this is a bad time or bad day for the other person. I no longer always have to be right. It also has me ever mindful that I am frequently wrong.

Many times my misperceptions led me to react in the most unpleasant ways. I used to say, "I am a reactor." I react to what I think are slights or when things don't go my way. Today, thanks to Step 10, I try to act—and act reasonably and responsibly in all areas of my life. I often fall short of the mark, and when I realize it, I can and do promptly admit it. Correcting the wrong, whatever it was, in the appropriate way, is my way of removing resentment clutter from my life. This Step has been a wonderful tool in my recovery—where I used to have resentments and harbor anger, letting it live rent free in my mind, body, and soul, I now find peace of mind and contentment in decluttering them daily or as soon as I can. This process also has taught me which areas or people in my life I might need to let go.

There is a saying that if you can't practice these principles in all your affairs, you'd best change your affairs. This Step has been invaluable in teaching me the areas of my life that need decluttering.

Happy Stepping.

Step 11

Holiday 2008

Rick M., MD

Step 11—*Sought through prayer and meditation to improve our conscious contact with God, as we understood God, praying only for knowledge of God's will for us and the power to carry that out.*

Having decluttered ourselves of those things that keep us from the "sunlight of the spirit," we are now better able to connect with that source of spiritual help. We do this through prayer and meditation. We define prayer as talking to our Higher Power and asking for help from that power. Meditation implies listening for whatever guidance this power has to offer.

This is a program of spiritual progress, not perfection. So we seek to improve our spiritual connection, to the best of our ability, on a regular basis.

Step 11 was first presented in *Alcoholics Anonymous* (the "Big Book"[4])—the basic text for the original 12-Step Fellowship of Alcoholics Anonymous. The authors knew they had no monopoly on the subject of prayer and meditation, but they made some useful suggestions that are still applied today by those people who have successfully recovered from their alcoholism. How can we apply these suggestions to recovery from our addiction to clutter?

First of all, let's keep in mind that we must continue to turn all of the defective thoughts and actions over to our Higher Power. Without doing this, our heads would be so filled with clutter there would be no room to let God in! So we must continue to take inventory, which we addressed in our discussion of the 10th Step in the last issue. The Big Book suggests we continue this inventory process in our 11th-Step practice.

> *When we retire at night, we constructively review our day. Were we resentful, selfish, dishonest or afraid? Do we owe an apology? Have we kept something to ourselves which should be discussed with another person at once? Were we kind and loving toward all? What could we have done better? Were we thinking of ourselves most of the time? Or were we thinking of what we could do for others, of what we could pack into the stream of life? But we must be careful not to drift into worry, remorse or morbid reflection, for that would diminish our usefulness to others. After making our review we ask God's forgiveness and inquire what corrective measures should be taken.*
> (*Alcoholics Anonymous* [The "Big Book]," p.86, paragraph 1)

Once we have turned these over to God's care, we are free to meet God more directly.

> *On awakening let us think about the twenty-four hours ahead. We consider our plans for the day. Before we begin, we ask God to direct our thinking, especially asking that it be divorced from self-pity, dishonest or self-seeking motives.* (A.A. Big Book, p.86)
> *In thinking about our day we may face indecision. We may not be able to determine which course to take. Here we ask God for inspiration, an intuitive thought, or a decision. We relax and take it easy. We don't struggle. We are often surprised how the right answers come after we have tried this for a while. What used to be the hunch or the occasional inspiration gradually becomes a working part of the mind....we find that our thinking will, as time passes, be more and more on the plane of inspiration. We come to rely upon it.* (The "Big Book," p.86, paragraph 1, pp.86-87)

We [clutterers] are undisciplined. So we let God discipline us in the simple way we have just outlined.

> *But this is not all. There is action and more action. "Faith without works is dead."* (The "Big Book," p. 88)

We will discuss Step 12 in the next issue.

Working Step 11

Holiday 2008

Gloria S., NY

Step 11: *"Sought through prayer and meditation to improve our conscious contact with God as we* *understood God, praying only for knowledge of God's will for us and the power to carry that out."*

Step 11, the meditation part, did not come easily to me—my mind, like my home, had been cluttered for a long time. And decluttering my mind has taken longer than the decluttering of my home and my emotions. For, you see, I am a thinker; I analyze everything, and I store up my thoughts and fears and resentments. I also like to be in control. But, after working Steps 8, 9, and 10, I felt a lot freer. I was able to start on my quest for a true relationship—a partnership with my Higher Power, whom I choose to call God. My God, who has no gender, is all loving, all accepting, and wants only the best for me. Always. This concept in itself took me years to grasp.

They say Step 3 is asking in prayer, and Step 11 is listening for the answer. Being still enough to hear that answer is what this Step is all about. The decluttering of my mind was the goal of this Step work. I needed to be clear enough to hear, to know the truth of the matter for which I sought guidance. There were times in the beginning I really thought I would get the answer loud and clear, that it would be that simple and immediate. Sometimes what I thought was God's voice was really just my own, trying to justify what I wanted. It took me a long time to realize that the answer did not necessarily come right then and there. It could, and did at times, come in the form of an intuitive thought right away. More often it came later, while listening at a meeting or talking to my sponsor or to one of my sponsees. It could happen—while watching TV, talking to people, reading something unrelated—that the truth of the matter and the path became clear. The funny thing was it came when I let go of the demand for the answer or solution, and I knew it when I heard it. I heard the truth. It is just awesome!

So okay—now I have the knowledge, how do I get the power to carry it out? The answer is really so simple: I let God do all the work! He has all the power. All I do is show up, with no attitude, no agenda, no preconceived idea of how to get things done. I get out of my own way. I let go and let God. I let God work through me and get His work done. For you see, today—whatever I do—I do it as if it were service to God. No ego involved, no longer needing to be in charge or to be the star. No fear to paralyze me. Because the outcome is no longer in my hands and I am not in control. I never was. Today I can accept that the outcome, even if I don't like it, is what my Higher Power has in mind. Can I do this, act this way, feel this way all the time? Of course not. I'm not perfect and never will be. I am trying to grow along spiritual lines. The Steps are meant to be taken over and over again. I take them as needed, just like any other medicine. For, to me, the answers to all my problems are in the Steps. The Steps are my daily medicine to keep me clutter free in my mind, body, and soul, and, of course, my home.

Happy Stepping.

Step 12

Twelve and Twelve–Step 12

Spring 2009
Rick M., MD

We have been studying Steps 1 through 11 in this series in CL*Arity*. To review, we saw that our way wasn't working and that our solution had to be spiritual in nature. Once we decided to try the spiritual solution to our problem, we had to follow a course of action. We had to declutter our minds so our souls would have room to breathe and our Higher Power could lead us to better things.

First, we had to examine which aspects of self were getting in the way of our having the spiritual awakening necessary to be freed from the bondage of our clutter addiction. We shared this with God and another person and became willing to let God remove our character defects. We cleaned up the mess we had made and fixed what we had broken. We made restitution to those we harmed through our addictive behaviors. Now that we had cleaned our spiritual houses, we maintained them in Step 10. We now had room to listen for guidance from our Higher Power.

We found, however, that we could not rest on our laurels. This program requires action and more action. We were able to take these Steps because someone in the Fellowship was kind enough to carry the message of recovery to us. We found that in order to keep what we had received, we had to give it away. Now it was time to pay it forward.

Step 12—*Having had a spiritual awakening as the result of these Steps, we tried to carry this message to others, and to practice these principles in all our affairs.*

This Step can be divided into three parts.

- "Having had a spiritual awakening as the result of these Steps…"—This awakening has occurred over a period of time as we have gone through the process of taking the other 11 Steps. It is continual.
- "…we tried to carry this message…"—It is from this principle that the practice of sponsorship evolved. A person who has taken the 12 Steps and has successfully worked the program shares his or her own experiences, strengths, and hopes with someone who has less experience. "In order to keep it, we have to give it away" is a saying that is often heard in 12-Step meetings.
  (*Alcoholics Anonymous* [The "Big Book"[4]], Fourth Edition, page 89) puts it this way:
  > *Practical experience shows that nothing will so much ensure immunity from [cluttering] as intensive work with other [clutterers]. It works when other activities fail. This is our twelfth suggestion: Carry this message to other [clutterers]! You can help when no one else can. You can secure their confidence when others fail….*
  >
  > *Life will take on new meaning. To watch people recover, to see them help others, to watch loneliness vanish, to see a fellowship grow up about you, to have a host of friends—this is an experience you must not miss. We know you will not want to miss it. Frequent contact with newcomers and with each other is the bright spot of our lives.*
  >
  > *The sponsor does not preach to the newcomer. We state the problem, then the solution, and then the plan of action that has been presented in these articles about the 12 Steps. We do this by telling the person our story. We say, "This is what worked for me."*
- "…in all our affairs."—As a result of the growth we have experienced from taking the 12 Steps, we can apply these principles in all our affairs. These include our interactions with our family, friends, neighbors, and associates; those we work with; and our community overall.

I would like to end this series of articles on the 12 Steps with a passage from the "Big Book," page 164. In a chapter called "A Vision for You" the authors write:

> *We realize we know only a little. God will constantly disclose more to you and to us. Ask Him in your morning meditation what you can do each day for the man who is still sick. The answers will come, if your own house is in order. But obviously you cannot transmit something you haven't got. See to it that your relationship with Him is right, and great events will come to pass for you and countless others. This is the Great Fact for us.*
>
> *Abandon yourself to God as you understand God. Admit your faults to Him and to your fellows. Clear away the wreckage of your past. Give freely of what you find and join us. We shall be with you in the Fellowship of the Spirit, and you will surely meet some of us as you trudge the Road of Happy Destiny.*

May God bless you and keep you—until then.

Working Step 12

Spring 2009

Susie S, CA

Step 12—*Having had a spiritual awakening as the result of these Steps, we tried to carry this message to others, and to practice these principles in all our affairs.*

When first asked to write this article, I declined because—although I've completed Step 12 in three other programs—I have not officially worked this Step in CLA. Then I remembered what I have learned in 12-Step Fellowships: Anyone can start immediately working any Step that begins with a digit 1 (meaning Steps 1, 10, 11, and 12). We can all start doing a 10th-Step inventory, do prayer and meditation (Step 11), and be of service (Step 12), no matter how new we are to the program.

I think of Step 12 as having three parts; first is "having had a spiritual awakening as the result of these Steps." I have definitely had many spiritual awakenings, which have helped me to change my life in so many positive ways and have enabled me to create and maintain clutter-free zones in my kitchen, bedroom, car, etc. I have been able to keep my home in such good order that a visiting child recently said "you have a nice house," something I never imagined possible.

The second part of Step 12 is, "we tried to carry this message to others," which is something I definitely love to do. I'm so thrilled with this program that I share about CLA with anyone I feel might benefit from it! I believe that my life's purpose is to heal from my addictions and then inspire others by sharing my experience, strength, and hope. If I were to write a book, it would be titled, "There Is Always Hope," and I love to share about the hope to be found in CLA!

It helps me to see how my experience can benefit others and to know that my cluttering now has had a purpose. Service is so rewarding, whether by sponsoring, leading or sharing at a meeting, or calling a newcomer. As the saying goes, "in order to keep our recovery, we need to give it away."

When I heard that there was a need for a workshop presenter at the Clutter Free Day in Los Angeles (7.5 hours away), I had to overcome my tremendous fear of traveling in order to be of service and was very happy I did so. I was grateful to be able to share my recovery story and "before and after" photos. Being of service has certainly strengthened my recovery.

I feel very fortunate to have a sponsor in CLA and have found it very rewarding to be a sponsor as well. One of my sponsees lives in Jerusalem, which is very interesting, because she is starting her day as I am ending mine!

The third part of Step 12 is "practice these principles in all our affairs," and I definitely strive to do so. I do my best to practice these principles—including honesty, willingness, and service—on a daily basis, in all areas of my life. I encourage us to remember that we can start Step 12 today—even if we are new to CLA.

Other Articles About the Steps

The Importance of Working the Steps

Fall 2009

Rick M., MD

For the past two years or so, I have been offering a series on my understanding of the 12 Steps and how we can apply them to our clutter problems. So when I go to CLA meetings and find very few, if any, of the members of our local Fellowship have actually taken the 12 Steps to recovery, I am greatly saddened. When we go around the room to check in, people often share the small successes they've made with their clutter. I still have to question how much progress is really being made.

Even when significant accomplishments have been made, success is slow and does not seem to last. Why? In Alcoholics Anonymous, there is a saying that "the same man will drink again." What does that mean? It means that unless there has been a significant change in the person from the inside, he or she will end up drinking on the outside. Likewise, if a clutterer does not declutter from the inside, the clutter will continue to exist and grow on the outside.

So why do people resist doing the work that will free us from the bondage of our clutter addiction? Why this lack of commitment? I think many of us suffer from what I like to call "underachieving perfectionism." I think I'm supposed to do this perfectly. I will never be able to meet this standard of perfection, so why try? The 12-Step program is one of spiritual progress, not spiritual perfection. I don't need to do it perfectly. All I have to do is do it to the best of my ability, one day at a time, and continue to practice it in all my affairs. Many of us see the 12 Steps as some esoteric, mysterious thing that we could never possibly accomplish! If I waited to perfect a Step before going on to the next one, I would never get through them in this lifetime. Step 3 is merely about making a decision.

We are clutterers. We tend to complicate things. Hence the saying, "The 12-Step program is a simple program for complicated people." This program was meant to be simple (though not always easy—it required a commitment—something many of us avoid). It is my hope that this article will demonstrate how simple the program really is, if we put some effort into it.

In Step 1, I identify the problem. Once I start acting out on my clutter, I can't seem to stop. I get a physical craving because I've triggered my own body's brain chemistry (such as dopamine and serotonin). When I'm not acting out on my cluttering behaviors, I go through withdrawal from these chemicals. Despite the negative consequences of these actions, I am powerless to stop once I start.

Abstinence from these unhealthy behaviors is obviously my best bet. Then why do I find myself going back time after time? I get uncomfortable in my own skin and forget how bad the consequences of my clutter were. I remember the good feelings I get when I act out on these behaviors. I tell myself, "This time I will control it." Of course my "last time" always seems to become my first time (again!). Once again, I've completely lost control of my behavior once I start.

My life is unmanageable because I can't "manage" my mind enough to act sanely. Sometimes I can control my urge to act out. Sometimes I can't. And I don't know when I won't. It's a futile situation. I've already lost a lot. If I keep going I could end up evicted, fired, bankrupt, divorced, etc., as a direct or indirect result of my addiction to clutter. I might eventually end up dead. I can die a mental, a spiritual, and eventually a physical death (that's the direction I'm heading). That's how serious this disease is!

Step 2 identifies the solution. Despite how bad my problem has gotten, I have absolutely no power over this condition. I've tried everything—therapy, antidepressants, yoga, change in diet, new exercise program. These have been helpful, but they have ultimately been insufficient to keep me from acting out with clutter. There has got to be a Power greater than myself that can and will restore me to sanity. That Power is named God by many.

If we get down to causes and conditions, my main problem is my "self." All of my actions have been based on self-centered fears. This is the root of all my problems. It has kept God out of my life because I think I'm the "director." But life doesn't go according to my plans and I am not at peace. This makes good fodder for another relapse, which I can't afford. Why? I don't want to suffer the negative consequences of my behavior. I don't want to lose any more. I want to live. So I have to make a decision:

Am I going to continue to live life on my terms—or God's terms? Step 3 is not about turning my will and life (otherwise known as thoughts and actions) over to God. It's about making a decision to turn it over to God. If I don't take the rest of the Steps (including Step 12), then I haven't really made a decision to do it God's way because I'm still doing things my way. The problem is I keep getting in my own way. I have to find out what it is about me that keeps cluttering up my path toward a spiritual awakening.

Hence Step 4. This is the beginning of my housecleaning. I must investigate the flaws in my own makeup that keep me from the "sunlight of the spirit." These include resentment, dishonesty, impure thoughts and motives, self-centeredness, and fear. I must look at them honestly and share them with someone in my 5th Step. Once I've identified what they are, I become willing to have God remove this clutter from my mind. If I'm not completely willing, then I pray to become willing. And I ask God to remove them in his own time and in his own way.

Whether or not I want to admit it, I've harmed people whenever I've acted out on my clutter addiction and the self-centered fears associated with it. I have to clear the wreckage of my past. I have to fix whatever I broke to the best of my ability. I have to right these wrongs wherever possible, unless, of course, they would cause further harm to them or others. Not to me. To others. The A.A. Big Book[4] actually says we must be hard on ourselves, not others. We should not shirk from our responsibilities.

By this time, a spiritual awakening should have occurred. I have cleaned my house. There is now room for me and my Higher Power to communicate. I maintain my house in Step 10 by working Steps 4–9 on a daily basis. This way I don't amass any more garbage in my life or anyone else's. I must do this because my sobriety is contingent on the maintenance of my spiritual condition. I cannot rest on my laurels! If I do something wrong, I ask God to remove it and ask for guidance. I share it with my sponsor or someone else in the program to whom I can be accountable. And I make amends if I need to.

I have been purified by this whole process. I no longer carry the heavy heart I once had. When my own house is in order, I can ask God for guidance in prayer. I will then have room to listen for guidance during meditation.

One of the problems in CLA is that, in many places, good sponsorship is not readily available. Persons who have not taken the first 11 Steps are not in the ideal position to sponsor others. We cannot give to others what we don't have in ourselves. If, on the other hand, I have taken the Steps to the best of my ability (again, this is not a program of spiritual perfection but a program of spiritual progress), I have had a spiritual awakening. I realize that I cannot keep this thing unless I give it away. My sponsor guided me through this process and saved my life. Now I have a responsibility to pay it forward. This is how I actualize Step 3—my original decision. If I refuse to do this, then I am still being self-centered, not God centered.

It is in giving that we receive, so I'm being a little selfish when I attempt to persuade people to practice these principles, so I can see others enjoy the same quality of sobriety that I have today.

Peace and God bless to everyone.

Editor's Note: It is important to work the Steps with the help of a sponsor.

Why We Work the Steps

Fall 2011

Kathy H., CA

Every CLA recovery meeting reads (or at least should read) the 12 Steps and 12 Traditions of CLA. Having originally come from another 12-Step program, I am well aware of the importance of doing the Steps. But in my years in CLA, I have been somewhat disturbed to find many members strongly resisting even discussing the Steps. They seem to think they are just an unimportant adjunct—or they just plain don't want to bother.

Once a member told me she didn't want to read the Steps because they were boring. I was flabbergasted. The Steps are the whole basis for our program of recovery—although I am well aware that many of our members don't seem to get that. If they just want to share tips, there are probably other organizations where they can do that. But just sharing decluttering methods does not get to the root of why we clutter—so most of us just end up cluttering again, even if we had been able to declutter in the first place.

I am not trying to say that other programs and methods don't have value; they obviously do for many. But our program is built upon the spiritual recovery to be gained from working the 12 Steps. This does not mean that you can't also use various modalities in your personal life, but they are not the basis for CLA.

Gaining recovery by working the Steps can involve a lot of emotional energy and time. So why do we do it? This is a method which can put us in touch with our Higher Power and with our own inner drives and hangups. It offers us spiritual recovery. In other words, we work on our underlying strengths and weaknesses, our resentments, our motivations, and our fears.

Tips and tricks and organizational methods involve only the surface of things. They do not deal with why we clutter. They do not deal with why we procrastinate. They do not give us the motivation to declutter or tackle the fears that keep us from dealing with our clutter. Learning to trust our Higher Power and keeping our lives on track by working the Steps can do all of this.

We work the Steps with a sponsor, who helps to guide us through them. Generally, this process involves some writing about our feelings, motivations, resentments, etc. Having gone through all 12 Steps, we continue to work them in some form. For instance, I know that I need to focus on the first three Steps every day. In other words, I need to remind myself that I am powerless over clutter and allow my Higher Power to help me recover. When I start thinking that I have it all under control, I tend to slide back into my old ways.

Step 12 does tell us to practice these principles—i.e., the principles embodied in the Steps—in all our affairs. My sponsor has urged me to do two things daily: (1) upon waking, to meditate upon what I need to accomplish that day, and (2) before going to bed, to review the day to see where I went wrong and what I can improve. That way I am able to keep my day on track and also to make amends and correct behaviors when necessary. It helps me to keep in touch with my Higher Power and to remember what it is that I want to accomplish in the long run, instead of putting everything off until the next day. Without working the Steps, I would not have made the decluttering progress that I have. So every day I give thanks for this program.

Working the Steps with a Sponsor

Holiday 2012

Kathy H., CA

The 12 Steps of CLA are the backbone of our program. These Steps, adapted from those first formulated by Alcoholics Anonymous, guide us to improve our "insides." I do believe that without first tackling the underlying issues we have, we will be hard put to make a lasting success in tackling our clutter.

My first experience in working the Steps was in another program. Having begun reading 12-Step literature and talking with others in that program, I had achieved a solid belief in the successes of those working the Steps. I wanted the same serenity they were experiencing.

Not being a religious person and tending to be very literal, I had a bit of trouble initially with Steps 2 and 3—especially since I had begun running from all the well-meaning people preaching their religions at the drop of a hat.

So, my sponsor had me doing quite a bit of writing on these Steps, which helped me eventually to form at least a bit of a relationship with a Higher Power. Also, I resented the words "restored us to sanity" in Step 2. I was not insane, I said. But she made me realize that, although in most respects (including legally and medically), I was sane, it was not sanity to keep expecting a different result from doing the same thing that had not worked. This realization also later helped me tremendously in working my CLA program.

Then I came to Clutterers Anonymous. It took me several years to find a CLA sponsor, partly because I was not aggressive enough in asking. But, eventually, I did find one in a different state, and I began working the Steps once again.

My CLA sponsor had a different approach to his writing on the Steps. His lists of very specific questions, on which I shared written answers, were more focused on practical results. He used a format similar to that of early A.A., which had me going through the Steps within a month or two. Originally, A.A. had members work the Steps before they attended a meeting.

I cannot say which sponsor's approach was more helpful to me. They came at different times in my life, and I probably had different needs each time. All I can say is that both were helpful, but I need to keep up with the process more than I have.

Lately, I have lapsed in talking with my sponsor and have begun thinking of finding another in my area. But isn't that one of our problems in CLA, that there aren't that many willing to be sponsors? I have decided that if I don't find one locally, I will approach the sponsor I had been working with and ask to begin again. I do have faith in him; it's just that I do better face-to-face than on the phone.

Working the Steps can sometimes be easy, sometimes wrenching; but I have always found that, when I do, I am left with more joy and serenity. When I continue each day to work the Steps, my life seems to run much more smoothly.

While I do not formally do Steps 4–9 daily, Steps 10 and 11 do cover working on our inventory and amends more quickly and casually each day.

And I find that I get into trouble if I don't keep giving at least a small amount of attention each day to Steps 1, 2, and 3. I start forgetting that I am powerless over clutter and forget to ask my Higher Power for help. So, for me, taking a few minutes each day to meditate on these things keeps my life on track.

Without working the Steps, I would still probably be swimming in clutter and not be mostly decluttered the way I am now.

Steps and Traditions from a Sponsee's Viewpoint

Summer 2013

Alison B., NJ

A few years ago I had a serious CLA sponsor for approximately eight weeks. He had a group of sponsees and held conference calls to go through the Steps within this short time span. Apparently the original A.A. members had handled the Steps by learning the basics before they even attended their first meetings. We had written homework each week. I became stuck at Step 9, with a list of resentments toward a past boyfriend who wanted me to never contact him again. Of course, it's hard to make amends under these circumstances. All I can do is work on changing myself for the better, and I do try very hard—when I'm not depressed, that is.

I couldn't stay with this sponsor. There were many reasons. One was the mere fact that he was a man—an opposite sex alliance is frowned upon within 12-Step circles. After I met him in person, he did, in fact, push my boundaries. I know I'm responsible for my part in that. So, ex-sponsor, if you're reading this, I totally apologize for my own piece in that incident, which unfortunately caused me to judge you in a very negative way before I was able to let it go. I know I cannot afford to carry a resentment, so I did try very hard to continue the relationship. But it was obvious to me, at least, that this quandary was getting in the way.

Then there was the time when I tried an arrangement where two of us sponsored each other. Every day we would spend one free minute saying hello and checking in with our feelings. Crosstalk was allowed, but only for that one minute so that we could get it out of the way. Then we spent seven minutes each making that day's commitments and reporting on the previous day. In retrospect, that was more like a "buddy" partnership. I have not met that person. That one lasted about three months. I wanted all the energy to be focused on me, which is why it didn't work for me. And she wanted the same thing for herself. That was upsetting because I had wanted to delve into the 12 Steps on a deep level. Eventually we were going to do that.

Incidentally, the Traditions have been ingrained in me due to my service work at WSO. We have to use them to figure out how to do the "next right thing" for the group and to educate the Fellowship about them. I used to think they were incredibly boring and useless. Now I am in awe of them and how, if they are followed properly, teamwork becomes intriguing and even fun at times. Not only that, I have found I can apply them to my personal life!

When I became chairperson of WSO, I found a woman on the phone lines who sponsored many people as a hobby. She sent me, by email, her version of working the 1st Step. It was too complicated for me. It wasn't her fault. She had to make it up herself. I did not stay with her, so the sad truth is that for much of my leadership time I did not have a sponsor. We in CLA desperately need our own Steps workbook, like the ones I have seen in other programs. We can still do them the "Big Book"[4] way, but that version does leave something to be desired for clutterers—an inventory of physical items, for one thing. My own belief is that we have to start from the unofficial Step Zero, which is to "put down the clutter." What do you think?

The Importance of Steps 1-3

Fall 2014

Kathy H., CA

Some time ago, a CLA member expressed the view that the Steps may not work for clutterers because—since Step 1 states that we are powerless over clutter—it implies there is nothing we can do to recover. That might have some validity if we stopped with the first Step. But doing so ignores the other 11 Steps. When working a program, we immediately follow Step 1 with Steps 2 and 3—acknowledging that our Higher Power can help us to recover from cluttering, and allowing him to help us.

Step 1 is important because it requires us to acknowledge the fact that we are clutterers. When we do not recognize that we have a problem, we see no need to deal with it and experience no recovery.

For many years before I came to CLA, I used to make sporadic efforts to clean up my clutter. I would set goals and sometimes even begin working on them. But I would never be able to stick with it, and the clutter got worse.

It was only when I admitted to myself that I was powerless over my disease that I started attending CLA (which I had known of for a few years). Without the realization that I was unable to lick the problem on my own, I would still be in despair because of the clutter. So I started attending meetings and working the CLA program, and gradually the situation began to improve.

Step 1 has been very important to my recovery from cluttering, and I often find I need to work it daily. When things are going well and I am able to keep up with the chores in my life, it is so easy to feel that I have the problem licked. I begin to ignore the clutter (physical and nonphysical), and it seems to magically appear again. The piles start accumulating, bills do not get paid, and I begin ignoring my health needs.

When that happens, I find it helps to stop and remind myself that I have this disease which leads to the clutter and that I am powerless over it when left to my own devices. But I don't stop there! That is the time I most need to turn to my Higher Power for guidance. For me, this includes meditating, attending meetings, bookending, talking with my CLA buddies, and putting attention on my ultimate goal.

Our literature has a sentence that I love: "Discipline is remembering what we want." To me, this means that I must keep my ultimate goal in mind and not give in to the momentary urges that stand in the way of achieving that goal. I believe I am attuning to my Higher Power's guidance when I do this, and it brings a sense of joy and satisfaction. In other words, I realize my Higher Power can help me, and I make the decision to turn to him for help.

Twelve Steps FAQs

Spring 2013

Kathy H., CA

I came to CLA for help to stop cluttering my house and my life. Every week in my meeting, we read the 12 Steps of CLA. What do those have to do with my clutter?

The CLA program has its "Tools of Recovery,"[19] which aid us in dealing with our clutter. We can work with a buddy, find support in meetings, read the literature, and so forth.

But most of us have found that, unless we work on our insides, we cannot change our actions for any length of time. In other words, until we deal with our emotional and spiritual issues, we are unable to deal with our outer manifestations of clutter.

The 12 Steps are a spiritual approach to working with ourselves and a sponsor to solve those inner problems that lead us to clutter. They are the heart and soul of our program of recovery.

I know this is true in my case. For years, I read every article I could find on organization. I read self-help books. I made resolutions not only to reduce the clutter, but to keep up on the maintenance—put things away, clean regularly, etc. However, I wasn't able to keep any of these resolutions for any length of time. Habits are hard to break—and let's face it, my primary problem is procrastination, so I always tend to put things off.

When I came to CLA, I made some progress, just by attending meetings and trying to incorporate the Tools,[19] including networking with a CLA buddy. But I made greater strides in dealing with my clutter when I began working the Steps with a sponsor and striving to incorporate them into my daily life.

What does it mean to "work the Steps"?

Most people work the Steps with the help of a sponsor. Generally, the sponsee will write about each Step in succession, often as answers to a list of questions provided by the sponsor.

There are many different lists of questions used in 12-Step programs. Sometimes, the sponsor will ask for a more general, open-ended way of studying each Step—in other words, what the Step means to the sponsee and how he or she is using it to change behaviors.

Then the sponsee will share this writing with his or her sponsor. The sponsor will give feedback and answer questions. This continues through all the Steps. But working the Steps is not a one-time action. A long-time 12-Stepper has usually worked the Steps all the way through several times.

Working the Steps (especially 4–10) has often been difficult, but the changes in my life have made it well worth it. Each of my sponsors varied in approach—one asking me to write about the Steps in a more general way, the other directing me to write answers to a set list of questions. Both methods gave me some help in improving my life and gaining serenity.

There are those Steps I work every day, to keep my focus on my program and maintain my serenity. They are Steps 1–3, which remind me that I am powerless over clutter but that my Higher Power can help me. Also, I briefly touch on Steps 10 through 12. I review my day each evening to see what I can change, I admit when I am wrong, I work on improving my relationship with my Higher Power, and I try to carry the message of recovery to others.

When I remember to work the Steps each day and keep my program firmly in mind, I accomplish more and am able to maintain my serenity.

Summer 2013

Kathy H., CA

I've heard members say that they work Steps 1, 2, and 3 to deal with issues in their lives. What does this mean?

Step 1 says: *We admitted that we were powerless over clutter—that our lives had become unmanageable.*

Step 2 says: *Came to believe that a Power greater than ourselves could restore us to sanity.*

Step 3 says: *Made a decision to turn our will and our lives over to the care of God, as we understood God.*

The first three Steps are a foundation for working the rest of them successfully.

Take Step 1. If I do not admit that I have a problem, I will do nothing to solve it. When things start going well and I am taking care of my clutter, it is so easy to start thinking that I have the problem licked—and when that happens, I slip right back into my cluttering ways. So I need to remind myself daily that I have a problem with clutter in order to deal with it.

Steps 2 and 3 are related. I can't turn my life over to a Higher Power without first believing that my HP will help me. These two Steps have always been the most difficult for me. I am not a religious person and have trouble trusting in something I can neither see nor hear. Although I worked on trying to define my Higher Power, that has always eluded me. I have found, however, that it works for me to "act as if." I don't try to decide who or what my Higher Power is, I just have to listen to that bit of guidance, and somehow it works for me (when I let it, that is).

Without listening to this guidance, I start drifting and become lost.

How will working the 12 Steps benefit me?

Our physical clutter is an outward manifestation of an inner spiritual and emotional problem.

Without working on our inner problems, we are unable to deal with the clutter for any length of time. I know that for years before I came to CLA, I kept trying to deal with my clutter. Sometimes I would have great success for a week or two, only to fall back again. There were times when I believed that learning better ways of organizing would solve my problem, but that wasn't enough.

I have benefitted in many ways from working the 12 Steps. I have been able to find a Higher Power to lean on, which has helped me to rise above my problems of procrastination and lack of motivation to some extent.

While working Steps 4 through 9, I have been able to clear away some of the old mental garbage by looking closely at my resentments—including finding my part in them and dealing with that—and also seeing where I needed to make amends and doing so. Dealing with resentments and making amends has freed up some of the clutter in my mind, leaving me more free to live my life and deal with other problems.

It is a truism that when you teach something, you learn it better. It seems to be the same with recovery. Step 12 not only says to continue practicing the principles of the program, it also tells us to carry the message to others. It is this principle which underlies so much of the program. We find that when we help others, we help ourselves. So we work with other CLA members, as well as giving service, to aid our own recovery. I know it has worked for me. It helps to keep my mind on the program, on my Higher Power, and on my recovery.

But why do I need to find a Higher Power to trust in, anyway? I have read many books and articles on organizing. I have devised methods for controlling my clutter. I have promised myself that I would no longer be so messy. But those things alone never seem to work for me. They never helped me with my problems of procrastination and losing motivation. This is where I need the support of the CLA program, the Steps, and a Higher Power to lean on. These have made all the difference in my life.

Fall 2013

Carol N., CA

Will working the Steps conflict with my own religious beliefs?

It is natural to feel threatened by the thought that something will be imposed or forced upon oneself. Some feel strongly about religious beliefs. Feeling threatened, we naturally resist.

The founding fathers of A.A.'s 12-Step program realized that this fear might be a stumbling block to many people. Although many of the first 100 were Christians, they wanted to construct guidelines that were broad enough to include all faiths, even those that took no position on faith or religion.

The phrase, "God, as we understood Him," was added to the 3rd Step. This meant that any believer could apply program principles to his or her behavior, using his or her own concept of God, and be confident of a positive result, provided that they continued the practices outlined in A.A.'s 12 Steps.

But what about the unbeliever? Could a person who doubted or outright disavowed the existence of a supreme being still have a chance at recovery? Many people seeking recovery have chosen to rely on something outside of themselves without referring to that something as God. That something is often another person (sponsor or buddy), the power of the group, the forces of nature, or even Good Orderly Direction. These can give focus to a struggling newcomer, while also offering a feeling of safety and support.

The founding fathers also took the focus off pleasing a God, or gods, who might be either punishing or benevolent, and put it on what seemed to work for them: the cosmic laws of cause and effect.

These principles have been taken from many past cultures that have been applying parts or all of them through the ages. What the Steps do is forge a specific path.

There is something for everyone in working the Steps, whether one has an established faith or not. Still, it does require a bit of faith to even begin, to believe that recovery is possible and that it can be for you, too.

Can the Steps work for me if I have no belief in any deity or religion?

Yes, because CLA is not based on any particular religion. It is a spiritual program based on many concepts, some seemingly religious, associated with "religion," but which are, in reality, very practical. Belief in a deity is not a prerequisite for realizing you are going down a path you don't want to be on and deciding to change direction. However, this is easier to do with the help of others and a reliance on something other than only ourselves.

The word "God" is first mentioned in Step 3 (regarding turning our will and our lives over to the care of) and mentions "God as we understood God." This is after coming to believe in a power greater than ourselves, that could restore us to sanity. The mention of God in the following Steps can be as broad as you want it or need it to be. It is still understood that we're talking about a power outside ourselves—something we can lean on and rely on.

Also—in addition to Supreme Being—the word God, or small g (gods), is defined as an image of a deity, idol, or any deified person or object.

When I put my trust in clutter, I am giving it the same power over me that a personalized deity would have. I trust deep down that my clutter will somehow make things better for me. It is even the answer to all of life's problems. It isn't until I'm willing to let my Higher Power guide my life, at least in part, that things do noticeably change.

Holiday 2013

Kathy H., CA

Can I work the Steps without a sponsor? Will working them with a buddy help?

It is always recommended that you work the Steps with a sponsor. A sponsor is a CLA member who has already worked the Steps and is willing to help guide you in working your own program.

It is difficult to work the Steps successfully on your own. Those few I know who have tried it have had little success. I know that I have gained so much more when working with a sponsor. Sponsors not only help you with your Step work and listen to your inventory, they also provide an ear to listen to your problems, especially your problems related to clutter. Most members call their sponsor at frequent intervals—daily, weekly, etc. Since many of us have busy schedules, some sponsors and sponsees have worked out set times for the sponsee to call. Of course, even if you have a sponsor, outreach calls to other clutterers at any time are always helpful.

There are those who have been unable to find a sponsor and have worked the Steps with a buddy. If the buddy is just providing a sounding board for your Step work, it can be of some benefit—but nothing like the relationship between a sponsor and sponsee. A buddy isn't a replacement for a sponsor but can provide some good value in working the Steps and can help to give emotional support.

It is worthwhile to put forth the effort to find a sponsor. Without a sponsor's aid, working the Steps can be less productive. If you are totally unable to find a sponsor, a buddy may help until you do find the sponsor.

I have found it difficult to find a sponsor in CLA; is the Fellowship doing anything to help with this issue?

Sponsorship is an integral part of a 12-Step program. Actually, the idea is a part of Step 12: "…to carry the message to others." The importance of this was realized after the founders of Alcoholics Anonymous found that, even though they had followed all the other Steps, they were unable to stay sober unless they helped other alcoholics to do so. In other words, we help other clutterers (which includes sponsoring them) in order to maintain our own recovery from clutter.

Unfortunately, CLA has not developed a strong pool of sponsors. Sometimes it is easier to find CLA members who have sponsored in another 12-Step program and are willing to guide CLA members through the Steps. It seems to be a recurring cycle: If we had more sponsors, we would have more sponsees, who would then be able to become sponsors.

Possibly another cause of the dearth of sponsors is a tendency on the part of many clutterers to overcommit, which makes them shy away from other commitments. Also, our procrastination often plays a role: "I will do it later," but later never comes. And there is the problem some of us have when we feel unable to do things, even when we are capable.

Members of the CLA Fellowship have often discussed the problem of lack of sponsorship. Two solutions which have been considered are holding sponsorship workshops and writing literature on sponsorship. Actually, such literature is high on the agenda for the CLA Literature Committee—but it does take a long time for literature to get written and approved, so it may be a while before it makes it to print.

Do you have any ideas on how to jump-start more sponsorship in CLA? If so, please share them with the rest of the Fellowship. You can use any of the contact methods listed in the front of this book.

Spring 2014

Kathy H., CA

What would help me work the Steps?

Working the Steps is not always easy, but it can be a path to joy, serenity, and freedom from the chains of the subconscious mind.

What would help most in working the Steps? Doing it with the aid of a sponsor and learning to rely on your Higher Power. To get any real benefit from working the Steps, it is important to be open and honest with oursleves.

Generally, working the Steps involves writing about them. Until the Literature Committee publishes a workbook on working the Steps, many sponsors use material from other 12-Step programs to guide their sponsees in working the Steps.

Most sponsors use a series of questions, while others have few questions but use a more open-ended writing format. If a sponsor does not seem to be working out, try to find one who's more suitable. At present, CLA has few members who sponsor, and it may take some effort to find another one, though it is well worth it.

How much benefit we get from working the Steps depends largely on ourselves. If we answer questions or write about the Steps in a superficial way, we may gain little. If we are willing to search deeply for our answers and be honest with ourselves, we may gain an amazing sense of freedom and joy. The biggest keys are honesty, openmindedness, and willingness. Most people in this and other Fellowships have to go through the process of working the Steps many times during their lives, each time being able to learn more and gain greater freedom.

However, we don't work the Steps once, be cured, and then never need to visit them again. In order to get the benefit, ultimately we need to continue with Steps 10 through 12—meaning we use them daily. In other words, we continue to take a quick daily inventory, admitting promptly when we are wrong, seek to follow the will of our Higher Power, and carry the message to others. It is through this continuous daily use of the Steps that we attain true peace and contentment.

What are the benefits of working the Steps with a sponsor?

It is difficult to work the Steps successfully without the guidance of a sponsor. Perhaps it is partly because there is no quick, cut-and-dried way to work the Steps—which can be seen by the various approaches sponsors use with their sponsees, although almost all involve some writing. Most people need someone to listen when they are struggling through a process which involves searching their innermost feelings and actions. A sponsor is not a therapist, but rather a fellow clutterer who can act as a mentor and guide.

But what is it that a sponsor does for a sponsee?

A sponsor is a person who has experience in working the Steps and is able to guide someone through the process. Since each of us is unique, our feelings and experiences will vary.

Our sponsor can help us to shed light on our underlying issues, which may be holding us back from recovery, and help us to incorporate the growth we have gained from the process into enriching our daily lives.

A sponsor is someone we can trust to talk about our inner feelings and listen to our clutter problems. He or she can act as a sounding board for new insights and ideas. A sponsor is a mentor who will listen when we need someone to talk to. We can also turn to them for feedback about Step and clutter issues. After all, they have probably been through the same problems with clutter as we and can always share their own experience, strength, and hope.

In the next issue, we will give ideas on ways to find a sponsor.

Summer 2014

Susan M., NC

How much should I write when working each Step?

How much you write and how long it takes you to work the Steps is up to you and your sponsor—and your Higher Power. There are no set rules or guidelines. You will work with your sponsor to determine how much detail to include.

One exception is Step 4, where you will have to be fearless and include as much detail as you can. Often, when you feel you are done writing on a Step, it is time for you to move on. The bottom line is that it is individual to your journey of working through the 12 Steps.

*The Third Step Prayer, is from *Alcoholics Anonymous*[4] is commonly known as "The Big Book"

†"What Is Clutter?" is part of the "CLA Meeting Starter Kit[7] and "Recovery from Cluttering: The 12 Steps of Clutterers Anonymous"[14]

12 Traditions of Clutterers Anonymous

The Traditions help with the smooth functioning of the group. They work hand-in-glove with the Steps. It is difficult for members to follow the principles in the Traditions without having had the spiritual recovery embodied in the Steps. The Steps and Traditions are the cornerstone of the CLA program.

Tradition 1

Twelve and Twelve–Tradition 1

Fall 2009
Rick M., MD

Tradition 1—*Our common welfare should come first; personal recovery depends upon CLA unity.*

The long form of Tradition 1 is found in the A.A. *Twelve and Twelve:*[16]

> *Each member of Alcoholics Anonymous is but a small part of a great whole. A.A. must continue to live or most of us will surely die. Hence our common welfare comes first. But individual welfare follows close afterward.*

Page 17 of *Alcoholics Anonymous*[4] (the "Big Book") says:

> *The feeling of having shared in a common peril is one element in the powerful cement which binds us. But that in itself would never have held us together as we are now joined.*

The tremendous fact for every one of us is that we have discovered a common solution. We have a way out on which we can absolutely agree, and upon which we can join in brotherly and harmonious action.

Tradition 1 is based on the concepts of unity and humility. We are a group of individuals who suffer from an addiction to cluttering behaviors. We have tried to stop through our own self-will but were not successful. Our bondage to our clutter was zapping the life out of us. There had to be a way out. Some of us found a solution to our problem—the 12-Step program. We had a common problem. Now we have a common solution to our problem.

We cannot punish members or groups who deviate from the Traditions. There are no "musts," only "oughts." If a person or group deviates from the Traditions for too long, they will naturally suffer the consequences of their behaviors. They are operating on self-will instead of spiritual principles. This lack of humility will lead to further acting out through clutter. If the clutter addiction gives a person enough pain, he or she will hopefully come back to CLA, humbled and willing to work more closely with the spiritual principles of the program.

The purpose of the CLA Fellowship is twofold. One is for the newcomer to gain hope from the old-timers who have found the solution to their problems by working the 12-Step program. Its second purpose is to give old-timers an opportunity to find newcomers to whom we carry the message of the 12 Steps. Groups are formed to carry on our 12th-Step work. In the process, we find we need each other. We can do together what we cannot do alone. If we are clutterers of the hopeless variety, we cannot survive without each other. So, even though the individual is important, because it is the individual who is being helped, we find that the individual cannot be helped without the Fellowship. In that respect, we must learn to sacrifice the desires of our self-will to the desire of the group—humility. By working the 12-Step program within the structure of our Fellowship, we learn to think less of ourselves and relate to God and to our fellows. We realize that we are "a small part of the great whole."

Unity and humility are founded on the principles of mutual cooperation. We must work together or suffer alone. We have a common solution to our mutual problem. That solution is the 12 Steps. We "old-timers" must work together to take the Steps so that we can carry the message to the newcomer. Any CLA group that deviates from this is a 12-Step Fellowship in name only.

Working Tradition 1

Fall 2009

Alison B., NJ

Tradition 1—*Our common welfare should come first; personal recovery depends upon CLA unity.*

I am an officer of the CLA World Service Organization. This year I'm the Communications Coordinator. I love working for the good of the group—and by "the group" I mean the whole of CLA. I've always wanted to "make a difference," and I've begun to realize that I have the capacity to have a profound effect on the growth of this remarkable Fellowship. Am I special? Yes—as special as every individual who takes Tradition 1 (and all the Traditions) of this program seriously. Why is it so serious? Because if we don't stick to it, groups will fall apart. I've seen it happen.

A healthy group has a lot more experience, strength, and hope with which to help the individual. A healthy individual is one whose life has enough balance to give back to the group what has been so freely given—although that, in itself, is not enough. Those of us who feel the call to service must encourage other members of their home groups to give of themselves also and to allow the group to make informed group decisions.

The group that allows its one and only leader to do all the work suffers at the level of the individual. From my 24 years in various 12-Step Fellowships, and my 6 years in CLA, I genuinely know this to be true. I try hard to do the "next right thing" for the good of the group. I truly enjoy knowing that I am amongst those who are also working on themselves and coming together whenever we can to help build a strong foundation for my friends who suffer so much from the energy drain of being clutterers.

I do this because it helps to heal me and because I truly feel that clutterers are some of the nicest, albeit most misunderstood, people I have ever met—and I am one of them! I do it because I struggle, and helping others gets me out of my own way. I continue to learn the meaning of "tolerance for those with different struggles," and it's a practice I adopt daily to counteract the fear and shame issues that I work so hard to overcome.

In order to help with our common welfare, we need to gain experience with Steps, Traditions, and even the 12 Concepts[17]—which I had never heard of before, but they pertain to service. Taken together, all of these embody a way of life that keeps me spiritually, emotionally, and physically balanced, and what is good for me is good for the group. I have learned not to bring in literature that isn't approved by A.A. or specifically written by CLA. If I did that, everybody else would feel they have permission to do it as well, and that way there would be too many choices floating around.

We in CLA have a problem with choices and are here because we know we need to limit them. Let's keep our groups pure, everybody—we are all on the same side here—to carry the 12-Step message of recovery to the clutterer who still suffers.

Tradition 2

Twelve and Twelve–Tradition 2

Holiday 2009
Rick M., MD

Tradition 2—*For our group purpose there is but one ultimate authority—a loving God as expressed through our group conscience. Our leaders are but trusted servants; they do not govern.*

When Bill W., the cofounder of Alcoholics Anonymous, originally wrote about this Tradition in a magazine article in January, 1948, he was assuming that the members of each group had already worked the 12 Steps. In order for God to "express" Himself through the group, the individuals needed to have a spiritual awakening as a result of working the Steps.

It is hard for a group to make spiritually informed decisions if the individuals in the group have not had this spiritual awakening. It is much harder for God to work through people still caught up in the throes of their disease and in their active addiction. Therefore, when a group of individuals who are growing spiritually come together, God can work through each of them in an informed group setting. Individuals sustain growth by working the Steps. They continue to take inventory and when wrong, promptly admit it. They seek to improve their conscious contact with God, asking only knowledge of His will and the power to carry it out. Likewise, a group should continue to take inventory of itself, constantly seeking ways to find what works best for each particular group. Group members ask for God's help during this process.

This being the case, there is no need for executives or directors to run the show. Decisions are made by democratic principles. The A.A. book, *Twelve Steps and Twelve Traditions,*[16] 1981, page 132, says:

> *Where does A.A. get its direction? Who runs it? This, too, is a puzzler for every friend and newcomer. When told that our Society has no president having authority to govern it, no treasurer who can compel the payment of any dues, no board of directors who can cast an erring member into outer darkness, when indeed no A.A. can give another a directive and enforce obedience, our friends gasp and exclaim, "This simply can't be. There must be an angle somewhere." These practical folk then read Tradition Two, and learn that the sole authority in A.A. is a loving God as He may express Himself in the group conscience. They dubiously ask an experienced A.A. member if this really works. The member, sane to all appearances, immediately answers, "Yes! It definitely does."*

Each individual should have an opportunity to be heard on whatever issue is being discussed, no matter how strong or meek the personality. The majority rules on the decision. Ideally, members will respect the decision of the group, whether they had initially agreed or not.

Working Tradition 2

Holiday 2009
Mary P., NY

Tradition 2—*For our group purpose there is but one ultimate authority—a loving God as expressed through our group conscience. Our leaders are but trusted servants; they do not govern.*

This Tradition can seem difficult; but in practice, it provides useful, time-tested guidance for the day-to-day functioning of a CLA group. To people new to a 12-Step program, the 2nd Tradition sounds counterintuitive. In my experience, it can actually work very well.

I first encountered it in, as we say, "another program," the one after which CLA has patterned itself, the one with decades of experience in bringing together very disparate bunches of people who have only the goal of recovery in common.

When I first came to CLA, I had the benefit of having taken the 2nd Step—having found a Higher Power I could somewhat understand and believe in. This made it easier to believe that a group could be and should be under the benevolent guidance of that ultimate authority, a Higher Power. I realize that some people are put off by "the God stuff." I've heard that the Higher Power can be the group itself, or that it can be anything, so long as it's not me.

The CLA group I joined was fairly well-established, and meetings were running quite smoothly. Crosstalk during members' shares was not allowed, and the idea of timing each share was arrived at by group conscience.

Occasionally, someone would bring in the latest book on clutter and ask us to include readings from it or would want to have an outside speaker. The group decided, based on the Traditions, that these were outside enterprises, and we shouldn't include such things during our meetings.

When the facility where we met decided to raise our rent, we decided by group conscience whether we could afford it. Eventually, this group decided to relocate.

After our move, we had fewer people attend at the new location; therefore, a few of us had to take on the role of group leader or chairperson. We've tried to remember to ensure limited terms and rotation of positions.

A person can grow in each servant leadership role and help the group become more cohesive, more in sync. This is how the 2nd Tradition guides us.

We've had to encourage people, without pressuring them, to take service positions. This sometimes means people have occasion to grow beyond their comfort zones, especially if they tend to be shy or retiring.

Previously, I served as secretary and literature person. Personally, I have to fight a tendency to be bossy, and the group has proved a good antidote, providing good practice in principles before personalities (as emphasized in the 12th Tradition).

I'd be lying if I said we all look forward to our group's monthly business meeting. Sometimes things get a little heated, as we discuss some change to our format or procedures. The 2nd Tradition, with its emphasis on the Higher Power, mutual trust, and service, can help us reach our group goals.

Tradition 3

Twelve and Twelve–Tradition 3

Spring 2010
The CLA*rity* Team

Tradition 3: *The only requirement for CLA membership is a desire to stop cluttering.**

In the early days of Alcoholics Anonymous, groups proposed many membership rules. It was found that if all these rules had all been enforced at every group, there would be no members at all! This eventually led to the principle embodied in Tradition 3.

The long form of Tradition 3 (Alcoholics Anonymous, *Twelve Steps and Twelve Traditions,*[16] copyright 1981, page 189) states:

> *Our membership ought to include all who suffer from alcoholism. Hence we may refuse none who wish to recover. Nor ought A.A. membership ever depend upon money or conformity. Any two or three alcoholics gathered together for sobriety may call themselves an A.A. group, provided that, as a group, they have no other affiliation.*

Our desire to stay sober is our membership card. But it is the only reason for us to come together. This is not the sober softball team. We are not the sober bowling league. We are not here because of the quality of fellowship. We walk in the door with a desire to stop acting out in our addictive behavior. It is what we have in common with the newcomer the day he walks in the door.

The following is from "The A.A. Grapevine, Inc.,"[2] copyright February 1948.

> *The Third Tradition is a sweeping statement indeed; it takes in a lot of territory. Some people might think it too idealistic to be practical. It tells every alcoholic in the world that he may become, and remain, a member of Alcoholics Anonymous so long as he says so. In short, Alcoholics Anonymous has no membership rule.*

Why is this so? Our answer is simple and practical. Even in self-protection, we do not wish to erect the slightest barrier between ourselves and the fellow alcoholic who still suffers. ...If we raise obstacles, he might stay away and perish. He might be denied his priceless opportunity.

So when he asks, "Are there any conditions?" we joyfully reply, "No, not a one."

All of us are equal members. Our status is not measured by our profession or our position in life. It is not measured by our CLA service positions. It is not measured by how we are dressed. It is measured only by whether we have a desire to stop cluttering.

We do not wish to deny anyone his chance to recover from compulsive cluttering. We wish to be just as inclusive as we can, never exclusive.

**Editor's Note: This Tradition was originally worded, "The only requirement for Clutterers Anonymous membership is a desire to eliminate clutter and bring order into our lives." It was changed by a vote of the World Service Organization on March 25, 2006.*

Working Tradition 3

Spring 2010

Carol N., CA

Tradition 3: *The only requirement for CLA membership is a desire to stop cluttering.*

When I was new in another program, it took me years to decide that I really belonged there. During that time I clung to Tradition 3 as a way to gain legitimacy within that Fellowship and be able to participate. I had doubts for a long time, but I kept coming back.

I could feel the disapproval of some when they heard my story, but I did have a few supporters—one of whom (a man) said that if the only 12-Step meeting in Timbuktu was Pregnants Anonymous, he'd go. Fortified with that support, I stuck around, tried to work the Steps, got a sponsor, and gradually came to believe.

I was fortunate when I came to CLA in that I already knew I was a "real" clutterer. I didn't need a defense against those who might say I didn't belong. In fact, I had been in 12-Step programs long enough to forget that such prejudice might still exist. And yet, I heard about it soon enough. I heard some say that people had no right to call themselves clutterers when they didn't identify as a physical clutterer, but rather a time clutterer. This kind of talk makes me feel dismayed, as I remember my early time in the other program...it takes some of us longer than others to come to our own truths. Nothing was actively done, though, and this member continued with us for a long time.

CLA is not so old that we have generations of sponsors. I have been to many meetings that attract newcomers, only to find them soon fall away. It would be easy to feel that we should allow only those who are really serious about doing this program. After all, why should we waste our time giving it away to those who obviously don't want what we have? Even if someone doesn't come back to our meeting, it's no indication that they will never come back into a CLA meeting. Or that they reject or haven't heard what we are telling them. They may be just taking a long time to make up their minds. Ideally, group members will continue putting the program out there, no matter what the reaction of the newcomer(s).

That might be said also for the so-called troublemaker. If we really believe that you are a member if you say you are, then all attendees should be treated with respect and tolerance, even if they voice opinions different from ours. The key to having the patience to do this lies in understanding the full meaning of the 3rd Tradition. If every member is able to self-diagnose, we can truly make the person who shows up feel and less like an outsider by being patient.

Can we uphold and forward 12-Step ways without making someone feel unwelcome? I remember a very effective little old lady who got across her point by saying very sweetly, "We don't do that here, dear."—over and over. Then she would take time to talk to the newcomers, and gradually they fell into line. I often think of what someone once said to me...that time spent with another human being is never wasted.

Tradition 4

Twelve and Twelve–Tradition 4

Summer 2010
Rick M., MD

Tradition 4: *Each group should be autonomous except in matters affecting other groups or CLA as a whole.*

With respect to its own affairs, each CLA group should be responsible to no other authority than its own conscience. But when its plans concern the welfare of neighboring groups also, those groups ought to be consulted. And no group, regional committee, or individual should ever take any action that might greatly affect CLA as a whole without conferring with the World Service Organization. On such issues our common welfare is paramount.

Every CLA member should have a home group, which is the group he or she regularly attends. Members are asked to take on service positions (i.e., secretary, treasurer, literature person, delegate for WSO, etc.)

The home group periodically holds a group conscience to vote on important matters that affect the home group and CLA as a whole. Each group has a right to pick the format, its time and location, and its particular focus. Some groups focus on speaker meetings, where a person shares his or her experience, strength, and hope about what it was like before coming into CLA, how bad it became, and how life has changed since working the 12-Step program of CLA.

Some groups choose a topic and hold a Round Robin discussion, where everyone has the chance to speak on the topic. If certain members feel strongly enough against a group conscience decision, they have the right to, and are encouraged to, start their own groups. In the A.A. Fellowship, where coffee and donuts are often served, there is a saying that to start a new group is easy. All you need is a coffee pot and a resentment!

In a sense, Tradition 4 embodies the previous three Traditions. Much of what we have just discussed is covered in Tradition 2, which states that: "For our group purpose there is but one ultimate authority—a loving God as expressed through our group conscience...." Each group conscience pertains to that particular home group. It is independent of all other individual CLA groups.

The paradox, however, is that they are not entirely independent of CLA as a whole. Each group must be careful to consider the effect of its decision on the rest of the Fellowship. It is therefore recommended that each group consult with WSO around any issues that could be considered a potential danger to the integrity of CLA as a whole. Though the group conscience of one group is independent of the other groups, it is important that we continue to bear in mind our first Tradition. Tradition 1 states that: "Our common welfare should come first; personal recovery depends upon CLA unity."

Working Tradition 4

Summer 2010
Cindy S., CA

Tradition 4 states: *Each group should be autonomous except in matters affecting other groups or CLA as a whole.*

The principle behind Tradition 4 is that the freedom enjoyed by individual groups carries with it the admonition to protect the Fellowship as a whole.

Each group ought to have the freedom to learn from its own mistakes, except when its actions affect the welfare of other groups or CLA as a whole. So, each CLA individual meeting has complete freedom to decide for itself. Some of these decisions include whether the meeting will be open or closed, when and where the meeting will be held, changing its meeting format, and how its funds are spent. In these matters, each group has total freedom; it's entirely up to the membership of that individual group.

And the second part of this Tradition reminds each group that it also has the responsibility to the worldwide Fellowship to adhere to the

Traditions and principles of the program. Each group can assure that it will not stray too far from the program's basic tenets. So, the autonomy provided in Tradition 4 does not mean an individual group has the authority to reword the Steps or the Traditions, or even to create its own literature. Nor should a group introduce and sell outside literature at its meeting place. Many a meeting has gotten away from the look and feel of its primary purpose by using literature that is not Fellowship-approved, showing videos of popular self-help speakers, or allowing treatment professionals to speak at open meetings on the latest therapy techniques. There is a saying that there is no right or wrong way of holding a meeting, but a group could cease carrying the message if it strays too far away from the Traditions and concepts. But other than that, groups have complete freedom to design their programs for the needs of their members, which can result in a wide variety of formats.

Our Tuesday morning meeting has gotten so healthy that people have suggested in the business meeting that we use the new Starter Kit,[7] and we changed the format for running the meeting. I've been going to this subcommittee meeting where we are looking at the new Starter Kit and at the new recipe suggestions for how to do the meeting, and it's been interesting and challenging and painful. So, the bottom line that this Tradition speaks to is that the meeting has the choice of what it wants to read or not read. However we change the meeting format, as long as we are cognizant that we are serving the purpose of CLA and operating within its Traditions and principles and that how we change the meeting is not going to hurt any of our other local meetings or CLA as a whole, then we are at liberty to change it within the structure. It's not about doing it right, or doing it perfectly, or conforming to a specific vision. I have found a lot of freedom in applying this principle in sharing with other people that there isn't a wrong way to do it, as long as we're being respectful and conscientious about the choices we make and how they are going to affect not only our membership, but other meetings.

So, thank God for this program!

Tradition 5

Twelve and Twelve–Tradition 5

Fall 2010

Rick M., MD

Tradition 5 *(Long Version): Each [Clutterers Anonymous] group ought to be a spiritual entity having but one primary purpose—that of carrying its message to the [clutterer] who still suffers. (From the long form of Tradition 5 according to Alcoholics Anonymous.)*

Bill W., one of the founding members of the original 12-Step Fellowship, began his essay on this Tradition by stating that "...it is better to do one thing supremely well than many things badly...we shall never be at our best except when we hew only to the primary spiritual aim of A.A.—that of carrying its message to the alcoholic who still suffers alcoholism."

The only thing that Clutterers Anonymous can do well is to carry the message of hope and recovery to the clutterer who stills suffers from the unending compulsion to clutter. Tradition 5 ties the 12 Traditions to the 12 Steps, especially Step 12.

"That the man who is making the approach has had the same difficulty, that he obviously knows what he is talking about...that there are no fees to pay, no axes to grind, no people to please, no lectures to be endured—these are the conditions we have found most effective. After such an approach, many take up their beds and walk again." (*Alcoholics Anonymous*[4] [The "Big Book"], pp. 18-19)

Bill W. also compared our efforts to those of a team of researchers looking for a cure for cancer. Each individual may have his or her particular specialty, but all biases and efforts based on self-interest must be set aside in order to unite in their efforts toward this common goal.

The difference between these researchers and us is this: The doctors may feel guilty if they fail in this effort. We, on the other hand, may be doomed to continue living as slaves to our compulsive behaviors if we fail to carry the message of recovery.

The purpose of the original 12-Step Fellowship was twofold: (1) Newcomers could find hope for themselves by hearing the experience, strength, and hope of the "old-timers," who had experienced a spiritual awakening as a result of working the 12 Steps; (2) "Old-timers" could find newcomers to work with.

The newcomer is the most important person in the room. What is said in our meetings should be nothing other than our 12-Step experience, strength, and hope—and how to apply it to daily living. When we talk about problems clutter has caused us, it should be so that the newcomer can identify with us.

A newcomer certainly has the right to ask questions of anyone in the group, but it's best to reply offering opinions only on one's own program of recovery.

Newcomers are encouraged to work with a sponsor whenever possible and direct most questions to that person; but they can seek help from others in the group in the absence of adequate sponsor support.

A 12-Step Fellowship is not meant as a place to dump lifelong woes and sorrows; therapy is better suited for such purposes. The newcomer already knows how to act out. What he or she now needs to hear is how to recover.

Real recovery takes place when one recovering compulsive clutterer sits down with another and shows that clutterer how to work through the 12 Steps. In order for the 12-Step message to be carried to the newcomer, those carrying the message have to have taken the Steps themselves.

It's not necessary to work all 12 Steps before sharing experience, strength, and hope with newcomers. But if we have no strength or hope to share, then we probably need to keep our experience to ourselves until we are more advanced in recovery.

We grow through working the Steps and by continuing to share our recovery—and nothing more—with newcomers and others in CLA.

CLA does not endorse in any of its meetings any techniques, cures, gurus, motivational speakers, books, etc. on the topic of clutter. Perhaps some may find these outside resources helpful, but they are outside the scope of the CLA program.

We have only one message: that we had a spiritual awakening as the result of the 12 Steps and that we practice these principles in all our affairs. If we do not carry this message—or if we carry any other message—then we are a 12-Step Fellowship in name only.

Bill W. sums up the issue in this way:

> *Sobriety [freedom from compulsive cluttering] through the teaching and practice of the 12 Steps is the sole purpose of a [CLA] group. Groups have repeatedly tried other activities, and they have always failed.... If we don't stick to these principles, we shall almost surely collapse. And if we collapse, we cannot help anyone.*

Bill W., "The A.A. Grapevine, Inc.,"[2] February 1958. (Affirmed as a guiding principle of A.A. and approved by the A.A. General Service Conference in 1969, 1970, and 1972.)

Working Tradition 5

Fall 2010

Colleen C., CA

Tradition Five: *Each group has but one primary purpose—to carry its message to the person who still suffers.*

As individuals, we all have so many different types of gifts and talents; we each have our purpose in life. However, as a group, it is very important that we keep our focus on CLA's purpose. I believe the 5th Tradition is of utmost importance in helping us to stay on track and grow as a Fellowship of recovery. If we involve ourselves in objectives and responsibilities that are outside of our realm, we could eventually fall apart.

Tradition 5 is a reminder that we, as recovering members of CLA, need not possess any special qualifications to carry the message. Our program has nothing to do with level of education, training, or even having a "perfect" home. There is no textbook or predetermined list of outside requirements we must have in order to be of assistance to our CLA groups in carrying the message. This Tradition also has everything to do with our own personal recovery. It reminds us that, as we read in our literature, "We keep only what we give away." This means that as we strive to carry the message and help the clutterer who is still suffering, we also gain and further our own personal recovery and happiness in the process!

The inherent meaning of this Tradition is that our groups don't venture into areas that are outside of our primary purpose. For example, as it says in our literature, "Some people come to CLA expecting housekeeping hints, tips on sorting and filing, lectures on time management, or the like. To their surprise, they find that this is not CLA's purpose." We are a program of spiritual recovery, and even though addressing the physical manifestation of clutter is an essential part of recovery, we don't involve ourselves with these outside issues.

Other examples would be a CLA group intruding into a member's personal and family affairs or involving itself with recommending religious institutions or beliefs, professional organizers, or housecleaning companies. I would like to clarify these statements so as to avoid any confusion; this is not to say that we don't help each other with decluttering. We do help other members with the ways and means of addressing the various types of clutter we struggle with in our disease. In CLA, we have "clutter buddies," for example, and there are times when we do offer very tangible help to one another. As clutterers, many, if not most, of us have struggled with the physical manifestation of our disease, in addition to the emotional and spiritual turmoil. Maybe we help to organize a room in a fellow CLA member's home, assist with filing paperwork, or discuss our time plans with one another. These are examples of how we, as individuals in recovery, use the Tools[19] of the CLA program, and I don't believe any of these examples go against Tradition 5. There is a difference between the examples I just mentioned and the group itself taking on outside responsibilities.

Further, I believe it is important to take as much care as we possibly can in providing resources to our newcomers. At my home meeting, we are very mindful about welcoming newcomers, and our meeting format includes a detailed newcomer's section that offers an explanation of CLA. We reserve time at the end portion of the meeting for newcomers to share, and we welcome them with a newcomer recovery chip, if they choose to take one. Many of us were hurting and confused when we attended our very first meeting. (I know I definitely was when I walked into my first meeting on May 28, 2005, and I really "didn't get it" at first.) Furthermore, as we read in our literature, many of us in this program have been accustomed to taking care of other people and neglecting our own needs, which may have resulted in our cluttered, unmanageable lives. By remembering Tradition 5, we as a group can maintain a strong bond, and lovingly represent and explain to the newcomer what we're all about as a recovery Fellowship! We remember our primary purpose and keep the focus there. We encourage members to keep coming back, and we also remember that it's progress, not perfection.

I also find that I can apply the message of Tradition 5 to my own life. The aspect of Tradition 5 that we help ourselves when we help others has become a very important new part of my life in recovery. When I came into CLA, I was spiritually broken and had so much to learn, particularly about service and helping others. I have come to understand that our program is a continual process of recovery, learning, and self-discovery; that it's progress, not perfection, and I won't suddenly be cured or fixed in one day. But today I can look at my life and see the recovery I do have, and I have this program to thank. As a clutterer and a hoarder, I found that my thinking was crippled, and I didn't understand that as I give to the world, so the world will give to me. When I gave to others, it was often a way to avoid responsibility for my own life, or it was a form of manipulation, to bring about an end result that served my purposes. As I work the Steps of CLA, I am realizing each day that I'm here for a purpose. Today, I am motivated to be of service to others, and I'm committed to the spiritual program of CLA. In my interactions with my family members and friends and in my professional life, I am able to give much more freely to others, and I am discovering the paradox which is mentioned in A.A.'s *Twelve Steps and Twelve Traditions*[16]—that it all comes back to me. As I live each day, I find myself keeping the focus more and more on what my primary purpose in life is.

In terms of my physical clutter, my CLA program and my Higher Power show me how my life has been so deeply impacted by clutter. In the past, physical clutter suffocated me and blocked my spiritual channels. As I keep Tradition 5 in my daily living, I am reminded how this disease can pull me away from my primary purpose in life.

I see other practical applications of Tradition 5 in my own life every day. In situations at work or with family members, I am reminded that I'm part of a group. I can ask myself, "What is our primary purpose in this case?" and remember to keep the focus there, rather than getting off track and involving myself in affairs that are outside of this realm, or focusing too much on my own interests and my own agendas. Tradition 5 helps me to take a step back from things, reconnect with my Higher Power, and determine where my focus should be.

I'm also very thankful for my home CLA group, the Newport Beach, California, meeting on Saturdays at 4:30 pm. We are a small but dedicated group of individuals, and we have a primary purpose on which we strive to focus. We are there for the newcomer, we are helping each other to recover, and in turn we help ourselves.

Tradition 6

Twelve and Twelve–Tradition 6

Holiday 2010

Rick M., MD

Tradition 6: *A CLA group ought never endorse, finance, or lend the Clutterers Anonymous name to any related facility or outside enterprise, lest problems of money, property, or prestige divert us from our primary purpose.*

Tradition 6 (from the long form of Tradition 6 according to Alcoholics Anonymous):[16]

> *Problems of money, property, and authority may easily divert us from our primary spiritual aim. We think, therefore, that any considerable property of genuine use to A.A. should be separately incorporated and managed, thus dividing the material from the spiritual. An A.A. group, as such, should never go into business. Secondary aids to A.A. such as clubs or hospitals which require much property or administration, ought to be incorporated and so set apart that, if necessary, they can be freely discarded by the groups.... Their management [of these special facilities] should be the sole responsibility of those people who financially support them. For clubs, A.A. managers are usually preferred. But...places of recuperation, ought to be well outside A.A.—and medically supervised. While an A.A. group may cooperate with anyone... [it] can bind itself to no one.*

The focus of Tradition 6 is our Fellowship's relationship with money and property. It suggests that our groups should never go into business nor ever lend the CLA name or money credit to any outside enterprise. Even clubs should not bear the CLA name. Instead, they ought to be separately incorporated and managed by CLA members.

In practicing this principle, we are able to separate the spiritual from the material. We are able to confine CLA to its sole aim—to carry the 12-Step message to the clutterer who still suffers. It is okay for individuals from our Fellowship to engage in business ventures where CLA meetings may be held, but it should not be a CLA group enterprise. It is a business venture, so the individuals involved are allowed to make some money from their efforts. But no matter how wealthy individuals may become, it is important that CLA itself always remains poor. We dare not risk the distractions of corporate wealth.

Because we still have some self-centered attributes, we have often quarreled violently about money, property, and its administration. Money, in quantity, has always been a dangerous influence on group life.

Money is not the lifeblood of CLA. With us, it is very secondary. We are better off using only what we need—no more, no less.

The core of CLA procedure is one clutterer talking to another, whether that be sitting on a curbstone, in a home, or at a meeting. It's the message, not the place; it's the talk, not the charity.

These are the spiritual attributes which do our work. Just places to meet and talk, that's about all we really need. Beyond these, when we look to the future, we may be able to have a few small offices, a few secretaries at their desks, a computer or two, a few dollars apiece a year. These await a time when there are more trusted servants, and funding will easily be met by voluntary contributions. Our material needs are only secondary to CLA's success. It makes more sense for us to lead our organization based on spiritual principles as our primary foundation.

Working Tradition 6

Holiday 2010

Kathy H., CA

Tradition 6 states: *A CLA group ought never endorse, finance, or lend the Clutterers Anonymous name to any related facility or outside enterprise, lest problems of money, property, or prestige divert us from our primary purpose.*

Tradition 5 defines our primary purpose: To carry our 12-Step message of recovery to the clutterer who still suffers. Tradition 6 tells us that groups should stick to that primary purpose and that involving the group in outside enterprises could divert us from it, thereby limiting recovery for our members.

Outside the meeting, CLA members are free to use any method. However, whatever system or professional help is used, it does not belong as a part of CLA and should not be talked about during the meeting or in the meeting room directly after the meeting.

Many clutterers come to CLA for the first time expecting to be handed tips, to be given a bibliography of outside literature, or to be referred to a therapist or professional organizer. They seem surprised when we tell them that this is not the purpose of CLA—that our focus is on the spiritual program of recovery embodied in the 12 Steps. Many of those newcomers leave after that first meeting, not having found the quick fix they envisioned. Some do return when they find no other way to solve their problem. If they were to do so, only to find that in the meantime we had abandoned emphasis on our program of recovery by incorporating other methods, we would not be helping them, but rather harming their chances of recovery.

If reading articles, books, etc., on organizing and clutter were able to solve my problem, I would not have come to CLA at all. What I lacked was motivation to declutter; I needed the spiritual approach of the 12 Steps. All of our literature and ideas are born from the experience, strength, and hope of CLA members—those like ourselves who really understand.

As clutterers, we tend to think that adding more items to our already-cluttered lives will give us satisfaction or that adding more items to our programs will aid in our recovery. But by letting the group go in all directions, we create another form of clutter. Except in this case, we are cluttering our recovery programs, and our CLA message of recovery gets lost in the chaos. This diverts us from our primary purpose and can lead to misunderstanding and confusion within a group. We cannot be all things; when we try, we end up being nothing.

Endorsing outside enterprises or literature implies that CLA as a whole endorses their ideas. But they do not reflect the experiences of CLA members. Some outside enterprises may endorse CLA; that is perfectly fine. What they do is their business. But CLA can never endorse them, no matter how worthy.

Often, getting involved in outside enterprises leads to individuals investing so much energy in a proposal that they lose sight of Tradition 12, putting principles before personalities, and are unable to let go of their ideas. If others have backed conflicting ideas, it leads to fighting within the group.

One thing should be avoided at all costs: CLA is not a forum for professionals to drum up business. There should be no advertisements, business cards, or announcements by professionals at meetings. Nothing can break up a group faster than having money issues come between members.

A professional who is also a clutterer is free to be a member of the group and attend meetings but not to promote a business within the group.

No matter how worthy we feel an outside enterprise is, it has no place inside a CLA group. By sticking with this Tradition, we protect our identity and preserve our unity.

Tradition 7

Twelve and Twelve–Tradition 7

Spring 2011
Rick M., MD

Tradition 7: *Every CLA group ought to be fully self-supporting, declining outside contributions.*

Tradition 7 Long Form[16] (From the long form of Tradition 7, according to Alcoholics Anonymous):

> *The A.A. groups themselves ought to be fully supported by the voluntary contributions of their own members. We think that each group should soon achieve this ideal; that any public solicitation of funds using the name of Alcoholics Anonymous is highly dangerous...that acceptance of large gifts from any source or of contributions carrying any obligation whatever is unwise. Then, too, we view with much concern those A.A. treasuries which continue, beyond prudent reserves, to accumulate funds for no stated A.A. purpose. Experience has often warned us that nothing can so surely destroy our spiritual heritage as futile disputes over property, money, and authority.*

We may ask ourselves where we are going to come up with the money which must go to rent for meeting space, production of literature, and maintenance of the website. If we are working our program properly, chances are we are saving and possibly even making more money as a result of not squandering it on unnecessary purchases or money invested to counteract the results of our cluttering, hoarding, and disorganized behavior. We find that the amount of money invested in keeping our meetings going is only a small fraction of what we are now able to earn.

What if there are people who want to and are able to contribute large sums of money to our cause? Think of all the things we could do with that money! We could produce even more literature, pay for more public service announcements, put on more conferences in our efforts to spread the message of hope and recovery from the insanity of our obsessive/compulsive natures that dooms us to repeat our cluttering behaviors. Or, we might say to ourselves, "We are a pretty small group just getting started. We are pretty broke. We sure could use that extra money." What could possibly be wrong with accepting large sums of money from people who are willing to offer it to us?

Well, for one thing, let us not forget that our primary purpose is to carry the message to the clutter addict who still suffers. If we were to accept large sums of money from outside sources, we would run the risk of being influenced by outside interests, which are not directly connected to our primary purpose.

In addition, let's face it—we are human. Money can go to our heads. In the early days of the 12-Step Fellowships, there were bitter controversies among the members of various groups over what to do with large sums of money that were offered to them by members and outside sources. One person would want to invest that money into major projects to further the cause. Others would rather hoard the money and watch it accumulate. This is the kind of stuff our addiction feeds on. Such practices could, therefore, tear us apart.

When we were active in our addiction to clutter, many of us bought and held on to things. We were takers. Now that we have a program of recovery that helps us to become responsible and productive citizens, we want to turn our attention toward expressing our gratitude by focusing on the act of giving.

So, it has been found through trial and error that it is best not to accept large amounts of money that could potentially divert us from our primary purpose. Nor should we save up large sums of money for the same reason. When two or more clutterers meet for the purpose of carrying the message of recovery to one another, we have a CLA meeting. We do not need a lot of money in order to achieve this. The early pioneers of the 12-Step movement found it better to live by the principle of "corporate poverty."

It has been recommended, however, that we keep a prudent reserve of money that equals from one to three months' worth of operating expenses. Such funds can help ensure our survival in tough times, so that we may be able to continue carrying the message to the clutterer who still suffers. But we should have no more and no less. Remember, we are now living on spiritual principles. We are acting in the spirit of giving but doing so with humility and gratitude. One clutterer helping another is all that is needed for us to recover.

Working Tradition 7

Spring 2011

Betsey K., NJ and Kathy H., CA

Tradition 7 states: *Every group ought to be fully self-supporting, declining outside contributions.*

Tradition 7 follows naturally from Traditions 5 and 6. To fulfill the primary purpose of our Fellowship, which is to carry its message to the clutterer who still stuffers, we must remain free of outside influences. That would be difficult to do if we accepted outside contributions.

We have no dues or fees; a group's funds come from voluntary 7th Tradition contributions. Each group is responsible for supporting its own group expenses, as well as CLA services. It is entirely up to group conscience to decide how much the group will contribute to intergroups and WSO. This support benefits all CLA members.

Groups and CLA service bodies are always guided by this Tradition. Adequate support from all the groups helps both intergroups and WSO decline outside contributions, whereas accepting them would change the entire structure of the CLA Fellowship and destroy its basic spiritual concept.

Also, it is never the policy for one individual to be the dominant group support, either monetarily or with service commitments. This often leads to that person expecting to have more say than other members in group matters.

Learning to be fully self-supporting is important for CLA groups and recovering clutterers. Our program teaches us to depend on a power greater than ourselves for our security, rather than on other people. With the help of our Higher Power, we learn to take care of ourselves and our groups, physically, emotionally, and spiritually.

CLA groups do have legitimate expenses, such as meeting places and literature. Intergroups may have expenses such as literature, publishing meeting lists, telephones, websites, and Clutter-Free Days. The World Service Organization provides other vital services: publishing CLA literature and worldwide meeting lists, maintaining website and telephone services, answering questions from groups and CLA members, and responding to inquiries from all over the world about the CLA program. All of this is paid for by CLA members and groups who make 7th Tradition contributions. Without such services, the newcomer often could not find CLA or its meetings.

Recently, we have been faced with a decision on how to handle our checking account because our bank will soon be charging monthly service fees. One option was proposed: In order to avoid a charge for the CLA*rity* bank account, we could link it to the personal account of a member. After much discussion, we realized that this would not be in keeping with our Traditions. It was pointed out that, according to Tradition 7, we do pay our own way, and that includes bank fees. So it was decided to leave things as they are and pay the fee.

When we look closely, we realize that this Tradition deals with one of the basic tenets of CLA's program of recovery. When we as individual members and groups understand that we are responsible for our own survival and progress, we discover a great spiritual strength in ourselves and in the group. Often, our willingness to pay our own way is a sign that we are recovering and maturing emotionally.

We learn to rely on our Higher Power to become self-supporting and let go of our unhealthy dependence, and we develop healthy relationships with others.

When we look at the fuller meaning of the 7th Tradition, we find that, if groups and individuals are to be fully self-supporting, they need to take on their share of the service work as well. When meetings give back some of the help they have received in the program, contributing whatever support they can when they are able, then they become fully self-supporting. A group functions best and is able to foster a better environment for recovery when all of its members feel they can get involved.

There are healthy limits for giving service, just as the amount of money any one member donates to CLA is limited.

Meeting our responsibilities to the group and the Fellowship, financially and by doing service, helps to bolster our self-esteem. When we do not take part or when we fail in our responsibilities, our self-esteem begins to falter.

Most of us are glad to contribute to keep our own groups and CLA itself functioning. When all is said and done, we realize that CLA is our means of recovery from compulsive cluttering. When we contribute to our group and the Fellowship—by giving money, time, and effort—we tend to feel more as if we belong. We have more of a stake in the program and in our own recovery.

When we first come to CLA, we clutterers have often begun to fail in keeping up with our responsibilities. Becoming responsible for our contributions to the group, whether financial or with service, we begin to learn responsible habits.

By declining outside contributions and accepting our responsibilities as CLA groups and individuals, we keep ourselves and our Fellowship free of the complications that would arise were we to accept funds from outside sources. It preserves CLA's unity and equality.

Tradition 8

Twelve and Twelve–Tradition 8

Summer 2011

Rick M., MD, and Kathy H., CA

Tradition 8: *Clutterers Anonymous should remain forever nonprofessional, but our service centers may employ special workers.*

Tradition 8 (from the long form of Tradition 8 in the Alcoholics Anonymous book, *Twelve Steps and Twelve Traditions,*[16] 2009):

> *Alcoholics Anonymous [CLA] should remain forever nonprofessional. We define professionalism as the occupation of counseling alcoholics for fees or hire. But we may employ alcoholics where they are going to perform those services for which we might otherwise have to engage nonalcoholics. Such special services may be well recompensed. But our usual A.A. [CLA] Twelfth Step work is never to be paid for.*

Clutterers Anonymous will never have a professional class. "Freely ye have received, freely give." Money and spirituality do not mix. When we try to professionalize our 12th Step, we always defeat our primary purpose.

Our Fellowship gains its strength from the simple act of one clutterer talking to another. Our 12th-Step work with the clutterer who suffers is based only on the desire to help and be helped. When a CLA member talks for money, whether at a meeting or to a single newcomer, it can negatively impact both of them. Doing 12th-Step work for money can compromise the whole process.

But what about those who serve us in other capacities? If we were to have cooks and custodians, they would not be considered CLA professionals, since these are not 12th-Step jobs. These people are often doing tasks that no CLA member can or will do.

Twelfth-Step work cannot be sold for money, but when we declare that our Fellowship cannot hire service workers nor can any member carry our knowledge into other fields, we are acting out of fear. If these fears ever get too strong, none but a saint or an incompetent will work for CLA.

Our few paid workers perform only those tasks that our volunteers cannot consistently handle. They are not doing 12th-Step work, but they make more and better 12th-Step work possible. Secretaries at their desks are valuable points of contact, information, and public relations. That's not CLA therapy; it's just a lot of very necessary, but often thankless, work.

But if a member accepts employment with an outside agency dealing with cluttering, is it considered professionalism under the CLA Traditions? The answer is no because members who select such full-time careers do not professionalize CLA's 12th Step.

This was a concern of early members of Alcoholics Anonymous. In A.A.'s *Twelve Steps and Twelve Traditions,*[16] the authors recount the following:

> *At first, we couldn't see the real issue involved. In former days, the moment an A.A. hired out to such enterprises, he was immediately tempted to use the name Alcoholics Anonymous for publicity or money-raising purposes. Yet not a single one of them had been hired to do A.A.'s Twelfth Step work. The violation in these instances was not professionalism at all; it was breaking anonymity. A.A.'s sole purpose was being compromised, and the name of Alcoholics Anonymous was being misused.... We cannot declare A.A. such a closed corporation that we keep our knowledge and experience top secret. If an A.A. member acting as a citizen can become a better researcher, educator, personnel officer, then why not? Everybody gains, and we have lost nothing.*

There is a clear distinction between "organizing CLA" and setting up, in a reasonably businesslike manner, a few essential services. This will allow the clutterers who still suffer to continue to get the help so many of us already have. Let us continue to give the helping hand these fellow sufferers deserve.

Working Tradition 8

Summer 2011

Rick M., MD, and Kathy H., CA

Tradition 8 states that *Clutterers Anonymous should remain forever nonprofessional, but our service centers may employ special workers.*

This Tradition confuses some at first glance. If the program is nonprofessional, doesn't that conflict with hiring workers? But what it means, essentially, is that we don't hire anyone to do 12th-Step work (such as a sponsor). We don't hire buddies. We don't hire speakers for our groups. We don't pay anyone for service positions either (secretary, leader, chairperson, treasurer, etc.).

Intergroups and WSO may have need for professional services that are outside the scope of our spiritual program. When WSO had need of someone to maintain its website, a webmaster was paid on a contract basis. That is a task which is completely outside of our groups, any 12th-Step work, or any service positions.

What special workers do is to enable members of the Fellowship to make 12th-Step work possible. However, the principle is that people who serve this kind of function are not paid to do 12th-Step work, which is helping to take people through the 12 Steps; but they're making the organization run smoothly enough so that we can do the 12th-Step work.

Can clutterers be members of CLA and also be therapists, professional organizers etc.? Yes, as long as they keep their professional lives separate from CLA meetings or any 12th-Step work they may be doing. In other words, they wear two hats, but when they go to meetings, they put the professional hat on the shelf. Is it a problem if they use what they have learned in CLA in their professional lives?

No, they are simply using Step 12: "...practicing these principles in all our affairs."

I know one CLA member who has also worked as a lifestyle counselor and, occasionally, as an organizer. Some other members, upon learning of her outside occupations, criticized her for getting paid for such work. However, she is still acting within the Traditions, since she is not mingling her outside work with her CLA 12th-Step work; she treats them as two different compartments of her life (the two hats mentioned earlier). She has talked about her work outside meetings with some other CLA members who are friends, but that does not involve CLA whatsoever. Were she to be told she couldn't be in CLA and undertake this profession, we would be trying to control her life. That is never the purpose of CLA.

Our primary purpose is to carry the message of recovery from one clutterer to another. Our Fellowship is spiritual in nature; that's the reason why we get together.

We are not a counseling service nor are we a church, but we have elements of spirituality, and we have therapeutic elements as well. But what makes it so powerful? When done right, if one clutterer is getting healthier by working the 12 Steps that this Fellowship is based on, then it's an obligation for us to carry that message to other people.

Our gain is not in material profit, but in spiritual growth, increased sanity, and freedom from clutter. These blessings would be lost were we to bring money into the process.

Tradition 9

Twelve and Twelve—Tradition 9

Fall 2011

Rick M., MD

Tradition 9: *Clutterers Anonymous, as such, ought never be organized, but we may create service boards or committees directly responsible to those they serve.*

Tradition Nine (from the long form of Tradition 9 in the Alcoholics Anonymous book *Twelve Steps and Twelve Traditions,*[16] 2009):

> *Each A.A. group needs the least possible organization. Rotating leadership is the best. The small group may elect its secretary, the large group its rotating committee, and the groups of a large metropolitan area their central or intergroup committee, which often employs a full-time secretary. The trustees of the General Service Board are, in effect, our A.A. General Service Committee. They are the custodians of our A.A. Tradition and the receivers of voluntary A.A. contributions by which we maintain our A.A. General Service Office at New York. They are authorized by the groups to handle our overall public relations and they guarantee the integrity of our principal newspaper, the A.A. Grapevine. All such representatives are to be guided in the spirit of service, for true leaders in A.A. are but trusted and experienced servants of the whole....*

(The following is based on the writings of Bill W. and modified for the CLA Fellowship.)

The least possible organization, that's our universal ideal: no fees or dues, no rules imposed on anybody, one clutterer bringing the message of hope and recovery to the next. What do we mean when we say "no organization"?

Did anyone ever hear of an organization that had no membership rules or regulations, where compliance was not enforced, and disciplinary actions (including expulsion from the group) were implemented only when deemed necessary? Don't most organized structures give authority to some of their members to impose obedience upon the rest and to punish or expel offenders? CLA does not conform to this pattern.

Fortunately, Clutterers Anonymous and other 12-Step Fellowships seem to be the exception. Neither the World Service Organization nor the smallest individual group can issue a single directive to a CLA member and make it stick, let alone mete out any punishment.

Officers and members alike have found they

can do no more than make suggestions, and very mild ones at that. Instead of giving orders to individual members and smaller groups, CLA does better to respond by saying, "Of course, you are at perfect liberty to handle this matter any way you please, but the majority of our experience in CLA seems to suggest...." We have learned from experience that clutter addicts can't be dictated to—individually or collectively.

Our more conservative members will surely see to it that CLA never gets overly organized. Our more ambitious members will continue to remind us of our terrific obligation to the newcomer and to the many clutterers still waiting all over the world to hear of our Fellowship and what we have to offer.

We shall, naturally, take the firm and safe middle course. We do not like the idea of any general organization. Yet, paradoxically, we insist upon organizing certain special services, mostly those absolutely necessary to do effective and plentiful 12th-Step work.

If, for instance, a CLA group elects a secretary or rotating committee; if an area forms an intergroup committee; or if we set up a foundation, a general office, or a CLA*rity* newsletter—then we need to implement organizational structure for these services. It is these organizational committees that make sure we are able to send out CLA literature. We also need them to provide meeting places and make our conventions and other special events possible.

We should never name boards to govern us. On the other hand, we shall always need to authorize workers to serve us. It is the difference between the spirit of vested authority and the spirit of service—two concepts which are sometimes poles apart. It is in this spirit of service that we elect the CLA group's informal rotating committee, the intergroup association for the area, and the World Service Organization of Clutterers Anonymous for CLA as a whole.

These service structures and the people in them derive no real authority from their titles. Universal respect is the key to their usefulness. This is the key to our survival.

Unless each CLA member follows to the best of his or her ability our suggested 12 Steps to recovery, he almost certainly falls back into relapse and the misery of active addiction. These are not penalties inflicted by people in authority; they result from personal disobedience to spiritual principles.

This also applies to the group itself. Unless we comply closely with CLA's 12 Traditions, the group, too, can deteriorate and die. So we do obey spiritual principles—first because we must, and ultimately because we love the kind of life such obedience brings.

Just as the aim of each CLA member is personal recovery from clutter addiction, the aim of our services is to bring sobriety within reach of all who want it. If nobody does the group's chores, if the organization's telephone rings unanswered, if we do not reply to our mail—then CLA as we know it would stop. Our communications lines with those who need our help would be broken.

Though Tradition 9 at first sight seems to deal with a purely practical matter, in its actual operation it discloses a society without organization, animated only by the spirit of service—a true Fellowship.

Working Tradition 9

Fall 2011

Larry E., CA

Tradition 9: *Clutterers Anonymous, as such, ought never be organized, but we may create service boards or committees directly responsible to those they serve.*

I learned of CLA when there was only one meeting in Simi Valley, California. I wanted to start one in Orange County, California, because I needed help, and a 12-Step program worked for me. Some friends and I started the meeting, and it attracted others—we exchanged our experiences and provided each other support. We had some readings that came from the Simi meeting, and we used A.A. literature as well.

So, at that time—1990 approximately—CLA was not organized, and there were no committees or service boards. What happened was this: a local Simi Valley newspaper wrote an article (which was later syndicated) about the Simi Valley CLA meeting. That meeting started getting inquiries from Hawaii, Guam—and all over. Some members of the group made up meeting starter kits[7] and information packets and mailed them out. The Simi group became so overwhelmed that the group secretary asked us in Orange County to handle some of the mailings, which we did.

At that time, almost no one had even conceived of a recovery program for clutterers (or "pack-rats," as I'd identified myself previously). One morning I received a phone call from Nicole, one of the two CLA founders: Would I please start up a CLA World Service —for the purpose of carrying the message of CLA recovery to all clutterers. I think I replied that it was an interesting idea and would get back to her. I remember speaking to the other CLA founder—Varda—for guidance She had had much 12-Step experience and was a gifted writer.

A group of CLA members met and elected a WSO board—myself included. Now new meetings formed in Los Angeles County, as well as New Jersey and elsewhere. The CLA board met quarterly, and delegates from CLA meetings attended to help decide what we would do.

The main things, as I remember, were: write literature, get approvals from CLA groups, and publish and distribute literature and all-important meeting starter packets. Also, the WSO maintained a PO Box, and, for a time, a telephone line and answering machine. We wrote bylaws and they were approved by the groups that we knew about. We also obtained permission from the A.A. Central Office to adapt and use the 12 Steps and 12 Traditions.

As a group, we adhered to the 12 Traditions in good faith. Tradition 9 is crucial in how the service board should function. Reaching consensus and following the group conscience is important.

I've tromped on Tradition 9 (and Tradition 2) during my involvement in CLA WSO. And I saw what harm comes from it. I learned humility, and I am reinforced in my belief in the 12 Traditions as the foundation of our program.

Tradition 10

Twelve and Twelve–Tradition 10

Holiday 2011

Rick M., MD

Tradition 10—*CLA has no opinion on outside issues; hence the Clutterers Anonymous name ought never be drawn into public controversy.*

Tradition 10 (from the long form of Tradition 10 in the Alcoholics Anonymous book, *Twelve Steps and Twelve Traditions*,[16] 2009):

> *No A.A. group or member should ever, in such a way as to implicate A.A., express any opinion on outside controversial issues—particularly those of politics, alcohol reform, or sectarian religion. The Alcoholics Anonymous groups oppose no one. Concerning such matters they can express no views whatever.*

Let us remember the purpose of the 12 Traditions. They were adopted for the express purpose of our survival as a Fellowship. Without the fellowship of people who have found a common solution to our problem, our chances of recovery are severely compromised. Although we are made up of individuals who may disagree on many things, we must maintain unity when it concerns our primary purpose, which is to carry the 12-Step message of recovery to the clutterer who still suffers.

The fact that the 12-Step movements have survived and grown over the last 76 years has been a true blessing. But we cannot rest on our laurels. We have to be careful to avoid unnecessary controversy. Bill W., one of the founding members of Alcoholics Anonymous, the granddaddy of all 12-Step Fellowships, studied what worked and what didn't work in groups that successfully treated addiction but were unsuccessful in staying together. One of these groups, the Washingtonians, began in a tavern on Mount Royal Street in Baltimore, Maryland, in 1840. Three drunks were sitting around drinking, when they decided to take a pledge to give up liquor for good. They met on a weekly basis and supported each other. They brought in more people and ended up being the most successful fellowship to treat alcohol addiction at the time. By 1860, they were all but gone.

Why? What happened?

The Washingtonians began to address outside issues, such as abolition, which was a hot topic at the time. (Remember, this was a big issue to influence the American Civil War at that time.) Members were attacking one another, which led to disunity. Perhaps they could have survived this conflict. Unfortunately, they also became crusaders trying to reform drinking laws and habits overall. Again, this was an outside issue that brought in a lot of controversy between members, as well as the public at large. These actions led to disunity, which weakened their effectiveness.

We in CLA run the same risk if we align ourselves with any religious, philosophical, and/or political causes. These are the things that divide us. If we are to survive, we must not be distracted by outside issues but continue focusing on our primary purpose—to carry the 12-Step message to the clutterer who still suffers.

Working Tradition 10

Holiday 2011

Kathy H., CA

Tradition 10 says: *CLA has no opinion on outside issues; hence the Clutterers Anonymous name ought never be drawn into public controversy.*

Tradition 10 expands upon Tradition 6 by emphasizing the need to keep CLA free from organizations and systems outside of the program. This allows us to concentrate on the recovery offered by CLA without becoming embroiled in the conflicts of the world. While we must admit that no group can be entirely free of conflict, by following this Tradition we can learn to live with a minimum of strife. We don't oppose other entities or causes, either. We have no opinion one way or the other.

Newcomers to 12-Step programs are often surprised to find that a Fellowship which supports our personal recovery from cluttering refuses to give its support to other good causes. Some members may want to include them as group discussions or as topics for sharing. But were we as a Fellowship to take a stand on outside issues, we would begin to alienate some of our own membership and lose the positive atmosphere needed for recovery in our meetings.

The issue of support for outside organizations has cropped up in CLA. In a few places around the country, there are organizations known as hoarding task forces. There is one such in Los Angeles County. When a member wished to give it support in the form of free literature, others took exception to the idea—both because it violated Traditions and because we would be giving this support to only one area of the country while ignoring others. Also, were we to do so, we would be putting a certain amount of effort into helping the task force rather than supporting our own members.

The result of a group conscience was to refrain from providing them with free literature. Some individual CLA members are involved as private citizens, which is perfectly fine. However, CLA itself cannot participate, no matter how worthy the organization may be.

Having no opinion on outside issues also means that meetings do not use or sell anything other than CLA Fellowship-approved literature (which includes A.A. conference-approved literature). We do not talk about outside systems or methods in the meetings, either.

CLA literature is the product of the group conscience of CLA as a whole and was developed, edited, and reviewed by committees of CLA members, reflects feedback from the various groups in the Fellowship, and was approved by WSO. Of course, not every member will agree with everything in the literature. But our literature focuses exclusively on CLA principles and on the CLA program of recovery from cluttering through the 12 Steps.

In my experience, this has been one of the thorniest issues in our Fellowship. I have often heard members not even wanting to mention the Steps at meetings. Instead they talk about every book they have read on organization and decluttering. It may be one reason why many CLA meetings have not progressed very far in their recovery. We do have our own program of recovery; it will not prosper if we set it aside in our collective conscience for every other method a member comes across.

Of course, as individuals we are free to work for any cause, join any religion or organization, and even use any organizing and decluttering system we wish. But we should not bring these things into CLA meetings, lest we destroy ourselves with controversy and drift away from the purpose of our group, which is to carry the message to the clutterer who still suffers.

Tradition 10 reminds us again of CLA's reason for existing: to help compulsive clutterers to recover through the 12 Steps. We need to avoid anything that would interfere with carrying out this purpose.

Tradition 11

Twelve and Twelve–Tradition 11

Spring 2012

Rick M., MD

Tradition 11 states: *Our public relations policy is based on attraction rather than promotion; we need always maintain personal anonymity at the level of press, radio, films, television, and all other media.*

As with other 12-Step programs, CLA is different from other organizations regarding public relations policies. Most non-12-Step groups will use sensational advertising to promote their movements. How many infomercials have we seen that promote the latest diet, exercise program, or organizational methods? How many professionals and others are broadcast offering the latest organizational techniques? How many commercial testimonials are given touting success? CLA does not carry its message in this fashion. Why don't we?

Our policy is to attract people to come to us as a result of the recovery we embody, rather than self-promotion. Before we came to CLA, some of us could not have friends in our homes due to embarrassment. We could barely find anything because whatever we were looking for was buried under piles of clutter. We even know of at least one case where a clutterer has died when the house caught on fire. The clutter was so bad that the firemen were unable to get through it to save the person's life.

When we came to CLA, we were offered support and fellowship by people like ourselves who understood our predicament and had found a solution. We learned life skills to help us manage our approach to clutter. We were so grateful to be given this lifesaving program. Wouldn't it make sense for each of us to go public and tell the whole world how CLA saved our lives? Wouldn't it be much more effective to advertise to the public at large what CLA has done for us and broadcast testimony of how Clutterers Anonymous pulled us from the brink of despair? Wouldn't more people be reached through these traditional forms of informing the public?

The founders of Alcoholics Anonymous discovered that it was problematic. Along the way, many 12-Step groups have gotten a lot of participants from vigorous advertising. Although this worked at first, it influenced some members to promote themselves for less-than-honorable reasons or for financial gain. Some of the members were doing so more out of self-ego building or to associate the movement with outside products or ideologies that were not directly connected. And when these members relapsed, it opened up the program for controversy.

We seek to avoid these controversies. We have found that the results will speak for themselves. It is because of this that we have gained the respect of therapists, doctors, journalists, etc. We have found that our friends in these areas have been our best promoters and referral sources. When speaking at the public level about CLA, whether it be through the press, television, radio, or the Internet, we use our first names and surname initial only. We do not put the full name of CLA on envelopes sent through the mail. Some of us do, however, use our full names inside the meetings. We realize, of course, that this is an individual choice for each member.

What do we do if we are trying to start a local group, and people don't even know we exist? Are we allowed to advertise? We can put small notices in the community section of local publications.

We have found that it is acceptable to put out public service announcements, such as the example below, for one purpose only—so people will know we are available to help those who suffer from clutter addiction and to find out where to obtain more information about CLA.

> Is clutter a problem for you?
> Perhaps Clutterers Anonymous can help.
> Contact us at (give mailing address, phone number, website, etc.)
> Weekly meetings open to the public at the XYZ Building (address) on Sundays at 8 p.m.

It is because of the safety and humility found in the principle of anonymity (for Tradition 11, we are speaking about the public level), that we have found that:

Our relations with the outside world should be characterized by modesty and anonymity. We think A.A. ought to avoid sensational advertising. Our public relations should be guided by the principle of attraction rather than promotion. There is never need to praise ourselves. We feel it better to let our friends recommend us.

(The above was taken from the long form of Tradition 11, as found in A.A.'s newsletter, "The Grapevine,"[2] October 1948)

Workng Tradition 11

Spring 2012

Compiled from a presentation given by Kenny P. of California during the CLA Traditions Seminar on September 12, 2010.

Tradition 11 states: *Our public relations policy is based on attraction rather than promotion; we need always maintain personal anonymity at the level of press, radio, films, television, and all other media.*

Often, people believe that this Tradition is about members' personal anonymity, to protect the individual; it's to protect the program of Clutterers Anonymous. However, we don't need to keep the program anonymous. There are a lot of organizations that would support CLA, but they have to be able to find us.

In my home group, we read questions from a Traditions list adapted from one printed in the "A.A. Grapevine" years ago.

The first question on that list is about not promoting CLA so dramatically that it is unattractive. When I talk about the program, I talk about the Steps and what they have done for me and how my life has changed. The only way for somebody to see how it works is to see a person change; then they can try it. It's all about the attraction of the program, about the inside change in us showing on the outside.

The second question is about being able to keep confidence reposed in CLA members. Mainly I talk about this Tradition being about protecting the group, but it's also not my place to break anyone else's anonymity. So I need to remember that my job is my recovery and not me talking about what other people have said.

That leads to the next question about being careful about not throwing CLA names around, even within the Fellowship. If I hear people talking about stuff that I want to share with somebody, I can say, "I heard this in a meeting" or "I heard this from an individual."

The fourth question is about being ashamed of being a clutterer. For a lot of years, I was ashamed of my cluttering. But I have found that if I don't share about my cluttering with friends who are clutterers, they'll never hear about the program. What many of us do in meetings is keep our names and phone numbers to ourselves, and then we wonder why we're not recovering. There are a lot of Tools, and for us to use those Tools, we have to be available so people can get in touch with us.

The fifth question asks where CLA would be if not guided by the ideas in Tradition 11. I think what would happen is that we would end up being affiliated with all kinds of organizations, which is against our other Traditions. Also, we may risk our existence, because if I were to talk about Clutterers Anonymous in public—building this big picture around me and my recovery—and then slipped and started cluttering again, everybody would see my cluttering and say the program doesn't work. But one person's recovery has nothing to do with what Clutterers Anonymous as a whole is doing.

And, finally, the last question deals with whether my recovery is attractive enough that a sick clutterer would want the same quality. Am I doing the things that will attract someone else to me so that they will want what I have? Am I working the Steps in a way that is changing my life—not just the physical clutter, but the mental clutter and the time clutter? I've been around 12-Step programs for a long time, and one of the things that I've learned is that I need to work on me and get myself to the point that other people want what I have.

Tradition 12

Twelve and Twelve–Tradition 12

Summer 2012
Kathy H., CA

Anonymity is the spiritual foundation of all our Traditions, ever reminding us to place principles before personalities.

The long form of Tradition 12 from the Alcoholics Anonymous book, *Twelve Steps and Twelve Traditions,*[16] states:

> *And finally, we of Alcoholics Anonymous believe that the principle of anonymity has an immense spiritual significance. It reminds us that we are to place principles before personalities; that we are actually to practice a genuine humility. This to the end that our great blessings may never spoil us; that we shall forever live in thankful contemplation of Him who presides over us all.*

A.A.'s book, *Twelve Steps and Twelve Traditions,* says:

> *The spiritual substance of anonymity is sacrifice. Because A.A.'s Twelve Traditions repeatedly ask us to give up personal desires for the common good, we realize that the sacrificial spirit—well symbolized by anonymity—is the foundation of them all. It is A.A.'s proved willingness to make these sacrifices that gives people their high confidence in our future.*

Long experience in the program of Alcoholics Anonymous, as well as CLA and other 12-Step programs, has led to two realizations, which form the backbone of this Tradition.

First, if CLA members, especially newcomers, fear that their anonymity will be broken, they would rightly feel that their trust had been broken and likely leave the program. In fact, if this breaking of anonymity were to become widely known, it would begin to turn newcomers away. In this regard, it is also important that we never discuss outside of meetings what other members have shared.

Second, when anonymity is broken at the public level, the potential for great harm to be done to the program is enormous. If the member whose anonymity is broken in the media later has a slip, people begin to lose faith that the program works.

This was one big reason for A.A.'s developing Traditions regarding anonymity in the first place, as discussed in their *Twelve Steps and Twelve Traditions*:

> *As this tide offering top public approval swept in, we realized that it [publicity] could do us incalculable good or great harm. Everything would depend upon how it was channeled. We simply couldn't afford to take the chance of letting self-appointed members present themselves as messiahs representing A.A. before the whole public.... If even one publicly got drunk, or was*

lured into using A.A.'s name for his own purposes, the damage might be irreparable. At this altitude (press, radio, films, and television), anonymity—100 percent anonymity—was the only possible answer. Here, principles would have to come before personalities, without exception.

Another negative result of members forgetting to follow the spirit of anonymity—even if not publicly—is a tendency to place "egos before principles" instead of "principles before personalities."

Instead of acting as a CLA member, the clutterer starts acting as a CLA show-off. This also means that members should never use their professions, job titles, or spiritual positions to influence other program members.

In working the program, it's okay to let friends, family, coworkers, etc., know of your CLA affiliation. These quiet conversations can sometimes let others who are in need know of the program. As A.A.'s *Twelve Steps and Twelve Traditions* [16] states: "Though not in the strict letter of anonymity, such communications were well within its spirit."

Our work, however, does need to be publicized. That is why we sometimes cooperate with the media, always taking great care that, when identified as a CLA member, no individual's full name or picture is publicized.

Anonymity is a spiritual quality which embodies humility at work. A.A.'s *Twelve Steps and Twelve Traditions* says:

As we lay aside these very human aspirations, we believe that each of us takes part in the weaving of a protective mantle which covers our whole Society and under which we may grow and work in unity. We are sure that humility, expressed by anonymity, is the greatest safeguard that Alcoholics Anonymous can ever have.

Working Tradition 12

Summer 2012

Carol N., CA

In times past, there was a lot of stigma attached to admitting to being an alcoholic, and so it has been with clutterers. There has been much advancement in the scientific field regarding recovery from the disease of cluttering, and we are now where A.A. was early on. The purpose and results of anonymity are spelled out in the chapter on Tradition 12 in A.A.'s book, *Twelve Steps and Twelve Traditions*. The spiritual substance of anonymity is sacrifice.

I know that when I'm with a group of program people, the temptation to discuss someone else's business is great. There's such a fine line between gossip and sharing information. Anonymity should be practiced with regard to the wishes of the person being discussed. When no request is made, it's always safe to assume that they don't want their business told, unless it is obvious that they don't mind.

In the case of A.A., I am reminded of the story of a famous personality from the 30s and 40s. Hollywood made a very famous movie which detailed much of her life and ended with her subsequent recovery. Unfortunately, she later got drunk, which negated any positive influence the spectacularly dramatic story of her life had achieved. In effect, it actually harmed A.A., instead of helping. So far, to my knowledge, CLA can't claim a member of such prominence. However, local media sometimes highlight the lives of people we know or are marginally acquainted with; and the temptation is to tell our friends that we know these people, even if we don't mention how we know them.

How anonymous should a CLA member be? That's a good question, on both the individual and group program levels.

So the question becomes when to speak and when not to speak about CLA. The essence here is the phrase, "when opportunities to be helpful come along." The very heart of this is, again, humility. In my own life, I don't disclose to everyone asking, but occasionally I do—if the person asking is receptive and not just curious for sensationalism.

CLA has received requests for speakers at events, interviews for newspaper articles and broadcast programs, and participation in reporters' series on hoarding. The question of how anonymous we should be always comes up on a case-by-case basis, and for this reason we have a public information officer who is very well-versed in the Traditions.

CLA is beginning to feel the tide of media approval, as A.A. did years ago before it was widely established. It's going slowly, and some of us are impatient and want it to be more. A.A.'s experience, however, tells us that too much, too soon, would not necessarily be a good thing. One meeting had so many newcomers following a positive news article that there weren't enough old-timers to handle the new people, so many of them didn't come back. Growth is desirable, but sudden growth can be a challenge.

Step 7 gives a greater in-depth look at the acquision of humility. In my own life, I took on the job of chairperson at World Service many years ago—firstly, because no one else wanted it, but then, because I began to have a vision of what I could do for the organization. I was seduced over time by my marginal successes in wanting to make a name for myself. When I saw those same traits in someone else, I was forced to come back to earth and see my service as a way of helping everyone. It was important to give others their due and let them have a turn in the spotlight, too. That awareness helped me to get more life-sized, as it says in Step 7. The 12th Tradition of anonymity also covers when I should learn to keep my mouth shut and when I should speak.

The backbone of all the Traditions is anonymity, with its concept of humility. When I read that, it really opened my eyes to realize that this Tradition is, indeed, rooted in sacrifice. When I think of sacrifice, I have to think of what I have to give up by being anonymous.

Newcomers learn about the concept of anonymity at program level, but it takes a while to get to the concept on a personal level. I have to be anonymous in other peoples' lives instead of trying to get their attention by talking over them, or trying to get more recognition for myself instead of letting God work through me. It's sometimes a hard lesson to learn, because God lets me go ahead and do those things. And I realize by how I feel when it's working and when it isn't working. Most of the time when it's self-will, it isn't working.

So, then—when I go back to the book and I read more about humility, more about how sacrifice works, and more about these things that are in the *Twelve and Twelve*[16]—I get a chance to use them in my daily life. I try to remember what they are, so that I can be conscious of the lesson that I'm learning. A lot of times I don't remember until after the deed's already done. I've said the hurtful thing, or I've done the hurtful thing, or I haven't forgiven somebody for their doing the hurtful thing. It took me a while to get into wanting to learn about the Traditions. A lot of people think the Traditions are boring and stuffy (and they probably are when you read through them and you don't really understand what they're saying). But once you get past a certain point and you're ready to have the lessons come in, they will.

Other Articles on the Traditions

Twelve and Twelve–Traditions

Summer 2009

Gloria S., NY

The Traditions are to protect the Fellowship from our own egos. They are based on those of A.A. and were a product of trial and error, of what worked and did not work for A.A .as a whole. As the Fellowship grew, the members were tempted to do all sorts of crazy things.

The 1st Tradition has to do with unity. It states that our common welfare must come first; we are all in this together, no matter where we are located or how large or small our groups are.

The 2nd Tradition has to do with governing and the idea that the only authority is a loving Higher Power as expressed by group conscience. No one person is in charge, and no one person can govern us in any way.

Third, the only requirement for membership in our group is a desire to stop cluttering. All are welcome, and no one can keep anyone out.

Fourth, each group is autonomous and has the right to decide for itself how its group operates. There are no rules as long as the group's actions do not affect another meeting or CLA as a whole.

Fifth, the group's one primary purpose is to carry the message of recovery to another clutterer.

Sixth, as a Fellowship, we do not endorse, finance, or lend our name to any related facility or outside enterprise. In that way, we can never compromise our integrity or divert ourselves from our main objective.

Seventh, we are self-supporting through our own contributions—neither asking nor accepting funds in any way from anyone but our members.

Eighth, while we are nonprofessional in our recovery work, we do pay people who do professional work for us.

Ninth, we are never organized, but we do create service boards or committees directly responsible to those they serve. And, they serve the groups as trusted servants and have no real authority.

Tenth, we do not engage in any public controversy, and as an organization or as members of CLA, we have no opinions on outside issues. We mind our own business. As individuals we are free to do what we want, but we do not bring our affiliation with CLA with us.

Eleventh, we attract members to us, but we do not promote ourselves. We maintain personal anonymity at the level of press, radio, films, television, and all other media. We also protect the anonymity of other members.

Twelfth, anonymity, having a spiritual significance, reminds us to place principles before personalities. This ensures humility and gratitude for the recovery with which we have been blessed.

So you see, although these Traditions may sound strange, they serve a very important function. They keep the focus on recovery of the individual who comes in looking for help.

Respectfully yours in service.

The Importance of Practicing the Traditions

Summer 2009

Alison B., NJ

You've heard them read at meetings, but they go in one ear and out the other. You don't really pay attention. Why should you? They don't apply to you…or do they? Believe it or not, they apply to each and every one of us as individuals as much as to the welfare of each group. They are serious, and they are there to help us avoid trying to reinvent the wheel.

Just think about it: they have kept thousands of A.A. groups together successfully because they were written from the experiences, good and bad, of the early A.A. groups. They can help us too, but we do have to study them, learn them, and apply them.

I can already hear you saying that you are already overwhelmed with all the decluttering you have to do. Well, is it working for you? If you have a sponsor, or at least some kind of ongoing support between meetings, then the answer will undoubtedly be yes because you are serious about your recovery. But each group has to have a solid foundation, just like the foundation of a building; or, just like a building, it will wobble, crack, and finally collapse.

This means that it is the responsibility of every member of the group to help with the smooth running of the group. This is what we call "service," and it is very important for your own recovery. Service means helping the group in any way you can. Aside from practical help like setting up chairs, bookkeeping, and leading a meeting, the best way you can help your group is to understand the Traditions and contribute your opinions at business meetings, based on this knowledge.

The Traditions will help you to learn how to cooperate within the group; and this will, in turn, help you learn how to cooperate with people in the rest of your life.

Without applying the Traditions, CLA would crumble and fall apart, so let us always remember something that a founder of A.A. said: that our common unity comes first, but the welfare of the individual follows closely behind!

Viewpoint on Traditions

Holiday 2009

Lorraine, CA

If a meeting wants to be included in the CLA Meeting List or a phone meeting wants to be on an officially recognized CLA phone bridge and code, then the meeting needs to follow CLA Traditions and guidelines. Callers—especially newcomers—should have an expectation of hearing the Traditions, 12-Step philosophy, and CLA-approved literature. This is designed to preserve the CLA groups as a whole for the future survival and growth of CLA and its primary purpose. A prime example is the phone line, (712) 432-3900, with access code of 727176.*

While people in various support groups tend to come and go (each one with personal opinions and desires, which often conflict with each other), the survival of CLA as a whole is paramount, especially for those yet to come. And practicing the Tradition of placing principles before personalities is vital to the program in attracting the newcomer, as well as current members.

While a format can be extremely simple (such as for the shared activity sessions), it needs to be in adherence with CLA Traditions—and, once adopted, should not be altered in a non-CLA way. A lot of dedicated service goes into planning and evaluating a CLA format, and this work and service should not be compromised or diminished.

Endorsing outside literature, organizations, philosophies, workshops, or businesses (especially "for-profit" types, including self-help books) at any meeting serves only to confuse newcomers (and even those who have been members for a while) as to what CLA is truly about. There is no need to add to or water down the existing program, which already has so much valuable information. Too few of our members as of yet know the CLA literature or the 12 Steps and the 12 Traditions (adapted from A.A.), which are the heart of our program of recovery. Newcomers are especially vulnerable to any ideas which may sound good. These "good ideas" often contradict the CLA philosophy and the 12 Steps, and using them in a CLA meeting or activity session violates our 12 Traditions.

Whenever any group tries to be all things to all people, it fails in having or sustaining a primary purpose, and eventually self-destructs—an example being the Washingtonians (100 years prior to A.A.). Allowing any CLA group to adopt a flavor-of-the-day mentality (with instant group consciences or leader's choice), causes confusion—and often disenchantment—when a CLA member or potential CLA member calls in expecting CLA recovery through the 12 Steps and instead is met with confusion and no assurance of any continuity, structure, or guidelines that remain consistent. As already stated, members will come and go in any program, so the survival of a program itself depends on its having and maintaining its primary purpose; and when it is a 12-Step program, its survival also depends on following the 12 Traditions. Keep in mind that this is a program of attraction, not promotion.

And while CLA (like other 12-Step programs) has adapted the 12 Steps and 12 Traditions of A.A. to CLA's primary purpose, which is to carry its message of recovery to those who still suffer, CLA is not affiliated with or answerable to A.A. And by the very nature of CLA's different problems, needs, and primary purpose, it does not need to replicate A.A. Nor does it need to follow what an extremely small part of A.A. might possibly allow in their meetings. So the focus needs to be off A.A. and only on CLA and how it believes it can safeguard its primary purpose. Therefore, if any meeting decides it does not want to follow CLA's Traditions, then it is their obligation to not pronounce their meeting as CLA, and to ask to be removed from the "CLA Meeting List" and, if a phone meeting, to acquire a different conference bridge and code.

But, rather than any group fighting for whatever it wants (regardless of the detriment to CLA as a whole), why not ask how it can meet the guidelines of CLA and be of maximum service to its meeting participants, as well as all CLA members (current and future)—such as using CLA leaflets and approved 12-Step literature—as the focus of the meeting. An example would be to read five or more of the CLA Recovery Affirmations[20] prior to each "quiet time" during a shared activity session. This provides a recovery tool and hope to the participants. The CLA Fellowship will benefit from experience, strength, and hope!

The Importance of Practicing the 12 Traditions

Fall 2013

Kathy H., CA

The Traditions were first developed by Alcoholics Anonymous (A.A.) some years after it came into existence. They were distilled from the hard experience of A.A. groups. It is often said that the Traditions are to the group as the Steps are to the individual.

But why are the Traditions so important? They are a guideline for the smooth functioning of Clutterers Anonymous groups and service bodies. Ignoring one or more of the Traditions often results in discord within the group and the Fellowship. The Traditions are so important that most groups read them out loud at every meeting. Also, some groups use a Tradition as a topic at certain meetings, and there are groups which study one Tradition each month.

Often, when a group breaks one or more of the Traditions, it is because the members are not well-informed. This can be remedied easily. CLA does not yet have a book on the Steps and Traditions, although one is being planned. However, it would be helpful for more members to study the Alcoholics Anonymous book, *Twelve Steps and Twelve Traditions.*[16] It is a good starting place to learn how the Traditions work. There have also been many articles written on the Traditions in the *A.A. Grapevine*,[2] as well as many other sources.

Many problems can be prevented by following the Traditions. Groups that ignore the Traditions usually run into trouble in the long run. In fact, as we begin to understand the Traditions, we find that they are a good guide in dealing with others, even outside the Fellowship. I know that, for myself, when I am in the habit of behaving with the principles of our Traditions in mind, my relations with others improve, and I am able to attain more serenity and isolate less.

I think of my own CLA home group. Once we had a member who refused to have anything to do with the Steps or the Traditions; she would not even read them during the meeting, instead tuning them out when they were read. She insisted that they were boring and refused to learn anything about them. We struggled with her often-expressed desire to bring outside methods, systems, and literature into the meeting; and we had to often repeat that the 12 Steps are the basis of our recovery. (Of course, we also discussed the "CLA Tools of Recovery"[19] in our meetings.) Eventually, this member dropped out of CLA altogether.

Our group is small, but it functions in a spirit of loving support. Were we to put anything before our personal recovery (Tradition 1), the group would no longer be the place to come to share our problems and triumphs. Everyone in the group has the same voice in meeting affairs; no one person dominates (Tradition 2). We refrain from bringing outside issues and materials into the meeting, and we do guard the anonymity of our members.

Tradition 5 tells us that each group has but one primary purpose—to carry the message of recovery to the person who still suffers. Were we to put our time and energy to any other purpose but that of furthering the recovery of CLA members, we would be hard put to carry out this primary purpose.

When we keep our Traditions in mind in all the dealings of our Fellowship, we find that we are more able to support all the members of the group and avoid letting personalities run riot over principles.

CLA Literature and the Traditions

Fall 2009

We have found that there is much ignorance in our Fellowship about the CLA Traditions. Because of this, Clutterers Anonymous World Service Organization has set up an ad hoc committee to help educate the Fellowship in this area.

In that spirit, the CLA*rity* team has decided to include an article on a matter that has currently engendered much controversy: that of using outside literature. In our meetings, we use only CLA Fellowship-approved literature or that of other established 12-Step programs. It has recently been suggested that we limit the latter to A.A. literature to avoid confusion and bewildering choices. Also, there are some programs that do not follow all the Traditions as set forth by A.A.

Why do we follow the Traditions of Alcoholics Anonymous when our program is for clutterers? A.A. is the founder of all 12-Step programs; it has more than 70 years' experience in learning how the program functions.

The efforts on the part of early A.A. groups to establish mechanisms for managing groups and the organization as a whole eventually evolved into the Traditions as we know them today. In short, we use them because they work. To understand fully, it is important to read further. Since CLA does not yet have a "Twelve and Twelve" book, we refer to that of A.A. The following references are from the book, *Twelve Steps and Twelve Traditions,*[16] by Alcoholics Anonymous. On page 146, (Tradition 4) it states,

> *Over the years, every conceivable deviation from our Twelve Steps and Traditions has been tried.....Children of chaos, we have defiantly played with every brand of fire, only to emerge unharmed and, we think, wiser. These very deviations created a vast process of trial and error which, under the grace of God, has brought us to where we stand today.*

The problem is that in trying to do too many things, we lose sight of the program. Page 150 states:

> *"Shoemaker, stick to thy last!"...better do one thing supremely well than many badly. That is the central theme of this Tradition [Tradition 5]. Around it our Society gathers in unity. The very life of our Fellowship requires the preservation of this principle.*

Page 157 says:

> *These adventures implanted a deep-rooted conviction that in no circumstances could we endorse any related enterprise, no matter how good. We of Alcoholics Anonymous could not be all things to all men, nor should we try.*

Some Thoughts on the Traditions

Holiday 2014

Mary P., NY

It's been said that the Steps exist to keep us from killing ourselves, the Traditions to keep us from killing each other. The Traditions guide the way a CLA group can run smoothly and fairly, from week to week and even in business meetings. Their message is one of participation and moderation: being right-sized, knowing your right place, having the right motives, and doing the next right thing.

Consider the 1st Tradition: "Our common welfare should come first; personal recovery depends upon CLA unity." Consensus and the common good should be the goal. We should ask, "Is this good for the group?" not "Is this best for me?"

Similarly, the 2nd Tradition stresses the group conscience and reminds us, "Our leaders are but trusted servants; they do not govern."

We must guard against overly dominant or controlling leaders—in other words, people who take advantage of CLA's loose structure for their own purposes. Meetings that don't have regular elections or rotation of leaders run the risk of being "Mike's meeting" (or "Maggie's meeting"). No group ought to assume that theirs is the only way to run a meeting. As Tradition 4 states, "Each group is autonomous except in matters affecting other groups or CLA as a whole." The smoothly functioning group does depend on everyone's participation; it's a cop-out to say, "Oh, I just don't like business meetings."

Other traditions define how the group relates to the outside world. CLA groups, the 6th Tradition states, "ought never endorse, finance, or lend the Clutterers Anonymous name to any related facility or outside enterprise, lest problems of money, property or prestige divert us from our primary purpose" (which, Tradition 5 has specified, is to carry the message to the person who still suffers).

The 7th Tradition, concerning self-support, warns against accepting any outside contributions.

Further delineating this distinction, Tradition 10 states that CLA has no opinion on outside issues and must avoid public controversy.

All the Traditions are encapsulated in the 12th and final one; we are reminded to place "principles before personalities." If we do that and keep the emphasis on the "we," not the "me," our group should run fairly and smoothly.

Anonymity, which is very close to humility, will always be our guiding principle.

How the Twelve Traditions and CLA Changed My Life

Summer 2016

Nancy W., CT

In our CLA meetings, we say that the Steps are to the individual as the Traditions are to the group. Well, I always knew I had a problem and that I wasn't like other people. I did not then know what I had was a disease and that I think differently from other so-called normal people. I think it was being in another Fellowship that made me ready to start facing the reality that I could not continue to live the way I had been living.

Living by the 12 Steps is extremely important to my recovery. What I didn't realize is how the Traditions have helped me to accept my need for CLA. You see, I was always like a character in one of my favorite TV shows: a person who struggled to pick up after herself and kept bringing things into her environment.

To paraphrase *Alcoholic Anonymous*[4] ("The Big Book"), I am a clutterer of the hopeless variety. Trusting that the group conscience of the CLA Fellowship is led by a Higher Power (Tradition 2) was the answer for me. This Fellowship is very different from the other ones I am in. First, this Fellowship is truly a "we" program. Not only do meetings help, but we are blessed to have the Action Line to live the program. Could I book-end if there was no one on the other end of the phone line to take my commitment? We need each other. This disease is so insidious that it is difficult to define abstinence. This disease tells me to be ashamed and that my recovery is a matter of will-power. I have to surrender and learn from every-one else's experience, strength, and hope.

Also, I find, as a clutterer, I am extremely sen-sitive. So when I feel someone is judging me, my feelings tend to get hurt. Or if I hear some con-troversial discussion, I become very uncomfortable and shut down. Tradition 12 tells me to place principles before personalities. I feel that clutterers are extremely passionate people. Each one of us is here to help and to carry the message to the new-comer (Tradition 5). We are here to live.

I know if I don't change, this disease will kill me. Therefore, I cannot take anything personally but have to trust and keep following the sugges-tions of the program, as well as work the Steps. This is crucial in my life because I had to realize that most of my family will not believe me or trust me that I'm in this Fellowship.

I have tried many, many things to help my cluttering, and nothing has helped. I have bought all kinds of different books, I tried to change my character defect of laziness, and I promised over and over that it would be different for my family. Again, when my family doubted my intentions, I had to look at principles before personalities. Because, in my heart of hearts, I know that if I do what CLA members tell me to do, eventually I will see progress.

CLA has given me hope. I am so grateful to all who participate in this Fellowship, and the Tra-ditions teach me to cherish everyone's opinions, even if I don't agree with them. I can learn some-thing from each person. Unity is the answer, and I am very grateful to be a member of Clutterers Anonymous.

*Phone meetings may have changed focus, meeting times, phone numbers, and access codes since this writing. Check the "CLA Meeting Directory" at ClutterersAnonymous.org for current information.

Clutterers Anonymous Program

While the basis of CLA's program of recovery is working the 12 Steps, there are many other aspects to the program. These include the CLA Tools of Recovery,[19] Affirmations,[20] and Slogans.[21]

Newcomers

Advice to the Newcomer

Fall 2015

CLA*rity* asked a few long-time CLA members how they would guide newcomers to the program. Following is a compilation of their comments.

It has been suggested that newcomers try at least six meetings before deciding whether CLA is for them. It would be helpful to study the "CLA Tools of Recovery" and use them. Read as much CLA literature as you can, and get a sponsor to mentor you through the 12 Steps and the program. If you attend face-to-face meetings and cannot find a sponsor at your meeting, try going to a few phone meetings to see if you can find one there. Get involved in service and consider attending open meetings of another 12-Step program to boost your recovery.

Attend meetings, either face-to-face or over the phone, and if you relate to another member, ask him or her to be your buddy. For the definition of a buddy, see the "CLA Tools of Recovery" located in two pieces of CLA literature: the leaflet, "A Brief Guide,"[5] and the booklet, "Is CLA for You? A Newcomer's Guide to Recovery."[12] Then actually call that new buddy so you can start becoming accountable for your decluttering actions.

If you're not comfortable asking someone for this sort of help, it may be helpful to call in to one or more of the Phone Activity Sessions or the Commitment Line. Here you can share about your decluttering in a safe environment and discover the advantages of being accountable for your actions. One member shared that this helped her enormously in the beginning and left her feeling not quite so alone with her clutter. You might even find a buddy through your participation in these sessions.

Writing about cluttering issues for CLA*rity* seemed to jump-start another member's decluttering efforts. She's not suggesting that you have to write newsletter articles, but the benefit of writing is that you have to think through cluttering issues and sometimes even research them. It's a great learning experience. She wrote an article about procrastination which really made her think about her reasons for procrastinating, a habit common to clutterers. You don't have to show your writing to anyone.

If you find it helps, great; if not, maybe it's not an effective tool for you. But it may be worth a try.

If your clutter seems too overwhelming, try taking action on only one piece of clutter. It's better than not doing anything. Some members have had success in using a timer for 15-minute intervals. In other words, they "played" for 15 minutes, then worked for 15 minutes. Another member has had success with decluttering at least ten items daily. Others have found success creating "clutter-free zones." These are spaces that you designate and commit to keeping free of clutter before you go to bed each evening. As you progress, you can expand the size and number of clutter-free zones. It may be helpful to envision how you want each space to look after it is clutter free.

And remember, "we start where we are." We can't expect to go from "overwhelmed" to "completed" all at once; it takes consistent effort over time. As we say in CLA, "progress, not perfection." That is the goal.

Abstinence and Measuring Progress

Finding Abstinence: One Member's Journey

Holiday 2007

Kathy H., CA

After participating in many discussions among CLA members, I have come to the conclusion that defining abstinence is an important aspect of the program. CLA currently has no definition of abstinence from clutter, but it is a concept that is in development by the Literature Committee.

Since our cluttering problems are so varied, the actions that constitute abstinence for one member are different than those for another. Because of this, I believe that CLA members should be encouraged to find personalized definitions of abstinence to help them with their own problems by working with a sponsor or a buddy. This can be a difficult issue, and it is probably better not to figure it out on your own. Through working the CLA program more than five years, I have begun to realize that finding what constitutes abstinence for myself is more complex than I had thought previously.

I have made quite a lot of progress in decluttering. However, I now recognize that in order for me to maintain my house in a manner in which I would be comfortable I need to identify just which behaviors constitute cluttering for me; therefore, I am beginning to develop an abstinence plan. I will list the specific behaviors that lead me to clutter or delay decluttering, as well as those behaviors that aid in my recovery. By implementing a personal abstinence plan, I believe I can do a much better job of decluttering and, thereafter, keep my house clutter free.

CLA Tools of Recovery

Buddies

Summer 2008

Kathy H., CA

The CLA "Tools of Recovery"[19] state: *Buddies are CLA members and helpmates in recovery. We may call them with our daily plan or ask for help with a project.*

Some people maintain their relationships as CLA buddies purely on the telephone, while others visit each others' homes. Although the telephone is also a tool in itself, buddies are a little more systematic. You may call many CLA members occasionally, but a buddy is an ongoing resource in working on a decluttering plan and in giving moral support or advice. Buddies may help us with prioritizing and devising a decluttering plan of action or by physically helping one another to declutter. Sponsors and buddies do differ. While sponsors may also fill the same functions as a buddy, they also guide the member through working the 12 Steps.

In my experience, just having a buddy at the house is a help in decluttering—even if they do no work at all. One time my buddy was sitting in my house reading. I felt uncomfortable, since I had been telling her I was going to declutter a particular spot and hadn't even begun. So I decided to start the job, so that I wouldn't have to confess complete failure. I went back to find her asleep. Just having her there helped me to find the motivation to finish my decluttering task. We have both had the same experience at other times; it seems that having another person there can be the catalyst just to be able to start.

We also have helped each other with making plans of action. The chores seem to go a lot faster with help and much more gets accomplished. I have found that my decluttering is more successful when I plan out the steps needed for a complex chore. Certain tasks have to be done before others can be undertaken. Otherwise, I end up just spinning my wheels. As in so many things, organization is the key to efficiency and success, at least for me. Of course, the other key is dealing with my procrastination demon—and a buddy can really help there! Finishing this article is a case in point; I couldn't seem to get motivated until I discussed it with one telephone buddy. Then, once I got started, it seemed to flow. This just goes to point out how important it is to maintain contact with my buddies, as well as with my Higher Power.

I have, a few times, worked as a buddy on a short-term basis with groups of three or four CLA members. This is certainly easier to do when it involves other clutterers, who are in the same boat.

I was able to let go of my embarrassment and ask someone to come to my house within a few days of joining CLA. However, this particular buddy is also a long-time friend and had already seen part of my clutter. Some members may feel resistance to having anyone over for quite some time after they join the program. I have seen some who are able to admit a buddy right away. The important thing to remember is that the buddy is also a clutterer and should not express judgment about your problem. This knowledge usually lessens the embarrassment factor.

I do feel that the concept of buddies works best when both members are willing to accept and give help. When it becomes one-sided, it tends to lead to discomfort or resentment.

In short, without having a buddy in CLA, my recovery from decluttering would not be nearly as far along!

The Telephone

Fall 2008

Don A., CA

If we look at our lives as a path that we must travel as the poet said ("Two roads diverged in a yellow wood..."), there are many choices which we will be called upon to make.

I used to overthink all the time. Then an old-timer at a Clutter-Free Day advised me to "make three phone calls a day."

That simple advice carried me through my early months in CLA. I accepted that I was powerless to change my life without outside assistance.

But how and when do I choose to use the telephone as a part of my recovery, rather than as an escape from my discomforts?

The way I used to make most decisions was impulsive and reactive. It's not surprising that I would want to find a quick way to fix the problem and take an action to try to resolve the discomfort. Any action is better than doing nothing, I used to think. Not true!

Really, what I needed to do was to take the right action. But I was riddled by self-doubt and shame; I felt frozen, angry, and confused. I certainly wasn't sure about much. Except that my life wasn't serene! So, I thought to apply the program thinking to my use of the telephone.

First, ask: What have I been doing with the telephone?

Then, ask: Has that been working? How do I feel about it? Do I want to continue with the same approach?

Next, take action. (Yes, I want to take action, but what?) Two things that have worked for me are: (1) Bookending—calling a buddy, calling the Check-in Line, or writing it down—and (2) making a committed phone call to someone who has asked for one or whom you had promised to call.

Change is always an exchange, and there is usually fear at letting go of the familiar.

My CLA Toolbox–Sponsorship

Spring and Summer 2009

Cindy S., CA

The CLA "Tools of Recovery"[19] state:

Sponsors are CLA members who are committed to recovery through the 12 Steps and 12 Traditions A Step sponsor leads us through the 12 Steps of recovery. We choose a sponsor who has what we want. The sponsor and buddy may be the same person.

When I found CLA initially, phone meetings were hard for me because I could hide my shame and not pay attention nor stay focused to listen. I am visual, and it helps me to view a person's communication in order to remain engaged. I found that when it comes to things that are emotionally threatening, I will take any distraction and not reveal the truth about myself. On the phone I can stay in my head, but at in-person meetings I am forced to come out of isolation and be seen. Miraculously, in my desperation, I started an in-person CLA meeting with someone I met at another 12-Step Fellowship who had shared about a problem with cluttering. I knew I could get myself to in-person meetings, and it was simple to set it up using the Traditions and with the support provided by CLA WSO.

Because we were all new to CLA and, for many, our meeting was their first exposure to a 12-Step program, we had no available sponsors. In another program, I have had a sponsor with whom I speak daily. I yearned for such support in CLA. I knew I did well with structure, but I could provide none for myself, even though I could organize someone else and had worked my way through college as a personal assistant and executive secretary.

I desperately wished for someone to be witness to my commitments, to provide feedback from his or her own experience regarding the reality of my intended projects, and to show me the way. I don't have good judgment when it comes to how much time it takes for me to do something. I don't know how to take care of myself. I have absolutely no idea how much energy I have. I think that I am depleted before I even begin to deal with paperwork. (It had taken me seven years to send my husband's death certificate to my accountant. I constantly misplaced my children's birth certificates and sent for them several times, only to lose them again.)

I had promised I would find a CLA sponsor and then was embarrassed to admit when I didn't do it. I became ashamed of myself and felt I had let the meeting down by not being a good role model. It was an intervention from my Higher Power that got me down to Los Angeles for the Clutter-Free Day. Out of nowhere, I got a call from someone driving down. I went with the intention of finding a sponsor. I had hoped there would be discussion around this tool.

I heard people communicating about how their minds were a jumbled mess, just like mine. I was surprised, relieved, and disappointed to find that I was not alone in not having a sponsor and also in refusing to sponsor someone else. People who I judged to have it "together" in their appearance spoke my concerns about not considering themselves "advanced enough" in the program and definitely not able to assist someone else's recovery.

I took home with me that all we need to be is "one Step, one action" ahead of someone else in order to be a sponsor.

I established a sponsor relationship with someone I met in Los Angeles, and I agreed to sponsor someone who had asked me repeatedly at home. I will sponsor as long as it supports my recovery. I must get more from sponsoring than I am giving, so I sponsor to be reminded of what I am committed to in my recovery from cluttering.

As a sponsor, I share how I work my program, and I sponsor someone who wants to work the program in a similar fashion. This is unnerving at the beginning, because we get to learn to tell the truth and trust someone else with intimate details about our living situation. As I gain the ability to do this daily, I am finding that I deserve to give myself attention, and I can trust someone else to be understanding. Here's what works for me:

I write down my mantra that I can view during the day, when I forget who I am and what I am committed to. I email it to my sponsor, and sometimes I look at it 25 times during the day. It looks like this:

I am a compulsive clutterer. I am abstinent and grateful today because I don't add anything unless I remove something first. Daily I commit to my sponsor my plan of action. No matter what happens today, I know that I am working my program to become clutter free. I make my bed when I wake up. I put away everything I take out. I do one act of decluttering. I clear my sink before I go to bed. I write down my schedule and assign a timeframe to each task. I ask for help to bookend and turn over my anxieties when I get stuck.

It has been amazing to me to see how much I do when I write it all down and how much easier it is when I turn it over to someone else. I ask my sponsees to do the same for themselves.

It is much easier to sponsor than I feared, because daily I get a phone call about someone else's decluttering progress, and I get to be witness to their spiritual and emotional growth. They are so grateful when I point out their obvious progress. It strengthens my focus, and I know I am not alone because I have a sponsor to whom I am turning over my goals as well.

Before, I noticed only what didn't get done, and now I'm relieved of that critical judgment because I have someone else "holding the space" for me to recognize how much I have done as well. I am learning to measure my time and choose where I invest my time, energy, and resources. I am learning to say no to things and people. I am recognizing that I am obligated only to my own program, and my own commitments come first. I heard someone say that CLA is a "selfish" program, and I think it is true for all of recovery—we must mind our own business.

No longer do I have to struggle, stay stuck, or keep something that doesn't support me. Every day I am reminded to take care of myself first, turn over my plans to my sponsor, and let my Higher Power support me. I don't have to do it alone because today I have Tools of the program, as well as the Steps and the Fellowship. It is simple, but not easy. I am truly grateful for the 12 Steps and "CLA Tools of Recovery,"[19] especially the Tool of Sponsoring and being sponsored.

CLA Toolbox–Bookending

Holiday 2009

Alison B., NJ

Bookending is talking to another person or group of members for support before and after taking any action, especially when it's about a difficult step in recovery or doing a challenging task. Bookending is helpful in completing the task or offers support toward progress.

I would have to say that Bookending is my favorite Tool. For one thing, it gives me an excuse to call someone. Then it's easy to say, "Hi, friend, how are you doing today?" I have always been a bit scared when it comes to initiating phone calls—in fact, I used to say I had a phobia about phones—so I really prefer it when I can legitimately say that I have a valid reason for calling. Thus, I know ahead of time what I'm going to say: "I need to bookend doing my laundry," for example.

I specify: "This means I will work on it from start to finish—from sorting to putting it away. I will call you back in two hours and let you know that I have completed this task."

Now it's up to me to get off the phone as quickly as I can and not let myself get distracted from my primary purpose. Sometimes the person at the other end needs to bookend, too. I think it's always better when the support is mutual.

Many times, I have used the Bookending Tool when I've needed to do filing. This is because I don't enjoy this chore, and somehow I feel much better if I can get a pat on the back once it's done. Calling back after a reasonable amount of time spent working on a task is a crucial part of the completion cycle for me.

In some instances, I have called a person who didn't pick up the phone, so I simply told the voicemail that I needed to bookend and would call back once I'd finished. It's not my preferred method, but it does work in a pinch.

I have noticed that I tend to live my life, for the most part, by making commitments to others for the things I have to do. It's partly because I have trouble making decisions and partly because, if I don't have someone to report to, apathy and rebellion tend to set in. There are many times that I have sabotaged my own efforts by promising myself to do something but then "forgetting" to do it, such as paying bills. When I tell someone else—and put an immediate time frame on it—I make myself accountable. This works for me.

I am very grateful to the CLA program for giving me this Tool. I am also grateful for the list of other CLA Tools[19] and Affirmations[20] which, when used properly, assist me in doing my Higher Power's will and help guide me along the arduous road of recovery.

The tasks that I am learning to do through bookending tend to be the actions that will help me to achieve my goals in the long run.

Meetings

Summer 2010

Colleen C., CA

Meetings: *We attend meetings to learn how the program works and to share our experience, strength, and hope with each other* (CLA Tools of Recovery).[19] On May 28, 2005, I walked into my very first CLA meeting in Orange, California. I had never attended a 12-Step meeting before and didn't have an understanding of how this program of recovery works. As a newcomer, I thought CLA was a "decluttering club" where I would find tips on becoming more organized, housekeeping hints, and simply a place to complain and commiserate with others about the clutter! I had many misconceptions about CLA when I first came to this program and just as many frustrations and setbacks, but I am glad I listened to the members who said, "Keep coming back."

There were times when I became discouraged and questioned whether it worked at all. However, I knew that I felt better after attending a meeting, sharing, and making a commitment to one doable action for the week. Meetings were all I knew thus far, and so I made it a top priority to attend. If I was traveling, I would try to find a meeting in that city or attend a phone meeting. I still continued to struggle in my recovery for some time, but I kept coming back to the rooms of CLA. I kept an open mind as I listened to others share their experience, strength, and hope, as well as their missteps. I began to hear the message from those who have found recovery in CLA and other 12-Step Fellowships. By attending regular meetings, I have also been motivated to keep coming for the newcomers who walk into our rooms.

Today, I am grateful for the members who come each week and share at my CLA home group and for all of the groups in our Fellowship. I actively work the program of CLA with the help of a clutter buddy who has worked the Steps in other Fellowships and has found recovery. For me, attending weekly meetings continues to be one of the most valuable Tools of recovery in this Fellowship. When I didn't fully understand how to work this program, I learned from listening to others that I could "act as if" and keep coming back, week after week. Recovery for me feels like an uphill battle sometimes, but meetings continue to be a touchstone, a vital part of my ongoing recovery process, even if the group is small. I have found that if I stop attending meetings, I put myself in danger of starting to slip back into cluttering. Many others in the Fellowship have shared the very same thing. Meetings are an essential part of CLA, not only in our own recovery, but also in helping to ensure the program is here for those who follow in our footsteps. Keep coming back, it works if you work it—and to borrow a slogan I heard in another 12-Step Fellowship, "Meeting makers make it!"

CLA Toolbox–Earmarking

Holiday 2010

Susie S., CA

We provide a place for our possessions and return them there. We create a home for anything before bringing it in. When we add a new item, we release an old one. For accessibility, beauty, and peace of mind, we keep some empty space.

Earmarking is one of my very favorite Tools[19] in CLA, and so when asked to write this article for CLA*rity*, I readily agreed. It has been my experience that any opportunity to be of service is always going to benefit me as well, and contemplating this topic has helped me to apply it to my life to an even greater degree. Earmarking has helped, not only with my physical and mental clutter, but also in regard to spiritual timing, including how I schedule my activities.

I had an eye-opening experience related to earmarking a few months ago when I was about to do my timed decluttering commitment, which I do each morning with a CLA buddy. The thought crossed my mind that if I were to earmark each item in my room—if each item had a home—it would no longer be clutter! I hope I can articulate how much this Tool has helped to simplify my decluttering process. All of a sudden it seemed so simple to tell myself that I just need to create a home—to decide where an item belongs—and that I can keep whatever I need as long as it has a home. And after using an item, I then need to return it there. This felt so comforting and reassuring and lifted a lot of the fear, overwhelm, and paralysis surrounding my clutter.

Earmarking has also been a very helpful Tool to apply in scheduling my activities. I earmark—create a place in my schedule—for daily prayer and meditation, exercise, handling errands, emails, phone calls, service, rest, leisure activities, etc. Having these activities earmarked has really helped eliminate the mental fog associated with indecision and time clutter. In addition to simplifying, it has brought much joy and purpose to my life. I am able to enjoy guilt-free leisure time because it is earmarked in my schedule!

My first CLA sponsor also stressed the importance of using this Tool in regard to my activities. She said that if I were to add a new activity to my schedule, I would need to release another and "keep some empty space" in my schedule. In applying this to physical clutter, I was quite impressed to hear how a CLA buddy was very diligent about releasing an item of clothing for every item she brought into her home, something I'm still working toward!

I am very grateful for the Tool of Earmarking and look forward to discovering new ways to apply it to my life and to bring me the joy of a less cluttered life!

My CLA Toolbox–Trust

Fall 2011

Carol N., CA

Trust is a recent addition to the "CLA Tools of Recovery."[19] When I first discovered it had been added, I wasn't immediately accepting of the idea of considering Trust as a Tool. I've gradually come to a changing of my understanding of the dynamics of "trust"—the word definition, the process, and the results.

One of CLA's cofounders, Varda, was the author of most of the first leaflets, one of which expounded on the "toolbox" concept. In the CLA literature stockpile, our ten "Tools of Recovery" had survived for almost 20 years without change. It was only a few years ago that the tools were expanded to 12 to include Trust and make Bookending a separate Tool.

The Tool of Trust, as written in our literature, states that "...we simplify our lives, believing that when we need a fact or an item, it will be available to us." But how does one go about "believing" or even learning to believe? And how does this enable me to let go of clutter I don't need? How useful, anyway, is this concept of trust in regard to the rest of my life?

When I was younger, I put my trust in people and institutions too easily and was consequently hurt when they let me down. This led to my living with the uneasy feeling of being alone and afraid in a hostile world and a certain wary cynicism that was largely on the unconscious level. That hardening of my heart kept me from the intimacy I longed for with other humans, especially those I love. When it became unbearable, I would flip-flop and rush to confide in people who were sometimes complete strangers and then feel hurt and stupid for opening myself up to the betrayal I felt.

I believed that in order to trust others, they had to somehow prove to me they were trustworthy by never doing anything I could perceive as negative. However, since I was constantly looking for proof, sometime down the line there would inevitably be a misdeed, and I would feel either rewarded for "finding that out in time" or feel sorry for myself for having been betrayed yet again.

This cycle continued a long, long time. I didn't know that I was practicing a character defect and that I had any choice at all in the matter. I thought I was at the mercy of every honest face because I really wanted to believe in people, but it seemed that my trust was misplaced a lot of the time.

This lack of trust was not only in my fellow man, it was in myself, in keeping my own word to me. It became symptomatic. Lower trust in myself served to lower my trust in others—in humans and in God and the way the world worked in general. I felt depressed a lot of the time; and I know now, looking at myself through their eyes, that it affected my relationships with others.

As with all character defects that cause enough pain for action, it eventually culminated in a kind person pointing something out to me. I must have been ready to hear it because it stuck and enabled me to begin to make a change in my life. What this person told me was a little hard to grasp at first, but I kept thinking about it. I thought about it a lot over time and came to some hopeful conclusions. In a nutshell, he said that it was one thing to do or not do something regarding another because I wanted to or didn't want to—but quite another to have to do or not do something with that person out of fear because I thought I had to. Somehow I equated that with having to do with trust issues of others' motives, and it began to dawn on me that I had been missing the boat regarding the dynamic of trust.

I had looked at trust as something to do with the other person's performance, that I had no part in it. I painfully began to desire to see the truth, the truth about the part I did play in my unhappiness regarding trust. I came to the conclusion that I was doing the "not trusting," and that it really didn't matter if I didn't know who was trustworthy and who wasn't because all humans (including myself) will eventually fail me anyway. So I could stop waiting for them to fail me and waiting for proof that they wouldn't, and I would stop worrying about my decisions and put all my attention to what I was going to learn about myself.

I've found that accepting that my "trust muscle" needs to be exercised every day keeps me moving forward in my quest for complete recovery. What also keeps me moving forward is a greater degree of acceptance of my circumstances and trust that things will be okay in the desire for a willingness to find out more and more about myself, especially the bad, as the good is more inclined to reveal itself with more ease.

Self-appraisal done on a regular basis doesn't undermine one's self-worth—it enhances it. Others can't hurt or surprise you by using their information about you if you already know it and accept it as a part of you. Knowing yourself is how trust develops, even toward your own person and circumstances.

Remember that this is a lifetime job, one that gets easier over time, provided you use the Tools[19] from the CLA Toolbox and those that life itself has given you to use freely. They're there if you search for them daily.

The ability to trust is so much more than just being able to call up a fact or item when you need it. That's just a fringe benefit. Being able to trust deeply—in yourself, your fellow man, and your Higher Power—will bring you out of isolation into the sunlight. Our literature talks about life becoming richer and more joyful. The more that becomes true for you, the less you will feel the need to protect and defend your clutter. ▲

My CLA Toolbox–Literature

Spring 2012
Gladys H., NY

Home: Our Sacred Place[11]

The CLA lavender leaflet, "Home: Our Sacred Place," was so revolutionary for me. My whole attitude and outlook on life changed on a Sunday afternoon as I read it while facilitating a Focused Action Line phone session. Home was a place I had spent my entire life running from (and oftentimes for good reasons).

The belief that my home could become a friend and a "sacred" place—if I allowed the "Spirit of the Universe" and "Infinite Love" to flow through me and my home—was difficult to believe; however, I was more than willing to believe it immediately after our sacred work session.

I meditated on the idea of "home" as my "sacred place." The following thoughts emerged as the meditation moved me from room to room.

First, it was my bedroom. My bedroom is a sacred place to be shared with the man whom God has given me to love, respect, and revere as a holy man, worthy of the best from me in a harmonious, clean, decluttered, well-ordered, and beautiful space. This is a place to share love, intimacies, hopes, dreams, and pain; a place where we will treat each other with respect, love, and high regard. I pray to always remember that when we're in this sacred space, I am in the presence of infinite love.

Next, it was the sacred place of the kitchen. It's where health, strength, and nourishment for the mind, body, soul, and spirit is to be created daily, not just once in a while. Here is a space that requires a real commitment and functions as the heartbeat of the home.

The sacred space of the bathroom was a mind-opening experience. The bathroom is a space for cleansing, cleaning, soothing, moisturizing, relaxing, and reflecting. A place and a chance to "let go and let God." To ensure that good will come in. To let out the negatives, fears, hatred, indifference, worries, and concerns. And to let in faith, hope, trust, encouragement, new ideas, and healing. A place of renewal.

And lastly, it was the living room as a sacred space. This sacred space is for good conversation. For sharing with good friends. For having good times. And for making good memories.

"Home: Our Sacred Place" has forever changed the way I view myself, my home, and the people I love. Thank you God, CLA, and the Focused Action Line—for it is with this love and support that we help each other create the loving and orderly life of beauty, harmony, and peace. Today, my home is a constant reminder of God's love and presence in this home, in my relationship, throughout the world, and in the universe.

My CLA Toolbox–Service

Summer 2012
Anonymous

The HOW of Service

Physical clutter is often caused by a cluttered life and mind. As a "trusted servant" (Tradition 2), in doing service I must conquer not only my clutter but its causes, which I do by working Steps 4 through 9 in my daily life. An inventory of my clutter and resentments is a good start but does not go far enough. I must inventory my performance as a servant. I must ask myself if I am practicing **HOW**— Honesty, Openness, and Willingness. Each day I give myself a quiz:

H—How *honest* am I with myself, my sponsor, my group, and CLA as a whole? Do I readily admit my faults and failures? Do I try to hide them or make excuses for them? Do I share my weaknesses and tell how I have worked the Steps to correct them? Is there anything I hope no one finds out about, or have I made a complete amends (Step 9) and do I now have clean hands so I am trustworthy?

O—Am I *open* to new ideas, no matter where they come from and which person in CLA proposes them? Am I placing principles before personalities (Tradition 12) in my life and service work? Do I argue or listen carefully and thoughtfully to what is said, even if I don't like it? Is it best for just me or CLA as a whole? Do I treat my fellow members with respect, and am I willing to put aside differences for the common welfare of CLA? (Tradition 1) Am I open to placing the results of group decisions in my Higher Power's hands? Do I try to control the results?

W—Have I experienced a spiritual awakening? (Step 12) Do I follow what I believe is my Higher Power's will in my service work? How *willing* am I to do service work, or do I feel "stuck" because it appears that few people are stepping forward to help? What can I do to make others feel comfortable and welcome in giving service? Does my group play musical chairs with the same faces, just different titles, or does my group practice true rotation of service by asking for assistance and helping those people become ready to advance in their level of service by sharing how things have been done in the past and are currently being done? Is it okay to "let go and let God" when a position becomes unfilled, or do I rush to fill it, even if I am not qualified and don't know what I am doing? Are the group and I willing to ask for help from those inside and outside CLA who have specialized knowledge? If a position remains unfilled, do I leave the success or failure of the group to my Higher Power, or do I try to rescue the situation by shaming people into service? Do I exercise my authority by doing double duty? Am I a one-man show? Am I tempted to "govern"? (Tradition 2)

I am sure, if you give it some thought, you can come up with additional or perhaps better questions to estimate your level of service and how well your group is doing in this area. I am grateful for all those who attempt to do service.

My CLA Toolbox–Streamlining

Fall 2012

Alison B., NJ

We honor what we own by setting limits on our possessions. We keep only those items we use and for which we have space. We realize that the more we acquire, the less we enjoy what we already have.

When I came into CLA, I decided not to create new clutter. I stopped buying almost everything except food. There were clothes all over the floor in one room. I had so much that I only needed to do laundry every eight weeks.

It was no wonder that I hated doing it. First, I began weeding out underwear and socks. I decided not to keep those that were damaged in any way. That meant I could no longer go so long without washing them. Also, I gave myself permission to throw them away without worrying about recycling. Clothes with holes or stains also went into the garbage and those I was keeping "just in case" got put into black plastic bags and taken to donation drop-offs. I know the universe will provide—it's in our literature. But knowing this emotionally has been another story. I sorted through my clothes many times 'til I could fit them all in my closet. I threw out all my metal hangers and replaced them with white plastic, which is much easier to handle. I turned all the hangers the same way so the clothes looked better. I even started putting them in categories, though I'm not very strict about this. I no longer have clothes in drawers—it's quicker to do laundry if I hang them over a chair when they come out of the dryer and then hang them up. It's exciting to have eliminated that nasty folding process! Underwear goes into large zippered plastic bags which are also hung up. I've bought some clothes along the way—then the rule is that I must eliminate a similar item. Sometimes I do miss certain items, but I'm proud that I chose to let them go.

Having success with my clothes has helped me in other areas. Now that I've discovered services that pick up used items to give to groups of needy people, it's been much easier to release all sorts of things. I now have a minimal number of shoes. I resist letting go of certain books, but I've given away at least four boxes. I have visions of cataloging the rest and then releasing them. I love music—but I would much rather listen to broadcasts than hear recordings that I own, so why keep them? It's comforting knowing that others are listening, too. The same goes for watching movies. I collected certain VHS tapes and then realized that was pointless so I released them, and I never bought many DVDs. Most of the cassettes I kept are ones on which I recorded my own singing. A huge, prerecorded boxful is now gone. Giving away all my vinyl records was gut-wrenching and still hurts because some were from my teenage years, but they were taking up precious book space.

As for papers, I finally invested in a good shredder, and I'm slowly going through my bulging files. I've given away two drawers' full of bed linens that were given to me. I've gotten rid of pots and plates that I haven't used in years, and I'm happy knowing that someone else will use them. Where my computer is concerned, I keep many files online so I don't worry about losing them, and I regularly streamline the hard drive with utility software.

I still have a long way to go—photos and CDs to be sorted, a large box of mementos, drawers and closets that contain unused things.

Streamlining for me goes way beyond mere possessions and into how I approach tasks. But that's another article!

My CLA Toolbox–Focusing

Summer 2013
Kathy H., CA

Our goal is to do one thing at a time.

I am writing this article on a long plane flight, having put it off and having trouble focusing on what I want to say. It almost sounds like I am writing about procrastination, but I am really writing on focusing, which I think relates to procrastination. Although they have different meanings, I tend to think of the two things together. When I am focusing on something, I am not putting it off. Of course, this article is about one of the CLA Tools of Recovery,[19] Focusing.

This Tool says that we do one thing at a time. This means a couple of things to me. First, it means I need to focus on a current task, without letting my mind wander on every momentary thought (which has everything to do with my problems in writing this article). Second, I believe it refers to doing one activity at a time, rather than multitasking. But I also use focusing to remind myself to work on one project at a time, finishing that one before I go on to another.

I used to have no trouble concentrating on one thing, blocking everything else out of my mind. As clutter began to accumulate, I began to be lazy in my thinking. Attending CLA meetings is helping me, once again, to stay on track.

In modern society, we seem to revere those who can multitask. But I've realized that I can't give my best performance on something if I am thinking about something else. If I were to try writing an article during a long, involved conversation, I would not be able to do justice to either the article or the conversation. There are many things that require my total concentration, so I need to focus on them to do them well.

It is possible for me to do a rote job while carrying on a conversation, watching TV, etc. It is no great trick to talk on the phone while making the bed or washing dishes, for instance. To me, this type of job, since it requires very little concentration, can easily be done while focusing on something else. I do find, however, that when I do certain things, I cannot spare even the little bit of attention those jobs require.

Then there is my tendency to have more than one project going on at once. This usually happens because I want to accomplish more than I ultimately manage to do. I have active hobbies, such as sewing and woodworking, which require the use of materials. Before coming to CLA, I would often start one project but not finish it on time. Then I would start a different one, so I would put the first project aside and begin on something else. Often, I never got back to the first, so the materials would pile up and add to the clutter in my house.

A few years back, I went through all those old projects, finished a few, and either threw away or gave away the materials for the others. Now I try very hard to avoid starting a project when there is an unfinished one. Of course, I am not perfect. Sometimes, I still procrastinate too long and need to start an urgent project before another is completed. But at least I don't let them accumulate for years the way I did in the past. I try to keep my ultimate goal firmly in mind—attaining a clean, decluttered house. Or, I could say that I focus on having a home I can live in happily.

Sometimes, during meetings, I feel I want to "zone out" during the readings I have heard many times. But without regularly hearing about this Tool of Focusing—as well as the other Tools[19] and all the readings—I start to slip away from the precepts I have learned in the CLA program. All the Tools have become important in my decluttering efforts. When I keep in mind the lessons I have learned from using the Tool of Focusing, I live more in the moment and avoid accumulating clutter.

The Joy of Buddies

Holiday 2013

Wendy L., IL

A clutter buddy understands you like none other. Can't bring yourself to throw away those cute pink socks? You know the ones. They have never matched anything you own. But you save them just in case. She gets that. Feeling completely overwhelmed by that pile of paperwork? She can relate to that, too. Clutter buddies get it and can be invaluable friends and allies in the war against clutter and space-wasting pretty socks.

CLA literature defines clutter buddies as clutterers who are "helpmates in recovery." I think of them as lifesavers. When my clutter is overwhelming or my life is in chaos, they buoy me with words of support and encouragement. Buddy relationships can be like personal extensions of CLA recovery meetings but where feedback is allowed. We talk about our successes and stresses, joys and setbacks. Unlike me, both of my buddies work strong 12-Step programs and share how that helps them deal with their clutter.

I met my buddies by calling each one after they had left their phone numbers on the Focused Action Session phone line. But boy, were those first phone calls tough. I wasn't sure what to say or how they'd react. Luckily, both turned out to be friendly and receptive, and we related to each other. But not all members I called worked out as buddies. It seems to be like any sort of friendship in that you need to click with each other and find common ground.

One of my buddies was happy to bookend with me and I gave it a shot. Per CLA literature, we bookend "when we talk to other CLA members before and after taking difficult steps in our recovery." My buddy and I let each other know what we hope to accomplish in a set amount of time.

Although it helps me enormously to be accountable to someone, I don't always achieve all my goals. My buddy understands that and doesn't reprimand me in any way. It's a gentle relationship, not a punitive one.

Having buddies doesn't mean everything always goes well. Some days I'm overwhelmed by my to-dos and piles of stuff, and I just don't have the physical or mental energy to do a thing.

It gets so bad that I can't even bring myself to call my clutter buddies. I feel as if I'd have to talk forever and I don't want to burden them with that. On those days I might send one of them an email, as writing helps me think through what's bothering me and why I'm so paralyzed. I get back words of gentle encouragement that lift my spirits and give me hope that I can tackle my clutter, one day at a time.

My life is still filled with clutter but I don't feel so alone now, due in part to the two beautiful clutter buddies in my life. I don't mean to always gush about CLA, but it's what brought us together and what keeps us connected. For those of you who don't have a clutter buddy but would like one, take a look at those names and numbers you collected at CLA meetings. Then make a call. It can pay off in many ways you'd never expect. Pink socks or not.

My CLA Toolbox–Meetings

Spring 2014

Alison B., NJ

There's something about going to a face-to-face meeting that gets my heart pumping. First, it means I have to get ready. I mean, it's not as if I can pick up the phone and greet everybody wearing pajamas. These people who stare at me every week are going to look into my eyes and see my wardrobe, not to mention my body language.

Here's where I can't hide from who I am. In order to get myself there when I would not otherwise feel like going, I used to have a commitment with another member to pick her up every week. This would ensure that I got myself out of my home because if I didn't do it for myself, I did it for her. Also, the time we spent in the car was enjoyable and was our only bonding time of the week.

Amazingly, this arrangement lasted over 10 years, but recently it hasn't been tenable and I sorely miss our time together. Lately, I have been opening up for the group instead, and this service position has kept me showing up. I put the kettle on for tea, open up the room, and pull out the meeting formats, timer, and other items needed to run the meeting. Now someone else is doing that for a while, and already I am making excuses not to attend the meeting—although to be fair, the weather has been excruciatingly cold lately!

We strongly believe in rotation of leadership in our group, which is why a different person leads the meeting each week. One item on our agenda is to write a list of weekly commitments and then read them aloud. The following week we report on whether we have completed them or not. Then we take this one step further—on a separate piece of paper, we write our commitments, names, phone numbers, and the date. We fold this list several times and put it into a can which gets passed around.

Each person takes a piece of paper and then, during the week, calls the person whose name they chose. You'd be surprised how much this helps if it's done right, though people making the calls tend to procrastinate and not call until the day before the meeting.

Over the years, we have had different types of meetings. My favorite was when we used to choose a leaflet, read it from beginning to end, and then share on it. Once a month we always have a business meeting when enough people are present. Now we take one week to read the Step of the month and one week for the Tradition, and then an open week. We can also have open shares at any time.

We have only a very small core group of people, and I'm not sure this latest format is working too well, or if it's just the time of year when people are extra busy.

We have our meeting in a beautiful location. The garden is delightful, the sanctuary is serene, and there is a surprisingly large indoor circular labyrinth which I have walked several times when I have been in a bad mood. It does help to put things into perspective. We don't even have to pay rent—we just have to make a very small donation. However, the place is not without its trials and tribulations, and they do challenge me.

There is a young girls' group, for instance. They meet only once a month, but they are gleefully noisy. They have taught me that I can concentrate on the meeting even when there are distractions. Then there is the theater group. Every so often they put on plays at the church and have intense rehearsals. I love to act and I am often frustrated by envy, but this has taught me absolute loyalty to my group, which comes first. We were displaced from our usual room: another group needs our large space more than we do.

The situation is teaching me to have more patience, be more flexible, and go with the flow. Every lesson I learn is slow and painful, believe me.

Fortunately, the members of the group are my friends, and I am glad to know them and be with them on our life journey.

I go to service meetings over the phone, too. I used to be involved in a lot of them. Now I'm on just the CLA*rity* Committee, which is extremely fulfilling for me. Although it's not a recovery meeting as such, it has taught me the value of teamwork, friendship, and loyalty and the importance of practicing the Traditions. We meet weekly. I love the team, and working with them is always a pleasure.

We have just started our eighth year of CLA*rity*, and I'm proud to say I've been with the team since the newsletter's inception. Here's to another eight years!

My CLA Toolbox–Service

Summer 2014
Colleen C., OR

In Loving Service to Clutterers Anonymous

As I try on a daily basis to work the spiritual program of CLA, I make a conscious effort to incorporate all of the Tools of Recovery[19] in my life. Looking back over the past several years in my journey toward an uncluttered life of clarity and serenity, Service is a Tool that has been a consistent part of my program from very early on. Before I had even developed an understanding of the 12 Steps and embarked on working the CLA program under the guidance of a sponsor, I began to learn the importance of service.

I've come to realize that it is not just about giving back to the Fellowship of CLA so that our program will continue to be here for others. I've also realized that I gain so much in my own recovery when I am of service to others and the Fellowship as a whole.

Having helped to start up a brand-new group when I was still very new in CLA, I learned the importance of service positions to keep the meeting running smoothly each week. I also came to understand the great value of rotating the responsibilities to different members. Rather than one person being "in charge" of a group, the rotation of service and leadership greatly helps to keep our meetings healthy. Over the years, I have had the opportunity to serve as group secretary, treasurer, literature person, and WSO delegate. In addition, on many occasions, I led meetings and served as timer during the sharing portion. One of the many ways service helps my own recovery is by keeping me accountable. Holding a position of service to the group helps me to keep showing up, week after week.

I have also learned that it is possible to overcommit and take on more than I can realistically handle, and overdoing does not help my recovery. Several years ago, I had expressed interest in serving at the WSO level, as web mail correspondent. However, I quickly realized during a period of learning the responsibilities of the position, that I was not ready for this role. In this case, the service position required a level of recovery with email accountability and responsiveness that I had not yet attained. Recovery has allowed me to be more honest about whether or not I'm able to take on a new activity or service role, without being overly self-critical or risking relapse by overdoing and overcommitting.

Continuing on the journey, I am always aware of ways in which I can be of service to CLA and others in general. Living a life of service has made me so much happier compared with living out numerous patterns of cluttering habits and the obsession to acquire more stuff. I have learned that the CLA Tools, such as Service, are not the means to an end. These Tools do not singularly define my recovery. For many years, I attended meetings and did service in CLA without doing much else to work a program, specifically working the Steps and understanding or using the Traditions. I found that the real recovery and positive changes in my life began when I got a sponsor and worked the Steps and began to sponsor others. Service, however, will always continue to be a very important Tool of recovery for me. As I give to CLA, the program of CLA will give to me.

My CLA Toolbox–Daily Action

Holiday 2014
Kathy H., CA

I first joined CLA more than 12 years ago. For a time, my progress was somewhat slow. But when I started really using the program—the Steps and the CLA Tools of Recovery—I was able to make inroads into my clutter and disorganization.

Then I started using the Tool of Daily Action: *We do something each day to further our recovery, doing what we can, no matter how small. Our goal is progress, not perfection.*

At first, I looked upon doing "something each day" as referring to physical decluttering only—and that did help. But then I considered the word "recovery" and that it also applies to our spiritual development, which involves working the Steps. So I began to put some effort into focusing on the Steps in my daily life. I did get a sponsor for a while, which helped tremendously, and I am currently searching for a new sponsor.

I feel it will be time fairly soon to start another formal session of working the Steps with a sponsor. But I do try to work Steps 10 through 12 every day by briefly reviewing my day, meditating to stay in touch with my Higher Power, and trying to carry the message of recovery to others. I also focus on the first three Steps to remind myself that I do have a disease over which I am powerless, but that my Higher Power can help me manage.

One thing my previous sponsor directed me to do was to review my day each evening before going to bed and, when I wake up in the morning, to list the things I intend to get accomplished that day. This morning review helps keep me on track.

I have tried various methods of dealing with the physical clutter. Sometimes I have just kept in mind that I have to do some work on my house every day.

But it is so easy for me to put it off until it is late, so there I have employed some techniques from time to time which help.

Sometimes I have great decluttering success by focusing on one room or one area. That is how I was able to declutter my bedroom, by focusing on one closet, one drawer, one shelf, or one box at a time. There was a time I decided to rotate two tasks that were onerous. I would do one until I really didn't want to look at it again and then switch to the other for a while. In time, both tasks were completed.

I had a great deal of success when I decided that I was going to declutter at least ten items each day. I would keep a count in the back of my head as I went through the day until I reached ten. Some days, I probably did 20 or 30 or more—but I made sure I did at least ten.

Although I have used varying methods to declutter, they all have one thing in common: Do something every day. I have spent time analyzing why this works for me. I think it is because of two reasons:

The first is because, over time, things add up. Take the "ten things" concept. If I declutter ten items each day, that is 70 items a week, and over 200 items in a month. So when I do something each day, I am slowly chipping away at the mountain of clutter.

The second—and more important—reason daily action works for me is that I am changing my habits. I am strengthening the part of me that wants an orderly home and weakening my tendency to procrastinate. I find that when I put off doing my chores for even a day, I tend to drop back into my old habit of letting things go. If I don't do anything for two days in a row, it is even harder to get back to it—and the resistance to doing anything on my house increases the more I don't do anything. So I try to work on my house every day, even if I am able to spend only 10 or 15 minutes on it. It keeps me on track and sets up good habits to tackle tomorrow.

And I try to keep in mind that "Our goal is progress, not perfection." Done less than perfectly is better than not done at all.

My CLA Toolbox–Trust

Spring 2015

Alison B., NJ

My kitchen table is clear! Lately that has been a rare occurrence and has happened only when I've worked hard to file papers that I haven't handled on a daily basis.

Dealing with mail, I've discovered, involves a great amount of trust in my Higher Power that my identity won't be stolen. Several months ago, I became terrified because I began to think that anything with my name and address could be used for identity theft. I ripped my name and address off envelopes and other papers to be put through my shredder. I stockpiled them to shred all at once but never shredded them.

I became paranoid to the point where I wouldn't even open my mail. I had to wait for my friend to come over and do most of it for me after it had piled up. But he left the open mail in piles on my kitchen table, and it stayed that way.

Let me tell you, that's not a good way to live. I would wait until the next batch of mail piled up and then invite him over to help me again. Finally, after three rounds of this, my patient friend complained that he was enabling me and refused to help me again. He said I could bookend with him instead.

There was a time, also, when I was convinced that if I left the mail long enough, most of it would just need to be thrown away anyway. What I didn't realize was that I was missing important things, like renewal of my car registration. (I ended up paying a fine on that!) I never worried about bills because I always pay them automatically through my bank, but even they need to be filed. However, I caused myself problems. I believe that 90% can be thrown out, but it's much better to do that the day it arrives. It saves having to spend several hours on it months later.

When I came into CLA 12 years ago, there were huge piles of mail on my kitchen table. Some papers were 18 months old. I managed to get it all in order by building a proper filing system, but I still kept papers that I probably didn't need. I didn't trust that if I needed them again, they would be made available to me. I know now that there was a lot I could have thrown out then. I still have many papers left over from years gone by that I could throw out and never miss.

At my Monday night CLA group, I have faithfully made commitments every week to open my mail on a daily basis, but there have been many months, years even, when I haven't stuck with it. I know now that this is the only way to keep up with it properly. The rule for me is that I must deal with it completely—open it, fill out a form, file it, throw it out, shred it, whatever needs to be done—there and then—and that I can simply throw out the junk mail without shredding it. I have to trust that there is no danger. For things that need to be done in the future, I put them in a folder; but I try not to do that too much because I tend to forget about them.

It was only a few weeks ago that I started dealing with my mail on a daily basis again. Coincidentally, it was right after my friend gave me that tough love. Funny how that works.

I tried to keep the papers off my kitchen table by buying a cheap desk for another room. When that didn't work, I bought a secretariat (an antique desk), thinking I would enjoy that better. Now I have two desks not being used. It seems that I like working at my kitchen table; but as I said at the beginning, it's clear now, because in order to write this article, I went through my piles of mail and papers and, thankfully, sorted them all out in one afternoon. I got rid of most of them. I trust I won't need them.

P.S. I just found a bag full of papers and mail underneath the kitchen table. A clutterer's work is never done!

My CLA Toolbox—Daily Action

Fall 2015

Kathy H., CA

We do something each day to further our recovery, doing what we can, no matter how small. Our goal is progress, not perfection.

This Tool has been so important to my recovery. Since procrastination is one of my major character defects, working on my problems every day is critical to my success—for my spiritual recovery, as well as physical and time clutter recovery.

After analyzing how things work for me, I believe that the reason Daily Action is so crucial to my physical decluttering efforts is twofold.

First, when I spend time decluttering daily, all the small tasks completed each day add up to one big task. For example, if I declutter for ten minutes each day, that is 70 minutes per week and over five hours in a month. That is not to say that I never spend more than ten minutes in a day—I often do—but that those small efforts daily combine to a lot of effort over time.

Also, forming good habits is so crucial to my decluttering efforts. Each day that I do not do maintenance makes it harder to get started on the next day. But if I keep doing something every day, it is much easier to get started. Think of a dirt driveway after the rain. When you first drive a car over it, tracks are laid down. The next time, it is a little easier to drive right in those tracks. Pretty soon there are deep ruts, and it is difficult to drive anywhere but in the ruts. I like to think that my actions are wearing ruts in my brain, the same as the car is wearing ruts in the drive. These ruts then form into habits, which are hard to break. In CLA, I have been putting effort into forming the ruts which help me, rather than those that hinder me.

Many of the same principles seem to apply to my spiritual recovery. At the end of the day, before I go to bed, I review my day—the good and the bad—and note if there are any amends to be made (which I try to do the very next day). When I wake up, I take a few minutes to go over what I wish to accomplish that day. These two actions, along with a conscious effort to work the Steps, put some emphasis on my spiritual program daily. When I keep my spiritual program foremost, the physical and time clutter seem to diminish.

Often, after making great strides in decluttering, I decide to take a breather and congratulate myself on my success. But if I forget about Daily Action, the clutter begins to pile up again. Take my dining room table. Years before I came to CLA, I had given up trying to eat at the table. At times, it has been piled so high, I could barely see the surface in places. I have decluttered this table several times during my years in CLA, but the clutter still seems to accumulate whenever I get complacent about my success and stop focusing on my program.

So now, although I do revel in my successes, I try to get right back into the swing of things, doing something each day on my house and on my spiritual program. As long as I keep this Tool in mind, I will be able to enjoy my home and my life and let the beauty, peace, and serenity of the program infuse my life.

My CLA Toolbox–Earmarking

Holiday 2016

Kathy H., CA

We provide a place for our possessions and return them there. We create a home for anything before bringing it in. When we add a new item, we release an old one. For accessibility, beauty, and peace of mind, we keep some empty space.

Remember the old adage: "A place for everything, and everything in its place"? Well, the first part of this Tool says exactly the same thing. I have completely agreed with this concept all my life—so why is it so hard to do?

When I was 20, my clutter was much more manageable. I didn't have so much stuff; but, although I had a place to put almost everything, I would struggle with the motivation to put things away once I had used them. However, since the total amount was not overwhelming, I would take a couple of hours each weekend to put things away. In this way, I maintained a house that was somewhat liveable, but I always worried about someone coming over between cleanup times.

As the years passed and I accumulated more possessions, it got harder and harder to keep up with those cleanup periods. The problem was twofold: first, I had too many things for the space; and second, I was out of the habit of putting things away. Over the years, I had become more and more lax, and the time between those once-a-week cleanup periods lengthened and lengthened again. It had gotten so bad the earlier two-hour cleanup period had now become days or weeks—too much to handle.

There are actually four parts to this Tool.

The first part is "We provide a place for our possessions and return them there." I can't think of how many times I have spent hours looking for a needed item because I had not put it away in its designated spot. My old habit of handling items once I had finished with them was to set them down wherever it happened to be convenient. Bit by bit, since coming to CLA, I have been replacing that habit with one of taking the time to put things away once I am done with them. I have not totally succeeded, but more and more, when I look for things, they are where they should be. How wonderful it is to look for something and find it immediately where it should be!

The second part is "We create a home for anything before bringing it in." I still sometimes struggle with this part of the Tool. I tend to think, "Oh, I need this. I'll get it now." Sometimes the location is obvious: I bought a new little kitchen tool; it goes in the drawer with others like it. But if that drawer is already full or if there is not an obvious spot to put the item, then I have to find someplace to keep it. However, since I don't often do impulse buying any more, this is not usually a big problem. But it does work much better when I figure it out before making the purchase, which I often do now—and when I don't, I try to take care of it right after getting it home.

The third part is "When we add a new item, we release an old one." I don't always consciously do this part, and I am working on doing better at it. However, what I do is to go through my possessions every few months to clean and reorganize; and in so doing, I find things I no longer need, and I take them to the thrift shop. In a given period, I am usually releasing at least as much as I am buying (not counting consumables).

And the last part is "For accessibility, beauty, and peace of mind, we keep some empty space." This is something I never put effort into before coming to CLA. Instead, I would see how I could organize the space I had to fit more into it. But being a visually-oriented person, I totally agree with the concept. If everything is filled to the brim, nothing stands out, and what you are left with is not only physical clutter but visual clutter as well. I learned this when I learned how to design printed publications. One general rule is that white space is very important. I see how it translates to my home and am working on getting that same resting space for the eyes that I sought in my work. Although it has been slow going, I am getting to the point where I can do that.

While I sort of ignored this Tool at first, it has become very important to me. Along with other aspects of the program, it has been helping me to gain a more comfortable and pleasant living space. Thank you, CLA.

Sponsorship

One Person's Experiences with Being a Sponsor

Spring 2007

Beryl W., NY

In CLA, I sponsor others; I have no sponsor, purely from negligence on my part. There are a couple of people I think would be good sponsors for me, but due to the procrastination part of the disease I have never asked.

I also sponsor in other programs, and my time is limited. I also try to be generous with my time when people call on an ad hoc basis—often for a month or so. (They might be, actually, trying me out as a sponsor and decide I'm not for them!) And I am most glad to do this.

I also wonder if people should just ask others from other programs they like to sponsor them.

Should sponsors stand up at a meeting when asked? I have had successful sponsors identify themselves at local meetings by raising their hands or making a mark on the phone sheet. I listen to people. I call them a few times to ask for their experience, strength, and hope. And, if their suggestions resonate with me, I ask if they could sponsor me. Sometimes they can (yea!) and sometimes they can't, or don't want to. The point (doing the footwork) is for me to get off my duff, look for a sponsor, and ask.

I know for a fact that the first person who asked me (years ago in another program) asked me even though I had checked "no" on the phone list. I had to think for a moment or two if I felt I had enough recovery to help. I said "yes," and also said I was unsure if I had the recovery and gave the person full permission to move on at any time. I sponsored her for a few years. This was a wonderful, humbling experience. (Actually, the person who I sponsor in CLA also asked me before I thought I was ready.) Mostly because of her willingness, I found that a wonderful experience!

Maybe the sponsor problem is not that sponsors are not self-identifying, but that CLA members are not asking for sponsors.

Having a sponsor requires a lot of willingness and initiative. One must be "entirely willing." It is not a process that should be spoon-fed. Having the courage to ask someone to sponsor—even if they have not identified themselves as a sponsor—is an important part of the process. Looking at one's defects, looking at parts of one's actions that need to be changed, and then changing them (or asking God to change them!), takes a lot of courage.

I don't think the lack of self-identified sponsors is a problem. I think it is a good obstacle in the path of one who wants a sponsor, a training element for the steep 12-Step road ahead.

Let's encourage our membership to ask. And ask, repeatedly and often! Until HP puts them in contact with the perfect person, the searching and rejection are part of the process. Eventual success is in God's time and plan, not ours.

A Fellowship of people who are actively looking for and/or using sponsors will be a strong, beautiful thing. Let's encourage people to ask, ask, ask, and then work, work, and work!

Affirmations

Fall 2011

Betsey K., NJ

I allot more time than I need for a task or trip, allowing a comfortable margin for the unexpected.

For much of my life I have been known for being late for commitments. When I was a child, I would have to run to get to school on time. Often I was able to get rides from neighbors. A number of years later, my street was designated as one-way—in the opposite direction—so I would have been out of luck, since cars could no longer be driven in the direction I was running to get to school.

In recent years, however, I have learned that it makes a lot of sense to allot more time for a task or trip than would seem to be necessary. Such a practice reduces the stress of wondering whether I will be on time for an appointment or meeting and allows for extra time in case of unexpected traffic delays, for example.

About ten years ago I was planning a vacation trip with my son. The goal was for us to fly to Dallas and arrive by noon on Wednesday to meet up with my brother, who was driving. We decided to leave home on Tuesday evening and booked a motel room in Dallas for that night for the three of us. Because of stormy weather, our flight was delayed. When we did finally get under way, the airline had changed the plan: Instead of continuing on to Dallas after a stopover in Atlanta, the plane was being diverted, and we were told to take another plane to continue to our destination. We arrived in Atlanta after the last outgoing flight and spent the night in the airport. The next morning we were able to get a flight and did arrive in Dallas by noon. Had we planned to leave home on Wednesday morning, we might not have arrived by noon if our flight had been delayed.

When I plan a lunch date with a friend, I allow an hour to arrive at our meeting place, even though I expect the trip to take only 45 minutes. I can often drive to my CLA meeting in about 30 or 35 minutes, but I allow at least 45 minutes because of possible heavy rush-hour traffic.

For a recent trip to an unfamiliar destination, Internet directions estimated the time as 2 hours and 15 minutes. I decided to allow at least three hours and arrived in plenty of time. I would have been quite embarrassed if I had arrived late.

Arriving early leads to less stress and more peace of mind. Of course, it is impossible to allow enough time to cover all possible delays. A major traffic accident might result in the closing of a road for several hours. Such delays are not predictable, and one cannot allow that much extra time just in case of such an unpredictable situation.

Holiday 2011

Kathy H., CA

I participate with my clutter by putting my attention and action on it in the present moment.

The character defect that has always given me the most trouble is procrastination. As I was preparing to sit down to write this article, I noticed that my office trash can was overflowing. My inclination has always been to say to myself: "I don't want to bother with this now; I'll take care of it later." Of course, later would probably be days later, when the trash was strewn all over the floor and causing a bigger problem. I would think: "It's not good, but at least there's nothing rotting or stinky in the office trash; I'll worry about it later."

But this time, thanks to trying to keep the CLA program in mind, I stopped right then and emptied the trash into a bag, put it next to the door to take outside later (since I wasn't dressed for outside at that time), and then got ready to write.

I felt good. It felt like progress because I didn't have to deal with a mess on the floor. Putting my attention and action on the clutter in the present moment was such a departure from the habits of my lifetime!

After nine years in CLA, with most of my house decluttered, I still struggle with putting away items now, not later. I may struggle all my life—but at least, with the help of this program (the Steps,, the Tools,[19] Affirmations,[20] and all the literature; the meetings; my sponsor; etc.) I am, most times, able to take care of household problems as they happen or shortly thereafter, rather than putting them off until they have escalated into big problems.

So, I like this Affirmation and hope to keep it in mind and action as I go about my daily life.

Summer 2012

Kathy H., CA

I participate with my clutter by putting my attention and action on it in the present moment.

It has always been so easy for me to ignore my clutter; I just don't look at it, even when it is piled haphazardly right in front of me. I have tended to spend a lot of time visualizing my house when all the big projects are completed; of course, this visualization just automatically assumes that the clutter will have been taken care of. I would often spend a lot of time on this, mentally planning out details of how I wanted things to be. But unless I pay attention to the conditions that exist now and take action in the present, the clutter just gets worse (and the projects don't get done, either).

For instance, even though I have decluttered much of my house, dealing with the daily mail is an ongoing struggle. So now, instead of glancing at the mail and setting it aside for later, I try to deal with it when I take it out of the mailbox. Of course, sometimes I don't have the time to handle it right away when I bring it in. In those instances, I need to set it in a prominent place, pay attention to it as soon as possible, and take care of it the same day. When I put the mail off until another day, it starts to make piles that add to the clutter (and important things sometimes don't get taken care of when they need to be handled). So—attention and action in the present moment; that is key. This also leads into the CLA Tool of Daily Action. By doing something to forward my recovery each day, I nudge myself into focusing on my clutter and dealing with it.

When I pay attention to my clutter, I find that I clutter less and declutter more.

Spring 2013

Alison B., NJ

I set reasonable goals, remembering that my first priority is my well-being.

Originally, I decided not to write about an affirmation for this issue. Why? Because I had already committed to writing one article—and one article per issue seems like a reasonable goal to me. However, I did not receive a firm response when I asked others if they wanted to write for this column. In the interest of my own well-being, at least I did not take this on before I had completed my other assignment. If you want to see the work of other authors, please consider making your own contribution. It's not hard—I mainly write as I speak, and then others edit it.

I know my own limitations—that I am apt to become stressed whenever I undertake a writing commitment. I know I'll probably leave it 'til the last minute. Somehow, in my mind it becomes a huge mountain to climb; every single time I attempt this feat, I think that I don't have the requisite skills to write anything interesting. I am highly perfectionistic, and I don't want to make any mistakes. However, I have managed to learn over the years that if I don't write anything at all, I will end up being disappointed with myself—and that nothing I write will ever be perfect. All I can do is give my best effort for CLA*rity*.

I tend to make myself just as stressed over other sorts of problems. It is only by working through my fear of the unknown with the less important things in life that I am able to learn to relax in the face of bigger fears—or at least learn how to pace myself, so that my stress level is manageable.

I try to write lists and then put individual tasks into a time frame. I actually have to write things down, like "eat breakfast," or else I end up not eating until 4 p.m. I also schedule break periods and time on any given day for my favorite hobbies. These things are part of my well-being. So are trips for supplies, doctors' appointments, and exercise activities.

My idea of getting things done is very black and white— either I want to challenge an endless list of goals, or I want to deliberately do something mindless for hours. That kind of instant gratification does not contribute to my long-term wellbeing—but on the other hand, my mind needs the rest.

Fall 2014

Alison B., NJ

As I let go of what is insignificant to me, I am better able to enjoy those things that are important to me.

An affirmation, to me, is a meaningful sentence I can say over and over to myself until it gives me ideas—on many levels. This particular affirmation is important on spiritual, emotional, and physical levels; but it is interesting that when I first looked at it, it was only about clothes for me!

I obsess over clothes a lot. No matter what I wear, nothing hides the weight problem. I went through my wardrobe recently. There were still two dresses there from when I was very thin that I will probably never be able to get into again.

But I live in hope—especially since these two items have sentimental value to me. I did get rid of all the rest of that size, and I am focusing on losing weight. I have lost ten pounds and definitely hope to lose more.

I had gained about 20 pounds previously (and I was already heavy); so I have been scouring garage sales and thrift shops in search of larger plus-size clothes, which are difficult to find. I know I am supposed to have places earmarked for items I bring in, and I also know when I bring an item in I'm supposed to release an equivalent one. Well, there was a time when I released a lot of items, and it got to the point where I really didn't have enough clothes.

Now, many of the clothes I have are a bit too small for me, and it's so hard to believe they are insignificant and that the universe will provide what I need, when I need it. Obviously, I am not ready to let them go yet.

For today, at least, I put them in a separate area in my closet so that the ones I am wearing are more at the front, and I filled up one big, black garbage bag to be given away to one of those places that picks up donations or one of those clothes drop-off containers.

As far as emotions go, I enjoy times with friends, and I have learned to let go of insignificant arguments that loom large to me, so that I can enjoy my time with my friends even more. That is probably the biggest thing that program has taught me: how to be serene around other people. Many times I obsess and have to work a problem through—sometimes writing about it—before I can let it go.

Spiritually, I know that in the face of my Higher Power, whom I choose to call the Universal Power, everything pales into insignificance and nothing else is important. That means I can rise above any problem and remember to put it all into perspective. It's like being in an airplane and looking down. Where are the people, the cars, the houses? I can't even see them until I get closer to the ground. Somehow they have become insignificant—and so have all my problems. And for the time I'm traveling, I forget all about my clutter!

Summer 2016

Kathy H., CA

"With every item I release, I create space in my life for more joy and energy, as well as new insights and experiences, to come in."

In reading over this affirmation, I remembered an incident from before the time I joined CLA. I love flowers and always enjoyed those my mother brought into the house from her garden. In those days I had very little spending money, and so it was an extravagance to buy flowers. But one time, I decided to spend the money and enjoy the flowers. I took them home, arranged them in a vase, and placed them on a coffee table. I enjoyed them in a few glances that evening, but before I noticed them again, they were long dead. They had become entirely lost in the surrounding clutter.

The other thing I have noticed is that living my life amidst clutter just makes it more difficult to function emotionally. Even when I ignore the clutter, it weighs on my spirit and drags me down.

Recently, I decided I needed to do another overhaul of my kitchen. I had begun to accumulate clutter there once again! It's too bad we can't work our programs once and be cured forever. Unfortunately—for me, at least—it doesn't work that way; it's an ongoing struggle. At any rate, once I started the kitchen overhaul, I began to feel wonderful. Every time I looked at those clean, uncluttered counters, I felt light and free. That left me feeling good enough to take on other things in my life that had been festering.

I have found that when I take a box of items to the thrift shop, I feel lighter as well. I only wish it meant I had lost pounds from my body! But what I feel is a sense of freedom—I have let go of physical items, but what they had really been doing was to drag down my spirit. Letting them go leaves me with a sense of peace and well being.

With clutter gone, I can revel in the beauty of flowers, as well as enjoy other things I keep just for their beauty. My life has become freer and more joyous.

Slogans

HALT

Spring 2009

Not thinking clearly? HALT!

Feeling frazzled, in a fog, or spirally thinking? Try this acronym I heard somewhere in a 12-Step program:

How it works for me:

1. Losing serenity? Say to yourself, "HALT!"
2. Take a quick personal inventory…
   Am I Hungry? H
   Am I Angry? A
   Am I Lonely? L
   Am I Tired? T
3. What action do I now need to take in light of these answers?
4. Congratulations, you just moved from *re*-acting to acting!
5. Still not sure what to do? When in doubt, explore it further.

Action Is the Magic Word

Summer 2009

Betsey K., NJ

I am reminded of the story of the man who had the utmost faith in God. When a flood threatened to wash his home away, he rejected the aid of rescuers who came with a canoe, a rowboat, and a motorboat, telling each of them, "The Lord will provide." Finally, he was swept off his roof by the rising water, and he drowned. When he arrived in heaven and recounted the story of what happened, he was told, "You're not supposed to be here; I sent you a canoe, a rowboat, and a motorboat."

In Step 3 we decided to turn our will and our lives over to our Higher Power. This does not mean, however, that we can just sit back and let our Higher Power do everything for us. We must remember that, although our Higher Power will guide us, we must provide the action. Just one small action each day will lead to amazing results over time.

It Works if You Work It

Spring 2010
Kathy H., CA

Attending CLA meetings, sharing, using the Tools,[19] and working on physical decluttering all have some benefit, but for greater recovery through the program you have to work the Steps.

In 12-Step programs, it is often said, "It works if you work it," meaning that if you take the time and effort to work the Steps with a sponsor, to write on them, and to apply them to your life on a daily basis, you will find yourself blessed with the benefits of recovery promised by the program. As it says in the A.A. Big Book,[4] "Half measures availed us nothing."

So try to work your program fully and honestly, and you will find the great joy this program has to offer and discover the other half of the saying, the one that people often end with in meetings: "...and you're worth it!"*

**Some groups may use a different version of this ending, or none at all.—Editor*

Easy Does It–But Do It!

Summer 2010
Alison B, NJ

Twenty-six years ago in another Fellowship, I first heard the phrase "Easy Does It." I thought it was wonderful—it took the stress out of whatever project I was rushing to complete. After all, I reasoned, I was working on my recovery, so I needed to rest sometimes. Unfortunately, my idea of resting was to "zone out" in front of the television and stay there for hours on end.

Years later, I heard an expanded version, "Easy does it, but do it!" I then realized I had developed an addiction to the TV; and, as a result, my projects were not completed and my accomplishments were few and far between. Now I have rules—I generally don't watch TV until at least 9:00 p.m. during the week. I know that I have an addictive personality, and I'm careful about the way I expend my energy. Unfortunately, I'm now addicted to computer-related activities, but at least that's more positive. It is definitely possible to go the other way and do too much, and there has to be a balance. Don't forget to rest before you get tired!

Wait Until the Miracle Happens

Holiday 2010
F.T., CA

Dictionaries define the (Latin) origin word miraculum as "an object of wonder" and refer to a miracle as "a marvelous event...exceeding the known powers of nature...due to the intervention of...some supernatural agency." I was raised in a free-thinking family. That eclectic background naturally led me to a nontraditional attitude towards spirituality. And yet, upon examining the 12-Step philosophy, I had no significant difficulty accepting the existence of "...a power greater than ourselves..." (Step 2). My CLA home group supported the nonreligious approach to understanding Higher Power (HP). And the specific language of Step 3, "...God, as we understood Him..." further convinced me that my beliefs would be compatible with the program.

My first miracle was that I could walk into a basement room with a dozen strangers and feel at home. "I need to come regularly to these meetings," I thought. Many times since, I have heard and repeated the idea that six meetings is a good goal to aim for when evaluating a new experience. Another piece of wisdom I have heard that reminds me of the logic of patience goes something like this: "It has taken more than a few years to get where you are today—why should changing yourself go faster?"

The ongoing gifts: A major object of wonder for me now is the patience and serenity that visit and revisit me as I continue to work the program the best way that I can; I can accept "good enough" and release perfectionism. There are still ups and downs, but I really feel and see my progress over time. I am becoming more willing to let go of the "people, places, and things I cannot change," and to let HP guide my journey.

Progress Not Perfection

Spring 2011
Andrew S., MD

This slogan has given me serenity many times. This phrase helps me to realign my expectations, so that good enough becomes my functional criterion.

This is especially helpful when I tend to get stuck in thinking about complex situations. "Progress not perfection" helps me to break down the planning into more manageable pieces and then to move into action, letting go of the "what ifs" as much as possible.

Overthinking can be a problem for me; I sometimes enjoy creating complex, theoretical projections, which are just too involved to know where to start or which feel undoable because of their scope. Too much of this thinking without action is inclined to become a waste of energy and time.

When I was striving for the ideal, ultimate plan or allowing myself to get discouraged if things didn't go as I had projected them, I was not satisfied or serene. Daily, I still need to practice letting go. And surprisingly, when I can release "perfect" and accept "good enough," often the next right action will come to me.

This simple phrase, like many program sayings, helps me to reprogram my thinking. I can stop and look and feel reality in a different way. If I can pull the camera back to a long shot, it is so much easier to see my progress than if I'm focusing on the details.

Completion Cycle: Get It, Use It, Clean It, Put It Away

Summer 2011
Kathy H., CA

Doing these few simple steps can make a world of difference. Think of it: Every item we don't put away becomes a piece of clutter.

Because I tend to procrastinate, I have always struggled with leaving clutter after undertaking a project. In the past, I looked upon each activity as being composed of only the "use it" part of the cycle. But if I think of a project as all four parts of the cycle, I tend to clutter less.

So, if I have a loose screw, I think of the whole cycle: get the screwdriver, tighten the screw, and put the tool back where it belongs right away. When I cook, I not only wash the dishes after I eat but dry them and put them back in the cupboard. When I sew, I need to get out the fabric, the patterns, and the tools right away, instead of over a period of time. Then I put everything away as soon as I have finished—rather than waiting until later.

When I treat all four segments of the cycle as a part of an activity—rather than thinking of the cleaning and putting away parts as separate tasks—I am usually able to return things to their designated locations. In other words, finishing a project includes putting everything away. This means that, not only can I decrease the clutter, but I can locate items the next time I need them.

A Decision to Decide

Fall 2013
Wendy L., IL

If I could sum up my clutter compulsion in a few words, it would be the CLA slogan, "Clutter is about decisions waiting to be made." Or, more simply put, clutter is unmade decisions. Pair that with my perfectionist tendencies, and I am the perfect clutterer.

Now this goes back many years for me. My mom reminds me that even as a kid, when we'd go shopping, I'd take a very long time to make my purchase decisions, if I decided at all. Not surprisingly, I'm still a bad decision maker. Only now I've been enlightened by CLA and understand that my unmade decisions create clutter in my life.

Be it piles of paperwork or unread emails, undone to-do's or unfulfilled dreams, it's clutter. And it boils down to my avoiding what to do with it all.

Take email, for example, which piles up into the thousands because I can't decide if or how to act on each one. Then there's the screenplay that I want to write, but I can't decide on the plot and plot twists so I put off working on it and it never gets done. Sometimes it feels as if I'm walking on an endless treadmill of indecision with no stop switch in sight.

The good news is that, because of CLA, I'm slowly but surely learning to make effective decisions, which cuts down on my clutter. Bookending and talking with other clutterers help enormously, as does writing for CLA*rity*, which allows me to explore my reasons for being indecisive.

That treadmill is finally starting to slow down. I'm not out of the woods yet, but I'm seeing the light. And I'm grateful.

Do One Thing at a Time

Holiday 2013

Kathy H., CA

I have to remind myself frequently to do one thing at a time.

It is often helpful for me to visualize how I want my home to be when I am finished decluttering, reorganizing, and rebuilding. But I run into problems when, even after I have decided on my plans, I spend too much time basking in what things will be like when they are done, rather than working on achieving my goals.

However, the main reason I need to focus on doing one thing at a time is to avoid getting overwhelmed by all the things I need or want to accomplish. In order to achieve any of it, I need to break it down into smaller pieces and then focus on only those parts that I want to work on today (or, sometimes, even this hour).

I remember that years ago I was able to help a friend in this way. It was a few months after she had moved, and she confessed to me that she was depressed because most of her things were still piled in boxes. She was unable to deal with any of it because the large amount of work was overwhelming her. I thought a while and suggested that maybe it would help if she just dealt with one box at a time and ignored the fact that all the other boxes still needed unpacking. A few weeks later, she happily told me that it had worked. All her possessions had been unpacked and put away.

Unfortunately, I often forget the advice I so easily told my friend. I think that's true of many of us clutterers—we can do things for someone else but have trouble doing them for ourselves. That is why, since joining CLA, I now put a lot of effort into focusing only on what I need to do in the present. It's amazing how much I can get done when I focus on doing one thing, as long as I also keep in mind the CLA tool of Daily Action, so I can at least get started on what I need to do that day.

Keep It Simple

Summer 2014

Wendy L., IL

Keep It Simple (some add the word "stupid" to the end, making it KISS) is an awesome concept that makes my life so much more manageable. It's so important to me that I really ought to hang it from a sign in my home.

Here's why:

I'm the opposite of simple. I was born to a dad who taught me to be perfect, which has led to my having a heck of a time making decisions. It's part of why I'm a clutterer. The options and possibilities can overwhelm me, and the worry that I won't get it right can be downright paralyzing. Many tasks require decisions, and that's where I get stuck.

It's when I'm struggling that a light goes off in my head and the words "keep it simple" come to me. I kindly remind myself to relax, and I take a deep, calming breath. Then I focus on what needs to be accomplished.

To get at the essence of any given task, I ask myself what is required and what I must do to get it done. This means boiling it down to its simplest parts and choosing a starting point. Sometimes I'll even consider what will happen if I avoid dealing with it. Fear can actually be quite motivating.

If I start stressing out again and find myself obsessing that I can't do this or I'll never get it done, I circle back to the essence and pick up where I left off, or I start over.

This has helped me deal with all sorts of things, from conducting personal business to confronting piles of paper. Simplifying things gives me the confidence I need to take action. It doesn't take away the stress completely but often brings it down a few notches. Sealed with a KISS.

Fake It 'Til You Make It

Holiday 2014

Alison B., NJ

I always used to have a sink full of dishes until I committed, at my local meeting, to doing them daily. But I had to trick myself. I started by putting my kettle on, and I would do dishes until the water boiled for my tea. It was probably less than three minutes. Then I found I could use my timer and in just seven minutes, wash the whole sinkful.

But, believe it or not, that was too much for me. I began to let the dishes pile up again for days at a time, and the sink became smelly, which I didn't like at all. Now I literally wash each dish as I'm finished using it. I love my current way of doing the dishes. Do I put them away? Not lately—I will have to work on that... again!

Literature

Literature is one of the CLA Tools of Recovery;[19] it is an important aspect of the program. This section includes articles that appeared in the "Sharing on Leaflets" column in CLA*rity* and other articles about CLA and A.A. literature and writing.

Sharing on Leaflets

Declutter Your Mind [9]

Spring 2013

Alison B., NJ

All the CLA leaflets were beautifully written, and I have more than one favorite. I chose to write about "Declutter Your Mind" because it has many creative and practical ideas to help me in my quest to lead a more organized life.

Firstly, the title itself reminds me that I may choose not to be perpetually confused by thoughts that, if left unchecked, tend to push and pull me in several different directions all at once. When I read the leaflet, I am reminded that there are actions I can take to help lift the "clutter fog." When I take those actions, my mind is definitely clearer, and I feel more confident about the way I interact with others because I know that I am striving to do my best behind closed doors.

I strongly identify with having my mind filled with trivia and failing to recognize what is really important. In my case, it's often deadlines. My low self-esteem tricks me into thinking that I can't handle things like paperwork forms. I have now learned that I can break tasks down into doable segments and take breaks in between so that I don't have to tackle everything in one sitting. I often use a timer for 10 or 15 minutes at a time, and I bookend to help myself get started when I don't feel like doing what I know I must.

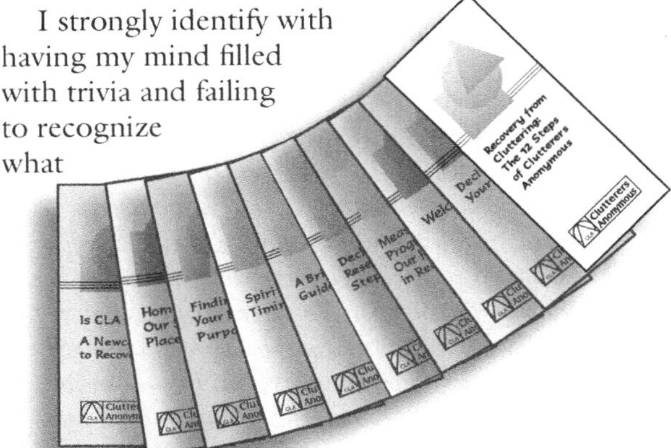

I try not to multitask, except when I'm waiting for something to cook or for laundry to finish its cycle, and perhaps I can use that time to get some filing accomplished or to declutter a surface. According to the leaflet, I'm supposed to use those periods for reflection, but I believe I have to use my common sense here because, when left to my own devices, I tend to use most of my day for thinking, and the result is too little action.

I have read this leaflet more times than I can count. Each time, I learn something new. I have learned to make daily and weekly lists; put all these items into a planner and make a loose time plan; prioritize the most important things and do them when my energy is high; pat myself on the back for every task I complete; get myself validated by others; empty my pockets, purse, and car as often as possible; try not to carry today's problems into tomorrow because when I do, I don't seem to sleep very well; write a list in the evening for what I have to do the next day so that it's not on my mind overnight; not beat myself up if I don't accomplish everything I thought I would in one day;

not take on another project if I haven't completed a similar one recently; and recycle or throw out anything unused when I bring items of equivalent value into my home.

One extremely important thing I have learned is that I cope much better when I take more time than I think I need for a task or trip. For example, I get out of bed two hours before I need to go out. People look at me strangely when I tell them it takes me two hours to get ready, but during that time I am relaxing, taking quiet time, meditating, singing, making myself look and feel the best I can, and generally enjoying my time alone so that I may feel comfortable and show enthusiasm in the presence of others.

We are told CLA does not give us decluttering tips. However, when I study this leaflet, I realize that all the decluttering tips I will ever need are actually included here, and all I need to do is take the actions described. It's not easy, and I have to work hard to stick to a regimen that doesn't come naturally to me. Often, I fall short. There is not enough space in this article to point out everything this leaflet has taught me. I hope you have the opportunity to read it for yourself.

Finding Your Life Purpose[10]

Summer 2013

Carol N., CA

We believe we are here for a purpose—we are meant to do more than struggle with clutter. ("Finding Your Life Purpose," paragraph 2)

For so long, I have yearned to find my place in the universe—where I fit in—and to contribute to life in a meaningful way. Much of that time, I felt alone, on the outside, unable to decode the clues to living that others seem to grasp with ease. I was blessed to find the 12-Step way of life and eventually, through other programs, found my way to CLA.

I don't remember when I got the leaflets that were CLA literature at that time; it may have been at the meeting, maybe later. I knew right away, though, that they were important to my feeling better. Although I didn't fully comprehend the deeper meaning of the writings, reading the leaflets made me feel better. Maybe that was because they talked in spiritual terms, and I felt like they were there to show me something, instead of just telling me something. Over time, I have learned a lot from them all, and all have been a special focus at one time or another.

Currently, my favorite leaflet seems to be bent on helping me find my life purpose. I have succumbed to the desire to allow myself to go deeper into understanding myself. It is ironic that the revelation of understanding comes only after I become aware that I am unsatisfied with results.

Sometimes I have to have the same results and the same dissatisfaction many times before it dawns on me that there is another way. The leaflet, "Finding Your Life Purpose," is where I get support in feeling that it is okay to want satisfaction, and it is also okay to actively seek it. I do that by being hungry to learn spiritual principles.

Trying to reconcile spiritual concepts with the obvious "workings of the world" is sometimes very trying. The "Finding Your Life Purpose" leaflet is a very practical guide to reconcile these two worlds and assist in how to utilize cosmic principles for everyone's good, not just my own. It talks about purpose, action, signs (that it's working), recovery, and realizations. In fact, the last paragraph is often read at the closing of CLA meetings. These principles, when I take them out into the world, enable me to be integrated into humanity because I see how and why I fit there.

I learn something in this leaflet every time I read it or hear it.

> *As you declutter, we hope you will remember that you are not merely finding lost keys and bankbooks, not only discarding obsolete projects, not just making space for guests—you are finding yourself. You are clearing away the wreckage of your past. You are being responsible for small things so that you can be entrusted with larger ones. You are making room for your true purpose to emerge. Go with God and know you are blessed.*

Home: Our Sacred Place[11]

Holiday 2013

Alison B., NJ

I live in this apartment alone. That wasn't supposed to happen. I first moved in here 20 years ago from a smaller apartment in the same building, along with a boyfriend and two cats. This place was definitely full of love until my boyfriend became my fiancé and then ultimately abandoned me. I never quite understood it, nor did I ever completely recover.

That was when my cluttering began to get out of control. I was so depressed that I left my apartment only once a week to attend an Al-Anon meeting, and that was only because someone picked me up. Thank goodness for that meeting. I suppose I went food shopping—I don't even remember. For the most part, I watched TV for at least 15 hours a day and slept the rest of the time.

Then I got my first computer. I still pined over my ex-fiancé, dreaming about the day he would come back as he had promised. Then this apartment would truly be a home. Or we would move into a new home together, maybe in Florida where he is living now, near his mother. When I found myself cyber-stalking him, I realized it was time to get a life of my own, so I sought out a 12-Step program for messy people. I was so excited when I found CLA that I threw myself into the program with complete abandon, even getting deeply involved in service work at the World Service level.

I have read all the leaflets many, many times over. When I read "Home: Our Sacred Place," I realized that I never really moved into this apartment, that it never did become a sanctuary for me—so over the years, I have been working on making it more comfortable. There was a time, for example, when there was nothing on the walls, so I have tried to choose my artwork carefully. It is tough because I'm on a strict budget, but I have a great piece of art in my living room that is three pieces surrounding my window. Although I don't really count myself as a visual artist, there are a few things on the walls which I did myself and of which I am very proud. In the leaflet, this comes under "Please Yourself."

I realize that when it came to decorating tips, I had my mother's voice in my head, and it took me many years to get rid of that voice. I think I was always looking for acceptance from her, even though she lives far away from me. The "Inner Change" mentioned in the leaflet is taking me years to accomplish and is slow and very painful at times. I still work on "Self-Acceptance"—it comes and goes. It's often tied in with weight loss and how much money I have at any given time. I'm now working on my feelings of "Entitlement" in that I believe I'm entitled to a nicer apartment. I try to have gratitude for this one with its cracked walls and old carpets that can't be cleaned, but I often fall short.

Over the years, I have replaced all my metal hangers with white plastic ones and decluttered many clothes by giving them away to an organization that helps veterans. I've given away many other items, too. It feels wonderful, yet scary, to release items I know I will never use but someone else will. How will I manage without them? Usually I forget them completely!

I'm still uncomfortable letting people in, and I have to remind myself that another person's attitude is not my concern. I've been fortunate enough to visit other clutterers' places, so I know this to be true. My home is slowly becoming my sacred place.

Another article about "Home: Our Sacred Place" is printed in the CLA Program Section, p. 65.

Decluttering Resentment: Steps 4-10[8]

Summer 2014

Kathy H., CA

This CLA leaflet discusses freeing ourselves from the baggage of grudges and resentments. It says: "Whoever or whatever we resent controls us by limiting our ability to love, including loving ourselves. Even if we don't believe the person is worthy of our loving thoughts, we are."

Whew! So, let me see, if I hold a grudge or continue with a resentment, the person I am really hurting is myself. Somehow, I always knew that, but just knowing it doesn't necessarily make it easy to get rid of these festering wounds.

We free ourselves of this old baggage by working the Steps, especially what are called the "housekeeping Steps," Steps 4 through 10.

In writing our 4th-Step inventory, we list not only who and why we resent, we also list our own part in it.

For example, I had many resentments toward my husband, now deceased. In many ways, he was a wonderful person—caring and intelligent—but he had many emotional problems which often made him difficult to deal with. It was always so easy to think "It is his fault; he has the psychiatric problems." But was it all his fault?

In order to let go of these resentments, I had to realize that I had responsibility in the relationship also. For instance, the arguments had became too much trouble, so I would give in—which meant I didn't do my part to set boundaries. I realize now that I expected him to be "normal" and reasonable, even when he had demonstrated in the past that he couldn't be, so my expectations were unreasonable. I probably could have found a better way to deal with the problems than to keep expecting him to do what he couldn't.

Also, in order to keep peace, I really did deny my own needs, which added to the resentment. Looking back on that relationship, I can let all the resentment go by both realizing that he did the best he could and acknowledging my part in it. Letting go of the old garbage is like releasing a weight that was holding me down.

In doing my inventory, I have let go of many resentments. Of course, it is not always as easy as saying: "I have this resentment, and I see my part in it, so it is gone." The leaflet gives many techniques for being able to release ourselves of our old resentments and prevent new ones from forming. One that really hits home to me is the idea of giving myself what I want from others first, then giving it to them. I can't think of how many times in my life I have felt hurt because others did not give me what I needed and wanted. I am trying to take care of myself first—then, if I do not get what I want from others, at least I will have it from within. It is a process that needs daily reminders, but I expect it to reap very worthwhile results.

There is one thing I have learned from working these Steps. The simple act of writing and sharing our resentments does not by itself release all the inner turmoil, although it does help. Once we have done so, we need to keep doing so daily by working Step 10 and finding methods that work for us to release the resentment. That is when the true miracle of the Steps begins to happen.

Spiritual Timing[15]

Fall 2015

Lauren R., NJ

When I reread "Spiritual Timing" for at least the 30th time for the purpose of writing this article, I realized that it is my issue. Yes, I have way too many more possessions than I can keep track of or care for properly. Yes, these possessions impinge on my optimal functioning, but I do not have CHAOS (Can't Have Anyone Over Syndrome), and my home is cozy enough to use all the rooms almost all the time for what they are meant for: I can cook in my kitchen, eat at the table, use my bed, bathrooms, etc. (CLA is a help in reminding me to clean up.)

But the biggest detriment to my functioning is the way I overbook my time. I do all of the forms of time clutter listed:

- Overdoing (I have so rarely rested before I got tired.)
- Experience greed
- Not silencing self-hating thoughts
- Avoiding confronting problems (big time!)
- Busyaholism
- Inability to refuse invitations for fear of missing out
- Perfectionism
- Overachieving to impress people about my importance or worthiness and trying to make up for my underachieving past
- A busyness stash, ensuring that I'll always be distracted
- Information overload—Sometimes I think having a smart phone alleviates this; other times it seems to aggravate it.

Often, I have some activity after work each night of the week. Every Monday is my face-to-face CLA meeting; other days are more varied, but I belong to too many organizations, and I don't want to quit any of them. I enjoy the communities. I just agreed to another few years serving on the board of trustees at my temple. I get a number of action items or assignments from these groups. I have a hard time delivering the items I've promised—partly because I greedily agreed to do too much, and partly because of my unpredictable work schedule.

My work is a real feast-or-famine situation. There is no regularity, just swings between urgent overwhelm and scarcity that induce a panic that I might be laid off again. I also have a couple of side jobs that mix in unpredictably. But I don't want to quit them because they are a back-up if my regular job dries up again.

At home, I need time to do laundry, cook, declutter, putter, and rest. I need time to do my physical therapy exercises and dye my hair. Rest eludes me when I have such action-packed plans.

Yet, it is essential. The time to sleep, meditate, and just sit still is beginning to attract me more than ever. But every night, I have to do just one more thing before I go to bed, then another one more thing. Then I'm just too exhausted to sleep, but I lie down and my restless mind starts up.

I'd like to make a habit of my occasional practice of scribbling those last "one more thing" thoughts onto paper to free my mind from them until the next day. (My CLA group's commitment time is the only regular time I put these things on paper.)

Since coming to CLA, I have begun to change some of my habits. One big one is that I no longer talk on the phone while driving my car (not only mind clutter but a dangerous situation). I have become selective when doing two things at once; I do it only if they are things done by rote (such as washing the dishes). After all, one definition of multitasking is "not paying attention." Also, I have found that clearing out the physical clutter leads to more mental rest.

I have come to realize that the quality of my life is largely determined by the rest I get, so I have adopted several techniques to help me get the rest I need. I now set an alarm each evening to remind myself to stop doing things and to gradually relax toward my sleep period. Then I listen to a guided meditation tape, which says the words of my old yoga teacher, "There is nowhere to go, nothing to do." It helps me to let it all go and have a restful night's sleep.

Measuring Progress on Our Journey in Recovery [13]

Holiday 2015

Dody W., PA

We have new literature! CLA added a ninth leaflet to our literature set in April of this year. I'd like to describe the history and content for those who have not heard about it and then describe just a few possible ways it can serve members in our Fellowship.

History and Content

"Measuring Progress on our Journey in Recovery"was a response to the need many in our Fellowship expressed to have a definition of "abstinence" for our program. The literature committee received many excellent ideas and models from both face-to-face and phone meetings. Several drafts of an emerging model were proposed, until delegates from both phone and face-to-face meetings voted to accept the final one.

The majority of our Fellowship voiced a preference for the present title, rather than one containing "abstinence" because CLA is not a substance-based program.

The leaflet has three sections. The first section contains an overview of the purpose of this leaflet's tool and how an individual can begin to address and measure personalized progress with elimination of cluttering and/or hoarding behavior in the physical, emotional, and spiritual realms. The second section is a suggested Progress Guide containing three subsections which are blank but have the following headings: 1. Behaviors and habits that are blocking my recovery, 2. Behaviors and habits that are enhancing my recovery, 3. Behaviors and habits that are gray areas or depend upon circumstances. The third section portrays the same three subsections with examples a member might use as a guide.

Use as a Spiritual Tool

Clutterers are usually all too familiar with shame. We believe we have fallen short of both our own standards and the standards of others. Typically, we haven't been able to do what we originally thought we could. So we try harder. That helps a little, but not long term. More shame. So we apply our will more emphatically, read books on organizing, and try harder. Speaking for myself, applying my will alone leads to a maddening cycle of increasing shame.

Now about my will. I have a different perspective when I refer to a passage from page 85, second paragraph of *Alcoholics Anonymous* ("The Big Book"):[4] "What we really have is a daily reprieve contingent on the maintenance of our spiritual condition. Every day is a day when we must carry the vision of God's will into all of our activities. 'How can I best serve Thee—Thy will (not mine) be done.' These are the thoughts which must go with us constantly. We can exercise our willpower along this line all we wish. It is the proper use of the will." A very potent line from CLA's new leaflet is, "We recover in direct relationship to our surrender."

In using this leaflet as a spiritual tool, I first ask my Higher Power (whom I call God) for direction before beginning to write. In my *first* column, I personally frame the list of behaviors that block my recovery as my "*willful*" actions. I get some sort of payoff from doing them, and I can come up with rationalizations for each and every single one, but they are clearly *not* my Higher Power's gentle, loving will for me if my doing them prolongs and contributes to my continued suffering.

Behaviors and habits that *enhance* my recovery in the second column are more in line with my *Higher Power's* will. These behaviors often do not come easily, and often I must reconnect again and again, praying, "Thy will, not mine, be done." And God, please *help* me be to be willing! (In the spirit of Step 8 in the Big Book, page 76, "If we haven't the will...we ask until it comes.") When I do that, I experience a subtle difference. I may get more clarity of thinking, perhaps a sudden idea to bookend with a specific person via text, or a subjective but comforting knowledge that I am not alone.

Use as a personal compass

This is a gentle tool. The only standard to which you will be compared is yourself.

It can be used daily as part of a 10th Step inventory.

It can be used throughout the day to reorient you toward your preferred direction. When on track, you can check in with it and receive needed validation.

Use within the CLA Fellowship

Putting our personal realities in print can help break down our delusions and denial. This tool is even more powerful and convincing when shared with one or more members of our Fellowship.

When used as the focus in a literature meeting (face-to-face or phone), we can get a new vision for enhancing our recovery or seeing one of our own blind spots.

Please share with the Literature Committee ways in which you are using this leaflet. We will compile your responses to share with others in a future publication. Thanks for your help.

Welcome[18] Leaflet

Spring 2016

Alison B., NJ

I have a confession to make. I have been completely overlooking this leaflet, thinking it is for the newcomer. Well, the first thing I have forgotten is that we are all newcomers because—however long we have been in this beautiful program—"we start where we are," and we have only "one day at a time." I am celebrating 13 years tomorrow, and I can still be a newcomer every day by taking Step 1 and admitting that I am powerless over my clutter. I'm not saying that I do take it every single day...but I can!

We like to read the leaflets in our face-to-face group, and lately we have been taking them paragraph by paragraph and going around the room and sharing for two minutes each. One week, somebody chose this leaflet because we hadn't read it in many years. I wasn't thrilled with the idea, but once we started reading it, I was truly flabbergasted at how much food for thought there is packed into this small space.

First, there are the 25 questions to ask myself: "How Do I Know if I'm a Clutterer?" Just the fact that there are 25 questions written by clutterers tells me this is deadly serious and that I am in the right place. The questions are so clever and seem to hit almost every one of my weak spots. I think out of the yes/no questions, the only one I answered "no" to was about renting storage space—and that's probably only because I was born in England and stayed there into early adulthood, so I came over here with only two suitcases and some assorted hand luggage. Up until that point, I had not had a chance to accumulate much stuff because, in the way of space, I had never had more than a bedroom to call my own.

I would love to address all 25 questions in the leaflet, but there isn't room, so let me choose one question that really stands out, #11. "Do you have difficulty making decisions about what to do with your possessions, daily living, or life in general?" Er, yes, no, maybe. I often find life in general so confusing and overwhelming that I don't know where to start. The answer is that it's usually after I have procrastinated and the chores have piled up, (which probably answers at least two other questions). So the way I cope is to first make sure I have eaten and slept properly, or at least to the best of my ability. Then I like to connect with another clutterer for bookending, but I am shy about calling. If nobody is available, I occasionally go to the phone lines, but I must admit I'm very shy there, too. But I know what I have to do:

- Clear my kitchen table (again!) and put everything in plastic bags.
- Write down everything I need to do, in any order.
- Number things in order of importance .
- Take a calendar and write chores into time slots, putting some into different days to take the pressure off.

Then I must follow through and clean out the plastic bags, one at a time, with a timer. And I can report my progress on the phone as often as I'd like.

The leaflet goes on to ask: "What Does Clutterers Anonymous Have to Offer You?" I really think this should be on the first page. It says that some people come to CLA expecting hints and tips on sorting and filing and things like that. They are surprised to find that, instead, we offer unconditional acceptance and support. Then it goes on to explain that we have a threefold disease—physical, emotional, and spiritual. For me, it's emotional because of the bottomless pit which is definitely inside my head, and spiritual because I came to this program spiritually empty, trying to fill a huge, gaping hole inside myself. When I attended my first 12-Step program 30 years ago, I was agnostic. Now I believe there is a "Universal Power," so that the only way I can go is UP! (I also believe in a Higher Power and my higher self.)

Next, the leaflet briefly describes the 12-Step program of recovery in CLA, which offers healing on all three levels if you follow the "suggestions." I put suggestions in quotes because I know they work when I work them hard. I keep getting up to Step Nine in various programs, and then I get stuck. In one program, I wrote on 155 questions on Step 4 alone. There are no wrong answers.

Lastly, there is an equation: "Principles + Action = Recovery." The principles are found in the Steps. Actions are taken by using the Tools, which are found in our literature. Writing is not actually one of our tools, but I would like to get it added because it is a big tool in other 12-Step programs. It certainly works for me.

Recovery isn't easy, but the program is a worthwhile endeavor when it is broken down into manageable parts, which can be done with a sponsor, although I do not have a sponsor at present. I resolve to get another one this year. Yes, there is truly a lot in this leaflet. If you haven't read it in a while, you may enjoy a deeper study—I couldn't put it down! ▲

Welcome[18] Leaflet–Part Two

Summer 2016

Alison B., NJ

In the spring issue, I began exploring the "Welcome" leaflet. However, there was so much to comment on that I found myself answering only one actual question from the leaflet. Following are my answers to a few more.

Question One: This one really intrigued me: "Do you have more possessions than you can comfortably handle?" The no-brainer answer is: Obviously—that's why I'm here!

But I have a fantasy. I would like to whittle down my three rooms of belongings and furniture into two suitcases and a car and travel cross-country to live in Southern California. I say it's a fantasy because I haven't done anything about it yet. But these days I have fewer excuses, the main ones being the all-consuming finance problem, but mostly and especially the clutter that I'm emotionally attached to that's holding me back. Maybe I will have the strength to get rid of a lot more now that I am writing about it.

Question Two: "Are you embarrassed to invite (people) into your home because it is not presentable?" Yes. I clean up, but then I again clutter available surface space without meaning to. Also, when I moved in 22 years ago, management was supposed to replace the carpeting, but they never did; and now they won't, and it's dirty-looking and very embarrassing.

Question Three: "Do you find it easier to drop something instead of putting it away, or to wedge it into an overcrowded drawer or closet rather than finding space for it?" The short answer is yes. I prefer to do whatever is easiest at the time. However, because of CLA, I have changed some of my habits. I no longer leave clothes on the floor, and I either hang them up or put them in the laundry. I hang everything; I do not put any clothes in drawers. This makes it easier to see everything, though I still wedge other things into overcrowded drawers. I always thought that was putting them away...

Question Four: "Is your home or any part of it unusable for its intended purpose...?" I can't use my bedroom for sleeping because I can hear the superintendent below snoring (yes, really!), so I have turned that room into a junk room. This is really a shame because I have two nice desks in there. As if one desk wasn't enough for one person.

However, I'm much more comfortable doing my paperwork on the kitchen table, which is nearly always cluttered. I've thought about storing my paperwork in my antique secretary. My desktop computer, by the way, is in the living room along with my couch, recliner, and bed. I've heard that we are not supposed to have a computer in the same room as we sleep—but it does fit so nicely in that corner.

I am finding that writing about this leaflet is really helpful. I may ask permission to turn this into a series so I can continue to explore the leaflet.

Welcome Leaflet–Part Three

Fall 2016

Alison B., NJ

I decided to continue answering these questions because they're rather like an inventory. I'm finding out that, although I've come a long way in knowledge over the years, I seem to have cycled back to my earlier physical mess because I haven't kept maintenance habits in place. Please note that the questions are too long to type in their entirety—so, if you want to read them fully, you will need to refer to the leaflet.

5. Is clutter causing problems...in your relationships? Yes. Sometimes I am more of a hermit than I want to be because I'm afraid to get close to people in all sorts of ways.

6. Do you hesitate sharing about this...? Yes. I will tell people I am a clutterer. But, as the question says, I do feel embarrassment, shame, and guilt about it. Especially guilt. So I don't share that because it's so uncomfortable.

7. Do you have a weakness for discarded objects, bargain items...yard sales? I won't take discarded objects any more—not since I had a

bedbug episode, which was horrific. But I love bargains. My apartment is furnished with bargains. Actually, I need bargains since I live on a small budget; but in the past, I have tended to buy furniture items without paying attention to whether they match or blend. I would like to change that about myself. I do go to yard sales, but I am now very careful about what and how much I buy. And I know when I get home, I have to get rid of something of equal value. I used to be very good at doing that—now, not so much.

8. Do you use avoidance, distraction, or procrastination to escape dealing with your clutter? I use those to escape dealing with anything and everything. That's how I GET clutter!
9. Does your clutter create a risk of falling, fire, infestation, or eviction? Because I clean up for inspections, I do not think I would get evicted. I run the risk of falling in one room. I have a lot of wires but nothing near them. I use surge protectors with them. I've come to learn that everyone is at risk for infestation. I went though it with the bedbugs, and I have also had a roach infestation in the kitchen. That did not teach me to keep the dishes out of the sink, so I have to make a commitment to washing them on a daily basis. I no longer bring in second-hand furniture. I haven't got room for it, anyway!
10. Do you avoid starting assignments, miss deadlines...because you can't find the paperwork or material you need? I don't take on too many things with deadlines except writing and editing for CLA*rity*. Occasionally I miss the writing deadline, but I try very hard not to because I know it puts the editors behind. This time it was because I procrastinated and avoided. I have proper files in my computer. I am proud of this. I usually can find paperwork to start a project because I have it filed. Of course, I rarely throw it away! I'm kidding. I throw away a lot more than I used to, but there are years of past paperwork just waiting to be shredded. Materials are a different story. I was just asked to practice a song—one that I sang years ago. I do not know whether I have it on disc or tape or where I can find it. Luckily, there is the Internet...

Welcome[18] Leaflet–Part Four

Holiday 2016

Alison B., NJ

Hello friends. I'm up to question 11 in the "Welcome" leaflet. However, as some of you may remember, back in the spring—when I wasn't aware that I was going to be writing a series—I answered that question at random. Therefore, I'm omitting it here. Please be aware, once again, I am not typing these questions in their entirety; and if you want to see the full questions, you will need to refer to the goldenrod-colored leaflet.

Question 12: Do you rent storage space...? I am grateful to say no to this one. "There, but for the grace of God, go I."

Question 13: Do cleaning, organizing, follow through, upkeep, and maintenance all become daunting tasks, making the simplest of chores insurmountable? Yes, yes, yes, yes, and yes! I get very confused, especially when I see a mess around me. I write down lists of things I have to do, in any order, then I put them into a calendar. If there are things to be done while I am out, I batch them together. If I am pressed for time, then I give time-slots to everything. But while this sounds like a great recipe for success, I am not very consistent with it. I do not have the inner drive to get started.

Question 14: Do you bring an item into your home without designating a place...and releasing an equivalent one? I have brought in items without designating places. I have a small chest of drawers that still does not really have a place, but I like the artsy way it was painted, and so I had to have it. It doesn't have anything in it, maybe because I've never really considered it truly belonged to me. It's the old "I'm not good enough" story. But when I think about it, it's really more "me" than all the plain pieces surrounding it. I have put a moratorium on bringing in things without designating a place for them. My rule is that I must release at least one equivalent item, but often I procrastinate. It is tough if I am thinking about clothing, and I would rather give away a bag full than just let go of one item, for instance. I will bring in a book or VHS tape or CD without having sufficient space for it. I still have to let go of equivalent items in that case.

Question 15: Do you believe that there is all the time in the world to clean your house...finish those projects...read piles of...magazines and newspapers? I am certainly in denial about cleaning my apartment and the time involved. I do believe there is all the time in the world. My best friend died not too long ago. The building management put all his unwanted stuff in a dumpster. As for me, I took hardly anything. I have enough memories. I felt bad about his things, but it was his brother's decision. And now I know what may happen to mine eventually. I can live with that, but I would like to move from this place in the meantime, to a sunnier climate. That means getting rid of a lot of possessions—most of them, actually. And all I can do is complain that I don't even know where to get boxes. As for projects, I used to knit—but, sadly, I threw away my unfinished knitting when I had bedbugs. I haven't knitted in years. I have one magazine subscription (aside from CL*Arity*), and I hold onto the magazine usually until the next one arrives. Then I throw it out. I don't bother to recycle it. If I tried to do that, I would probably hold onto it even longer.

CLA Literature

New CLA Literature

Summer 2015

Measuring Progress on Our Journey in Recovery[13]

At the March 28, 2015, meeting of the CLA World Service Organization (WSO), a new leaflet, "Measuring Progress on Our Journey in Recovery," was adopted as CLA Fellowship-approved literature.

Many years ago, there was discussion in WSO about how to define abstinence. Some members felt that it was difficult for them to work a successful program without something to delineate abstinence. It was decided that there had to be some way that allowed variation, since different clutterers had different triggers and ways in which they cluttered. It was agreed that CLA should develop a method, but other projects had caused it to be put it on hold until recently. Since some members disliked the term "abstinence," the document ultimately became titled "Measuring Progress on Our Journey in Recovery."

The purpose of the leaflet is to address physical, emotional, and spiritual cluttering and hoarding. We do this by listing behaviors and habits that affect our cluttering so we may better track our progress and understand how these behaviors and habits help or hinder us in our recovery.

CLA invites members to purchase the new leaflet and work with the ideas within it. Some members' stories will be published in a follow-up booklet.

The leaflet, "Measuring Progress on Our Journey in Recovery," is available for purchase from WSO. As of this writing, there is no way to order it online, but it will be added at a later date. You can send your payment with a copy of the CLA "Literature Order Form." The form can be downloaded from the "Order Literature" page of the CLA website or requested via one of the contact methods in the box on page 2.

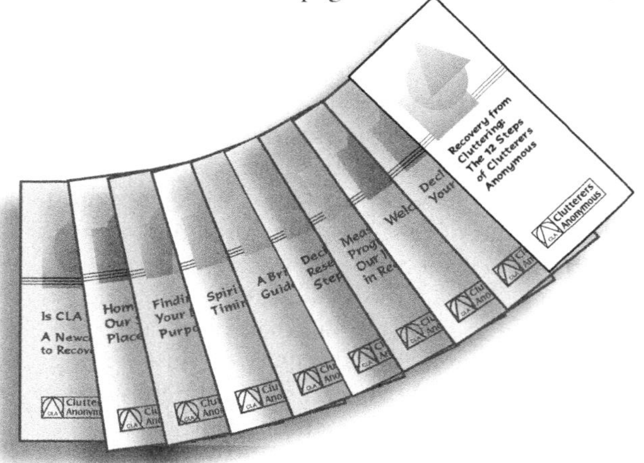

Writing

Clutterers as Writers

Fall 2013

Alison B., NJ, and Wendy L., IL

Writing styles take all sorts of forms that often get developed through trial, error, and study. Being a clutterer adds another dimension to the writing process, as writer/clutterers can be procrastinators and perfectionists. Here we explore both topics based on interviews with several CLA members who write for CLA*rity*.

Some people use certain formulas for writing articles. One person interviewed here is a frequent contributor to CLA*rity* and has learned which ways work for her. A favorite of hers is to free-flow. This means that the person starts where she feels comfortable creating her beginning and just writes anything that comes into her head, as long as it pertains to the subject matter. Sometimes this process helps her release poisonous feelings, and it takes some careful editing before she is satisfied that it is ready for publication. From there she knows she will have to write the middle and an end. At any time, she may make a series of bullet points to guide her and keep her on topic. These will not necessarily appear in the final article, although they could.

Editing her own work is optional because we have teams in CLA*rity* whose voluntary jobs are editing. Nevertheless, she likes to: "go through my own work and weed out the words that seem extraneous. Then perhaps I will strengthen my expressions by inserting more precise terminology where applicable." She knows there are those who like to make handwritten notes, but she prefers to type directly onto the computer. There are times when she will walk away and take a few days before she returns; but, being the clutterer that she is, she has usually waited until the final few hours before the deadline, and so she often doesn't have time to waste.

Some clutterers find that deadlines help them get motivated to write. One procrastinator shared that when her physical clutter gets overwhelming and she gets stressed about it, she finds it difficult to be creative and deadlines become critical. She needs to spend time decluttering, including bookending with other clutterers, to reduce her stress so she can write effectively.

Being a perfectionist causes other challenges. Those who have some experience have learned that there is no perfection; letting go of an imperfect manuscript for editing is a key, albeit an uncomfortable one, to recovery.

Another writer sometimes finds it difficult to decide on the organization, flow, and content of her writing pieces and struggles to decide the fate of her notes and drafts. Should she save them for possible future use in a writing piece, and how should she organize them? She has to create an effective filing system so her written and electronic documents don't become new clutter.

If you've never written a piece but have thought about doing so, there are some things you may want to consider. Nonfiction writing is based on your life's truths, and though you can get very creative here, you don't have to make anything up. So nonfiction writing might be a good starting genre for you. You may want to write about what you're most familiar with and try to emulate writing styles that you enjoy reading. Your first draft doesn't have to be perfect in any sense, i.e., grammar and flow, so just write and get something onto your paper or computer. Unless you have a deadline, you'll have plenty of time to edit your work and craft it into something you can be proud of. Good luck and happy writing!

Clutter and Decluttering

This section contains articles about clutter, including categories for Shopping and Collecting, Paper Clutter, and Nonphysical Clutter. It also has articles discussing our efforts to declutter, including Focus on Decluttering and Getting Unstuck and Motivation.

Getting Unstuck and Motivation

How Do You Plan to Get Unstuck?

Summer 2008 and Fall 2015

Alison B., NJ

The following list is excerpted from a presentation I made at Clutter-Free Day in the spring of 2007. It is based on some of the CLA Tools[19] and Affirmations[20] and has worked well for me as an aid to getting unstuck. To get a version suitable for framing, send an email to CLA*rity* at Clarity@ClutterersAnonymous.org.

- Eat and sleep well, and take care of your health.
- Abstain from creating clutter and negative thinking.
- Read CLA literature.
- Follow suggestions.

- Attend meetings.
- Do service for recovery.
- Establish buddy(ies) and a sponsor.
- Ask for help—physical, emotional, and spiritual.
- Jot down the first things on your mind and prioritize.
- Make reasonable goals.
- Bookend, for commitment.
- Use a timer set for intervals of 2–15 minutes.
- Reward/affirm when goal is attained.
- Declutter one section daily.
- Do 15 minutes' maintenance daily.
- Take action.
- Take it out? Put it away!
- Make a time plan.
- Underschedule—leave breathing space.
- Concentrate—do one thing at a time in priority order.
- Do not pressure others or yield to pressure.
- Take time to relax.
- Have patience.
- Live in the now.
- Preserve anonymity.
- Recycle when simple, throw out when necessary.
- Think you might need it in the future? Trust that the Universe will provide.

Motivating Myself to Declutter

Summer 2010

Excerpted from Clutter-Free Day Presentation, October 2007, by Beryl W., NY

About 2000, I found Clutterers Anonymous. One of the first things I did was an inventory of my clutter, writing it down room by room. I started with what bugged me the most, because that's the most bang for the buck. Doing that motivated me to go on to the next thing, and the next—until I had done the whole list. It does not happen overnight; you have to be persistent. But it does happen.

In order to motivate yourself, you do have to have a little hope. If you have no hope, it's very difficult to get the wherewithal to get up and do it. I recently got a good Higher Power and, for the first time, took Step 2 in a really profound way. But I had hope before—from the literature and the affirmations. I just figured there was a way out, and that was my hope. Along with hope comes self-esteem. Without self-esteem I think it's very hard to declutter.

When you finish something, give yourself a pat on the back. If you have a good experience at the end of a bad experience, you will be more willing to go back into it. When you finish the job, just sit and admire it. Then you will be motivated to do it again.

Do the worst first. One day I was sitting, not motivated to do anything. There was a phone call I had to make but didn't want to. I made the call, and I had all sorts of energy. So, do the worst first. If I can get my energy up, I can clear the clutter a lot easier.

Declutter your schedule; if you have a cluttered schedule, then you probably have a cluttered house also.

Something that demotivates me—if I always say I can't, I can't. Someone said, "If you think you can, or you think you can't, you're probably right." In the Big Book,[4] it says that when you look at problems, the problems get bigger; when you look at solutions, the solutions get bigger. When I am complaining, it's the same as I can or I can't. So I try to share the solution, and not the problem.

Find the fun. I love feng shui. If I want a relationship, I clear out the relationship corner; if I a want a job, let me declutter the career corner. For me it's very motivational. It may not work for you, but find what motivates you.

You have to decide you really want to declutter. I knew I needed to get rid of books; I had far too many. I couldn't do it. And then one day, I realized I had had those books ten years and never cracked them. I started taking things that I could release to the library. I haven't wanted one of them since. In Al-Anon they say, "Awareness, Acceptance, and Action." My part of that was "awareness, beat yourself up, paralysis." So, I was aware of the books, I accepted that I was not releasing them today, and eventually I let them go.

One barrier to decluttering is wearing your clutter as a badge—"I am such a bad declutterer, you have no idea." That is going to stop you from decluttering because that is what makes you special, but you will not ever get rid of it because that's your specialness. You're wearing that badge instead of developing real self-esteem.

Use the program. I do, and did from the beginning. The least we can do is attend meetings. Bring the body, and the mind will follow.

Read the literature. The first leaflet I really hooked into was "Decluttering Resentment."[8] I immediately got the connection between holding onto my clutter and holding onto my resentments. I got rid of so many resentments. It was wonderful; it was really liberating.

Service is key. If you don't know how to do a service position, ask, learn. Service: it's magical.

Take phone numbers and use them. If you are not taking phone numbers, you've got a problem.

Get a buddy; if possible, a sponsor.

Bookend—which means, I have a task I don't want to do, and I'm finding some resistance. So I call someone and commit that, within a stated time, I will have started, if not finished. At the end of that time, I call back and report: "Yes, I did it; no I didn't." Now, the trick to bookending: If you didn't do it, you're not a failure, you just didn't do it. You give yourself a pass, the same way I did with the books, and then you recommit. Judging yourself is as bad as using your clutter as a badge.

Make it easy for yourself. Not on yourself, but make it easy for yourself. I don't aim for perfection. I aim to do it. Find your bottom line. My bottom line: Basic 4. As a matter of fact, it doesn't take care of impacted clutter, but I'm not ever going to have new clutter if I do the Basic 4. Allow time to put things away.

Don't beat yourself up if you don't do it perfectly. You know, we're human, and the program asks only for progress, not perfection. Be patient, loving, and kind with yourself. Give yourself some pats on the back. Make the time. And have fun.

**Editor's Note: The Basic Four is not an official CLA Tool.*

How to Get Unstuck Using the CLA Program

Fall 2016

Bonnie W., NY

I struggle with being overwhelmed, being stuck and immobilized by clutter. I've been in the CLA program for many years, and I've decluttered and recluttered many times.

My clutter reflects many things—sometimes stress, anxiety, and depression; sometimes just hurry and bad habits; and sometimes exhaustion. Other times it's manifested in distraction and involvement with other more important issues or escaping to do less important things.

Last year, I specifically set aside a large amount of time to deal with it—once and for all, I imagined. I learned many things, the most important being that this is an ongoing problem which will reappear with amazing intensity at any time, but especially when I'm under severe stress.

This is an outline of what I learned. I continue to do the best I can, one day at a time. Often I struggle. The only thing I know for sure is that my Higher Power is my guide and salvation, and CLA is a source of support, inspiration, and hope.

1. First things First. When I am hungry, angry, lonely, or tired (HALT), or sick or stressed, I deal with that first. Honoring the true need for rest and self-care is crucial for a former workaholic like me.
2. Honesty. I admit when I am unwilling and unable. I say no to unreasonable requests, set boundaries, negotiate reasonable requests, and journal about feelings of unwillingness. I journal to let go of feelings of blame and shame that tie up energy better used decluttering.
3. Working Steps 1-3, 11, and 10 daily helps me admit the pain. I pray and meditate and evaluate what I truly accomplished.
    a. Before and during decluttering, I ask Higher Power's assistance with each step. Sometimes I'm directed to do something completely different from what I had planned. My Higher Power's plan is the perfect plan.
    b. Step 4 is used to inventory what I need to do, what I need to get it done, and how long I need to do it. I get help or pay help for the things I'm too overwhelmed to do. The best investment is getting it done and moving on instead of continuing to struggle for years with the same thing.
4. I face it! I don't run away! I work during high-energy time when possible—daily 5-15 minutes to start or intervals during the morning before work. Scheduling chore days for specific tasks works well for me. I eliminate distractions, cover areas not being worked on, and turn the cell phone off.
5. Maintenance of progress is the key to not backsliding and the most important part of keeping those surfaces clear. I guard those clear surfaces like gold!
6. In the spirit of Step 10, I keep a daily record of what I do to chart my progress and to not get discouraged.
7. Our program Tools:[19] Sponsorship, Literature, Meetings, Buddies, and Service keep me on track, as well as Step 5.
8. I expect challenges, setbacks, and times when there is just no progress. It is a normal part of

the process, although I sometimes get hysterical; but there is no need to do so.

9. Here are some other ideas that may work. Keep going. Make it fun. Declutter to favorite music. Have a throw-away-while-dancing party. Sing or say affirmations while working, or work while listening to an inspiring CLA tape or phone meeting. Play a game to see how much can be done or thrown away in 5-15 minutes or any set time. Have a decluttering party with Buddies. Take turns decluttering each other's projects. Throw a party or have a potluck after the work is done or each time you meet.

10. Finally, I celebrate any victory, large or small. With even the smallest step, progress is possible. Choose a reasonable self-nurturing way to celebrate daily. Some of the best celebrations are free—like listening to music, taking a walk in a beautiful area, talking to a favorite friend, or preparing a favorite meal. As we know, together we can do it one Step at a time, one day at a time.

See another article on this topic in the "Recovery Stories" section on page 128.

Focus on Decluttering

CHAOS (Can't Have Anyone Over Syndrome)–Conquered?

Spring 2008 and Summer 2013

Francis S., MD

The following is an attempt to organize, or pull together, my actions, feelings, and thoughts {for the past six months}. I tried to focus on the kitchen, although there were other big pieces that threatened to distract.

Over those months, especially at the beginning, my motivation towards "kitchen sanity" was inspired by the experiences of other CLA members. These "buddies" and acquaintances shared their commitments and goals, creating a jumping-off point for me and making the reclamation of my kitchen a possibility.

The idea of *committing* to cleaning up or clearing out my kitchen was too difficult and painful for me to get my mind around. At some level, I knew it was a challenge I needed to undertake, but I was reluctant to commit to any date or even to try to visualize what it would or could look like if it were a "normal" kitchen.

Over the last year, several Fellowship members had told me about their plans to host a group of people and had arranged events at their homes. I couldn't stop thinking: "I guess it's my turn. When will I pick the date?" I believe it was my decision to announce a housewarming in mid-January 2008 that really got me going.

True, I could get to the refrigerator and to the spot where the microwave and coffee maker were jammed into a corner, but there were only a few inches of clear, flat space in the whole room. I would say that the room, as a whole, was virtually unusable.

Perhaps 15 percent of the floor area was clear enough to walk on; the sink was just barely reachable over boxes piled in front and to either side on the floor. The stove, refrigerator, and island were topped off with more boxes, empty and half-empty bags—some chewed by mice or otherwise unusable—and a small hill of plastic deli containers in yet more boxes. The cabinets were blocked, overflowing, and chaotic. It was not a kitchen any more due to its cluttered state.

How many *hours of work* it was I don't know, because sometimes I could stand to work on it for only a minute or two.

Then, I wanted the sink to be clean, so I started to move the hundreds of things that were clustered near or perched on the edge of the sink or sitting in the drying rack. I had "found"—actually, I had created—empty flat space!

I "discovered" a beautiful ceramic bowl on the counter and thought how cool it would look with some fruit in it, so I cleared a little bit more counter space.

Once I had created some empty space, I

suddenly realized that I needed to change my unconscious habit of recluttering. I resisted the distraction of going to declutter other areas. I began to realize that I had to monitor myself.

The desire to again fill any space that I had created was almost overwhelming, automatic, and rather unconscious at first. In fact, the changes—decluttering and empty spaces—made me feel uncomfortable. I did get over this slowly, and the experience created a radical new awareness for me. And guess what, my attitude changed!

No longer wanting stuff to stay in my sorting and working spaces spurs me on to focused awareness. I am grateful that I was willing and able to feel without being judgmental.

I can now envision a beautiful kitchen, and it's not just some pipe dream. First, I stop and ask myself: "Is this something I need or will use?" If yes, put it away; if no, put it on the "trash" or "giveaway" pile now. Honestly, it's not quite that simple because there may be things that are too difficult to decide about, or ones which don't have a "home space." Sometimes it seems best for the pace of the overall goal to defer, revisit, or re-decide about some items. But I need to be very careful with this "later" pile, that it doesn't get out of whack with "keep," "give away," and "trash."

Next, I focused on the plastic containers—this was a challenge! I had even paid money for some of them, so the "waste not..." rule wanted to kick in. I challenged myself by separating out some containers (particularly those that I had many of, loose lids, etc.). And the height of the piles of boxes decreased. There was the floor! Visible progress encouraged me to expand my organization and disposal of plastic containers throughout the house.

Somehow, by focusing, I usually was able to minimize my tendency to get distracted by other cluttered areas in the house. I did this by (1) recommitting to the priority of the kitchen job, (2) breaking it up into smaller, "digestible" tasks, and (3) allowing limited amounts of time to work on other areas. In other words, I would take 15 or 30 minutes to make other areas tolerable, usable, and good enough, which acted like a break or a change of pace from the daunting size of the kitchen project.

What I learned: patience and gentleness with myself; balance, flexibility, and openness; and getting comfortable with "good enough" by renegotiating with myself.

Job Done! Not really. It's ongoing, one day at a time.

What's new? It's exciting that I can now envision a normal kitchen, and it's not just some unachievable fantasy.

Thank you, HP. Thank you, CLA.

Getting Into Action

Summer 2008 and Spring 2015

Bob M., Betsy L., and Parker B. of VA

Revisiting the Impact of an In-Home Action Team

On April 22, 2006, we shared about our experiences as an In-Home Action Team at the Clutter-Free Day in Metuchen, NJ. Now, two years later, we have been asked to revisit and give an update on working with each other in our homes. Below is our story.

The Story of What Happened

Originally, we had all been dissatisfied with our progress in decluttering. Organizing and decluttering had been a real grunt for us. So, after a CLA meeting, three of us decided to get together and go into each other's homes to see how that worked out. There was no commitment to a long-term group. On September 2, 2005, we met at Bob's for the first time. We did a lot of brainstorming and a little decluttering. We were excited by what was happening. We felt energy and power, and we were eager to continue. At the beginning, there was intense ambivalence. On the one hand, we desperately wanted help and energy from others; while, on the other hand, we feared having people in our clutter-filled homes. We felt very vulnerable. The experience of this vulnerability helped us to be more sensitive and empathetic when we went into each other's homes.

Betsy's was the second home we went to, and Parker's was the third. By that time, we knew we were onto something very powerful, and we were becoming committed to some sort of team action. We regularly shared our enthusiasm and ideas with our Wednesday night CLA group.

The primary benefit has been an increase in energy and motivation. We have confidence and faith that we can each have a pleasing, organized home. There is individual and group excitement. Not only do we declutter our physical stuff, we also declutter our minds and our spirits. A good part of our time is focused on the mental and spiritual. After more than two-and-a-half years of weekly get-togethers, the In-Home Action Team has continued to evolve. Below are some concepts we use when working with one another in our homes.

What Makes the In-Home Action Team Work for Us?

- Trust (confidential, emotional trust): No put-downs or emotional comments are made. Members feel safe around each other. There are no negative gut reactions to each other. No power struggles.
- Chemistry: There is natural, good chemistry among members.
- Respect: Members are careful to respect each other's ideas and opinions.
- Commitment: Members have the time available to commit. When one member can't make it, the others meet anyway.
- Host's agenda: The CLA team members are there to help the host and to respect and follow the host's agenda rather than to push their own ideas. They respect and follow the host's energy, direction, and lead.

What We Do:

- Brainstorm or get into action
- Declutter the stuff, as well as decluttering the mind

Red Flags:

- Difficult people
- High-maintenance people

Personal Growth:

- Problem solving
- Self-confidence
- Leadership
- Supportive social skills

It took a while to set up a group that worked. We had gone to the homes of several CLA members to help declutter; however, we feared having them in our homes. Therefore, we also suggested to several members that we stay on the phone while we decluttered; however, no one took the offer.

We also offered to drive from Virginia to help CLA friends in Philadelphia and northern New Jersey, but they declined. Finally, after a couple of years, we grew strong enough interpersonally to feel safe having others in our homes. It was lucky that the chemistry worked; it has worked very well. We are still meeting weekly, and we urge others to give it a try.

The Waiting Game

Spring 2013

Wendy L., IL

I was born late. And, as my mother reminds me, I still run late. I'm a life-long procrastinator. And it doesn't stop at being late. My procrastinating extends to other areas of my life, like making decisions and putting off stressful to-do's. This wouldn't be so bad except that it often causes me stress, and sometimes a lot of it.

Interestingly, I don't procrastinate too badly at the workplace, where I've developed successful organizational and time management systems. Of course, not being timely at work could cost me my job; I won't get fired if I don't do the dishes one day.

So what can I do about it? Let's take a look at some situations and solutions.

Running late. The reasons are varied. If I run early, I may not want to be alone with my thoughts, which may remind me of the clutter in my life. Or, if I'm on a roll with my current to-do's, I can't be bothered to stop and get myself ready. Avoidance of extreme weather is another excuse. So, how can I get my butt out the door on time? For me, it's all about the preparation—like getting all my paperwork together in advance. Getting dressed early is very important. Bringing an enjoyable magazine to read while I'm waiting for a doctor's appointment helps a lot. And using my remote car starter to get the heat or air conditioning going is a nice luxury.

Too many choices. You'd think that having tons of choices and options would be good. But for a clutterer, this can be a drawback. Take eye drops, for example. At the local drugstore, I counted 15 different bottles of drops for dry eye. All those drops for two eyes! How to choose? And around Thanksgiving I was shopping for a new computer, which is a pricier and much more stressful decision for me. I got so tense that I developed a tic in my eye!

It's easier to put off these decisions, but that doesn't help my eye problem or computer needs. So, I buy the most appropriate drops, which tend to be the most expensive. I look at it as an investment in myself. Oh, and I buy the drops at a store that has a very good return policy.

The new computer? I put the search on hold. At least my tic went away.

Servicing my car. I've been uncomfortable interacting with some gruff service guys in the past. How trustworthy are they? And what if they find something wrong and it's expensive, and I have to make a decision to do the repair? My resolution was to subscribe to consumer rating services, which I used to research local shops. I called the one with the most good reviews, and they sounded friendly enough, so I made an appointment. I liked the shop and will take my car there again. Additional solutions include asking friends for recommendations and giving a new shop a try by taking the car in for an oil change.

I have good days where I accomplish my to-do's and happily check them off my list. On other days, I feel overwhelmed or tired and don't do much checking off. CLA has been a big help, be it utilizing the Focused Action Session phone calls or talking with other clutterers.

There are solutions to procrastinating that take practice and perseverance. And slowly, but surely, I'm becoming a person who does less avoiding and more doing. Today, I am a grateful, recovering clutterer.

Happy Feet

Fall 2014
Ted S., NY

There was no deadline, no authority figure over my shoulder, no impending punishment if it wasn't completed. It just got done. It was done—meaning just now it got done. And also, wow, it's done!

Really?! Was it really started and finished in one day?

Well, not quite. It was physically started today and finished within an hour, despite being interrupted by a phone call and taking a short interval to clear the recyclables. Actually, the thought to do it first came Memorial Day weekend 2012, when they were getting put away.

Well, that must have been some project to take so long to complete!

Yes indeed, a huge undertaking, surpassing the will and might of the "armies of procrastination." It's no easy task to get by the self-imposed "landmines" of delay.

After each special event, I would make myself a promise to take care of this chore. All I needed to do was gather the items to be worked on, find the supplies and—most important—the time to do it. Not just time, but the right time, the proper time, the most convenient time.

Surely, there would be time before they were needed again (or at least there would be time to do them the actual day of the event). Oh, but wait...why not do them ahead of time? Well, they could become bruised or something before they were needed.

Now, there were plenty of other chores that needed completing but were also put off; so many, in fact, that nothing would get done. Still, it's better knowing that things have to be done than thinking they are but really aren't.

I knew how it usually would go, especially when an event was here: I'd expect them to be ready, but they weren't. So, then there would be this last-minute rush, and the anxiety panic would overwhelm me.

Thinking I'd finish them on the day of the event, I'd find there just wasn't enough time to do them. Then, a terrible feeling came over me, knowing they could have been done sooner. There was always a sadness while heading out to attend what usually is an enjoyable event.

Having not done them was another cape of clutter that wears me down with each activity that had been put off for another day. It makes me feel as if I'm a "heel." Putting things off causes such an embarrassment to my "sole."

I'm not sure how the impulse to do them now all of a sudden came about. All I am sure of is that it was time. I even questioned whether doing this now might be procrastinating about something else that had to be done.

I gave it a moment's thought and decided that no matter whether this was the best or right time or even the inappropriate time, it was the time they were going to be done.

Those get-all-dressed-up shoes were finally shined today; then they were carefully packed away to be ready for a special day.

There is a quiet serenity now that they're done. It's similar to having the perfect gift for a special someone, wrapping it all up ahead of time, and anticipating the look on the recipient's face when it's opened.

When my shoebox gets opened, that special someone in this case will be me. It gives me such a warm feeling that my eyes are welling up. Now there are happy feelings and it's done.

Now, whenever some special occasion arises, I know that they'll be waiting for me. All I hope is that I'll remember where I put them!

Summer Camp

Summer 2015

Kathy T., NY

I'm going to summer camp! I've never been before, and I'm excited. The arrangements were made over the weekend after I heard on the radio that the kids in New York City were enjoying their first day of summer vacation, now that the pools are open.

My camp is Kathy's "Learn to be Clutter-Free" Day Camp. I counted nine weeks from June 30 until Labor Day. *[This article was written in 2014—Editor]* (Weren't summers longer when I went to school? They seemed to stretch out to an infinite horizon.)

I have a Camp Counselor who is helping me every step of the way. We start with "Rock Climbing." That's my conscious contact before starting the day's activities, and I can rock-climb with the Twelve Steps, studying and practicing any time of the day or night!

Then there are all sorts of things to do. We go on field trips to places like the laundromat, the grocery store, the gas station, and the library. We get to practice gratitude everywhere!

And when we come back to the campground, there's KP! Wait, it's not what you think. It's Kitchen Possibilities! I get to clear off the tea cart (vintage 1950s stainless steel frame with enameled shelves, the top one removable as a serving tray). Then I get to set it up so it's useful to me. I can have access to my blender for those smoothies I haven't been able to have for years! How cool is that?

One session is "What's Behind That Door?" We'll find out what's in a closet. It'll be so much fun.

Then there's the "Find Things..." classes. Find things that are made of wood (glass, wool, plastic). Find things that are green (Whitman's "Leaves of Grass" counts!). Find things that begin with the letter "L." You get the idea.

We get to take walks and write down all the birds, animals, and plants we see (even the bugs, if we want). There's time to dance or do gentle stretching.

Confetti-Making 101 (shredding). Undersink Spelunking. Even Pile-Driving! That's when I get to reduce a pile of papers or magazines and drive them right out the door.

The classes don't have to be longer than ten minutes, and I get to do as many in a day as I want, keeping in mind the camp rules of "Rest before we get tired" and "My first priority is always my well-being." So on Dress-Up Day, if I try on only five items to see if they fit, are comfortable, loved and will be worn, that's all I have to do. If I do five items of clothing one day each week, that's still 45 items by the end of camp. That's great!

Nobody gets beat up at this camp ever. And the point is to have fun doing what needs to be done anyway. We even have "Pay It Forward." That's when we recycle stuff and donate it to help other people.

I can even worry if I really want to, but only during the five minutes of "Worry. Don't Be Happy."

I hope you can have a fun "summer camp" experience, too. Ttyl. (Talk to you later!)

Home Our Sacred Space

Fall 2015
Sandy, ME

Carrots, Coffee Filters, Old Cabbage Heads

Thanks to CLA and the grace of my Higher Power, I've received my earmarking habit. Almost everything has a preordained spot in my sacred home—my keys, jewelry, wet shoes, titles/deeds, mail, etc.

Of course, I'm a work in progress; not everything actually gets to its earmarked spot! My biggest challenge is paper—either creative projects jotted on the back of envelopes or "newsy" clippings with grand ideas. And because they often involve decisions, it's paper and mind clutter.

Nevertheless, there is one class of household stuff that always gets put in its rightful place. Can you guess what that is? It's all compostable materials—used coffee filters, expired bread and cereals, newspaper, old onions, the usual salad tidbits, and even paper towels (shredded a bit). Most materials are compostable but some exceptions include meat, dairy, and synthetics.

There are so many plusses:

1. I feel good about it.
2. I reduce trash volume and smell.
3. I let Mother Nature produce prime soil—a process that converts paper and veggies into flower blossoms or Swiss chard.
4. It's decluttering that I can truly enjoy.

A Move in the Right Direction

Fall 2015
Wendy L., IL

Moving to a new residence can be both a blessing and a curse. On the one hand, you get to start fresh in a clutter-free space; but on the other hand, you're forced to handle your old clutter. Not just some of it, but the whole shebang. Makes a clutterer not want to move!

Or you can always do what I used to. Just box up all your clutter and bring it with you, kind of like a turtle carries its home around with it. It's like clutter nirvana and nightmare all at the same time. And like double nirvana for those who have a storage shed or some such thing waiting at their new place.

Recently, I was in the very enviable position of being able to move and leave my clutter behind for sorting at a later time. So time was on my side. But even so, I brought over only what was absolutely necessary to manage a home. For the purposes of this article, I'm calling this "clean moving."

The thing is, I craved a clutter-free home so much that I decided I'd rather bring too little than too much. I still had access to my old clutter, so it wasn't as if I was walking on much of a tightrope. But still, I erred on the side of simplicity when it came to deciding what to take.

And I didn't get off leaving my clutter behind forever. I'm having to sort through it now. But I'm determined to justify bringing anything over to my new place. Take, for example, the commemorative mugs I haven't used in years. I felt some angst in discarding them, but it was trumped by not creating clutter at my new place.

After eight months at my new place, I can say that my home is picked up every day or two but have to admit that paper is still my Achilles heel. Those little receipts that barely fit through my shredder are my nemesis. But I keep my paper confined to a couple of areas and it's manageable. I can have people over after five minutes of cleaning up—a record for me.

Clean moving has not been without its perils, and there have been a couple of casualties along the way. Some surprising sadness remains for the sentimental objects I got rid of, but it's still better than the shame I would've felt by bringing them over as clutter. And there was some shake-my-head disbelief that I threw away a power cord. But after a couple of big sighs and mumbles, I can report that I'm surviving and learning to live without these things.

So, if you have the chance to move, take the opportunity to really start anew. Challenge yourself to be selective. And early does it, if you have the time. As cute as turtles are, try not to become one. Less is really more.

Focus on Decluttering

Holiday 2016

Ruthe S., PA

I have been in CLA for almost 16 years. During that time, I have both decluttered and recluttered my spaces. I have come to understand that my problem begins when I am under stress. All clutter is unmade decisions. Do I keep it or release it? If I keep it, where do I put it? If I release it, where do I send it? These decisions are incredibly hard for me to make, with the most difficult one being whether or not to keep it. There is something about trying to figure out if I will need it or not that gives me great fear. The best thing for me to do, which I have sometimes been able to do in the past, would be to have faith that Higher Power will provide what I need when I need it, as our literature states.

When I am under stress, it becomes almost impossible for me to make these decisions because my energy is being used to deal with whatever problem is at hand. My father died seven years ago and left me with a sick mother and a sick sister. At some point during this time, I did a lot of decluttering. Then I got married, which is a good stress, but is stress nonetheless.

After that, things intensified with my ill family. It became impossible to even pay attention to decluttering. Also, I had been using a professional organizer to help me, and during that time, I was unable to afford to hire her again.

As time went on, I got more and more depressed. I have learned in CLA that I actually hate clutter. I wondered how I would ever get my apartment back to where it was before. I decluttered little bits here and there, but it didn't look as if I had done anything. I felt a lot of despair. Finally, I was able to find the money to afford to have the organizer return.

We spent about three to four hours working in my living room. We consolidated things and threw things out. We also cleaned the surface of my coffee table. When we were done, things looked much better. We could see more floor and much of the table. I actually enjoyed throwing the bags of trash out and getting rid of the recycling.

After we were done for the day, I realized that my mood had lifted tremendously. I still had the same difficult things going on in my life, but I noticed later in the day I felt better. I realized that it was the decluttering that helped me. Although I had felt better after decluttering before, I think this was the first time I actually saw the direct link to my mood. I found myself looking forward to the next time I would declutter.

This reminds me of something an ADHD coach once said to me before I was in CLA. I told her that I was too tired after going to work, making dinner, and doing chores and errands; this made it difficult for me to declutter. The coach suggested that it was the other way around—that it was actually the clutter that was making me tired. That made a big impression on me then, and I see now that it is the truth.

CLA has no opinion on using professional help—Ed.

Various Articles on Clutter

Technology and Clutter—Part 1

Fall 2012
Kathy H., CA

In this article, I will cover ways in which I use electronic devices to aid in my decluttering efforts.

When I think of clutter and technology, I realize that technology has parallels to physical clutter. I have to ask myself, "When am I just a gadget junkie, and when am I using technology to enrich my life?" Using the principles in the CLA program—including the Steps, the Tools,[19] and other CLA literature—has helped me immeasurably to prioritize and declutter.

Using the resources of my computer has helped me to eliminate physical clutter. I have been able to recycle more than half the paper that had been in my filing cabinets. I decided I no longer needed some files, but others I scanned and stored on the computer, which allowed me to discard the original paper versions.

I scanned my entire 40-year collection of photographs and moved the printed photos from albums to file boxes, which freed up almost two shelves in my bookcase. I was then able to set up slide shows on the computer, so I can easily view the photographs whenever I wish. This has an added advantage—I was able to back them up on CDs, which are stored outside my home. So if my home were to be destroyed, I could still retrieve all my pictures. And I seldom print photographs I have taken with a digital camera—only when it is to give others a print. All this scanning did take time, but the end result is much less physical clutter.

It took quite a bit of time to do the scanning for both documents and pictures. But now that the initial job has been completed, I spend only a few minutes on it now and then.

When a company offers to email bills rather than send paper versions, I take them up on it—the same with flyers and notices. I have also requested that some firms I deal with no longer send me paper catalogs, since I can browse them online. In these instances, the computer has helped me by keeping papers out of my house altogether.

One last paper-removing item has been very helpful to me, although I realize that this solution is not for everyone. This works especially well if you have a smart phone that can synchronize with your computer. I keep my calendar appointments, my to-do lists, and my addresses on the computer and set it to wirelessly synchronize with my phone. That way, I have eliminated the need for a paper calendar and address book. Also, anything I add into my phone uploads to my computer, so the information remains the same without much effort on my part. It makes it easier for me to keep track of things and reduces paper clutter. That's a win-win for me.

Keeping appointments and addresses up to date requires attention, whether you use a paper or electronic method—although the time I spend doing so is actually very little.

All of these things lead me once again to appreciate the value of the Tool of Daily Action. As long as I keep up with the small chores of scanning an occasional document and keeping my addresses and appointments up to date, everything seems to run more smoothly. When I put it aside for later, it can take a lot of time to resolve the problems brought on by the resulting chaos.

Technology and Clutter—Part 2

Holiday 2012
Kathy H., CA

How do I ensure that using the computer is an asset, rather than a gadget that adds more work and frustrates me? Learning the operations of my computer and organizing the filing system have made it work for me.

The time I have spent in learning how to use my computer has paid off many times over. Because I take time to learn things, I don't become frustrated and waste time by being in the middle of a job and not being sure how to complete it.

Many years ago, I was learning to use my first page-layout program. The computer was given to me with software already installed, and I had no manuals. (This was before computer manuals were on CDs or online; one needed a printed manual.) I had gone through the quick introductory tutorial, so I did know how to set and move blocks of text. However, I needed to do hanging indents for some bulleted material and did not know how to accomplish this. Lacking knowledge of any other method, I set the indented material in a separate text block and moved it to line up in the proper location. It printed okay, but needless to say, it was a very time-consuming task. Subsequently, I purchased a printed "how to" book on the program and learned the easy way. That was such a relief! One simple little bit of knowledge saved me hours of work. After that, I always made sure I had instructions and took time to learn each new application.

Besides, when I know how my system works, I can often find a much quicker way to complete tasks. For instance, if I want to print a file, I have options. I can grab my mouse and move the cursor to the file menu and then choose "print" from that menu. But it is usually much faster to leave my fingers on the keyboard and type a keystroke combination. In the long run, these little bits of time add up to a lot of time saved doing mundane tasks.

I find it helpful at least to understand a little bit of how computers themselves work. Believe me, if you open your mind to a new way, it's not as difficult as many seem to think—but the key is to learn how your system works, including the file structure.

Modern computers have simplified what we see, but the file structure determines how files are written to disk and how they are retrieved. Your computer may have more than one drive or disk. Then, each drive contains folders and files (either ones placed there by the manufacturer or ones you have written). Folders can also contain files and other folders nested inside.

I am not proposing that you spend weeks or even days learning these basics; they can be grasped quickly. There are many good, short books on the market that can teach you the basics.

Technology and Clutter—Part 3

Spring 2013

Kathy H., CA

In the Spring 2013 issue, I will conclude this series by discussing how I organize my computer system and how I avoid computer clutter.

I have discussed ways in which I use my computer as an aid in my decluttering and how learning to use the computer has helped with my time management. In this last section, I will discuss how I organize my computer so that I can retrieve files speedily and what I do to avoid computer clutter.

Some type of organization is needed to be able to find computer files easily. Some people set up a naming system and use a "find" or "search" command to find the files they need. I prefer to organize all the files on my drives so I can find them easily.

For instance, I have added a folder for CLA to my computer's drive. In that folder are other folders pertaining to CLA items—my local group, various committees, etc. Many of these contain other folders. If I wanted to retrieve the file for this article, I would open the CLA folder, then open the CLA*rity* newsletter folder inside it. That folder would contain another folder for this issue of CLA*rity*, with the file inside. Organization can save a lot of time and frustration. Think of it as using the CLA tool of Earmarking—designating a place for items and putting them there.

I think about what kinds of things I save and how they relate to other items, then use this information to devise a filing system to fit my needs. Of course, I can always erase folders, create new folders, and move folders and files to other locations.

I also have put some thought into a standardized naming system for my files, which makes it easier to find them. For those who prefer to search for files rather than organize them into folders, it is even more imperative to standardize your naming system. Otherwise, it could take hours to find one file.

I find that I need to keep in mind the CLA tool of Daily Action when dealing with my computer.

To avoid having files and emails become clutter, I organize and declutter them regularly. Actually, it's easier to declutter computer data files than physical clutter—there's nothing to throw away or recycle.

My house isn't the only place I collect clutter; it's very easy to clutter the computer also. CLA literature defines clutter as "anything we don't need, want, or use that takes our time, energy or space, and destroys our serenity." I had to realize that, no matter how good my organizational system, the more documents I have, the more likely I will skip organizing them during a busy time and the more trouble I will have finding what I want—exactly the same as with physical clutter.

I was tempted to scan in every piece of paper I had removed from my filing cabinets (as discussed in Part 1). But before I started, I realized that much of what I kept about certain informational topics was now available online. Of course, there were some important papers—mostly legal—that needed to be kept. But I didn't need many of the others, either in my filing cabinets or on the computer. I haven't missed any of them yet.

Also, it's easy to cram a computer with too many applications. I try to look once or twice a year to see what I am not using and can remove.

I also do my computer maintenance routines periodically. I would rather run them in my down time than have everything mess up during a critical job. And I am careful to back up my files, so that if things do go wrong, I can always retrieve files. Doing these chores helps me keep my serenity.

Electronic clutter adds not only to the physical clutter of computer files, but also to time clutter and mind clutter. Everything I do takes time and emotional energy—and both my time and energy are finite. I keep in mind the Tools[19] of Streamlining and Earmarking. When I release an old item before acquiring a new one and when I keep everything in its designated place (this applies to both hardware and software), I find myself less rushed and more at peace in my life.

So, in conclusion, I am using CLA principles to deal with technology and clutter—utilizing the computer to decrease physical clutter, organizing it so I can retrieve things, and learning the basics that allow me to function with more efficiency and serenity.

Our Sacred Place's Sacred Place

Spring 2015

Anonymous

We frequently hear members of our CLA phone meetings and sessions report their "victories" in decluttering their homes. Of course, clearing clutter from our homes is one of our program's fundamental practices. As acknowledged in the leaflet, "Recovery from Cluttering: The 12 Steps of Clutterers Anonymous,"[14] "...what we [clutterers] yearn for are surroundings of beauty, order and serenity; a balanced life; and harmonious relationships," and that clinging to our clutter affects our ability to make that wish come true.

In addition, as we recover from clutter, we begin to honor our need for a safe, functional, and truly "sacred place" that supports our safety and health, our mental clarity, and spiritual roots. We acknowledge that a clean home is not in and of itself recovery. We then learn that we cannot achieve an uncluttered home without also releasing nonphysical clutter, including clutter in our minds, our time, and our relationships.

For me, my gradual recovery has allowed me to see expanding opportunities for clarity in my relationship with myself and my needs, as well as to people, places, and things in general.

Along with this increased awareness, I've come to question whether I'm truthfully decluttering my world when I thoughtlessly dispose of hazardous wastes and recyclables with the rest of my garbage when I might dispose of them more responsibly. After all, when I don't think about where my discarded objects will go, I'm shifting their negative physical effects to a space I share—even if it is outside my home in a landfill, dump, or incinerator.

This doesn't mean that putting my home in order is not a principle aim of my program. But when I eliminate physical clutter thoughtlessly, my actions may negatively impact my basic physical needs—shared with others—for uncontaminated and safe air, water, food, and land. So much of my serenity and that of future generations depends upon these things, as well as upon the indirect aspects of the greater physical world we inhabit, such as the beauty of the natural world, the shade of trees, and the ocean breeze.

While the entire planet is not my responsibility, when I ask for "the courage to change the things I can," I include in that request the courage and moral strength to responsibly divert empty plastic bags, water bottles, unusable electronics, flammable and toxic substances, unused prescription drugs, and other recyclable or toxic items. You can, too. Basic information on responsible disposal of all of these types of clutter is available to the public on various government and agency websites at the federal, state, and local levels.

At some point in our recovery, each of us can take a look at these sites, become more aware, and ask for the courage and strength to change the things we can in a manner that protects our lives and our world.

After all, our planet is the "home" to our homes.

When a Clutterer Loses a Loved One

Fall 2015

Judith N., CA

As I look back on my life, I realize that much of my clutter is actually composed of objects I received from my grandparents, my great aunt (who was my Godmother), my husband, and my aunt and uncle, the last three of whom died during the same nine-month period.

My grandparents represented stability in my life. I lived with them off and on until I completed seventh grade. I had also attended numerous schools during those early years. My grandparents had known many hard times, and they handled money carefully. I learned from Grandpa, "If something is worth doing, it's worth doing right." From my grandmother, I learned to appreciate the value of things—like fabric in an older garment that "still has a lot of wear in it"—good advice from folks who had gone through the Great Depression.

Great Aunt Liz was my grandmother's sister, a woman of the city. She bought nice clothes, and about twice a year she sent us a care package. She told us to use what we could and donate the rest. From the time I was in eighth grade, many of the clothes fit me. I have to admit, I didn't dress like the other kids at school because some of my clothes came from a 60-year-old woman. Aunt Liz dressed fashionably, though.

During the late 1970s, my husband and I built onto our house—partly because we had four children, and partly because I did not have room to put everything away.

I signed up for my first storage facility while my husband was still alive. And my second. And then even a third. My son and his family were crowded into a two-bedroom apartment, so I got them a storage place for their extra things. When they became "homeless" and moved in with other family members, I got the fifth space for their furniture and another for my excesses.

When my husband died in 2004, I left everything of his where it was. In October of 2013, my daughter came over and took many of her dad's things to her house, where she went through them and donated them for me.

A favorite aunt and uncle died later in 2004. I was invited to come up and take what I wanted. When I got to their house, it was with a rental truck. That was the day I rented the seventh storage space, "just for a little while," to hold their treasures.

It was during spring 2009 that my offspring did an intervention. Late one night, they told me they loved me, they were worried about my safety, and they were willing to help. Someone made arrangements for declutterers to come to my house. It was a day I will remember, the Saturday before the worst Mother's Day I've ever had. Rather than us working together as a team, they removed things without my knowledge.

At counseling shortly thereafter, it was recommended that I try CLA. I've attended pretty regularly since May 2009.

Then my mother died. I rented the eighth storage space for her belongings, again "just for a while."

Why am I writing this? I think it is difficult for clutterers to let go of things, but very difficult to lose loved ones. And, I suspect, holding onto the things associated with loved ones somehow fills the void. But it is not healthy. I recall my oldest son telling me, back in 2004, "Don't confuse memories of them with things." I thought that was very wise, so I wrote it down and posted it on the refrigerator. I still have that, too.

My children and grandchildren worry about me but do not nag. They fear I will trip or be killed in a fire. I can understand all of this. But there is a big difference between knowing and doing.

I make progress, but I'm so far from perfection. "Action is the magic word," but sometimes I do nothing, or very little. I rejoice over what I do get done, with the help of my Higher Power. Often, I can't start one thing until I complete another. Recently, I made a list of all the areas, and for each I listed a task I can do now, in preparation for others. This has helped me because it is easy to become overwhelmed. Focusing on one part of one area makes things manageable for me.

Speaking with a daughter-in-law last month, I mentioned that I am doing better. She reminded me that when my last aunt died, I bought the whole house. I had a good laugh because it is true. But the best part is that this vacation house is very clean and very tidy, thanks to the members of my family. I enjoy maintaining the place as a refuge, a place I can relax and simply maintain, somewhere I can entertain guests with no problem.

Not only is the vacation house a refuge—it is a good example of how to declutter and how wonderful it feels to experience a clutter-free environment. This motivates me to work with enthusiasm on my residence.

By the time I finish going through all the boxes at home and in my storage rooms, with God's help, and if I am still alive, I know I will enjoy both clutter-free houses. My new motto is not, "Can I possibly use this?" It is, "Do I need this?" What a difference words can make!

A Memento in Time

Holiday 2015

Wendy L., IL

Mementos can be lovely clutter—reminders of nice times that can morph into too much stuff. Because of their sentimental value, they are super hard to part with. So much so that throwing some of them away has caused me much regret and angst.

But why? I did some soul searching to find out. The results surprised me and will definitely make me think twice before I part with my most treasured keepsakes again.

Let me start with a couple of examples. For a while, I saved my entrance ticket stubs to such things as museums and excursions. The stubs reminded me of happy times spent exploring Europe and the pride I felt in visiting famous places. Consider also that I was with friends I don't often get to see now, if at all. And all this during a time when I was younger and in better shape.

Now, I can't remember the last time I was there.

Then, take the Christmas souvenir mugs I used to collect from a large department store on State Street in Chicago. These reminded me of times spent dining there with friends, sitting around the store's huge, beautiful Christmas tree. It seems these days I have to beg my friends to go downtown. Ah, perhaps I need new friends.

Anyway, it was as though throwing away these stubs and mugs was like tossing out little pieces of myself. But it also felt like I was hanging on to the past. So I decided it was healthier to create new memories and to collect new mementos, albeit selectively. I threw away my souvenirs and congratulated myself for being so good at decluttering.

But I was left with such a surprising amount of angst that it made me wonder what was really going on. Although it was uncomfortable, I let myself feel the pain and regret and felt back to when my parents had sold a beloved piano when I was 11.

Back then, I had had a mean teacher who had turned me off of practicing. My parents took that for disinterest and sold it when we moved. I was crushed. On top of that, it was then that we moved away from Chicago and I had to leave all my friends behind.

The losses had left me very sad, confused, and lonely. They weren't the only ones I suffered but were some of the deepest. Finally, I could start to see how the early losses in my life might be impacting the losses I was suffering as an adult. It was like the discarding of treasured things triggered the hurt all over again.

But although keeping my sentimental things might give me comfort, the accumulations can have the ugly effect of bringing on the shame and guilt I sometimes feel as a clutterer. It might sound like I'm being too hard on myself, but my serenity is now based on a clean home more than on mementos, as it used to be.

In hindsight, I'm glad I threw away the Christmas mugs, which took up too much space, and sad I threw away the ticket stubs, which were small and pretty innocuous. But I'm surviving without the stubs and instead throwing my energy into keeping my home clean and searching out new experiences.

I recently joined a writing group and just took a helicopter flying lesson. Gliding looks like a great time, too. Now I wonder if they sell tickets for that...

Shopping and Collecting

Saving the World

Holiday 2010

Kay R.

There I was, saving the world. Oh yes! Saving the world, one cheap, chintzy item at a time.

I have collected just about anything with a reasonably cheap price tag and have been loving it. Things I have no use for, except to say that I collected them.

Hats, caps, and bandanas have all had their uses. So have mugs, teapots, and spoons, to some extent. Dolls and collectibles of that nature can be understood. Porcelain figures are a popular item for many collectors.

Then there are the pink pigs of many sizes and materials. I even still lament the loss of the corduroy pink pig that a dog named Snickers ate years ago. This may well have been the start of that particular collection.

Nowhere do I seem to have drawn any sort of line. If one was nice, two were nicer. After three, I was looking for companion pieces—actively collecting, never giving a thought to where it would all go. Until suddenly, I was overwhelmed with boxes, baskets, and bags of stuff, not recognizing some of it, not enjoying any of it!

It came as a revelation that this was more of an illness than a lifestyle. Real collectors collect for the value of the objects—buying, selling, sharing, showing, and showing off.

"See what I have that you don't! Nah nah nah!" Playground nonsense brought to an expensive adult level. This is what collecting is about.

What I had been doing was filling in the gaps in my life with possessions. There are far worse obsessions, but I finally realized that I could not fit all this crap into my little apartment, and even if I could, I didn't really want to.

I bought it to make myself happy, and that just didn't work. Now that I'm aware, I have an enormous task of getting rid of it all. I can't simply throw it away; that would be an admission of guilt.

Guilt that I had bought useless junk! I just need to find someone who needs or wants it. Or at least someone who will carry it out of the place for me, as I can no longer manage hauling trash myself.

I had no problem carrying it all in; but again, I was busy saving the world.

The Return Blues

Fall 2016

Wendy L., IL

So I'm at a store shopping for a new shirt, and I've tried on a bunch of blouses and tops. It's been over an hour, and I still haven't chosen one. Frustration kicks in, and now I'm thinking I need to start a clothing design business because nothing here that's cute fits quite right.

I recognize that I'm a perfectionist, and most of these shirts won't fit quite right, but I really want a new one. Finally, I narrow it down to one and buy it, only to get home and have buyer's remorse.

The torture continues as I keep it but don't wear it, just in case I decide to return it. Occasionally, I'll try on what has now become pretty clutter, but I still won't commit to keeping it. It becomes spiritual clutter when I get mad at myself for struggling so much over a shirt. Just think if I had to buy a car. Actually, I've had to, and every time was a nightmare.

Finally, I decide to return it, and I put it in my car, but I don't actually return it. It stays in my car, taunting me. All I have to do is walk into the store, find the customer service desk, and return it. Honestly, I'd rather give a speech naked in front of ten thousand people than return this shirt or anything else in my car that needs to be returned. What's going on here?

In examining this behavior, I thought back to when I was 11. My parents had sold our house and told my sister and me we were moving to Arizona. Confused, I said goodbye to my friends and tried to look forward to the adventure ahead of us.

We visited many gift shops during our trip west, and I noticed that many of them sold round, hollow rocks called geodes. After a customer would choose a geode, the sales person would use a tool to crack it open, and the new owner would get to see its beautiful crystal center.

But, just like with clothes shopping, I kept looking for the perfect geode. Of course, there are no perfect geodes, or shirts, or pretty much anything else I can buy because all are a matter of taste and availability.

Well, my parents suddenly announced that our move was canceled, and we headed back to Chicago. I figured I'd find a geode at the next store where we stopped, but that was not to be the case. We were too far east, and the stores here didn't sell geodes. I never got to buy one and had great regret about that until many years later after I found recovery in CLA.

So now, to make up for never having chosen a geode, I buy things even though I'm not sure they're right for me. I'm afraid that if I pass them up, as I did the geode, I might want them back, but they might not be available any more. Sometimes the things I buy work out just fine, but many times they don't. I'm afraid to return them because, although they may be imperfect, I might regret letting them go.

So instead, they just sit around my house and car. It seems as if return equals regret for me. I assumed this behavior was purely because I am a clutterer. But in asking my non-clutterer (assumed) friends, I learned that some of them put off returning things as well. I was astonished.

Out of curiosity, I did an Internet search on "Why do I have trouble returning things?" To my amazement, lots of articles showed up, and I've decided to explore this topic further. At least now I don't feel so odd about this behavior. Turns out there's a lot of us.

See another article on shopping in the "Recovery Stories" section on page 120.

Paper Clutter

Powerless Over Paper

Fall 2009
Mary P., NY

A presentation from the Clutter-Free Day in New York, May 17, 2009

Why did I choose this topic? Because of what I've heard in meetings for the past seven years. Paper, in all its many forms, is our "number one offender."

Taking Step 1 is essential. We must experience powerlessness over clutter, especially paper clutter. "Without help, it is too much for us." Where can we get power? Step 2 talks about reliance on a Higher Power. It has been said that God = Good Orderly Direction.

Awareness and acceptance must come before action. Step 3 represents our first attempt to let our Higher Power in. We embrace Steps 1 through 3.

Step 4 "...has a double meaning for us in CLA. The traditional meaning is to make a written inventory of ourselves to discover our assets and character defects." (CLA leaflet: "Recovery from Cluttering: The 12 Steps of Clutterers Anonymous"[14]) In CLA, the 4th Step can also include a physical inventory of our possessions.

Making a list is a good exercise, and you can use it later when you decide what to do with each category. What categories of paper do you have in your life? I came up with 30-odd categories, such as advertisements, bank statements, bills, blank paper...newspapers, pamphlets...tax records, warranties.... "Miscellaneous," by the way, is not a good category!

Next, I wanted to examine what I have trouble dealing with and why.

Looking at my weakness for newspapers and magazines led to the idea of "Information Gluttony." Beyond this, I admit Pride comes into play; I want to be Ms. Know-It-All. I had to learn to dig deeper—to be searching and fearless. What does each kind of paper mean to me, at a deeper level? Is there magical thinking involved? If I collect every book and article on clutter, will I have power over my clutter? This is a rhetorical question. One of our leaflets speaks of Experience Greed, the totally unrealistic idea that you can do it all. It's been said that all clutter is delayed decisions and actions. Here's a good time to repeat the CLA Keep and Release Prayer:

God, grant me the serenity to keep the things I need to keep,
Courage to release the things I do not need,
And wisdom to know the difference.

Practice handling each paper item only once. *(OHIO = Only Handle It Once.—Editor)*

How do I process mail? I choose to designate a mail center. Research shows that about 80 percent of mail can be discarded immediately. Why not discard it right by the mailbox? I do. I suggest you have your trash bag or wastebasket near your mail center. Consider paying bills online. It will take time to develop a mail strategy that works for you. Mine has taken several years to fine tune.

I have chosen to create other action centers for different categories.

My system has three options: ART = Action, Reference, Trash. Three-ring binders with plastic sleeves or a file-folder system will work for most Reference and Action categories.

It helps me to have specific strategies for newspapers and magazines. You could too. Could you consider an information diet? Could you stop getting a daily paper, or cut down to one or two days a week? Could you consider throwing out the backlog, unread? (It sounds painful, but it's satisfying.) Or could you give yourself cut-off dates to "process" (clip and file) the articles you "need" to keep? Could you read things online, or read at the library? You may also need to develop specific strategies for coupons and catalogs, financial records and tax records. You can regain some power over paper, but it will take willingness and time.

I'll close with some useful items for you to think about: biggish wastebaskets, 3-ring binders with plastic sleeves or pocket inserts, 3-hole punch, shredder, folders, file cabinet or rolling file holder for hanging folders, timer, and prayer and the CLA Affirmations.[20]

Newspaper and Magazine Subscriptions

Spring 2011

Kathy H., CA

I used to subscribe to several magazines. I had great plans to read them all—but I never got around to reading three-fourths of them, so they piled up. I couldn't just throw them away, could I?

I also subscribed to a daily paper. Did I read it through daily, though? Not usually; most of it was added to the growing piles. Actually, I was able to get rid of the newspapers, usually within a few days or weeks, since most of the articles were about current events. But they did add to my clutter.

Then there were the how-to magazines, with articles on crafting and recipes. I would cut out articles and paste them in notebooks. It worked just great until I had so much it became clutter. Eventually, I could not keep up with them, so I began to have different piles—one for unread magazines and one of items already clipped but not placed—plus the notebooks themselves.

What I ended up with were boxes and piles of printed materials everywhere.

In CLA, I came to realize that all those subscriptions involved several kinds of clutter: the physical clutter of the stacks, the time clutter of trying to read too much, and the mind clutter of focusing on frustration because I couldn't read it all. So I learned to let go instead of trying to keep up. Now, when I find old magazines, I don't even try to read them. They go straight to recycling or to a thrift shop or lending library. Letting go has brought me a great deal of serenity.

It took me a long time to get most of it decluttered—fortunately, not as long as the years it took to collect the items in the first place—though there may still be a few old magazines left in my house in the last bit of stuff to be decluttered.

As for the notebooks for how-to items, I still have them, but I have realized that I will access only some of the items. So, I am planning to purge much of that material.

Where am I now? I maintain one magazine subscription—for my computer—which I rely on for tips and to keep updated. I periodically purge the shelf where the issues are kept, getting rid of anything more than a year old. I do not subscribe to a newspaper but prefer to get most of my news online. Most Sundays I buy a paper, which contains the inserts and opinion pieces I want. I usually stick to the rule of going through it on Sunday and putting most of it in the recycling bin before I go to bed. The remainder does not last more than a few days.

Oh, and I do subscribe to CLA*rity*, not only because I am on the committee, but because I want that recovery information close at hand, just as I keep all my 12-Step literature close. I keep my CLA*rity* issues in one notebook, so they don't add appreciably to the clutter.

I had stopped most of the subscriptions before I got to CLA, but it took working the program to get rid of the leftover detritus. And, boy, did it make a difference in my clutter. Thank you, CLA.

Nonphysical Clutter

Television and Time Clutter

Summer 2015

Alison B., NJ

Television can be entertaining and can also serve the important purpose of being an escape from life's stresses. But watched in excess, it can be detrimental to my relationships with others and in dealing with my clutter.

Television characters never let me down. They are as comfortable to me as family and friends—even more so, because they never criticize, yell at me, or take it out on me if they have had a bad day. They never make me do them favors or expect anything in return. Instead, they act their hearts out, telling me stories, allowing me to become totally engrossed in their lives without feeling as if I am intruding. Then there are the game shows, which entertain me and challenge my brain.

I'm sure many of you may feel I am completely wasting my time here. I bet you have your guilty pleasures, too. Or there may be others who are also addicted to these shows and who have never talked about them. At the CLA meeting I attend, we don't talk much about TV addiction.

Once I turn on my set, I am dragged into the vortex. It is excruciatingly difficult for me to turn it off. I let my voicemail pick up phone calls so I may watch my favorite shows. I get moody with my best friend if he interrupts during a certain murder mystery. Worst of all, I have missed opportunities to declutter so many times that my mess has become unbearable, and I have had to spend whole days sorting it out.

There have been times when I haven't gone out when I was supposed to, and relationships have suffered—all because I would rather stay home, glued to my make-believe world. Granted, that doesn't happen very often, and usually there is another factor at play like bad weather or not feeling well.

Since coming to CLA and in order to deal with this issue, I have deliberately made my life much busier than it used to be, although I still leave time for TV. Due to budget constraints, my lifestyle is limited to free activities, so much revolves around 12-Step meetings. I go to four per week and socialize after the meetings but don't really get close to anyone. I do have a sponsor in another program, though, and call her daily. I also do a lot of service work for CLA over the phone and Internet. Believe it or not, I have more friends through that work than anywhere else. Doesn't that say a lot for service work? Something else I'm doing is rehearsing to be in a play. Somehow, I think I'm rehearsing for real life!

Nonphysical Clutter

Summer 2016

Ruthe S., PA

Nonphysical clutter can be many things. For me, it was compulsive behaviors that I couldn't stop doing that often led to physical clutter. Many times, these behaviors were obsessive in nature and difficult to stop. I had to work on the nonphysical decluttering before I could get to the physical decluttering. I was very much afraid to stop these behaviors because I was scared of what would happen. Subconsciously, I think I was worried I would die. What I realize now is that I was afraid of the feelings I would get, and I was doing these behaviors to avoid feeling negative emotions like sadness, anger, fear, disappointment, etc. because I didn't know how to deal with them.

One example of my compulsive behavior was the fear I had of not having something if I needed it. This led to my taking a wheeled bag full of stuff everywhere, and I was embarrassed because people sometimes commented on it. I now consider it a sign of recovery if I leave something behind.

Another behavior I developed was "busyaholism." I was always going out to meet people or attend events. In addition, I was afraid of making the wrong choices about what events to attend and that I would miss something at another. This led to my going to everything. I would go to several things in one day, never enjoying any of them—but because I was running around all the time, I didn't have to face myself or my emotions.

One behavior that was particularly debilitating for me was videotaping and audiotaping TV and radio shows. I was afraid I would make the wrong choice of what to watch or would go out and miss something. I think I was worried that if I had a bad time wherever I was, I would regret missing a show. It was all about controlling my emotions.

Another example was "errands" that usually involved returning things I compulsively bought and then compulsively buying other items which I didn't have a home for. This led to clutter. This last one probably also falls under the heading of busyaholism. It also gave me a sense that I was getting some things done when, in reality, I was avoiding both feelings and doing things that were difficult and sometimes more important.

Also, I was getting the newspaper, even though I never read it. On top of that, I was addicted to watching certain shows on TV and going to the same events year after year, like film and music festivals. This was not necessarily a bad thing, but

I think for me it was comforting. I always had something to look forward to, my time was occupied, and I knew there would be no surprises.

Of course, all this led to physical clutter—with newspapers and tapes piling up and clutter from my compulsive spending lying around.

After finding CLA and another 12-Step program, I was able to begin to change these behaviors. I talked about them in meetings, with recovery people, and with my therapist. At some point, I stopped subscribing to the daily newspaper and started receiving it just on Sunday. I bookended this action with a recovery friend from another program. What I recall is that the first morning I didn't get a daily paper, I noticed it wasn't there, forgot about it, and didn't miss it. I also stopped buying so many magazines on the same subjects because I didn't really need them all.

I was later able to apply this to my TV watching and TV and radio taping. I forgot to tape something and decided that my Higher Power had given me an opening. This loss I noticed more than the newspaper, but after a few days, I was on to the next thing. I eventually stopped taping and even watching most of those shows. I realize now that those shows had become my friends, and I was afraid of losing them.

By working my recovery programs, I was better equipped to deal with negative feelings. I also had support while attempting to stop these behaviors. Maybe they were helpful at one time, but not any longer. When I stopped a lot of them, I found I had more space in my brain and more mental energy. I was able to identify thoughts and feelings more quickly. By realizing that, I was able to survive the loss of these things and the negative feelings that came with it. It snowballed and got easier and easier to let go.

I was able to rid myself of most of those behaviors, but not all. However, I am doing a million times better. I have been able to apply some of these principles to getting rid of physical clutter, but that has been much harder to deal with. I could not have gotten to the physical, though, without dealing with the nonphysical clutter. Sometimes I can't believe that I ever did all of those things. I am very grateful to CLA and 12-Step recovery in other programs for the gift of getting my life back.

Recovery Stories

Recovery from cluttering can be many-faceted: recovery from both physical and nonphysical clutter. This section deals with recovery in CLA not covered in other sections. It contains two categories: Qualifications and articles that appeared in the "Recovery Moments" column of CLA*rity*.

Qualifications

CLA Turns My Life Around

Holiday 2008

Cindy S., CA

In working another 12-Step program, I became aware that my life was unmanageable around clutter. For years, I had been paralyzed, overwhelmed, and oblivious about the boxes; piles; collections; unpaid bills; ignored correspondence; unfinished projects; unopened purchases; and unused items that filled my hallways, overflowed from my drawers, and spilled out of my closets. I knew that underneath all that was dust and filth—I didn't know there were also mice.

I had a good excuse: I was a widow raising three young children. I had moved to a much smaller house following my husband's sudden death. I was an Internet professional and had worked in volatile start-ups. I juggled my work, my special-needs daughter, my community activism, my 12-Step meetings, my insomnia, volunteering, driving my children to their various extracurricular activities, and Sunday school teaching.

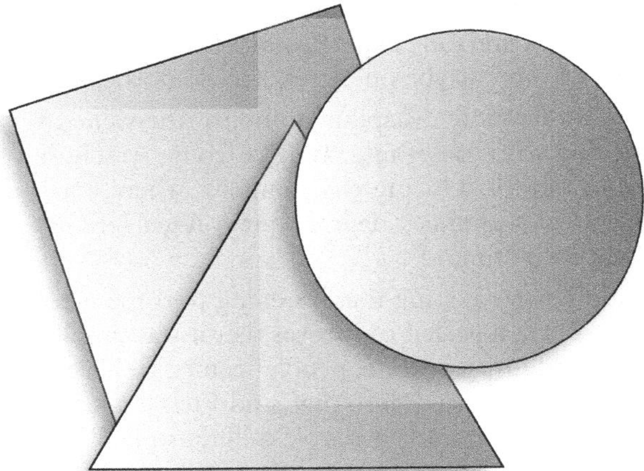

In retrospect, I did it by moving from one activity to the next without stopping to clean up from my last project or prepare for the next. I needed to be busy so I didn't have time to feel anything. By the time I got home every day, I was exhausted, angry, resentful, full of pride, and incredibly hurt. I was too tired to deal with laundry, cleaning, cooking, organizing, or maintaining a healthy home environment. I couldn't think straight in such a messy environment, but I could watch television and berate myself for everything that I was not doing and fall down a familiar, negative spiral of depressive thinking until I dropped off to sleep.

These self-pitying feelings originated in my traumatic childhood. I had survived by repeating the same patterns throughout my life—investing myself 110 percent to accomplish big things that helped others and got me recognition, all the while sacrificing my own needs. I got much approval from others, but I never approved of myself. I never counted myself in my priorities; I never noticed the good things I did—I did not think I deserved my own attention.

It was an intervention from my Higher Power that got me down to Los Angeles for the Clutter-Free Day. It was wonderful to put faces to the voices I have heard on the phone and words I have read in CLA*rity*.

I learned at the Clutter-Free Day that recovery is about "Progress, not Perfection." I heard that "You cannot think yourself into right action, but you can act yourself into right thinking."

It is uncomfortable and I feel guilty, but the more I say no to what I don't want, the more I am able to determine what does work for me, and the "free-er" I am to enjoy what I do choose to have in my life. This has been a long process—it's taken two years of going to in-person meetings to get to this place. Weekly, I work the Steps with a Step buddy. Some days it seems like two steps backwards instead of one step ahead, but I have another day tomorrow, and every day is a success if I do one thing that I said I would.

Every day, I am reminded to take care of myself first, turn over my plans to my sponsor, and let my Higher Power support me. I don't have to do it alone, because today I have Tools[19] of the program, as well as the Steps and the Fellowship. It is simple, but not easy. I am truly grateful for the 12 Steps.

Summer 2011

Kim, CA

I had a cluttered desk—everywhere I went I created clutter. Every time I tried to use a conventional means to become organized, I couldn't do it. It was like a guy in A.A. trying to stop drinking but unable to do so. I had read managerial books, etc., but I just couldn't get it.

I went to my first CLA meeting. It was a small group, but I was impressed as I listened to them share about clutter—both problems and solutions. That left me hopeful, and I attended regularly.

I began decluttering, but I couldn't continue going to that meeting. I was in my cluttered office, and a flyer arrived which said: "Are you having problems with clutter? Are you having too many problems?" It was CLA. I got in touch with a woman and had a nice conversation.

I am usually stressed, so when I go to a meeting, I am attracted to someone who has a problem like mine but remains calm. She was so calm. I was crazy—but I was so lazy, I never got to her meeting. But I did call her from time to time.

Then I started going to the Palms Park meeting, an outdoor meeting. What I really liked was the idea of sitting out in a park—it was such a contrast to my cluttered mind, my cluttered office, my cluttered living space, and my cluttered car. It was nice to share about our struggles and the progress we were making in such a free area. I met my sponsor, and he started focusing me on working the 12 Steps, along with using the tools. I also met people who were involved in service in this meeting; they were calm and focused on the miracles of the program, and that attracted me.

I started calling one guy with my to-do list. I didn't know where to begin, and he said, "Why don't you pare that thing down to about six items, and try to do about half, and then call me and share with me how you are doing?" So that is what I do, and I share how I am doing. Part of being restored to sanity is setting realistic goals. To do that, it's important to go to CLA meetings.

So my sponsor and this buddy got me to go to more meetings. One meeting introduced meditation, and that was cool. I went to the phone meetings. I already had some success working the program, but these meetings kept me connected, so I never lost touch with the Fellowship. I turned my life over to my Higher Power. I got so much help from the phone meetings. That's how I discovered the Basic Four,* which is my daily routine. If I had to do it by my own will, I wouldn't do it.

The first project I tackled was my office. I started to commit to declutter my file this week but couldn't do it. So I started breaking the task into parts. So finally I said, "I am going to do A" and came back and did A and B, and I felt good. Then I did C. And maybe one week I could do D and E.

I am learning discipline, humility, the value of sticking with something. It's like going to school again—but in a loving environment, where you don't get a graduate degree, but you get serenity and peace of mind.

So I started doing that, listening to those meetings. What appealed to me was that it was simple, it created order, and the people seemed to have peace. So I grasped onto that, and I felt less stigmatized, because you had people calling from all over, so I felt, well, that I was not alone. When I had looked at that stuff, I would feel bad about myself, and I would project that everyone else would feel the same way about me. The reinforcement I got from meetings was that I don't have to feel alone.

Another help was getting off other peoples' backs. A sibling and I own a house together, and I was always nagging her and washing her dishes and doing her part of the equation. For weeks I would talk about her. I just stopped that and realized it's about me. Then I started really making progress when I stopped focusing on the other people in my life. I can put my energy on others in the program who need help if they want it.

The house I grew up in was a three-bedroom house, and that place was cluttered all the time. My aunt had a fabulous place, and it was full of stuff.

First go to meetings, then reach out to people on the phone, then become uncluttered—simple things. The fellowship of people working on the program has always helped my growth. Then talking to another about picking up ten things a day has really aided my recovery. I have talked to others about picking up ten things a day, and it helps them because they are overwhelmed. If I have more time, I do more. So I put it away, give it away, or throw it away, and that has been helpful. And that is what I call the synergy of the program.

I have some deep-seated issues about my property and my sister, but I could go over there and pick up things. So I was able to put principles before personalities. Thank God I don't live in the same house anymore, but I have become willing to face this. I have learned all these healthy habits working in the CLA program, so I have been able to approach that. We really do learn compassion and empathy and to get along with other people.

**Editor's Note: The Basic Four is not an official CLA Tool.*

My Qualification

Spring 2016

Anonymous

My story begins with my Dad, actually. He was (and still is) a perfectionist and inadvertently taught me to be one, too. This would be great if I were a surgeon or a pilot, but alas, I am not. For years, I struggled to make decisions because I couldn't figure out the perfect answers. So instead of deciding what to do or where to put things, I put them aside and they became clutter. And speaking of planes, it was a bit like being on autopilot.

Add to that my just not handling stress well for most of my life, and I had a recipe for disaster. The more stressed out I got, the more I cluttered. If decisions were hard to make when I was relaxed, they became ten times worse when I was anxious.

My cluttering began in earnest in my early 30s, as I began to pick up more responsibilities at work. I started feeling overwhelmed and pressured, though it was of my own doing, as no one ever complained about my work. I'd get home and throw stuff aside, be it clothes, mail, or anything else. My mind swirled with unmade work decisions, and I obsessed about what I needed to do to get my work done.

This morphed into depression and anxiety, and my clutter became the visisble representation of that. I moved a couple times and took my clutter with me but never got around to sorting it. It got to the point where I couldn't have guests over, and I couldn't seem to stop cluttering. I began having health issues and often just didn't have the energy to declutter.

I discovered CLA through word of mouth and initially attended some phone meetings because there were no nearby physical meetings. But what helped the most at first were the phone activity sessions. There I could announce the decluttering action I wanted to take and then report back on how I did. There was something magical about being accountable for my actions, and I began to gradually declutter my stuff.

Eventually, I started writing about my cluttering and searched for patterns and explanations for why I cluttered. The entries that required research and soul-searching proved to be great sources of recovery for me.

For example, I discovered I often procrastinated or avoided dealing with my clutter. So I jotted down the reasons why I was doing this and discovered that, in some cases, I wasn't feeling in control of certain situations. So I started to identify ways that I could gain at least some control so I would feel less stressed.

About that time, I began learning how to better handle stress by using thought and behavior changes to reduce my anxiety. Being calmer helped me to feel happier and more confident than I'd ever been. I became more able to get rid of my stuff because I was confident I was making the right decisions and that the universe would provide what I needed if I got rid of something that I later required.

Today, I still clutter but am much improved. I let dirty dishes stay in my sink no more than one night before I clean them. My clothes get hung up within a couple days as well. I've had guests over and even hosted a group to watch football. I love my uncluttered home and get stressed out when clutter begins to form. Okay, so I'm definitely not perfect and have to admit that I've put some paper clutter in a couple of drawers, so that's our secret. But I do go through them periodically. I've come to terms with being a perfectionist, and "pretty good" is usually good enough for me now.

Today is the second of January and the start of a new year. Now that I have less clutter, I spend less time obsessing about it and more time doing fun things like socializing and going to seminars at my local library.

I've even started exercising, albeit slowly. Now if only I could make time go by faster while I'm using the exercise equipment. Unfortunately, CLA can't help with that, but at least I have a home for my workout clothes now. Ah, here's to celebrating the small successes.

Recovery Moments

Spring 2007

Anonymous

I spent time today honoring my needs and took care of my choices of what to work on, not what others presented to me. I equate a certain amount of stuff with comfort and ease. Anybody can clean up, but when not cleaning up becomes a way of life, it concerns me.

Leaving a time cushion to drive has been a real blessing to me of late. I had both my ears and mind open to what everyone said. I was finally able to laugh at my dis-ease for the first time.

Summer 2007

Anonymous

When I now invite guests into my home, their remark is, "What are you doing in CLA? It doesn't appear that you have any problem with cluttering." If they are trustworthy friends, I may give them a tour of my garage, junk room, and my bedroom (which houses my office); and they remark, "Would attending three meetings a week be too much for you?"

Recovery is slow. Recovery has meant more tolerance for myself. I am able to laugh and enjoy life. I have made wonderful progress, and there is much more to accomplish. Besides decluttering on a daily basis, I also include having *fun* in my life. I've given up being a *taskmaster*.

Fall 2007

Parker, NV

Like a magnet to steel, I frequented office supply mega-stores, proud to be a clearance section, bargain-hunting pro for over three decades. A third of my home office and storage unit stash was office supplies of all sizes and kinds.

As a buyer-hoarder junkie, I had file folders, binders, paper reams, hole punches, and more gadgets filling boxes and shelves.

Realizing the problem and ceasing the behavior is one recovery milestone I cherish.

Recently, walking across a large shopping center's parking lot, I stopped and smiled. I had been ignoring my "favorite" type of store, completely, painlessly, visit after visit. Now rehabilitated, reformed, and renewed, I surely have been granted the "courage to change my habits."

Holiday 2007

Kathy H., CA

Having been in CLA for several years, I long ago realized that the two biggest blocks to my decluttering are my tendency to procrastinate and a feeling of being overwhelmed by my clutter. Before I joined CLA, I had the feeling that I would never be able to motivate myself to declutter—which had depressed me to the point I let it stop me from tackling the job at all.

Several weeks ago, I was searching for some fabric, without success, in my sewing room. After having looked in the cupboard where I generally store fabric and in the piles that were sitting around in the sewing room, I decided to reorganize all of it and to work to prevent the problem in the future. I have made progress decluttering, although I have put off this task for several years—it just felt like such an overwhelming, daunting endeavor.

So I put some of the CLA Tools of Recovery[19] into action.

- Focusing: I decided to stick with this task until it was done (rather than finding my fabric and putting the rest of the job off to do something else).
- Daily Action: I made a commitment to myself to do something every day on the task when I wasn't traveling.
- Telephone and Buddies: I discussed my problems and my successes with another CLA member several times a week.
- Earmarking: I organized a place in the closet for each type of fabric and put it away in that spot. Also, I made two duplicate slips of paper, listing the fabric content, the size, and other information. One of these index slips got pinned to the fabric, the other had a snippet of the fabric attached to it and is organized into a notebook.
- Streamlining: I was able to release a large pile of fabric.

Now, all my fabric is easy to find and neatly put away; and what is more, it will be much easier to keep that way. I can find what I want by looking through the notebook and going right to the proper stack on the shelf without disturbing the rest.

So how do I feel after this progress? As I look at my fabric closet and all around the sewing room, I feel a wonderful sense of accomplishment and serenity. And, since the hardest part of redoing the sewing room is done, I have been energized to finish getting the rest of the room in order!

One day, one project, one room at a time, my house is becoming more decluttered and more livable; it is beginning to feel like a home again.

Summer 2008

Betsey K., NJ

This is one of the things read each week in the CLA meeting I attend:

Substitution—*We do not add a new activity without eliminating from our schedule one that demands equivalent time and energy.*

Recently, I received an email invitation offering me a position (effective immediately) on the district mission team of a church group to which I belong. Given my many service positions, primarily in CLA, my first inclination was to turn it down. Then I spent some time trying to figure out whether there was a way I could take on this commitment. By the end of the week, however, I realized that there was nothing I could give up at this time to enable me to accept this new position; therefore, I declined the offer.

Summer 2008

Kathy H., CA

Recently, I had been trying to declutter my kitchen and could not seem to get started. However, I found a solution for this: I was trying to do a difficult puzzle and was getting frustrated. I discovered that if I worked the puzzle until I was frustrated, I was able to stop and work on the kitchen. I kept this up for several hours and finished the whole job! Now, if I am unable to motivate myself to declutter, I try this technique of alternating it—not just with something I like doing, but with something I enjoy that also has a high level of frustration. It does seem to work.

Depressurized Shopping

Fall 2008

Anonymous

I have been more free to make choices since I have been working the CLA program. I used to "cruise for bargains" along a "route of stores" at least a couple of times a week. Whenever I knew there was a neighborhood yard sale day, I would be there. I would see a dumpster and feel it was necessary for me to look inside it.

Usually, I would return to this same dumpster to see what was new. Sometimes I would walk away with nothing. But most of the time, I found something to take home—whether I needed it or not. Compulsive behavior, do you think? At the time, it didn't seem to bother me.

These days, my "shopping" pattern is very, very different. I guess it happened slowly, but the key piece seemed to be that instead of reacting to some vague, inner pressure to get out and do something (nothing specific, just something), I was often able to stop and reflect. Maybe I would sit down for a few minutes to meditate, or I would plan my day or attend a 12-Step group.

Then, when I went out, I was more focused and deliberate. This recovering shopaholic was making decisions.

Often, the answer to my internal questions was no. If I were in proximity to one of my routes, I would decide each time: Shall I shop, or not? And if I did go in and went to the discount shelves, I would sometimes walk away with nothing.

No more buying stuff or picking it up off the street—just because it was cheap (or free). It had to be something I had a use for or needed.

Am I cured? Not yet. But I have changed, and I am continuing to change my old patterns. Listening to others in the rooms helps me; taking the time to be in touch with my feelings helps me.

Holiday 2008

Carol N., CA

The road to recovery means different things to different people. To me, recovery doesn't mean all's well that ends well. In fact, I prefer to think of my journey in CLA as progress, not merely recovery. Trying to judge whether, in fact, I am recovering can be a trap for me. I need encouragement from my peers, as well as serious guidance from a sponsor. Sometimes I can't see my own recovery (or my nonrecovery), and I need someone to remind me gently.

I recognize recovery in the newfound ease of doing a task, or in the willingness to change some small, ingrained routines. It is seen in my attitude adjustment, perhaps toward someone I regarded in a negative way, or a change of heart toward myself, bringing more self-trust and peace. It doesn't work to scold myself. The only person I need to compete with is me.

It gives me strength to pass along what I have been so freely given. People took their time with me. And as a former sponsor once said, "Time spent with another human being is never wasted." There are those before me (my sponsors), those after me (my sponsees), and those on either side (my peers). They hold me up as I go through this journey. I need to stay connected to them by going to meetings and making calls. I notice a big difference in my life when I do that.

Spring 2009

R.G., TX

I have always enjoyed travel, but for some reason preparing for a trip usually made me crazy. Especially packing, and especially packing for an auto trip. Here, I'll try to reconstruct how, through use of the 12-Step program ideas, I have made real progress.

The Three A's as the Framework: Awareness, Acceptance, Action

The beginning: **Awareness**—Packing had become unmanageable and made travel less pleasant. Anxiety, procrastination, irritation, missed deadlines, difficulty sleeping, and negative feelings troubled me. The program says that when we repeatedly encounter a problem situation, we should consider another approach: Ask for help or discuss it with others. (Don't *re*-act or rush into action; try to weigh your choices and discover the appropriate action, if any.)

The diagnosis: **Acceptance**—I shared my feelings and listened to others; I discovered I was not alone or unique in my frustrations. This basic realization encouraged me to keep exploring the internal territory of my problem, without being judgmental of myself or others. As I meditated on the situation, I suddenly felt a tangle of emotions and motives in the very core of my being. No wonder I was confused!

I started writing down the different feelings that came up when travel was on my mind (a kind of inventory, I guess). The experience of writing it all down granted me some relief. Now, I felt comfortable enough to think about making a plan and dealing with each part individually, breaking it down into digestable pieces. This change in my thinking made the task as a whole seem much less threatening.

Working out the problem: Appropriate **Action**—Here, my mind started operating faster and more creatively. I wasn't stuck and frustrated as before. Insights started coming to me. I saw that I had been cluttering my thinking. I complicated the job by including expectations or extra activities into the trip planning. So, I asked myself, "What is the primary purpose of this journey?" Focusing on that, I simplified: I didn't need to take papers that needed filing, golf clubs, or extra reading material.

I set aside enough time (days, not hours) for the entire process and worked on some part of it for at least a short period of time each day. I needed to declutter my car first. Then, I found I had enough time to vacuum it, too, before I packed. In order to find some maps and papers for this trip, I went through some of my files, got rid of duplicate or unneeded material, and organized my travel brochures and maps.

I had always made a list, but I realized it wasn't sufficient to keep me on track. This time I used a general list and adopted a simple but radical new approach: days ahead of the trip, I got out the suitcases and started to fill them slowly. This was heaven; there was virtually no time pressure. I even had time to *stop* and congratulate myself on how smoothly the process was going—a hit of serenity, a small miracle! It was also necessary to pause briefly, frequently, so I didn't get distracted by trying to declutter my whole bookshelf or the entire northeast corner of the basement, just doing what I needed to do to move forward on packing. I would ask myself, "Does this activity contribute to the primary purpose? In other words, is this the most important thing on which I need to concentrate?"

My sponsor suggested that I live life as if I were trying to assemble a jigsaw puzzle. This takes time if you want to achieve a satisfactory result. The analogy of a puzzle helps me to keep my mind on being flexible, patient, and gentle—which are not always my natural tendencies.

I used a step-by-step approach on the trip, starting weeks preceding my departure and continuing to this moment, as I sit here trying to describe the path I followed. And I'm still paying attention as I unpack my car and my bags, continuing to reflect on how it went, and as I start planning for my next adventure—one day, one step, one action at a time.

Leave Flat Spaces on Earth Alone

Fall 2009

Parker, NV

When I realized my biggest clutter trigger, that moment was as big a discovery as the age-old revelation that Earth's not flat. In fact, flat surfaces are the biggest challenge for my decades-long, pile-it-high, paper-clutter habit. My ex used to tell me, "If there's a flat surface anywhere within your reach, you will fill it with something."

My ex wasn't right about everything, but that point was a truism. Ironing boards, desktops, open counter spaces, tables—all were there for my conquest! It took only hours for me to start piles of papers and objects anywhere a flat surface appeared. I semiconsciously moved things from one overrunning, established stack to the newfound frontier of a wide-open, flat space. I told one fellow member, "I can prove the Earth is not flat, because if that were so, a paper clutterer would have filled it up in just three hours."

Well, upon realization of the facts, which were so true for me, I began to make changes in my habits. The CLA Tools[19] and literature, especially "Home: Our Sacred Place,"[11] give me reinforcement.

I've learned to recognize the patterns of my no-empty-space dis-order, as I euphemistically call it. My tendency has been to try filling holes in my life with clutter. But I can see it's okay for me to let that openness remain and allow myself to be at peace with its existence.

I am better able to resist the temptation to fill the empty spaces in my life with stuff. A bud vase with a flower, a cherished photo, or a single piece of artwork is becoming preferable and sufficient.

I even shifted my language to tell myself that I no longer want to collect piles of stuff: I now say I want to collect "spaces." I figure that by doing it that way, I can use a skill I'm already good at—collecting things—and turn it into a positive. So far, I have "collected" several flat surfaces and created the habit of reverse cluttering. I revere and respect open spaces more. Clear areas and now-usable flat surfaces are becoming my new positive "collectibles."

Holiday 2009

Karen, CA

Especially since joining the Clutterers Anonymous telephone community, I have had an opportunity to listen to meetings every day. This has proven very helpful for my recovery, resulting in many moments of awareness that facilitated growth.

One such moment happened a few years ago, when I was out running a few errands on a beautiful, rainy, dark California evening. I had walked into a bookstore, with the telephone in my ear, listening to a CLA meeting focused on the first three Steps. I felt warm and secure, confident in the understanding that I was "in the room" with others who were in the same position as I was.

Listening to the sharing going on at the meeting, I became all the more aware that I had turned to material items, especially books, to make my life somehow okay. I thought about my belief that yet another book would improve my sad life. I thought about how much better off I would be if I got rid of books, rather than bringing in more.

Then I heard the meeting facilitator read the question, "Are you now entirely ready to ask God to relieve your compulsion?" or something like that. This made an immediate and profound impression on me. I realized that all I needed to do was ask my Higher Power to relieve my difficulty, rather than continue bringing into my home the parade of books that had been cluttering it up without really giving me relief.

This moment of clarity stayed with me. It brought me out of the bookstore, into the nice evening air, and let me appreciate the walk home. I was able to enjoy the fact that I had made the right decision—not to bring home yet another book or magazine. I was grateful for the CLA meetings, for the training, the reminders, and the encouragement.

Spring 2010

Lauren R., NJ

One of my more dramatic recovery moments was when I cleared out my storage unit. The storage company cleverly doesn't permit its customers to use any on-site trash receptacles, so I had to take everything to my house first. There was an old-fashioned ice box I had painted with a zebra reversed into its stripes and which I had used as a cabinet. When I moved from my old apartment, a friend had suggested I dump it instead of storing it, but I insisted I would need it.

Wrong! After a few years of storage, it turned out that I did not need it. I also did not need to keep paying for my 10-cubic-foot storage unit.

The icebox was heavy, but all by myself I managed to tip it onto a dolly and into my car trunk, with a bungee cord keeping the trunk partially closed. Back on my street, as I wrestled it from my car, I felt very strong—not only physically but, especially, emotionally—strong enough to put it on the curb for heavy-day pickup. Thank you, CLA!

Summer 2010

Anonymous

Accompanying a friend to an art gallery photographic exhibit, I finished looking at the pieces before he did. I sat and looked at an array of magazines on the floor nearby and picked up one that featured a photo spread of a well-known film star and the details of how it was created. The subject matter was interesting to me, from my past glories as an enthusiastic amateur photographer who had delighted in developing his own film and printing the results in a converted bathroom.

I read the accompanying article and skimmed through the rest of this ten-dollar magazine. My friend had finished the exhibit and was talking to the gallery owner and was ready to leave. I just calmly replaced the magazine on the stack on the floor and left. I realized that I didn't have a reason to take it home with me as a souvenir. Even though I'd enjoyed it, it was easy for me to leave it where it was.

This was a supreme test of a recovery moment for me. Previously it would have been taken home, placed on a shelf with other important keepsakes, and rarely, if ever, looked at again.

After this art gallery, we went to another a few miles northeast, where I had completed viewing the original paintings. I sat down to read an art journal whilst awaiting my friend's similar pattern of looking at the art and chatting up the gallery owners. In the process, I managed to read the journal from cover to cover, and when he was ready, I calmly replaced it back in the bookshelf and left empty handed once more.

In both cases, I had no desire to bring home either of these printed pieces, in whose splendor I had devoted about half an hour apiece. I realized that I'd broken through an important habit, replacing it with the Tools[19] of CLA. I had no deep and abiding desire to bring either of these arts and entertainment printed materials home with me.

Free at last, great God almighty, I'm free at last!

Fall 2010

Sharon B., CA

I now realize something: I'm not done shopping until it's all put away. This realization, for me, incorporates time management and a home for my stuff. I don't have the time to shop unless I also have ample time to take care of my purchases when I get home. That is, I can't be rushing off to do something else or be too tired to finish the process.

When I return from shopping, I need to (1) take it out of my car, (2) get it into my home, (3) empty the bags, and (4) put everything into its proper location. Clothing purchases have to be hung or put into drawers; groceries must go into the refrigerator, freezer, or pantry. Next, I must put the receipt into its file or the paper-recycling bin.

Paper and plastic bags go into their drawers or reuse dispenser. Since I use fabric bags, I put those together on the front door knob. Finally, when I go out that door, I place those in the car's trunk. Then, my shopping trip is finished!

My new routine allows me to use the CLA Tool of Earmarking: putting our possessions in their designated homes. I also think this new routine helps eliminate time clutter and helps me grow in spiritual timing.

By being more realistic about all steps involved when I shop, I reinforce my desire to buy only from my list, and it helps me avoid wandering through stores and thrift shops, looking for that elusive bargain treasure. It strengthens my knowledge and growing trust that Higher Power has provided—and always will provide—what I need, when I need it. I am grateful to our program for leading me to more serenity and peace.

Fall 2010

Anonymous

Upon my first visit to the CLA website, I realized that I was no longer alone. I saw that there were others like me, all across this country; some had been recovering from cluttering by practicing this program for many years. Shortly afterward, despite my strong feelings that "I was no longer alone," it also became apparent that there were no meetings within 50 miles or so of my home.

I decided I would have to take action. (By this time, I had already pretty much worked through the process of awareness and acceptance to get into action.) So I contacted the CLA World Service Organization, told them of my desire to start a meeting, and ordered literature. Thus, I took my first, tentative steps toward recovery from cluttering.

I read each and every piece of CLA literature many times over the next year. I continue to read it, work the Steps, pray and meditate (talking and listening to my Higher Power). But, perhaps, what has really been of the utmost importance to my recovery is sharing with others in our still-small group. I believe that this is not a self-help program; I cannot do this alone.

A member once shared, "Just because something is good does not mean I have to have it." That was an epiphany for me!

Letting go of something, someone, some thought, some idea (or ideal!) when there is no space for it in my life at this time (even though it might still be "good" or of use) and trusting that if I really need it, it will become available to me—that has made for an amazing spiritual practice in my recovery.

Holiday 2010

Larry E., CA

Sometimes I get involved in working with the Tools[19] suggested by the program. In CLA, using such Tools as Daily Action, Earmarking, and Streamlining to dig out from under my clutter, I seemed to lose the conscious contact with my Higher Power.

Not only have I recently realized that these Tools are "power tools," now I realize where the source of the power comes from!

So, taking action with these Tools exercises the power I derive from my Higher Power.

Holiday 2010

Peggy A., CA

A few months ago, I made a decision which has helped me declutter. After listening to a fellow clutterer share her method, I made a commitment to pick up and put away or throw away at least ten items a day. These items can be of any size; each piece counts as one item. I did set a few conditions: Things that have not been in their current location for at least two weeks are not included, and anything moved as a result of working on a current project does not count. In doing this, I am right in keeping with two of the CLA Tools: that of Daily Action and that of attending Meetings (since it was in a meeting where I first heard of this).

At first, I noticed small improvement, but after a few weeks of doing this, it's amazing how much has been accomplished. For instance, in my dining room/office there were items that had been sitting on the floor all around the perimeter of the room for a long time. Now, the only things left are the trash can, recycle bag, and a few things on which I am currently working. Not only is it cleaner, but the room seems twice as large.

What a difference! Thanks, CLA, for helping me to achieve this wonderful space.

Spring 2011

Marianne, NY

One of my recovery moments occurred in 2007 while organizing a presentation for Clutter-Free Day. I remembered the message from a member in another 12-Step program about how we learn to keep the focus on ourselves. Yes, this is true, especially when we find ourselves obsessing about a person or situation that we can't control.

On the other hand, in CLA, I've learned that if I keep on sorting through too many choices without prioritizing them, I can't take an action, and I'm stuck in my thoughts and feelings. Or, if I keep on worrying about old resentments without journaling, the resentments stay stuck inside my body. Or, if I keep on worrying about how I'm going to resolve a misunderstanding without praying about it or without making a phone call and sharing about it, then I'm focusing too much on myself!

So, for my CLA issues, I have to get outside of my head and reconnect with people or the environment.

Fall 2011

Kathy M., CA

Decluttering feels fine. It is quiet time alone and gives me time to heal emotionally and physically while I have a cold. Decluttering was also fun when I cleaned out kitchen shelves, as a friend helped me and we laughed and laughed and took photos of us working! I find papers and phone numbers I need and feel like I'm cleaning up my life. I like it. I am organizing and learning to throw away what I don't need—especially papers.

Holiday 2011

Betsey K., NJ

Although I have served only one six-month term as secretary of CLA-East, I have been called on to write the minutes of various business meetings in the absence of the elected officer. I have also been recording secretary of a women's group at my church for most of the last ten years. Both these monthly meetings frequently take place on the same weekend. I have often been known to procrastinate transcribing my notes until the last minute.

Several years ago, when it was time to have the minutes ready for the next meetings, I could not find either set of notes. Finally, the night before the CLA-East meeting, I found my notes and wrote the minutes. The notes for the church group, however, were nowhere to be found. I spent several hours without success looking for that yellow pad on which I thought I had written them.

The next day, as I was getting my papers out of my bag five minutes before the meeting was scheduled to begin, I found the notes, which I had written on the back of a piece of white scrap paper.

A few weeks ago, I once again was faced with the task of writing minutes for the two meetings. This time, however, I decided to write the minutes before the end of the day and succeeded in doing so on both days.

I noticed that it saves so much time if I write them soon after the meeting while the events are fresh in my mind. And I feel so good that I have completed the task before I have a chance to misplace my notes!

Spring 2012

Marie K., CA

My recovery moment is about doing my physical clutter inventory, which is suggested in the CLA literature. I give it a try sometimes as part of Step 4. To count my own items in detail, as I've done in the past for a job, is something new. It brings me out of denial and vagueness, and I've learned new things about myself by doing it.

For example, in a lined notebook I listed (in various categories) 59 T-shirts I found in my house. (I seldom wear T-shirts.) Another page listed all the plastic bags in my kitchen: 14 large colored, 80 grocery with handles, 25 produce, 12 big flat, 3 big loose, and zippered ones—4 very large, 4 large, 8 small, 12 very small. Being this specific, truth to tell, can be quite uncomfortable.

I did an item-by-item inventory of my bathroom—medicine chest and all—on the way to turning it into a clutter-free zone. But there was resistance; inside me was a whiny little voice that wanted to go out and play and not pick up my toys. I gave it a smile and some love and called in to my grown-up CLA Action Line. With a deep breath, I finished my 15-minute commitment.

My clutter includes emotional fog and mental vagueness. Doing physical inventory grounds me in reality and gives me some sense of control in actually deciding what to keep and what to release. Each item I list in a column has a column space next to it for Quantity and one after it to indicate Last Time Used or Enjoyed.

Maybe others would like to use this tool on their paths to clarity, too. My love to all.

Making Do and Not Noticing

Spring 2013

J.N., CA

Initially, I was asked to write this article because of something I shared at our weekly CLA meeting. Of course, I procrastinated. Here is what happened and what prompted me to write now.

I had needed a place to stage things coming into and going out of my house. At the very same time, there was a kitchen table that had belonged to my aunt and uncle and had served my family of six for many years, taking up space in the family room. It was covered with miscellany—you know, other things I did not need but was "saving." Finally, after years, I put the two needs together and voila!, my son and daughter-in-law gladly helped me scrub the table and move it to the area just inside the front door of my house. The table has become an asset, meeting a real need, rather than taking up space. That is progress (not perfection).

Recently, I solved another problem of a similar nature. My knees are getting old, though I do not admit that I am. The folding chair I have been using at my home computer seemed to make the knees hurt more because it was a bit too low for even my short stature. One morning, I was determined to add a pillow to the seat, to raise myself a bit. Then I happened to think of using a dining room chair. It was empty except for a couple of bags hanging from the back. It would have seemed obvious to anyone else, I suppose, but I am now thrilled about being seated on the higher chair. And now that folding chair has been folded and is taking up less floor space.

I grew up with making do. I have saved so many things "just in case." It fills me with joy when I can use a resource that I have on hand rather than going out to buy something new.

Pushing Through Resistance

Fall 2013

Peggy A., CA

It's a common occurrence for me. I have a list of chores—perhaps some decluttering and cleaning, along with some business phone calls or computer work. But I find that there is one item on that list that I just don't want to do. Maybe I am afraid or embarrassed about what will ensue in a phone call. Maybe I don't quite know how to start a task, or I am ready to start one thing, only to be assailed by a feeling of inability to complete it. Or perhaps I just find the task boring and don't want to bother.

How do I get past this "bump in the road"? Sometimes I have been able to continue with other tasks but not able to tackle the one for which I have resistance. At other times, I seem unable to continue with any of them at all. But in all cases, it is easier to procrastinate, which leads to more physical and mental clutter.

Usually, if I can just get started on the problem chore, I am able to work past the feeling of resistance, finish it, and continue with the others. But how do I get past the resistance? Applying the principles of the CLA program has been helping. Sometimes I make progress just by turning it over to my Higher Power. Sometimes I need to bookend with another member. As our literature tells us, "Action is the magic word." Sometimes I just have to force myself to start, and then it is often easier to continue. In fact, I have often surprised myself by easily finishing after I have made this start.

If it weren't for the program, my life would be in much worse shambles than it is. Thank you, CLA.

Summer 2014

Sherry L., AZ

Do you have a task you dread doing?

One CLA buddy suggested a "45-minute challenge." She called and proposed that each of us work for 45 minutes on something we were dreading and then talk again about how it went.

It was great! The energy generated by knowing someone else was working at the same time spurred us both on. At the end, we celebrated our successes by talking on the phone again.

Another buddy and I have regularly scheduled challenges. Both of us have jobs, but on our common days off we have challenges. I have cleaned out the refrigerator and kept it clean. My apartment is neat enough to have maintenance people in. The clean bathroom and laundry room are easier to maintain. My bedroom is clearer than it has been since 2008. The clear space in my bedroom is large enough for exercising, which helps me meet one of my other life goals. Rather than looking at "attacking the clutter," I view it as "enlarging the empty space."

Thank you, CLA. The program works!

Changing My Attitude in CLA

Spring 2015
Kathy H., CA

You know those freebies you're always coming across? You go to an event, and they are passing out little tchotchkes. You go to a fair, and someone wants to give you free literature. You go to a play and are handed a free program.

They all seem to have value, no matter how small. And when you get them home, you can't just throw them away; they were given to you! So you end up with more clutter that you seldom, if ever, look at.

A while ago I was at an event and was given a small item. I didn't want to seem not to appreciate the gesture, so I accepted it. But I decided right then that it would be given away before I left for home. I don't want more clutter!

Then I realized something—my whole atttitude had changed since I joined CLA. For instance, my mother has been downsizing, and she asked if I wanted some of her old keepsakes. I was tempted because they had been in the family for awhile. But they were things I was not particularly attached to, so I told her thanks, but I had to decline because I had no room for them. When I went to a play a friend was in, I did not keep the program. I have had many other occasions in the past few years to decline items that would become future clutter.

I used to see such things as having value, and they were free, so of course I wanted them. Now when I am presented with free items, I see only clutter, so I decline them.

Why this change of heart? I think it is because I have replaced my need for things with the fellowship I have found in CLA. My interaction with people is far more satisfying than a bunch of clutter.

So I am able to keep my house that much more free of clutter. Thank you, CLA.

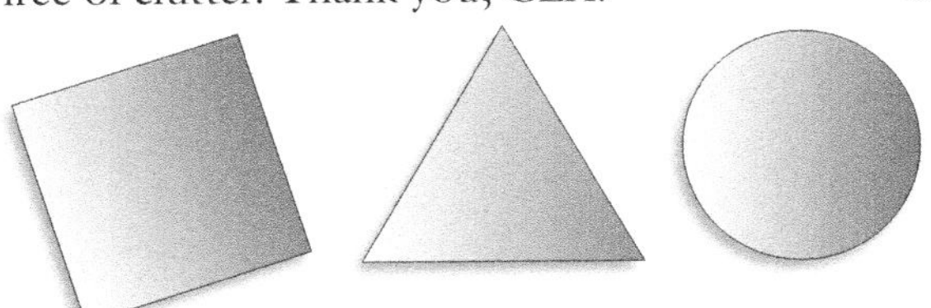

Finding Places

Spring 2016
Jean

Yesterday as I was emptying the dishwasher, I started wondering why I never hesitate to do this chore, yet the piles of paperwork on my dining room table languish for months. The same is true for groceries, which I put away immediately after purchase, perishable or not. Yet a box from an online merchant sits in the hallway for weeks.

My interpretation of this paradox is that dishes and food have designated places in the kitchen: pasta in its cabinet, vegetables in the fridge, pots in their drawer.

When I know where something goes, it's easy. So, contrary to what you might think if you walked into my house, it isn't the act of putting away that has me paralyzed. The issue is figuring out where to put the things that don't have designated homes.

Why this is an issue is still somewhat of a mystery. What's stopping me from assigning locations to items that arrive at the door, like mail, paperwork, and the contents of boxes that have been shipped to me? Part of the answer is that the obvious places are stuffed with items put away years ago. Clearing those drawers and filing cabinets of things that should be jettisoned is a job that cries out to be put off until tomorrow.

So, using the original serenity prayer and the Keep and Release Prayer, I've created another variation: God, grant me the stamina to find places for items to keep, the courage to release the things I do not need, and the wisdom to know the difference.

Holiday 2016
Alison B., NJ

Recently I had a leaky faucet. In order for a new one to be put in, I had to take out everything that was under my sink. Little did I know I was in for an education about myself.

I was astonished to find 12 pairs of rubber gloves still in the packages and 15 new cellulose sponges. Then there were the five containers of carpet cleaner, each purchased separately, to clean the extremely old carpet throughout my apartment. None of the cleaners were ever used. I decluttered somewhat but held on to more than I wanted to.

While I was working on that, I realized that I had bought a big professional carpet shampoo machine that I tried to use once with water only. Not to mention two carpet sweepers, a mini shampoo machine, and a vacuum cleaner that all gather dust, without picking up much dust.

I have two large file drawers stuffed full. I shred current papers, but I need to do more. I fully believe I could shred about 95 percent of it. If only I could get started....

I have bookshelves that are always overflowing. I get rid of a box of books occasionally, but it isn't enough. I will sometimes hold onto that box for a year or more before releasing it. Personally, I see no reason for this behavior, but I do it anyway. Then one day I snap and get rid of the lot. I don't miss those books at all. I give away only the novels, not the self-help books.

I gather clothes from wherever I can find them—thrift stores, garage sales, etc. I have two jam-packed closets. I used to have more clothes. I whittled them down to what the space could handle. I acknowledge that I need to buy better-fitting clothes and release ones that are too big.

So this is my conclusion: I am a hoarder. I didn't know. I may have been confused about my disease because I don't have piles of things from my floor to my ceiling like they do on those hoarding shows. But I am not supposed to compare. I am supposed to identify and accept. Well, it's taken me nearly 15 years in CLA to do just that!

Spiritual Recovery

CLA is a program of spiritual recovery, based upon the 12 Steps. Our experience has shown that without working on our spiritual development, most of us are doomed to clutter again, even if we have had some success in decluttering.

Willingness to Do Less

Holiday 2010

Marion, AZ

In CLA, we learn how to better handle all forms of clutter, not just physical. Here a reader submits her insights on recovering from time clutter. The original submission has been modified with the writer's permission for use in CLA*rity.*

> *...I've really found your CLArity articles and the CLA [literature] helpful...[with] many forms of clutter—time clutter, etc. ...I've had a long-standing struggle with being too busy and being unable to do less—I'm powerless over my addiction to "busyness." CLA has been very helpful. When I did the document about doing less and read it to my husband, he said "wow!" because he's seeing me beginning to actually do less.*

If I am *trying* to do less, this is a state of great confusion.
If I am *willing* to do less, this is a state of great humility.

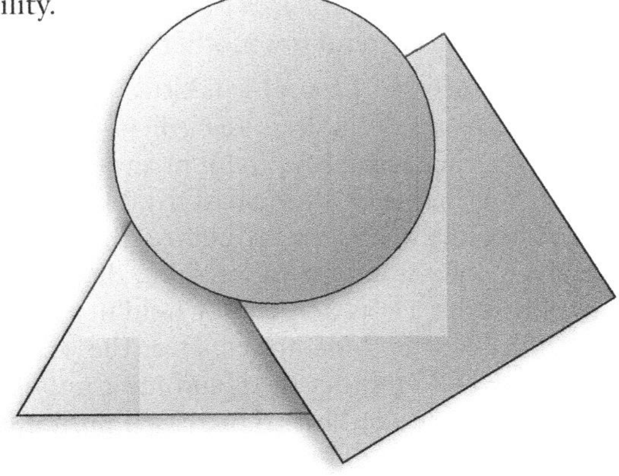

Trying to do less implies that I should be able to do it but am struggling with it.

A *willingness* to do less implies that I do not know how to do it, but I am willing to learn.
When I was *trying* to give up old ways and condemned myself for failing to do so, I simply became *willing* to learn how the old ways may be replaced with ways of peace.

When I was *trying* to do less, I feared not being able to do less and judged myself a failure.
When I am *willing* to do less, no setback is a problem, for I know that I will be shown.

When I was *trying*, I was attempting to surrender by myself.
When I am *willing*, I am asking for guidance.

Trying to do less places responsibility on me.
Being *willing* to do less places the responsibility on God.

Trying to do less is an act of separation from God.
Willingness to do less is, in a sense, a prayer.

When I *try*, there is resistance.
When I am *willing*, there is acceptance.

When I *try* to do less, everything is interference.
When I am *willing* to do less, everything is of assistance.

My free-will choice to do less is the most important decision I make each day because it speaks for my willingness to do less each day.

Outside of the will of God, there is no such thing as success. Inside the will of God, there cannot be any failure.

Losing the Shame and Pain

Spring 2012
Gladys H., NY

Action, action, and more action—that is what would make me better, I was told by so many experienced 12-Steppers. So upon entering CLA, I looked for opportunities for action because I feared that the pain and shame of it all would kill me. A social worker of mine always referred to the condition of my apartment as "it." She couldn't bring herself to say what she honestly thought and felt because she truly did learn to love me very much as a client. It wasn't until her supervisor threatened to fire her because of my clutter and hoarding that I decided I had to do something about "it." I finally took the plunge, and I shared for the first time about it in another Fellowship. That is where I learned about Clutterers Anonymous and that I was suffering from another illness. Thus began a new journey for me. Full of self-pity, I asked God why I had to bother with another 12-Step program. The pain this time was so great, I gave up the debate when I attended my first CLA meeting.

My 12-Step experience has taught me that no matter what the problem, I can read and learn about it, take action, and then come...come to... "come to believe" that things can, will, and do get better. So I began reading all the CLA literature I could find. Coming back from my cluttering relapse, I started over with the basics, reading, taking what small service commitment I was able to fulfill, and continued to attend meetings and talk with other compulsive clutterers. Only this time, to my surprise, I hit the pain of my core issues around this dis-ease. I found myself reading "Declutter Your Mind"[9] and "Spiritual Timing"[15] over and over again. Having my life surrounded by codependent people, battling with my perfectionism and my compulsion to worry, and having all of my energy zapped by emotional benders and clutter, I felt hopeless and helpless. But wait, wasn't I, too, one of those raging codependents? Did I not have the compulsion to be perfect and to prove to others that I was okay? Did I not think that I was in control of the universe by sitting and lying around worrying? My God, it was going to be an intensive inside job to get to the bottom of this matter.

Gradually, the mystery began to unfold. For two days, I found myself rolling in my bed, feeling deeply rooted emotional pain and shame about my cluttering. The repeated personal rejections, the physical fights and harm done to me, the reasons for homelessness or threatened homelessness, the destruction of relationships—with these memories, the flow of uncontrollable tears gushed down my cheeks. Acceptance of my disease, I knew, would be the beginning of healing and finding answers. And there it was.

It had its roots with living and growing up with alcoholism. Thoughts of my mother—a clutterer, a raging codependent, and battered woman, who I couldn't decide whether I loved or hated—came to mind. I found her death at the hands of my father traumatizing. Having had to move and live with my father's relatives, I found myself tortured by an alcoholic aunt who I vowed I would spend my life hating, and I did even until the moment of her death in recent years. I found this aunt and other relatives to be the most insensitive human beings I thought would ever walk upon the face of this earth. This particular aunt said horrible things about my mother because of her poor housekeeping and clutter. My God, I thought, my mother spent her life trying to stay alive and away from the danger of my violent father; when did she have time to play the happy homemaker and manage to keep a clean, decluttered home? Other relatives joined this aunt's criticism. I found myself not being able to grieve the loss of my parents because I was trying to defend my mother's honor.

To my surprise, I found I did love my mother very much—as all children, regardless of the type of parents they have, love them in a very special way. It was here that I retreated from life and family and became a loner in my bedroom. Bit by bit, I began to collect and hoard anything that reminded me of parents. I was desperately holding on to crumbs of love and memories. Over the years, one loved one after another died, and my compulsion to collect clutter and hoard increased until it grew out of control. So did my codependency. This discovery alerts me to the need to apply the sayings of "Easy Does It" and "One Day at a Time" and to allow my Higher Power to direct me, my life, my decluttering, and my total overall decluttering recovery. I have stopped feeling so anxious to share at meetings, and I have resolved to simply listen and learn.

Making Room for Love

Fall 2012

Anonymous

It didn't matter that I had not been a clutterer growing up. I realized I had become one and needed the help of the program. Character defects have been described as behaviors or personal qualities that have gotten out of balance in one's life, and I understood this completely.

My chosen career, which had been very rewarding and central to my life, came with an occupational hazard—paper clutter. When I would look at a pile of papers and say, "I might need this in seven years," I knew I was actually stating a fact. But as the piles grew all around me, I came to question what I was doing with my life.

Were all these papers making me happy? Over time, the answer became no.

This realization came at a time when certain professional setbacks led me to the conclusion that I wanted more physical space in my paper-cluttered apartment so that I could enjoy other aspects of life, beyond the professional world. For instance, I had stopped having people over long ago and wanted to be able to invite people into my space again. I also wanted to have more space inside myself, so I had room to enjoy these people.

My apartment, which for a long time had served me as a place of intellectual stimulation and protection, had started to become more of a prison, walling me off from loving connections to others in my home space.

With all these papers in miscellaneous piles, my home certainly did not feel like a sacred space. Our CLA leaflet, "Home, Our Sacred Place,"[11] reminded me that my apartment could be a place of serenity and support, a place of spaciousness and peace. But I had to be willing to work for it. A clutter buddy once asked, "What are you willing to trade in one area of your life to get what you want in another?"

The answer was to let go of the death-grip I had on my career so I could have space for more relationships and fun. And then start to take the time and energy to go through my things to lighten my load—using the CLA "Keep and Release" prayer. I'm discovering that there were many papers I thought I needed that I really didn't. And with each bag of papers that goes out of my apartment, there is more room for "eye rest" on my table tops. (With certain papers that have been very important to me, I find that I need to do a ritual to let go of them. For instance, sometimes I take them out to a campground and burn them.)

I had not had any space for a love relationship because I found the ideas written on my papers so compelling. But over time, this way of being got old. I was lonely. I started going out to meet people. I read a lot of CLA literature and called the phone lines often (both meetings and activity sessions). Somehow, a space inside me was getting created. It was growing. Then I met someone. I mean, I met someone! At that point, I had to decide, would I really make room for this person? It seemed that through my doing mental decluttering, working the 4th Step, realizing my situation, and taking action to change my situation, I was making inner space inside myself; this seemed to enable my Higher Power to create a situation outside that allowed me to connect with someone.

I am still doing a great deal of physical decluttering to make room for this new person in my home and in my life, but I now have much motivation to do the work. I also feel a certain sense of satisfaction (and at times, even joy) that has come about through mental decluttering. One of the best things that has come from this is that the person I've fallen in love with knows that I'm in the midst of creating space for us in my home—and brings a loving acceptance to this situation that helps let me be exactly where I am in the process. All I'm doing now is enlarging my circle of love. Thank you, HP!

Update: Since writing this article, the new person in my life has come into my home and says that she enjoys being in my space, which allows her to be in proximity to my spiritual self, and she feels safe and loved being in my home! The de-cluttering continues, but now I can enjoy actually having someone here.

Recapturing Me

Fall 2012

Gladys H., CT

I wasn't assigned too many chores around the house because my grandmother wanted to keep the peace. My aunt, whom I vowed I would spend my life hating, insisted on doing all the cleaning in the house and would put up a fight whenever I took the initiative to do some house-cleaning on my own. However, I did learn to do laundry, iron clothes, bake, and set the dinner table every day. (Recently, I discovered this aunt was like that because she was both an alcoholic and obsessive-compulsive with cleaning.) I really loved setting the dinner table because my grand-mother was "the hostess with the mostest," and I knew she was training me to become one. I loved entertaining in the home. I loved polishing the silverware, washing the fine china, decorating, and the special cleaning that was involved and the fact that I was allowed to participate in it.

Preparing the home for my favorite relatives, who would travel long ways to visit us, was so exciting. It was just as exciting to have friends from the community and church over for dinner. I guess I loved these times because that was when we treated each other the best. Home was not so depressing when we treated each other better. I also learned from entertaining in the home that family and friends were important and had lasting healing effects. That home doesn't exist for me any more, but I have spent a lifetime trying to find it and recapture it.

When I began decluttering my apartment, I felt sad that a very happy and important part of me had been lost in the pain and clutter. On Thanks-giving Day, a woman in the program without family was so afraid of being alone that I invited her over for the holiday. I'm glad I did. I enjoyed her company, and it was a healing experience for us both. Usually, I would run away from my home on a holiday to serve the homeless or to serve meals at church so I wouldn't feel sad and alone. I now realize I was also running from my clutter. I hope this has become a turning point in my life. I hope I am in the midst of recapturing the best in me that I always loved and appreciated about my family and myself. Thank you, God, for second chances.

Becoming a member of CLA gives me that second chance through its meetings, literature, service, and fellowship. As a result of being in this program, I have become more loving and gentle with myself, while others benefit from my new outlook on life. The leaflet, "Decluttering Resent-ment: Steps 4–10,"[8] has been the healing balm for my hurt and anger that were hidden under piles of clutter. I feel my recovery from living a cluttered life began when I read, "Even if we don't believe the person is worthy of our loving thoughts, we are." For the first time in my life, I felt free from the monster inside of me that could not "Let go, and let God." Recapturing me has not been easy, but it has been rewarding. I cannot wait to see what the future holds.

My G & A Journal

Holiday 2012

Anonymous

My owl-covered journal sits invitingly on the nightstand by my bed. Within its pages you'll find my highs and highlights, my proof and pride. Welcome to my Gratitude and Accomplishments (G&A) Journal. It is here that I record, usually daily, what I'm grateful for and what I've accom-plished during a day.

The origin of my G&A journal dates back to a time in my life when I was depressed and anxious and didn't have much hope. I didn't know about CLA and definitely didn't know I was a clutterer, though my life was very cluttered with paperwork, thoughts, and feelings.

My friends were very supportive, and one friend in particular really struck a chord with me.

She had faced her own demons and found serenity. She told me to write down, every day, at least five things I was grateful for and, when possible, to read each item on the list out loud. If I didn't feel grateful about anything, she told me to write about physical things, like "I'm grateful for my thin legs," and "I'm grateful for my eyelashes." What the heck, I had nothing to lose, so I started writing.

At first, my thin legs and eyelashes appeared in lots of entries. I had a roof over my head and a good place to live, so I added "my home" as a gratitude. My parents, friends, and cat were very supportive of me so they made it into my journal. I usually wrote in my journal at the end of the day and found it relaxing and soothing to end my day thinking and writing about my gratitudes.

As I started to recover, I found myself wanting a more spiritual life. I tried out a couple of 12-Step programs; at one meeting, I heard a member speak about being overwhelmed by her stuff. I spoke to her after the meeting, and she told me to search for "clutter" on the Internet, that there were organizations for clutterers.

My search led me to CLA. The only CLA meetings in my area were phone meetings, and I started calling in, albeit sporadically, to some of the evening phone meetings and daily activity sessions. I learned about breaking my to-do's into smaller, more manageable, parts. The term "baby steps" became my mantra, and still is, especially when I'm feeling overwhelmed.

Eventually I added my daily accomplishments to my journal entries. In the beginning, my accomplishments were very basic, like "brushed my teeth, washed my face, ate breakfast." As I healed, my accomplishments increased in number and responsibility, to such things as "shopped at grocery store" and "studied at library." I was proud and thrilled to add items to my journal. Even now, it feels good to write them down—to get them out of my head and onto paper where I can see proof of my successes. I don't judge or quantify my gratitudes or accomplishments in any way. So you won't see anything like, "ran errands but forgot to get bread" or "called the insurance company but the call didn't go well." What you will see is, "ran errands" and "called insurance company."

Today, I'm still cluttered but not as scattered, and I'm better organized. I use to-do lists that I get out of my head and into print via a notepad or into my smartphone. I feel so proud to check items off my list. My recovery is better and, consequently, I don't write in my G&A journal every day or write about common accomplishments, like brushing my teeth.

A sample entry looks like this:

9/21/12: bf/np (short for "ate breakfast/read the newspaper"), shopped at grocery store, worked on CLA*rity* article at coffee shop, emailed friends, called dentist office re: my bill. GF (short for "Grateful For"): courage, my home, my parents, my cat, the weather, patience, movies.

To add some fun and color to my journal, I buy some little cute, colorful stickers. For each activity that I'm really proud of, that took a lot of courage, I add a sticker next to the journal entry. Little dolphins, stars, and happy faces adorn my journal.

Though I don't often read through my journal entries, it gives me great comfort to see my journal by my bed every day. It's proof of my healing and growth. Some days I still feel overwhelmed by my clutter and have only a few entries to record. Even so, my journal still beckons and empty pages await my touch. One day at a time.

My Reality

Holiday 2012

Alison B., NJ

Each autumn, when temperatures fluctuate and days recede, I become fed up. I push people away and feel compelled to watch television reruns for up to 18 hours per day. "TV Addicts Anonymous" doesn't exist—I've checked. I had visions of sitting around and talking about how we couldn't possibly separate from our favorite characters.

At times, I put off daily chores until I'm overwhelmed, and I don't venture outside unless I have to buy food or I have a health-related appointment. I move sluggishly, and I'm hard-pressed to think clearly. It's definitely a pattern exacerbated by lack of money, thoughts of the holidays, the birthday blues, and possible expectations of gift-giving.

But I'm an old hand when it comes to 12-Step issues; several years ago, I discovered that underneath all my obsessions and addictions is really just the oh-so-human desire to be loved— the way I believe a woman is supposed to be loved by a man. And according to what I've read, even that can be called love addiction. Does it ever end?

All my life I've dreamt about becoming rich and famous. When I'm not watching TV, I'm imagining:

1. Having my own "reality" show.
2. Having a personal trainer for weight loss.
3. Having singing, acting, and dancing coaches who will transform me into a star in a fantastic rags-to-riches love story for the big screen.
4. Going on talk shows to discuss the broken mental health system as it pertains to me.
5. Doing infomercials with a holistic health organization.
6. Moving into a beautifully furnished, sparkling clean, and spacious location in a temperate climate. It would have gadgets in the kitchen, a recording studio, a gym, a whirlpool, and a balcony in the sun.

Here's the reality: I am grateful to have a roof over my head, but I'm uncomfortable in this apartment. It has never felt like home because I was abandoned here by the love of my life. We moved in before they could change the filthy carpets, which they've never let me remove. I've survived a huge roach infestation and bedbugs. I sleep on a camping bed because I had to throw away my real one. I have decluttered greatly over the years, but I know that in order not to repeat my patterns, I need to work the Steps. On a daily basis, I must remember my disciplines of writing lists and prioritizing. Meditation is really important to me, too. It helps me stay plugged in to my Higher Power. I talk to HP throughout the day.

Sometimes I think moving would solve everything, and then I remember I still have to take myself with me!

Wellness Check

Summer 2013

Wendy L., IL

Stress can make my recovery go haywire, and that often leads to increased anxiety and clutter. My serenity goes out the window, and my creativity tanks. So how can I stop this loop and regain my peace? Well, it's a little bit like living with the weather: I can't control it, but I can try to prepare for it by using umbrellas and wearing boots. Great, but how does that translate to living with stress?

It starts with awareness and lots of practice. First, I constantly scan myself for stress symptoms. Do I have muscle tension? Headaches? Difficulty falling asleep and staying asleep? Do I feel anxious or overwhelmed? Once I acknowledge that I'm stressed, I next determine what my stressors are and how I can address them.

Often, it's about one of my to-do's. What is it about the task that is stressing me out? Can I prepare for it? What action—physical or mental—can I take to lower my stress about it?

At this point, perspective is very important. What's the worst thing that can happen to me if I don't deal with this to-do? How important is this task in my life? Can I live without doing it? Will it be a relief once I accomplish it? Without perspective, I fall back to my old ways of being anxious much of the time, which is really uncomfortable.

Let's say my stressor is a phone call that I'm dreading. I research the subject matter so I know both the facts and my options. I write down questions I might want to ask during the call. I keep my notes in a file that I can easily find. I think through the negative, potentially overwhelming, what-ifs. What if I ask about A, and he disagrees? Then, I'll ask about B. What if I don't get B? Then I'll ask about my other options. On the other hand, what if I ask about A, and he agrees with me? I become my own cheerleader.

Staying in the present is critical. Let's say it's the night before the scary call. I can lie in bed awake worrying about it, or I can remind myself that I've prepped for it and there's nothing else I can do at this moment. Letting go is much easier said than done, and it has taken me a lot of practice. Sometimes, I need to visualize my stressor. I see it as a living ball of angry, black yarn that I place on a big, beautiful, green leaf. Then I watch the leaf and the ball flow down a stream and vanish from my view. I've let it go.

I often ask my Higher Power for guidance. Calling in to a focused action session or calling a clutter buddy to bookend about the stressor can be very motivating. Reading CLA literature can help put things in perspective.

Tried-and-true stress relievers can help—lighting candles, listening to soothing music, watching a funny TV show or movie, calling supportive friends, or hanging out in a coffee shop with a tasty beverage.

This is where I'm supposed to say I exercise, but right now that's not in my repertoire, sigh. Napping is a good escape—if not abused. Petting my cat, who feels soft like a bunny, soothes me.

Self-calming is a great tool for retaining my serenity in the face of stress and anxiety. So is keeping the stressor in perspective.

My mind is like a mental radar screen, scanning for anxiety blips. The sooner I prepare for the blips, the better off I am. And the less anxious I am, the more mental energy I have to be creative and enjoy life.

Managing Stress to Manage Clutter

Spring 2015

Wendy L., IL

When I was stressed out, I would clutter. What happened was that I would hit a snag in my life, got anxious over it, and then obsessed about it. This left precious little energy for dealing with the rest of my life, and clutter was the result. Adding insult to injury, the resulting clutter stressed me out, too. It was a vicious cycle and one that was oddly familiar.

Finally, and I must say after many years of struggling, I decided that all this anxiety was simply unacceptable. So I did something about it.

The key for me has been learning that I can control my thoughts and behaviors. And that it's up to me to change them in an effort to lower my stress and ease my anxiety. It's taken lots of practice, but this strategy has resulted in a lot less clutter, among other benefits.

Basically, I start by trying to figure out what I'm stressed about. Though it often feels like I'm just plain anxious, I find it almost always boils down to something specific. Next I take a good look at my thoughts. In times of stress they often get extreme, and I tend toward all-or-nothing thinking, or thinking in terms of black or white. For example, I need to eat better so that means I can never have chocolate again. Hmm. Okay, bad example.

Anyway, I discovered I was thinking in terms of negative what-ifs. Let me explain with an example. Let's say I have to call an insurance agency. What if the call goes badly and I don't know what to say? What if I say the wrong thing? What if they cancel my policy? So much extreme thinking and so little hope. No wonder I get stressed out.

So I started challenging my thoughts. Like—realistically, it's not likely that I'll lose the policy. The insurance company isn't out to get me. If I do get asked a question I'm not prepared for, I'll do my best to answer it and get back to the caller if need be. Most likely the call won't go as badly as I think it will.

So it probably won't be the catastrophe I first thought it might be. I start to feel better. Next come behavior changes, which means preparing for possible questions, rehearsing answers, and reading through my notes. I promise myself that I'll make the call when I'm at my most alert. As unfamiliar as it is to my cluttered brain, I realize that I now have a plan. And some control of the situation.

The payoff has been incredible. I still face stressors, and some can be more intense than others; but I think and act through them now and don't often let them get the best of me. Overall, my new strategy has led to increased confidence and optimism.

I have to admit that when something extreme happens, like a loved one getting sick, or when a big life decision needs to be made, it gets really hard to manage the stress because there can be a sense of a lack of control. But, ultimately, I still have to manage the stress or it will manage me.

I'm mostly able to lead a less cluttered life now, and I do eat chocolate. Okay, in moderation. Life isn't perfect but it's definitely more calm. And with my newfound mental energy, I've even started to act on my dreams and passions. The world is my oyster and I've found a pearl. Of wisdom, that is.

Mourning the Old Leads to Mornings New

Summer 2015

James C., NY

This is more or less a written summary of the talk I gave at Clutter-Free Day in Brooklyn, New York, on May 18, 2014. I can email the audio file and my written outline to those who are interested. *[To contact James C., please send a message via one of the contact methods listed on the Frontispiece.—Editor]*

How does mourning the old lead to mornings new? For me, (1) mourning my clutter, seeing it as a certain type of death, but then letting it go; (2) mourning the time, energy, and anxiety that decluttering necessarily draws out of me when I would rather do something else. These two "mournings," done consistently a little bit at a time, have led me to new "mornings" of greater order, peace, and space.

As seems to have been the case with others, my compulsion with hoarding and cluttering began with items like newspapers and baseball cards snatched away from me by others without my being able to decide whether to mourn and toss them or not. In reaction, I hoarded them in my room, and the clutter began to accumulate. People with whom I was living began to complain, and I realized that they had a point. I started going to face-to-face Clutterers Anonymous meetings. Hearing the qualifications and experiences of other clutterers and reading the literature, such as "Home: Our Sacred Place,"[11] helped me to see more clearly that decluttering would not only help mollify those around me but also give benefits that I myself could value, such as order, space, and peace.

But how to make the decluttering a success? For example, I treasured the information I found in newspapers, and I knew that I could not always find all of it on the Internet. I knew that the help and grace of my Higher Power were absolutely necessary. In prayer and meditation with HP, I realized that decluttering and tossing away the newspapers involved a sort of death to the positive information contained in them, and so a mourning of this was fitting. But this "death" would lead me to the beautiful morning-like attributes of order, peace, and space.

Similarly, the time and energy of decluttering implied a mourning of other activities I would rather be accomplishing, but again for the sake of a new life offered me by order, peace, and space. And I have found that I can sugarcoat the mourning by playing my favorite fun songs while I declutter. With the help and grace of HP, with meetings, with literature, and with a sponsor, I do find, a little bit at a time, brighter mornings coming my way.

Making Amends

Summer 2015

Kathy H., CA

A while ago, I was asked a question about making amends. This started me thinking about the subject of amends.

When we work Step 8, we "Made a list of all persons we had harmed and became willing to make amends to them all." Step 9 tells us to "Make direct amends to such people wherever possible, except when to do so would injure them or others."

This process of listing and making amends is integral to CLA's program of recovery. In doing so, we clear out lingering bits of poison in our minds to help free us of mental clutter. This may be one of the hardest things we do in our recovery process, but without taking this Step, it will be difficult to continue our spiritual recovery. It can lead to more freedom, serenity, and peace. It is important to first work Step 8 so that we clearly understand our own part in the situation and what we have to make amends for. Sometimes it takes some soul-searching to gain this understanding.

Often, all the process of making amends entails is a simple apology. Sometimes it requires more action on our parts. I have found that when I make an apology, I need to apologize for my part in it, without listing the wrongs done by the other person. There may be another time for a discussion of how I feel about what the other person did, but the amends should deal only with my own mistakes.

I discovered this when apologizing to my husband. I found I had no gains (either in our relationship or for my own peace of mind) when I would say, "I'm sorry—but..." Now, when I make an amends, I try to deal only with my errors.

Sometimes during an apology, the person I am making amends to apologizes for his or her own part in the situation—and we both end up feeling better. But if one of us didn't apologize first, we never would clear up our feelings about the situation.

I have found that putting off the amends just makes it more difficult. It is as if I have a little demon inside, who is telling me, "This is too embarrassing," or "This is too scary." The longer I wait to make the amends, the larger the demon grows, until the situation seems almost impossible to correct. I believe that this is the same character defect that sometimes keeps me from dealing with my clutter. In the CLA program, I have been learning not to wait—to make amends, declutter, or do my daily tasks. After all, one of our Tools of Recovery[19] is Daily Action.

What has really amazed me are the times I have put off making an apology, only to find that when I finally made the amends, the person I was making amends to had not even noticed or been bothered by the situation! Meanwhile, the need to clear the decks (make the amends) had grown and grown in my mind until it paralyzed me and totally destroyed my serenity. Had I done the amends right away, I would have saved myself a great deal of stress.

But what if the person we are making amends to does not want to accept the apology? We need to remember that we make amends for our own peace of mind. What the other person does is his or her business, but if we did our best, the mistake will not continue to fester in our minds.

This brings me to Step 10, which reads, "...and when we were wrong, promptly admitted it." I generally do what my former sponsor told me to do: When I go to bed, I review my day and determine whether I need to make an amends. Then, I try to make the amends the next day, before it grows so big that it destroys my serenity—although sometimes it does require further thought to determine the best approach. This helps free up my mind to accomplish other goals and to let the joy and serenity come through.

Dating as a Clutterer Some Peaks and Pitfalls

Holiday 2015

Anonymous

Dating can range from being thrilling to disappointing at warp speed and can touch on every adjective in between. Add to that being a clutterer, and you've got a recipe for, well, I won't say disaster but for some added challenges, at the very least.

If you're not single, you may just find yourself feeling a little more grateful for your partner. If you are single and not dating, well this will either encourage you to date or, more likely, give you cause to celebrate your singlehood.

As a modern-day dater, I mostly use smartphone dating apps or dating web sites to meet potential dates. That often means I have to write profiles about myself, and those need to include what I'm looking for in a man. Honestly, I'd rather walk on fire than write this stuff, and I'm a writer.

As a clutterer, I tended to write too much about myself, and my profiles were too straightforward. Boring. I'm still working on adding humor and color to my profiles, which is harder than it should be. But it can make one stand out from the crowd.

I must be doing something right because I'm meeting men, and some really interesting ones. Or at least I'm matching with a lot of them. Unfortunately, there's the whole fiasco of getting to know a man via email (bad) or texting (worse) before we get to the date stage.

Unfortunately, there are no nonverbal signals or voice inflections. And I have again made the mistake of sharing too much factual information about myself—clutter as it were. It can come off as dull and men sometimes just vanish, never to be heard from again. Ouch. The CLA slogan to keep it simple is key for me here and to keep it interesting and fun, which sure tests my electronic flirting skills.

Plus there are pitfalls in conversing with multiple men at the same time. I sometimes forget what I've asked one versus the other and occasionally can't remember what they've told me. This is partially because my head is so cluttered with the undone to-dos of my life that I forget things.

Lest you start wondering, I do make it to the date stage. So it helps to have clean, date-worthy clothes available. A couple of times I've put on a pretty shirt, only to find that it's stained. I scramble to find a plan B shirt, but often those are dirty or un-ironed because I'm a clutterer who doesn't always keep up with her laundry. Panic sets in here. I giggle and tell my date I'm late due to a wardrobe malfunction. Sigh.

When things are going well and I've gotten to know a man, I have him over to my home for drinks or dinner. Here it helps to keep a fairly clean home so I can actually do that. Not an easy thing for a clutterer. But thanks to my recovery in CLA, my home now tends to be mostly clutter free or can be freed of clutter fairly quickly.

Sometimes I wonder whether it would be better for me to date a clutterer or a non-clutterer. While I ponder that, I keep "swiping right" and "liking" potential dates online in hopes of meeting a great guy.

At the very least, dating forces me to keep a clean home. Ah, maybe dating should be added to the CLA Tools of Recovery.[19] Seriously though, they're fine as they are. Now for my profile, well, that's another story.

Asserting Away Resentment

Summer 2016

Anonymous

In one of my first jobs after college, I taught people how to quit smoking. Many of my participants struggled, quit, relapsed, and then repeated that pattern. To clutterers, it's common knowledge that cluttering, like smoking, is very hard to quit. Plus, I'd like to think it wasn't the teacher.

It was years later, and after I started identifying as a clutterer, when it occurred to me that something I had discussed with my smokers could be useful to clutterers.

It's that we choose to be assertive, passive, or aggressive in most situations with others. Common sense tells us that acting assertively is best, but this isn't always easy to do. Unfortunately, when we're unhappy with the way we behave, we might act out on our addictions to relieve the stress.

Anyway, it seems like a leap to say that when we're stressed out over the way we've behaved, we clutter. For me, it's more like I'm consumed and resentful over my stressful encounter and just don't have the mental energy left to make good decisions. Since much of my clutter tends to get created and maintained when I can't decide what to do with it, my indecisiveness can often lead to cluttering.

But let me back up for a minute to the bit about being resentful. Clutterers are not immune to this, and in fact, resentment is such a big issue that it's addressed in our leaflet, "Decluttering Resentment: Steps 4-10."[8] Here we learn that "Just as clutter consumes our physical space, resentment consumes our minds." I can tell you firsthand that resentment has caused me to become obsessed and neglect important things in my life, like order in my home. Hello, clutter.

The good news is that when I act assertively, I usually feel less resentful than when I act otherwise. Let me give you an example.

I had moved into a new apartment and was sitting in the living room when I smelled cigarette smoke. It eventually went away, and I thought (hoped) it was a one-time thing. Later that night, I heard what sounded like explosions and I thought it was thunder. I peered outside but it wasn't even raining and there was no lightning. Then I got a whiff of cigarette smoke again.

It turned out it was my downstairs neighbors playing video games and smoking. The last thing I wanted to do was have a confrontation with them. But I was feeling resentful about the whole situation and had started obsessing about it. My mind was cluttered and I couldn't relax.

I called the leasing office and unexpectedly learned that tenants were allowed to smoke in their apartments. So I couldn't complain about that. I was very nervous about going, but I did finally go downstairs to ask my neighbors to please lower the volume of their TV.

I felt good about being assertive and could feel my resentment lessen. Fortunately, for me, my neighbors moved out about a month later, and my new nonsmoking, non-videogame playing neighbor moved in.

Being assertive is not always easy for me. It can take courage and guts and may involve conflict or confrontation. But the flipside of not being assertive is being passive or aggressive, and both of those behaviors trigger resentment and mind clutter.

Also, the less resentment I feel, the more likely I am to think clearly. And thinking clearly is what I need to do to prevent or clean up clutter. It's definitely a win-win for me.

Sharing Our Abundance

Fall 2016

Terri J., OH

Feeding Where I Am Spiritually Fed

Our ninth leaflet has led me to look at what is working in my life to aid my recovery and what is not working in my life that hinders my recovery. I have been taught in my 12-Step recovery to feed where I am spiritually fed. I try to share this concept when appropriate at recovery meetings.

I realize that if I were at a 12-Step meeting and a basket were passed, I would reach into my pocket and share my abundance with the group.

I am in an area where there aren't any CLA face-to-face meetings, so a basket does not pass through my fingers. Many times I thought about sending in 7th Tradition donations at the end of CLA meetings when I heard our friendly reminder requesting support. It took me almost a year and a half in the program to reach out to share my abundance with a group that has spiritually fed me. Since I do not enjoy writing checks and since I was honoring myself with a CLA*rity* Christmas gift, I ordered a Meeting Starter Kit[7] and previous issues and a new subscription to CLA*rity*, and I also made a 7th Tradition donation. My donation took into account that I would most likely have put in a dollar or more at each meeting if a basket passed in front of me.

I have noticed in our financial report that in some months our donations are low, which makes me sad. I do not believe that we are unable or unwilling to share. I believe our clutter gets in our way. We forget where we are spiritually fed and forget the reciprocal energy that is created in our lives when we share our abundance.

Of course, making financial donations is not the only way I feed where I am spiritually fed. I first began sharing my spiritual abundance in CLA by reading the Steps and Traditions at meetings and later moderating meetings. It makes my heart sing when members eagerly offer to read at our meetings. The energy flows back to the leader and creates a circle of love and abundance among members.

I believe the energy created at 12-Step meetings is one of the most healing energies in the world. If you have ever led a 12-Step meeting, you are aware of the abundant love and healing that flows back to you magnified by our Higher Power. I believe in looking at my assets and defects and seeing where in the Fellowship I can share my assets and heal my defects, whether it is by being a positive member of our group, in reading or moderating at meetings, or taking on more of a leadership role in 12-Step committee work.

Looking at what is working and not working in my life helps me to see that if we look at various

12-Step Fellowships the same way, there are many things that aid them and some that hinder their missions. I think CLA will continue to grow and progress if we can look at our components and see what is working and, if it's not, what creative solutions will aid us in our individual and group recovery.

I know we all try our best and love our Fellowship. I have seen so much service by a handful of recovering members. I never would have imagined how much time it takes to plan a convention, write a piece of literature, and create bylaws. I am astounded at the love and need for our Fellowship and the continued commitment by officers and committee chairpersons.

I wish to thank all of you who have been of service over the years and who have kept our Fellowship going so it is here for me and others. I also hope many can think about giving back to the Fellowship by sharing their talents and abundance so CLA will continue to be here in the future.

Procrastination

Procrastination is one of the biggest common character traits among clutterers. It exacerbates all types of cluttering problems—physical clutter, mind clutter, time clutter, and relationship clutter.

Procrastination: If It Feels So Good, Why Does It Hurt So Bad?

Spring 2014

Anonymous

When it comes to clutter, procrastination is often our way out. We set out to get rid of an old treasured flute we haven't used in years. It's the one that's been taking up space in our closet. We'll give it away. There's someone out there just waiting for this flute.

But what if we want to play again? Panic sets in. Suddenly, sorting the laundry never looked so good. But we're left with flute clutter—much to the chagrin of our spouses and our psyches.

We learn from CLA that our clutter is a symptom of a problem and that we often engage in self-destructive behavior. For me, procrastination is one of those behaviors. According to the many articles on this popular topic, its causes can be quite complex.

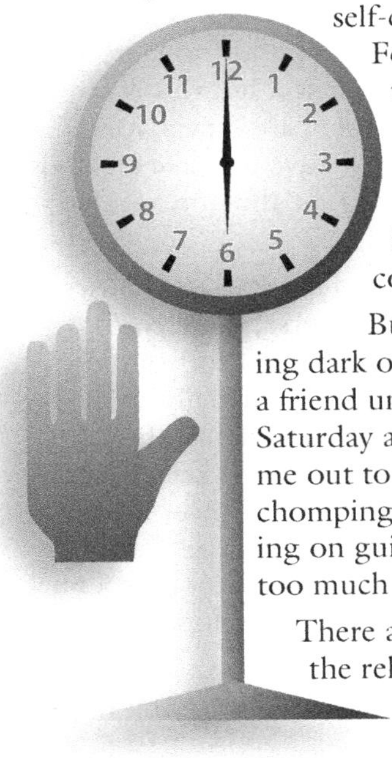

But sometimes it's nothing dark or deep. I love when a friend unexpectedly calls on a Saturday afternoon and invites me out to lunch. Now if I'm chomping on lettuce and chewing on guilt, this might not be too much fun.

There are other times when the relief of putting off a difficult task outweighs the guilt of not doing it. Sometimes I'm just prolonging the pain of whatever it is that's stressing me out. But hanging onto that task can clutter my mind and zap me of the mental energy I need to be doing other things, like enjoying my favorite TV show or pursuing my dreams.

If you talk to another clutterer or attend a CLA meeting, inevitably the topic of procrastination comes up. I've often heard other members say, "Well, clutterers are procrastinators" to explain our sometimes exasperating behavior.

Fear is often a top reason that we procrastinate. It can show up as the seemingly mundane fear of boredom to a more typical fear, like that of rejection.

Difficulty with decision-making is integrated with other reasons. In this example, decision-making is negatively affected by perfectionism: he can't figure out where to put the painting because he can't decide (fear of making the wrong decision) which location is best (perfectionism), so he puts off making the decision.

Below you'll find a list I've put together of why clutterers and non-clutterers alike procrastinate. This list is based on research and my own experiences.

Key Reasons for Procrastinating

- Fear: We're afraid to do something for some reason. This can be fear of: success, failure, rejection, the consequences, a confrontation, making a decision, making a mistake, etc.
- Decision-making: We're afraid of the consequences of our decision. We may also fear the pain of making the decision.

Other Common Reasons

- Rebelling: We don't do it because they told us to do it.
- Feeling overwhelmed: There's too much to do and we don't know where to start.
- Confusion: We don't understand something or something doesn't make sense.
- Perfectionism: We don't feel that we can do it perfectly.
- Carelessness: We can't do it because of errors on our part.
- Don't feel like doing it: It's too boring, dull, or not challenging enough.
- Don't know how to do it: We don't have the knowledge to do it.
- Can't handle it/do it: This one is a catch-all. For example, something unexpected or out of our control has occurred, or something is uncomfortable.

The above reasons may seem straightforward but can be loaded with unpleasant feelings such as anger, anxiety, frustration, and shame. For me, it's dealing with these feelings and their causes that makes procrastination so hard to beat.

As with cluttering, there are no hard and fast solutions for beating procrastination. For me, reviewing the CLA Tools of Recovery*[19] has been a good start, with bookending looking especially promising. To build awareness, I plan to catch myself when I procrastinate and identify which procrastination reason applies. I'll write down my findings and look for patterns. Hopefully, knowledge will be power.

There's also power in the experience, strength, and hope of other clutterers. In fact, CLA*rity* plans to share member stories about procrastination with you in future issues. So watch your mailbox for your next issue of CLA*rity*, where we'll continue discussing this popular unpopular topic.

*The Tools can be found in the leaflet, "A Brief Guide,"[5] and in the booklet, "Is CLA for You? A Newcomer's Guide to Recovery.[12]

Summer 2014

Alison B., NJ

In this article, we continue our discussion of clutterers as procrastinators. Here we have a personal account of one clutterer's experiences with mail and time procrastination.—Editor.

I'm truly surprised that I'm not putting off this article 'til the last minute—after all, there's still a week to go until the deadline. I had about two months to write it, and I had intended to start when I had some fantastic ideas to make it funny and poignant; but now, alas, these ideas have gone right out of my head. It serves me right.

Procrastination is truly a disease for me. I tend to push away an important chore by not thinking about it until fear overwhelms me because of time restraints, making it so crucial to get it done quickly. At some point, panic actually sets in, and by that time I feel as if I need someone to help me complete the task. Then I have to bookend because I just think I can't manage whatever it is; but underneath it all, I know I probably can if I break it down into small, doable parts.

My latest and not-too-greatest habit is letting the mail pile up for several weeks before I deal with it. This is because I have a lot of unfounded fear about dealing with mail. I don't know why. I tell myself that nothing bad will happen because I pay all my bills automatically and those are the only things of any consequence, but this is not strictly true. Sometimes there are crucial forms that I overlook, and then I have to make all kinds of excuses for myself and hope the bureaucrats will be accepting.

It's not the finest way to live life, as it causes even more stress. And, of course, there comes a day when I have to sit down and sort out all my mail at once, which I would actually enjoy doing if it weren't mine. It's the filing part I don't like. I never know whether to keep it or let it go, and I'm sure I keep far more than I need. Then there's the shredding. I have to fill a whole waste basket before I will do that. I'm now a bit paranoid about throwing away my printed name and address.

There are certain areas where I'm trying to get

ahead of my procrastination. I tend to run late because I have so many thoughts floating around in my head as I'm going through my morning routine. Also, I'm very slow in my movements. Now I try to time myself so that I can be ready ahead of time and, on top of that, give myself at least 15 minutes more to travel than I really need.

A checklist is also a wonderful tool that I sometimes use. If I need directions, I print them out several hours ahead of time or even the day before. I have a GPS, too, but I like to make sure I have two sets of directions. I'm still late some of the time because I can't seem to move as fast as I would like at home; but on the whole, this philosophy has saved me on many occasions.

I'm so proud of myself because I'm getting much better.

Procrastination–The Demon in My Life

Fall 2014

Kathy H., CA

In this article, we conclude our discussion of clutterers as procrastinators. Here we have another personal account of one clutterer's experiences with procrastination.—Editor

Why do I procrastinate? I have never been able to figure out why; I just know that procrastination has been at the root of most of my troubles: my physical clutter, missed deadlines, and even doing some things I wanted to do just for enjoyment.

My habit of procrastination has caused many roadblocks to a happy, fulfilled life. There was a time, before I joined CLA, when I became engulfed in debt—not because I charged outrageously, but because I kept procrastinating on paying the bills. The money was in the bank, but I would decide to take care of the payments another day. Of course, when another day came, I would forget until the bills were way past due—thereby generating late fees.

I also missed out on many opportunities because of procrastination, which sometimes caused me a lot of anguish. There was the time I had put off returning a phone call—for no particular reason, just my usual procrastination. When I finally did call a few days later, I learned that some relatives had been in town, but I had missed them because no one could get in touch with me. Had I returned the call right away, I would have enjoyed the visit instead of feeling an immense regret for the lost opportunity.

My difficulty keeping commitments has led to friction with friends, family, and acquaintances.

Of course, my physical clutter piled up because I usually put off doing things "until tomorrow." Often, tomorrow was many days, weeks, months, or years away. I used to procrastinate on putting away laundry. I ended up with piles of clothes at the foot of the bed, on top of the hampers, and on any other flat surface in the bedroom. It didn't help that my closets and drawers were overfull with clothes I could no longer wear but had not yet gotten rid of. Other rooms had just as big a problem, especially my sewing room and kitchen.

I kept trying to push away the thoughts of unfinished tasks and problems rather than dealing with them. All of this weighed on my mind so much that it added to my mental clutter and stress.

But how have I tackled this demon of procrastination? The CLA program has been my savior. I try to remind myself daily that my Higher Power is in charge, and I just need to follow that guidance.

Where does the guidance come from? Partly, it is a little voice that comes if I become still enough to hear it. Partly it comes from working the Steps and using the "CLA Tools of Recovery."[19] My sponsor has me doing two things: at night before I go to bed, I review my day to see what went right and wrong and where I need to make amends. And in the morning when I wake, I go over what I need to accomplish for that day. Reviewing the day helps alleviate the mental clutter, and having a firm goal for the day helps to set me on the path to accomplish tasks.

Often, when I find myself starting to procrastinate, I try to bookend with another CLA member. This has gotten me through some tough issues. When I use the Tool of Daily Action, I am not procrastinating on everything, at least.

Have I stopped procrastinating altogether? No; I still struggle, but I am trying to replace the habit of procrastinating with a habit of "get it done." I often have two people (or more) in my head: the one who wants to accomplish and the one that wants to ignore everything. I feel if I start going with the "get it done" one, that it will get strengthened, and the procrastination side will lose strength.

I guess in a lot of ways, it all comes down to what habits I establish. And thanks to CLA, I have started on the road of replacing the demon of procrastination with the angel of accomplishment.

Meetings and Sessions

The CLA Tools of Recovery[19] state: "We attend meetings to learn how the program works and to share our experience, strength, and hope with each other..." This section includes informative material about meetings and also articles from the "Group Stories" column of CLA*rity*.

Group Stories

Keep It Going!

Summer 2008
Andrew S., MD

Starting up the Baltimore Wednesday night group was a labor of love. The group started meeting in October 2005. Attendance was inconsistent for months. Sometimes the founder was there by herself, week after week.

She was there to welcome anyone who came to the meeting to join in reading CLA literature and to learn about the 12 Steps of CLA, and she continued to keep the room open. She posted notices and was patient and persistent. Slowly, the group attendance grew steadily.

When I first attended this, my home meeting, in a room at a church, there were about ten people seated in folding chairs around a table. This was a typical turnout, as I found out after attending several more meetings. From the first meeting, this group felt right to me. I felt as if I was with friends.

After the closing prayer, the group often met for food and fellowship at a nearby restaurant. At other times, a group of us might go elsewhere for coffee or refreshments.

Things sometimes change, though. These days, the average turnout is more like three to five, sometimes less. It's different with fewer newcomers. I may not like the change, but I still go whenever I can.

I have visited CLA groups in several states. Some have low attendance, others don't. Some groups close up after years of operation; others never seem to get off the ground.

The most important thing is that we are still a group. One thing that helps is communicating with other groups about our challenges and sharing ideas on ways to keep our groups going.

Fall 2008
Kathy A., CA

Editor's Note: This article shows how one member's recovery has been positively affected by improving the group dynamics in the North Hollywood meeting. They took three months to consider the problem engendered by a disruptive member, studied and discussed what to do about it, and counseled the problem member. In the end, they adopted a short but to-the-point meeting protocol and remained firm about implementing it, in spite of threats and manipulation. The result has been a meeting with much recovery and positive energy.

What I Learned at CLA

When I came to Clutterer's Anonymous (CLA), I thought that I would learn tips on cleaning and organizing. I didn't know anything about 12-Step programs or how they worked, so I had lots of questions about how the Steps would help me clear my clutter.

At first, I had a negative experience in the group and almost quit; there was low energy, judgmental comments, arguing about how the meeting should be run, and crosstalk (interruptions). However, I was fortunate to join at the same time as someone who had recovery in other 12-Step programs. She knew that the negative experience was not normal. By giving me her experience, strength, and hope and by my being open-minded and willing to allow change and learn more, I took responsibility for my experience and realized that I could expect better for myself and the other people in the group. If I wanted a more positive experience, then I had to take action that was loving and caring for myself and to others. We can't change what we don't acknowledge.

I learned that the goal is actually learning about myself through the 4th-Step inventory, and, for me, it was learning how I could get back to feelings of inspiration and hope instead of hopelessness. Learning to focus on my positive qualities instead of beating myself up all the time allowed me more happiness. I also found that sharing with others was working for me, making me realize I wasn't alone, and I didn't need to stay stuck in isolation and feelings of worthlessness.

In reading the 12 Steps and the references to God or Higher Power, I was a little leery because of my conflicting religious experiences, some negative and some positive. Yet by staying open-minded, and being tolerant when literature referred to the word God, there was an opportunity for me to grow and change.

My spiritual growth came through unexpected circumstances. Spirituality is our personal relationship with our Higher Power; we do not need to be religious in order to be spiritual, and if we are religious, it doesn't mean we can't be spiritual also, because it can actually enhance our religious experience. I now realize that as I got in touch with my spirituality, I learned that my mental (emotional) clutter was manifesting in my physical clutter and vice versa. My clutter can drain my energy, and as I release my mental and emotional clutter, I am better able to let go of my physical clutter. As I let go of my physical clutter, I find my energy and hopefulness returning. I now have a vision of my space becoming a place where I can relax and be inspired, a place where I can entertain.

I got excited about what I was learning and shared my experiences with the group, which seemed to appreciate my focus on more positive, growth-oriented language. I also shared what I learned about affirmations—that all our thoughts and words are affirmations. If our thoughts and language are negative, we would have negative experiences. Yet when we plant seeds of positive affirmations, we start experiencing positive changes, and those changes bring more positive experiences. It has been a great experiment to see the difference in my life from when I was focused on fear, anger, and resentments, to when I shifted to being more grateful, forgiving, and loving.

All of this work brought me to an understanding that often we may be looking for an outside reason, excuse, or cause for our clutter; however, the answer is actually inside each of us—in what we think about ourselves and how we perceive our surroundings. I have also come to realize that the more I isolated myself from others, the worse my clutter became. My 4th-Step inventory made me realize that I often focus too much on my shortcomings, faults, fears, and resentments, instead of on my talents and what I do well, which is my life purpose.

Learning that each of us has talents, which are meant for us to share with others and that I don't have to do everything perfectly—that is what it is all about. For me, TEAM = Together Everyone Achieves More or Together Everyone Activates Miracles.

I am so grateful that through the CLA literature and the people I have met at the group, I have blossomed into a new, better me. While I saw myself as a shy, meek, insecure person, I learned I actually have a lot of knowledge and talents that I can share with others. In learning about my positive qualities, I have become more confident. I realize that as I change my inner beliefs about myself, my outer environment also changes to reflect this growth. Yet, what I appreciated most was discovering that, because we all have the ability to change, there is always hope. I feel blessed having met each person who has come and shared experience, strength, and hope; and I can see each one for the divine person he or she is.

Thank you for allowing me to share my story. I hope that it encourages others to share their experiences because you never know who you can help by telling your story.

Holiday 2008

Nuala, England

I want to tell you about our struggles to start and maintain a group.

Let me relate how I came to realise I had a hoarding/clutter problem. A friend and I were talking one day when the subject of clutter was raised. She told me about her difficulties with clutter. I was fascinated, as this was the first time I'd heard anyone identify cluttering as being a "condition." She suggested I look up hoarding on the 'net and cautioned me to put OCD (Obsessive Compulsive Disorder) beside it; otherwise I would get facts about squirrels and nuts! This I did, and wow, a light bulb flashed in my head! I had this illness/disorder/condition. I was relieved and angry—relieved that I had a name for what was wrong with me and angry because I had yet another condition to battle with. The relief won. I did some more searching on the 'net and found interesting articles on the subject.

I came across CLA and noted there was a London contact. This would-be member and I had several phone conversations and decided to meet, which we did at a railway station in London. He was in touch with a member in California (and subsequently I was, too) who guided us patiently and informatively. Somehow we attracted a few more members. Unfortunately, one of our members turned out to be a total control freak; we had countless discussions with this person at the meetings over the following months. The numbers fluctuated greatly—sometimes there were five or six at the meetings, other times just two of us. This member became very argumentative and wanted absolute control over every aspect of the meetings. It was a constant struggle to try to explain that no one was "in charge." Finally, not being able to dominate and manipulate us was too much for this individual, who stormed off and has not been seen since. The person did, alas, scare some members away, and they haven't been back since, either.

Through other (non 12-Step) groups (OCD/hoarding), we attracted a few more members. Having been in other Anonymous groups for many a day, I find CLA the most challenging.

We meet on a fortnightly basis in a central London hospital café. We have printed out some "door guy" posters and intend to put them up in suitable places. We also have a CLA dedicated cell phone. We need to encourage ourselves to get into action.

We may be slow, but we shall succeed!

Summer 2010

Kathy H., CA

When I started attending the Friday night meeting in Whittier, California, it was a thriving group. There were three core people who had begun the group, with a healthy attendance from other members as well. I heard a lot of recovery there, with a lot of emphasis on the program and on the Steps.

Then, one by one, the original core people left. One started a rigorous university program and had to choose between CLA and another 12-Step group for his remaining time. One developed health problems and was not able to attend any meetings outside her home. The third moved to another state.

Gradually, as the composition of the membership changed, the meeting seemed to focus less on recovery and more on problems. Eventually, there came a time when there were only two of us regularly attending—and we are close friends who speak several times a week anyway.

When week after week passed with only the two of us attending, except for an occasional newcomer who did not stay long, we began to think it wasn't worth maintaining the meeting. After all, we talked about our problems with clutter on a regular basis, anyway. And we had to drive almost 20 miles to get to the meeting—in rush-hour traffic. We were seriously considering closing the meeting and opening one closer to home (in fact, we called other former regulars stating that if it didn't pick up, we would cease coming). But every time we were about to do that, another newcomer would show up for a few weeks or months, and we would feel compelled to continue in that location so as not to desert them.

Then, almost a year ago, another newcomer came who stayed, and she is with us today. Then another came. And another. Now, most weeks, we have six or seven attendees, with one or two more occasionally. This influx of people has energized and revitalized the group. Two people have trouble keeping the excitement and momentum going, but with more members sharing who are serious about their recovery, the meetings have become vibrant again. We are beginning to see some recovery in those who have been with us a while; and we still keep getting occasional newcomers, some who stay, and some who don't, but we now have another good core group.

I would like to say that we took certain steps, which led to this new group dynamic. But all I can state is that we had begun talking about recovery more than problems. And perhaps we just got a good mix of people. Somehow everything came together, and we now have a wonderful group.

Someone stated recently that one thing that keeps their group together is gathering for fellowship after the meetings. We have just started doing that again in our group, and it's wonderful to get to know the other members in a more personal way. We are also trying to have some contact with members between meetings, to keep the recovery flowing.

I think one of the morals of our story is that, when leaders leave a group, other members need to pick up and carry the banner. Also, don't just assume that things are okay with newcomers if you don't hear from them. Designate newcomer contacts, and call the newcomers to see how things are. Recently, two of our members agreed to call those on the list, and, as a result, one member has returned to the group. After all, 12th-Step work is one of the keystones of success in any program.

Los Angeles Civic Center Group

Spring 2011 and Summer 2016

Kim, CA

My sponsor in another 12-Step program shared that he had a plan for starting a business in his too-cluttered garage. So he went to CLA and with support was able to declutter it.

That got me motivated, and I went to my first CLA meeting. It was a small group, but I was impressed as I listened to them share about clutter problems and solutions.

That left me hopeful, and I attended that meeting regularly for a while. I began decluttering projects, but I couldn't continue going to the meeting.

I work at the location where our CLA meeting is held today. There are about three other 12-Step Fellowships that meet there, and I attended one. Some of those members were complaining about problems with clutter. So after the meeting, I asked if they had ever been to CLA and said, "The people there are cool."

It was like those old movies—like, "Hey, kids, why don't we start a meeting?" I think all the others were jazzed about it, but they didn't go when the meeting started. So I got a format from another CLA meeting and started the Civic Center meeting. Since I couldn't get to a meeting, I started one.

We have a nice meeting, and a lot of our format was taken out of the original leaflets. We set aside a period for each member to make a commitment for the following week. We make these commitments and put them into our God Box. We remember the principles involved in the 12 Steps and that each week is a new beginning. I started doing that.

It was basically just keep coming back, and keep on trying whenever you fail, and use baby steps—using slogans[21] that are universal to 12-Step programs, not only ours. It had a spiritual aspect: God was doing for me what I could not do for myself.

I did Step 1: I was powerless over clutter, and my life was unmanageable. By coming to the meetings, I came to believe Step 2: that a power greater than myself could restore me to sanity. Using the Tools[19] and making weekly commitments to do things, as we do at our meeting, is like Step 3—that was the active decision. That wasn't my will—I was inspired by hearing in the meetings that someone was able to make progress.

It's so encouraging to newcomers that all you have to do is show up, and with just a little bit of effort you can get some momentum. You can get the help that you need in CLA.

People heard about that little meeting we started (and it's still small), and they wanted to hear that we were doing great—and that motivates me. It's not preaching or like a religion. It's more like—I'm so happy I found CLA that I would like to share it with you.

When I began the meeting, people who had been remanded by the court started coming. One person was going to be put in receivership because of the cluttering. Some came because landlords had complained about them, and they were about to get evicted. The result of their cluttering was the unmanageable aspect of their lives, and they couldn't have friends come over. Being with other clutterers broke me of that self-obsession and absorption. It helped me to become compassionate and stop being so self-centered.

We learn to start with the simple things. First, go to meetings. Then, reach out to people on the phone. Then, become uncluttered.

I enjoy the experience of being there with other people working on their recovery. The fellowship of people working on the program has always helped my growth. And that is what I call the synergy of the program, which I could not get by spending money and going to a declutter-my-life class. I have become very encouraged about my own progress because of all this experience. I have learned all these healthy habits working the CLA program. We really do learn compassion and empathy and to get along with other people.

Springfield Groups' Expo Outreach

Spring 2012

The two Springfield, Massachusetts, groups put time, creativity, and team effort into organizing a CLA informational booth to "carry the message" at a local weekend women's expo on September 10–11, 2011.

First, the Friday night group spent two hours after their regular meeting developing the visual displays for the booth using brightly colored paper, glue, scotch tape, poster boards, and colored pens and markers. One was a framed collage depicting the topic "What is Clutter?"[22] and included photos of "a bed you can't sleep in," "a chair you can't sit on," and "a kitchen you can't cook in." The group framed letter-sized copies of "The Twelve Steps," "Affirmations,"[20] and "Am I a Clutterer?"23 from the CLA literature.

Second, the Monday group decided what to use for handouts. They chose the "CLA Meeting Directory," "Affirmations," "CLA Keep and Release Serenity Prayer," and "Am I a Clutterer?" One member got photocopies made and delivered before the event. Both groups donated copies of "Is CLA for You? A Newcomer's Guide to Recovery"[12] and CLA Literature Packs (consisting of the eight assorted, pastel-colored recovery leaflets) purchased in bulk a few months before the event.

Two members set up the booth on Friday during the day. All the tables and chairs, tablecloths, rugs, trash basket, and the filled candy dish were donated for the event by group members.

At the Friday night meeting, the group finalized the booth staffing schedule for Saturday and Sunday. One member covered each day, and other members provided periodic breaks and backup when needed.

Members enjoyed walking around at the expo to look at the other info booths and vendors but emphasized, "We tried very hard not to pick up all the free stuff and the free pens!"

Group members said they experienced a wide variety of questions and comments at the CLA booth, ranging from "outright laughter at the name Clutterers Anonymous" to people exclaiming, "I really need you."

One of the more challenging issues members encountered was general public "ignorance or misconceptions about clutterers." Some people initially thought it was a group of professional organizers. Other people asked if the members could provide much-needed "help and motivation to a family member" or friend of theirs who may have problems with clutter.

"We had to explain that we did not provide motivation for people. They had to want help," members said, adding that receiving the meeting directory, which includes face-to-face and telephone meetings, "gave comfort to some."

Many people inquired or commented about the TV/cable shows that focus on cluttering and hoarding—not surprising due to increasing media attention to the subject.

(Editors' Note: Tradition 10 states that "CLA has no opinion on outside issues," such as other programs, organizing systems, self-help books, celebrity speakers, professional methods, televised reality entertainment/education shows, and so forth.)

"Some clutterers have more clutter than others or different clutter," some members shared from their own experience. They referenced and presented literature to clarify for visitors that CLA is a 12-Step program patterned after Alcoholics Anonymous.

CLA's literature states that "anyone may join CLA, regardless of age, gender, race, color, nationality or creed." CLA's Tradition 3 states, "The only requirement for CLA membership is a desire to stop cluttering"—regardless of the amount, as clutterers may have varying quantities and types of clutter, degrees of or manifestations of cluttering.

The Springfield groups' expo display was for educational, public information purposes: "to carry this message of recovery to clutterers who still suffer," as the Preamble to Clutterers Anonymous states.

"All-in-all, the booth was a success. We ran out of copies of meeting directories, which we thought was a good sign." As one member concluded, "We planted a lot of seeds in the community, and we are waiting for some growth."

—Based on a submission from the Springfield, MA, groups

Summer 2013

Here are some of the tools we use at our group in Teaneck, New Jersey (everything is voluntary, of course, no pressure):

The commitment list is a very helpful tool. We take time to write our individual commitments for the following week. It helps us organize our goals regarding our clutter. We use our commitment form or a notebook to write our lists, and then each person reads theirs aloud.

A week later, we have a one-minute follow-up on the commitments, reporting our success and/or lack of progress. Lauren says, "At the same time as I know the group is rooting for me and I want to be successful in part for them, I also feel comfortable when I have failures because no one else in the world can empathize with me the way my group can."

Between meetings, we make a committed phone call to keep in contact and to support our efforts. We write our name, phone number, date, and commitments on slips of paper we fold up and all put into a can. Then we each pull one out and call that person during the week. We can review commitments or provide other support.

We pass around a "We Care" phone list so we can contact each other more casually as well.

Members of our group have socialized outside of the meetings, releasing us from 12-Step strictures. This strengthens our feelings of community.

Meeting Registration

CLA Votes to Institute Yearly Meeting Registration

Holiday 2011

Earlier this year, the CLA World Service Organization (WSO) voted to set up a committee to form a policy for instituting group registration. On September 24, WSO voted to accept the document titled "Meeting Registration Guidelines." The vote on the "Suggested Group Guidelines" was tabled until the December meeting.

WSO is now authorized to begin conducting yearly registration of CLA groups. Beginning next year, any group that wishes to be listed in the CLA Meeting Directory (formerly the CLA Meeting List), either in print or on the CLA website, must register with WSO. This will ensure that group information is more current than it has been in the past, and it will avoid many instances of clutterers being sent to meetings that either have changed time or location or no longer exist.

Information on the registration process, including the guidelines and registration forms, will be sent to CLA groups. Registration can be either by printed form or online, but the committee prefers that groups register online.

Registration Committee Update

Spring 2012

On September 24, the CLA World Service Organization (WSO) voted to accept the document, "Meeting Registration Guidelines." The document, "Suggested Group Guidelines," was approved at the January 28 WSO meeting.

Implementation of the registration process is on hold until a new webmaster is contracted to update the ClutterersAnonymous.net website. Registration forms will be available for submitting online or for printing and submitting by postal mail. Online registration is preferred.

Meanwhile, the committee will be working on procedures for registering delegates to WSO. The registration of delegates has several reasons: (1) to identify those people who are eligible to vote at WSO meetings, (2) to enable WSO to maintain better records, (3) to improve communication between WSO and the meeting delegates, and (4) to smooth the voting process. As with meeting registration, the final product will include both guidelines and forms for registering delegates.

Meeting Registration: It's No Trivial Matter

Fall 2014

Imagine this: You want to attend a CLA meeting as a visiting member or a newcomer, so you look for one. Good, there's one on the website or you see it in the CLA Meeting Directory and then travel there—maybe even driving an hour or more—only to find that there is no meeting!

After that unfortunate experience happened to several clutterers, the CLA World Service Organization voted to require annual registration of all CLA recovery groups in order for their meeting information to remain in the directory—both online and in print.

A Registration Committee was established to formulate a policy and oversee meeting registrations. The first registrations were due by December 31, 2013. Each subsequent year, meetings are required to submit a new Meeting Registration Form by December 31 in order to stay listed in the directory. The form is also used to update the group's meeting location, time, and any other vital information.

How can each member help with this? If you attend a regular face-to-face group, please double-check to make sure your meeting has sent in its current registration—even if the group is well established and has been in the directory for years, it must still register each year.

So that our meeting directory is accurate, group registration forms will be sent out annually to the meeting contacts on file, but if your contact information has changed, let the committee know. The Meeting Registration Form will be made available on the website.

By keeping an up-to-date directory, CLA hopes to eliminate the emotional stress and needless time clutter caused if a meeting is not where it states it is when newcomers or out-of-town visitors—or any clutterer who still suffers—go to the location based on the directory.

Be sure to register your group right away! To all the meeting contacts and members who are helping with this, the CLA Fellowship thanks you.

CLA Meeting Registration

Holiday 2015

As we are nearing the end of our second year of annual CLA meeting (group) registrations, it seems a good time to reflect on the process.

Since December 31, 2013, each CLA meeting has had to register yearly in order to remain on the CLA meeting directories. The directories—which list all CLA face-to-face and phone meetings—are located at ClutterersAnonymous.org and are also available in printed form.

It is by referring to the directories that newcomers and current members alike find CLA meetings to attend. Also, the voicemail correspondent (who responds to messages left on the CLA telephone line) and the webmail correspondent (who responds to emails sent to CLA WSO) use the information in the directories to help clutterers find meetings. So it is very important for a meeting to be listed on the directories to attract new members.

Yearly meeting registration wasn't always required to remain on the directories, so why did WSO begin requiring it two years ago? The primary reason is to keep the directories accurate. There have been instances in the past when CLA members or newcomers tried to attend a listed meeting, only to find, after arriving, that the meeting had moved its time or location or was no longer active. In fact, some meetings had been closed for years without anyone notifying WSO. With yearly registration, the directories should be more up to date.

Initially, meeting registration was due on December 31 of each year. Since this is often a busy time for many, WSO decided to move the deadline to March 1. Meetings will be sent registration forms by January 1.

At this time, the only way to submit a registration form is by (1) downloading it as a file, filling it out, and emailing it to the Registration Committee, or (2) by printing it and sending it via postal mail. It is expected that sometime in the near future, it will be possible to fill out and submit the forms online.

If the CLA Registration Committee doesn't receive the annual registration, that meeting may be removed from the directories. Every effort will be made by the committee to reach out to that meeting's contact person, but CLA requests that meeting contacts please complete and submit their registration forms by the deadline.

So talk to those at your meeting and remind them that your group contact needs to submit its registration form each year. If there are no changes, the contact person needs to fill in only the Group Service Number, the name of the person submitting the form, and check "yearly registration." If there are changes, all applicable sections should be filled in.

If there is trouble in filling out or submitting the form, contact the Registration Committee via one of the methods listed on the form, and help will be given.

Other Articles on Meetings

Hold the Line: CLA 12-Step Phone-Based Meetings

Spring 2008
Parker, NV

For years, meeting face-to-face was the only option for members of Clutterers Anonymous. Technology and member ingenuity eventually merged to create a new meeting environment—on the telephone. There are now phone-based CLA 12-Step Program meetings nightly, each with a different recovery focus and format.

The phone-based Fellowship is growing, partly because of the accessibility from all parts of the USA, as well as from other countries. The convenience and being able to connect without leaving home or office are just two reasons why many make phone meetings a part of their recovery program. The telephone is among the CLA Tools of Recovery.[19]

Phone-based meetings are also helpful for those who attend face-to-face meetings but want to increase their meeting frequency or who are shut in temporarily due to inclement weather. And phone-based CLA 12-Step meetings are sometimes the only way to connect for those who are homebound or otherwise unable to travel easily, such as members with temporary or long-term physical disabilities or other mobility impediments.

Phone conferencing companies use multi-caller lines and other advanced technologies, which allow the phone meetings to average between 15 and 50 participants, depending on the format and day. For some callers, there may be long-distance, per-minute fees or other charges, depending on their local telephone service carrier and long distance calling plan.

CLA literature reading is a part of nearly every meeting. Some meetings have Q&A formats, where the chair or organizer of the meeting—a member who does service by leading the meeting—reads prepared questions and asks for participants to write on the topic and then share.

Other meetings are sharing meetings, without writing, and often have a CLA member share his or her qualification. The speaker-qualifiers talk for about 20 minutes on any aspect of their CLA recovery or experiences with clutter. Newcomers are always welcome to attend any phone meeting and can also qualify, even if the time in recovery is short.

So, whether members attend local face-to-face meetings or phone-based meetings or both, the CLA phone-based Fellowship invites members to attend any of the following formats and days:*

- Sunday: Writing on Nonphysical Clutter
- Monday: CLA Literature Reading and 12 Traditions (one each month)
- Tuesday: CLA Steps 1–3
- Wednesday: Speaker-Qualifier/Share Topic
- Thursday: Reading on Nonphysical Clutter
- Friday: Q&A Writing and Reflections
- Saturday: "Home: Our Sacred Space"

To access the meetings any evening at 8 p.m.* Eastern Time, call (712) 432-2222, then enter 54576# when asked for the access code. Check the website, www.clutterersanonymous.org, for regular updates and changes to CLA meetings.

How to Start a Clutterers Anonymous Meeting

Holiday 2010

Order the "CLA Meeting Starter Kit"[7] from the CLA Literature Order Form or send $15† suggested donation to CLA, PO Box 91413, Los Angeles, CA 90009. All materials needed are contained in the Starter Kit; it's self-explanatory. Included are five complete sets of our recovery leaflets, a meeting format, and a copy of the new 28-page newcomer's booklet. Anyone can lead a meeting or read any of the included pages. If you can read, you can lead the group! Visit the website or contact Clutterers Anonymous World Service Organization (WSO) for international prices.

Learn about the program by reading CLA literature. Attend existing CLA face-to-face or phone meetings or meetings of other 12-Step groups (such as Alcoholics Anonymous) to see how the program works. For meeting information, check ClutterersAnonymous.net.

Find someone to work with you. It is easier to start a meeting if two or three people are willing to commit to attending regularly for a few months. Often we have friends who have too much stuff, such as we do! Ask if they're interested in seeking a support group for help. It is important that the group founders take their commitment seriously.

Good places for meeting spaces include churches of all denominations, temples, schools, hospitals, libraries, banks, and community or senior service centers (especially those that rent to other 12-Step groups). Ask what the organization requires regarding rent, key arrangements, insurance, etc. When newcomers show up, they need to find the meeting. Putting up signs and directions at the location helps direct people to the room you use.

You can attract new members through the following methods:

- Make announcements at existing CLA meetings.
- Display flyers in public places, such as libraries, churches, temples, schools, markets, bulletin boards, hospitals, banks, senior centers, and places where other 12-Step meetings occur.
- Contact local media to place free announcements. Be sure to follow the guidelines of Tradition 11.
- Register with the closest self-help clearinghouse, often listed in the telephone yellow pages or online directory.
- Get free listings in local newspapers and in online listings under 12-Step support groups.
- See about being listed in the printed schedule of the organization at your meeting location.

After your meeting begins, elect officers, such as secretary, treasurer, and WSO delegate. (See the Starter Kit[7] for more details.)

Fill out the "CLA Meeting Information Sheet" located in the Starter Kit and send to WSO to let it know of your existence. (See Frontispiece for contact information.) It will provide you with support and add your meeting to both the online and printed meeting lists. Don't forget to notify WSO of any changes in meeting information or contact person. WSO will make referrals to you from newcomer inquiries, as well as from those who are traveling or seeking to join a group. Please keep us informed of your new group's progress.

Enjoy the process. Share the work as much as possible. Call on WSO for help. Good luck!

Whose Meeting Is It, Anyway?

Holiday 2011

Katie M., CA

I didn't intend to write this article. At least, not this ending.

I'd been attending and giving service in other 12-Step programs for years. Clutter snuck up on me in middle age. I came to CLA in an abject state of "pitiful and incomprehensible demoralization." At my cluttering bottom, my mail, bills, and checks vanished for months on end. Overwork, health concerns, elderly and dying parents added to my frustration. I was running faster and faster to no avail. Depression, exhaustion, illness, and grief made even the most elemental tasks seem overwhelming. I was in danger of drowning in clutter.

A 12-Step friend told me about CLA. Clutterers Anonymous meetings were few and far between. I found some but was underwhelmed. They seemed to be stuck in a rut. I didn't hear the recovery, application of Tools,[19] working of Steps, and practicing of the Traditions I'd become accustomed to at other 12-Step meetings. However, my recovering friend had the compassion; commitment to recovery; and experience, strength, and hope I craved. We became clutter buddies.

With his example and support, I reclaimed my home. I banished the Can't Have Anyone Over Syndrome (CHAOS). I entertained. I dated. I was happy.

Then my friend moved far away. The dropping shoe kicked me solidly in the rear as it fell. Goodbye, clean home and happiness. Hello, major depression. Clutter came back with a vengeance, worse than before. I remember sitting in my car for 20 minutes, not wanting to enter my messy home.

Needing to know I was not alone, I returned to meetings, looking for a clutter buddy. Local meetings are few, far between, and small. I found people to bookend with and did clutter buddying work with someone for a while, until she quit coming to meetings. Sponsors? I didn't find any.

When A.A. started, it was one drunk helping another drunk. CLA is another kettle of fish. Yes, some of us may be agoraphobic, have mental health problems, be chronically disorganized, or have attention deficits. Severe clutter can turn even the most social person into a recluse. Whatever the reason, I have found attendance at meetings sparse and recovery hard to find. Old-timers have experienced months on end when they were the only people to show up at meetings. Twenty years after CLA began, it seems we are still toddlers. Maybe there's more recovery in phone meetings. I don't know. I doubted I'd find a local clutter buddy in a nationwide phone meeting. The program is only as strong as its participants. A meeting is only as strong as its members. From my perspective, we've got a long way to go.

Not only is it hard to find a clutter buddy or a sponsor at face-to-face meetings, rotation of service appears to be nonexistent.

How can we be a program of attraction when face-to-face meetings become irrevocably associated with their most assertive or long-time members? In my area, CLA members don't refer to the name, location, or date of the meeting (with one or two notable exceptions). Instead, it is "Member X's meeting" or "Member Y's meeting." Meetings become synonymous with the person who has ended up as secretary for life by default.

"Our leaders are but trusted servants; they do not govern." These words are read at every CLA meeting. It is agreed that our Fellowship encourages rotation of leadership. Yet in the absence of rotation of leadership and unwillingness of other members to step forward and take on service positions, it is so easy for officers and old-timers to forget that they do not govern. I've seen "Member Z" fail to implement a minor change in the meeting format adopted by group conscience and claim the change (which she opposed) was voted down. I've been yelled at by another member during the middle of a share on a Tradition for referring to A.A.'s *Twelve Steps and Twelve Traditions*[16] to quote a phrase relevant to my point.

I am pointing my finger at myself, too. I struggle with being a trusted servant—not a controlling autocrat—at meetings I care about deeply or those in which I hold service positions.

Six months ago, a friend and I started a new meeting. We designed the format to emphasize action, recovery, and service and to give people a reason to keep coming back. We elected a secretary, treasurer, literature person, CLA*rity* representative, and World Service delegate. Each week, the leader asks for a volunteer to lead the next week. We hold monthly business meetings. A portion of our 7th Tradition is donated to the World Service Organization to help carry the message to others who still suffer. We recite the CLA Responsibility Pledge before the closing prayer and "keep coming back."

After several months, we talked about what was working and what wasn't. We streamlined the format, discarding things which weren't working and trying some changes requested by members.

This discussion was hard for me. I'd invested my heart and soul in the meeting format. Some features I had thought essential annoyed a member who wanted to keep it simple. Unlike some other local meetings, this meeting asked for a show of hands to share. Sharing was initially limited to the week's topic, then opened to general sharing with time set aside for newcomers.

As we reviewed the format, an old-timer suggested we dispense with hands and just go around the circle. My body visibly tensed and a vehement "No!" escaped my lips before I was able to relax and really listen to the old-timer's comments. I needed, I absolutely needed, to attend a CLA meeting structured to emphasize shares on working the program and recovery. None of the other meetings in this area asked for a show of hands and topical sharing. This other member did not share my need. It took effort to relax, trust, listen, let go, and let God.

I'm sure my resistance affected the old-timer. I made amends the next day, but I feel the rift is still there. I'm making a living amends by letting go of my desire to control and micromanage the format.

Releasing the meeting to my Higher Power means stepping down as secretary at the end of my six-month term. I'd been planning to do that from day one. I'm willing to do service in another position. But continuing as secretary is not in the meeting's best interest or mine. The impulse to insist on things I want and reject suggestions that fly in the face of my vision is still there. We're a Fellowship of men and women with the common purpose of recovering from cluttering. Becoming the "stage manager," as referred to in Chapter 3 of *Alcoholics Anonymous* [4] (the "Big Book"), is a sure road to relapse.

Recently, the meeting held elections. No one wanted to become the secretary. Someone offered to take it over if she were not responsible for finding speakers. I offered to lend a hand in speaker selection if we established a Speaker Seeker Committee.

The next day, our new secretary decided she couldn't take it on. I offered to quit attending the meeting. My commitment to rotation of service and providing opportunities for leadership development trumped any founder's pride and emotional investment in the meeting. However, working with me was only one factor in the new secretary's resignation. She still wanted to step down.

Whose meeting is it, anyway? Certainly not mine. Absolutely our Higher Power's.

The answers will come when our own houses are in order. And I have no clue what the answer will be. All I can do is turn it over and show up.

At our next meeting, I plan to ask for a group conscience permitting us to suspend a portion of our format. We need to talk. If there is not sufficient interest in and commitment to the meeting, perhaps it's run its course. I don't know. It's the group's decision, not mine. All I can say now is "more will be revealed."

Release Victory Session

Holiday 2014

Kathy, NJ

On Sunday, February 23, 2014, a new tool was added to the CLA phone lines. It's a daily session that begins at 7:30 p.m. Eastern Time, where we share our daily release victories. Each person shares for one to two minutes on what was given away, recycled, thrown away, returned, or shredded that day—or since the last time he or she shared.

The session begins with the Organized Life Serenity Prayer and ends at 7:54 p.m. with the Keep and Release Serenity Prayer.

It began with an idea I had been thinking about for months that it would be nice to hear about the physical clutter CLA members released from their homes each day, in the hope that those shares would inspire and motivate others to do the same.

It was a quiet night on Saturday, February 22, in the After Meeting (after 9 p.m., following the 8 p.m. recovery meeting). The moderator asked if anyone had anything to share, so I felt it was a good time to throw out this idea. Everyone got so excited hearing it. Lorraine from California immediately came up with a Release Victory Session script and encouraged me to start this new session the following night, before the 8 p.m. nightly CLA recovery meeting.

Each night at 7:30, many CLA members join this positive session to share their release victories. The moderator congratulates the sharers on their successes of releasing physical clutter, wishes them success on future releases, and invites them to come back and share. We celebrate all victories, no matter how small. Each share motivates many listeners to release physical clutter. All it takes is hearing one person share about cleaning out a refrigerator, food pantry, medicine cabinet, makeup drawer, junk drawer, closet, car, etc.

Many listeners pick up that energy and come back the next night to say they were inspired and proceeded to clean out their own refrigerator or medicine cabinet or whatever.

Other sharers show up with long lists of items they released or the total pounds of paper released. I then started actually weighing my junk mail and was surprised to discover that I release 20 pounds biweekly. The huge amount of paper being released motivated many to get their names removed from as many mailing lists as possible.

Many CLA members share that they now realize their clutter is just "stuff" and are no longer attached to it. Our mindset is changing. We look forward to releasing and sharing our successes with all on the Release Victory Session. Some CLA members have said that this session is their lifeline in letting go of clutter.

We have CLA members who share their expertise in composting, recycling, or shredding, which has helped us all be mindful of the importance of keeping our environment clean.

Releasing clutter has never been so much fun! We are letting it go with a big smile on our faces and feel reNEWed. Please join us every evening at 7:30 p.m. on (712) 432-3900, access code 727176*. The CLA Tool of Trust says, "We simplify our lives, believing that when we need a fact or an item, it will be available to us."

Disruptive CLA Members and the 12 Traditions

Spring 2016

Unfortunately, members sometimes disrupt CLA meetings, business meetings and/or activity sessions. Most of the time, the disruptions resolve themselves. but occasionally, the disruptions interfere with the effectiveness of the meeting or session.

For the purpose of this article, we are using the word "meeting" to refer to CLA recovery meetings—both face-to-face and phone—and phone activity sessions.

It is important to keep in mind that clutterers who disrupt meetings are in recovery themselves and deserve to be treated with kindness and compassion in accordance with our 12 Steps and 12 Traditions.

Here are ways in which disruptions can conflict with some of our 12 Traditions.

Tradition 1:

"Our common welfare should come first; personal recovery depends upon CLA unity."

When disruptions occur, group unity is compromised. Disruptions may cause so much anxiety that members stop attending meetings or even leave the CLA Fellowship altogether. When this happens, clutterers may be unable to get the support they need from CLA.

Tradition 4:

"Each group should be autonomous except in matters affecting other groups or CLA as a whole."

Disruptions can potentially affect CLA as a whole by negatively impacting CLA's reputation as a welcoming 12-Step organization that offers hope to clutterers. Disruptions may also negatively affect overall group morale and may spill over into other groups as well.

Tradition 5:

"Each group has but one primary purpose—to carry its message to the person who still suffers."

Disruptions make it harder for members to carry that message because the disruption—and not recovery—often becomes the focus of the meetings.

Tradition 12:

"Anonymity is the spiritual foundation of all our Traditions, ever reminding us to place principles before personalities."

Disrupters may believe they know what's best for the group, when in actuality they do not represent the group's interests. Per Tradition 1, our common welfare should come first, not that of any individual member.

When followed, the 12 Traditions provide an excellent guide for the smooth functioning of CLA.

For more information on disruptive behavior, see the CLA-approved "Code of Conduct," which is printed on page 6 *[of the Spring 2016 issue]* and included in the CLA Meeting Starter Kit.[7]

Group Decluttering Project

Fall 2016

Mickey M., AZ

It came to our attention that a local newspaper sometimes has a list of charities requesting donations. Noting that clothing was being collected for an earthquake relief fund, it was announced to members of our face-to-face meeting and was met with enthusiasm. Two members also had a collection of 3-ring binders they wanted to donate. Yet another member had notebook paper to give away. The following Sunday the clothing, notebooks, and paper were gathered from the members, with the clothing going to the relief fund and the rest to a youth symphony orchestra.

One of the most pressing matters with clearing out clutter for many clutterers is the anxiety that the useful items do not end up in the landfill but instead go to people and organizations that need them. We were all happy to find excellent places for our donations. The best part of this drive was the worthwhile decluttering as part of the process.

Giving Away Items to Group Members

Summer 2014

The CLA*rity* team was asked the question: When we declutter, is it okay to either exchange items with other clutterers or to give them away (without trading)? During a discussion of this question, the following thoughts became clear.

Pros:

While some clutterers get to give away clutter, other group members are happy to receive items that they otherwise wouldn't have been able to obtain. It helps the environment if something is given away rather than thrown away. It could save time because it saves one clutterer a trip to a resale or thrift shop and another clutterer the time it would take to shop for the same item. Sometimes it could be a great experience.

Cons:

For the person giving an item away, there could be resentment if no one is interested in accepting the item—since we all have different tastes—or if another member accepts the item but never uses it. This may be more obvious when it concerns a wearable item. In the case of clothing, it could be difficult for the one giving it up to see another wearing a donated item, since the emotional attachment may still be pulling at the donor.

Also, some members in the group may have difficulty in saying "no" to something free even when they have no use or place for it, so it could create more clutter for the donee, who may end up feeling resentful because of it. Some members may accept the item and then keep it even when they can't use it because they feel guilty in throwing away a gift. Also, it could cause regret if a member doesn't accept the item and later has a change of heart.

Because of the emotional issues attached to the object for both the donor and donee, it could cause dissension in the group.

Conclusion:

Our comments were based on the collective experience and reflections of the CLA*rity* team. These comments were meant to be informational only and are not recommendations in any way. We hope that by presenting the pros and cons for sharing or trading one's clutter with other CLA members, you think about how this might apply in your own group. We understand that how we get rid of clutter is personal to every clutterer and what may work for one group may not work for another.

Has sharing or trading clutter with other CLA group members been a practice of your group? We'd love to hear how that has worked out for you. You can reach us by using any of the methods in the frontispiece.

---

*Phone meetings may have changed focus, meeting times, phone numbers, and access codes since this writing. Check the "CLA Meeting Directory" at ClutterersAnonymous.org for current information.

†Price of the "CLA Meeting Starter Kit" will be increased to $20 as of January 1, 2018.

Clutterers Anonymous Events

Various organizations in CLA hold periodic events. Clutter-Free Days are one-day events held by intergroups or local alliances of meetings. CLA periodically holds weekend conventions, which are attended by members from around the US and other countries. Occasionally, the phone groups hold declutterthons.

Clutter-Free Days

Clutter-Free Day in New Jersey Innovates

Spring 2007

The 11th semiannual Clutter-Free Day (CFD) filled St. Luke's Episcopal Church on April 28th, with a theme of "Envisioning your Personal Recovery." The Metuchen, New Jersey, conference was hosted by Clutterers Anonymous East (CLA-East), an intergroup of approximately 30 CLA meetings. A record New Jersey attendance of 101 folks from eight states included dozens of CLA "newcomers."

The all-day program included 11 separate presentations, nine of which were captured on audio CDs. The offerings included two keynote speeches and nine workshops on subjects ranging from mental decluttering to sponsorship. The all-conference album or individual recordings were sold at the event and will continue to be available.

The next CLA-East CFD event is slated for a Sunday in October, possibly the 14th. Subscribe to CLA*rity* now, and we'll try to keep you informed. (Then, when you're finished with the issue, pass it on to a friend. That's two ways to do important service for as little as $4!)

Want more information about CLA recovery materials? Contact the WSO Literature Department at CLA WSO, PO Box 91413, Los Angeles, CA 90009; go to clutterersanonymous.org; or talk to your group's literature person.

Eleventh Clutter-Free Day: A Members' Report

Holiday 2007

Kathy H., CA

The second Clutter-Free Day in 2007 was held in Brooklyn, New York, on Sunday, October 14. The theme of the event was "The Joy of Decluttering: If You're Not Having Fun, You're Not Doing It Right!"

About 120 attended the day-long event, which included two keynote speakers from New York—Naomi, followed by Frederick. It featured many workshops on various subjects related to CLA and many aspects of cluttering.

I was very pleased to attend this, my very first CLA-East Clutter-Free Day. Although I did spend some time helping to staff the CLA*rity* table (and also was the presenter of one workshop myself), I made sure to attend both keynotes and another workshop session. Since motivation has been such a big problem in my decluttering, I made sure to attend Beryl's workshop, "Motivating Myself to Declutter."

I came out of that session with a whole bunch of notes and the hope that, by using some of Beryl's ideas, I could tackle one of the biggest stumbling blocks to my decluttering.

Several attendees told me they were pleased with the sessions they attended as well.

I found the conference to be well-organized and insightful. However, the highlight of the day for me was talking to other clutterers, meeting many for the first time. There were even two clutterers attending from Mexico City. They were in New York for another reason but had heard about Clutter-Free Day. One of the women, who is in another 12-Step program, would like to start a CLA meeting in Mexico City. She had not known about CLA before and was thrilled to find an organization that could meet her needs. That conversation absolutely made my day!

All in all, based on my experiences at this Clutter-Free Day, I can happily report that CLA seems to be alive and well on the East Coast.

Clutter-Free Day Report

Summer 2008

Mary P., NY

"Spring Cleaning" was the theme as the CLA-East Intergroup hosted a Clutter-Free Day May 3, in Metuchen, NJ. Clutterers came from as far away as Virginia and Massachusetts to attend the all-day event, the 13th one sponsored by the intergroup.

Mari delivered an engaging keynote. More than 80 attendees enthusiastically responded to an array of presentations, ranging from Frederick's "Perfectionism and My Clutter" to Beryl's "Spring Cleaning My Mind." Recovery concepts were the subjects of other workshops, such as Ruthe's on phone tools, Bob's on mantras, and Mary Agnes' on journaling. Other speakers tackled more emotional issues, such as "The Original Pain of Clutter" (Elaine), "The Costly Emotions" (Serena), and "Am I Ready…to Cope With Clutter" (Peter).

Andrew and Alison led a discussion on commitment and doing service, which got people thinking about how they could participate more meaningfully and yielded some pledges of future involvement.

"Motivational," "powerful," and "inspiring" were some of the ratings folks gave in evaluations they filled out.

The fellowship aspect was, of course, key. "It's good to know that normal, intelligent people have the same problem," said one person. "Informative and helpful and a learning-filled day," added another.

The healthy lunch snacks (coordinated by Maureen) got rave reviews, as well. There was plenty of time for fellow clutterers to meet and chat. About a third were coming to their first Clutter-Free Day, while others had been at many previous events.

About 20 came as a result of seeing the event on a CLA website. People who attend some of the nightly phone meetings enjoyed their first "face-to-face" CLA experience. Others had seen flyers in such places as their local public library, while many were on a mailing list from previous events.

The event struck most as well organized, except for a couple of crowded rooms and a few technical glitches with the audiotaping of some workshops. CDs of select sessions are available from the company that did the recording.

The next Clutter-Free Day is being planned for New York City in the fall.

Southern California Clutter-Free Day

Holiday 2008

The Southern California Clutter Free Day was held on Sunday, October 12, 2008, at Antioch College in Culver City, California, and was attended by more than 60 people. The day-long event included a keynote speaker, a "Problems and Solutions" Session, a "Vision for the Future"

Session, and a presentation on intergroups and WSO. It also included the following six workshops: "Spirituality," "Newcomers' Workshop," "Mind Clutter," "Motivation," "Writing Workshop," and "Action and the CLA Tools." We talked with several attendees to get their impressions of this Clutter-Free Day.

"I especially loved the workshops I attended—presented by Susie S. and Bonnie K. I came away with the knowledge of how important it is to include prayer, spirituality, and working the Steps in order to have any success in dealing with my clutter. We cannot do it alone, and our Higher Power is part of the equation."

"I was very impressed, and I think it should be amplified."

"I thought it was really great. From the standpoint of someone who has attended all 13 of the CLA-East Clutter Free Days, it has given me some ideas of things we may be able to add to ours. There were some very interesting features, like the 'Problems and Solutions' Session and the 'Vision for the Future.' The workshops I attended were great. I also loved the entertainment session."

"We definitely should work on a CLA conference or convention that would be presented on a broader scale."

"I liked that the presenters gave a short talk before we chose which workshop to go to. Susie's workshop on mind clutter was awesome."

"I think it would be a good idea to tape all the workshops and sell them as a complete package. This has made an incredible difference in my life."

CLA-East Clutter-Free Day

Fall 2009

Mary P., NY

CLA-East celebrated the 20th anniversary of the Fellowship with a successful Clutter-Free Day May 17 in New York City. About 115 people attended the all-day event, which was held at St. Francis College in Brooklyn Heights.

Cindy S., of Berkeley, CA, was the keynote speaker. She told a powerful recovery story. The closing celebration included a guided meditation by Lori and clutter-related song parodies by Alison B. Fellowship followed, with an anniversary cake and a fruit platter.

Participants came from Massachusetts, Virginia, and points in between, with large contingents from New York and New Jersey. About a dozen volunteers helped with hospitality, registration, literature, and CLA*rity*. Those attending ranged from newcomers to CLA and Clutter-Free Days to Betsey K., who has attended all 14 events.

Returned evaluations rated the day's events as very successful. On a scale of 1–4, the overall rating was 3.65, between good and excellent. "Good connections between people" was the most-often-cited positive aspect of the day.

People who had previously known other participants as voices on the phone meetings met each other "in person" for the first time. One person found "a lot in common with the speakers, strategies that worked, info on phone conferences, hearing commonalities, people in multiple Fellowships…reassuring." Another noted, "I loved all the workshops I attended. I love the variety of topics that we get to choose from!"

There were three workshops at a time, in three time slots. The topics were wide-ranging, from Frederick's "Spiritual Timing" to Mary Agnes's "Book Hoarding." Beryl spoke on "Getting Motivated to Declutter," and Ruthe presented on "Nonphysical Decluttering." Peter covered Steps 1–3, and Naomi spoke on linking Steps to strategies to eliminate clutter. Tova's topic was "Tools of CLA," and Andrew dealt with "Clutter and Relationships." Mary tackled the topic "Powerless over Paper."

The evaluations and a wrap-up meeting of the planning committee revealed that the day was well organized and helpful for those who attended. The workshops and keynote were taped; contact CLA-East for information on ordering. People picked up meeting lists and copies of the leaflets and newsletter. A CLA*rity* subscription was the raffle prize, and some attendees took the opportunity to subscribe on the spot. All in all, it was a good chance for fellow clutterers to meet and to observe the 20th anniversary of the Fellowship.

The First Berkeley Clutter-Free Day

Holiday 2009

Cindy S. and Sharon B., CA

The first Berkeley, California, Clutter-Free Day was held on Saturday, November 7, from 10 a.m. until 5 p.m. at the Lutheran Church of the Cross, on University Avenue, right down the street from the University of California at Berkeley. The event marked the third anniversary of the Berkeley CLA Tuesday morning meeting and was a resounding success on all counts, from number of attendees, to information shared, to fellowship extended. There are currently seven San Francisco Bay Area meetings within a 140-mile range. About 60 people attended, arriving from near and far—including Alameda, Albany, Berkeley, Castro Valley, Concord, Costa Mesa, Danville, Davis, El Cerrito, Fremont, Long Beach, Los Altos, Los Gatos, Martinez, Menlo Park, Moraga, Oakland, Palo Alto, Rancho Cordova, Richmond, Sacramento, San Francisco, San Jose, San Ramon, and Walnut Creek.

The theme for the day was "Using the Tools of Recovery[19] in CLA." All attendees were treated to presentations by the CLA WSO chair, Kathy, speaking about "What CLA Offers" and Susie, from CLA telephone meetings, talking about taking "Action and the CLA Tools." Berkeley CLA members presented individual sessions that attendees could choose, including a newcomers' meeting; "Daily Action" by Cindy; "Clutter, Kids, and Parenting" by Ingrid; "Where Did All this Stuff Come From" by Joan; "Working Steps 1–3" by Wendy; and "Forgiving Yourself" by Uzuri.

Highlights of the day were Uzuri's singing the welcome, as well as her rendition of Q's lyrics from the 2008 Los Angeles Clutter-Free Day. People were still laughing all day after attending Joan's session, where she shared things from her home as examples of her creativity and rationale for keeping things too valuable to release. The day culminated with an open microphone, where people could share with everyone. Some things shared were:

"I'm a single mom who uses the tool of a sense of humor and laughter. I am with my people at a CLA meeting. I know I am not judged or criticized. Thank you all. I urge you to attend meetings."

"My favorite session was on forgiveness. I liked looking around that circle of people and seeing myself a bit in everyone."

"I am so grateful to the people I heard from today. Even though we have unique stories, there are always similarities. I learned how to really connect via the phone meetings in ways that I didn't understand fully before. Celebrate! I learned to let go and trust. Good connections with people here today."

"I didn't expect to laugh so much today. Joan's workshop was freeing by the laughter of identification. I was able to relax and let things make connections in my mind that I hadn't noticed before in my idiosyncrasies. Maybe Joan would take that on the stage! Her workshop really lifted me after challenges trying to get here."

"When I found the Berkeley group, I really thought I was at the end of my rope....My friend went with me to my first meeting. I found people like me who understood! Like, oh, the closet, the office filled from the floor to the ceiling. I had to move out of my home of 17 years. Those CLA women helped me....I was frightened to let them in. But it was such a wonderful, beautiful thing that they did, to help me clean and sort and box. They asked me, 'Do you want to keep this or do you think you can let it go?' Every time I let it go, they cheered. And I got hooked on the cheers. CLA is a wonderful place of love and caring. Each of you understands what this is about. We are all working together to get to that other place. I thank CLA, the Fellowship, the members who allowed me to do my work today—for letting me be myself today. This is wonderful! Thank you."

The day ended with a discussion on forming a Bay Area CLA intergroup and doing another Clutter-Free Day. Sharon agreed to set up an intergroup conference call.

Before leaving, people handed in their plastic nametag holders and evaluations. Across the board, every single person said that the day "exceeded their expectations," with some sessions being called "exceptional." Written comments included: "Today was fabulous—I'm no longer alone with my shame, guilt, and paralysis. I understand what 'together we can' means now." "I came here today for motivation and inspiration—important enough to clear my cluttered calendar. I found what I've been looking for and plan to be a participant in this group and hope to help and be helped."

Everyone was moved when they joined hands to recite the "CLA Organized Life" Serenity Prayer (which had not been used previously at Berkeley CLA meetings).

God, grant me the serenity of an organized life
with leisure time,
The courage to change my habits to ensure
these joys,
And the wisdom to be flexible.

And God, grant me patience for the changes
that take time,
Appreciation for all that I have,
Tolerance for those with different struggles,
And the strength to get up and try again,
One moment, one hour, one day at a
time.

The Berkeley CLA wishes to thank everyone who did service, including support from previous Clutter Free Day committees, and everyone who attended—especially those who came up from the Los Angeles area to support the event and share their experience, strength, and hope.

What Is Clutter-Free Day?

Spring 2010
Anonymous

The Clutter Free Day (CFD) is a once- or twice-yearly event where Clutterers Anonymous (CLA) members, including newcomers to the program, can meet as many as 100 or more people willing to share their growth and progress through working the 12 Steps of CLA. It represents a coming together and a demonstration of the various methods of recovery achieved by the several CLA speakers and workshop leaders demonstrating how they've successfully worked the CLA program. They have often come out of self-imposed isolation and dared to challenge themselves to change their self-destructive habits. As a result, many have gained the upper hand and begun a new, more orderly way of life, on a path towards a healthier, more productive way of dealing with their possessions at home or at work.

Newcomers can begin the slow journey towards their eventual recovery from the high probability of getting worse in their cluttering addiction. In extreme cases, some could even possibly be evicted without newer, healthier habits.

Each of these regional events—held in California, New Jersey, and New York so far—is a unique opportunity to identify with dozens of others who share their experience, strength, and hope, who often have experienced many of the same shameful and embarrassing reactions to having landlords, managers, superintendents, service workers, friends, and family see how they keep house.

How much does it cost? It costs an average of $15.

But it also may be the beginning of the end of:

- living a life alone,
- being afraid of getting found out,
- fearing inspections, and
- pretending not to be home when someone knocks on the door.

Coming to a CFD is often the very first step for some of these frightened people whose dread and fears are diminished upon finding dozens of others who are just like them. Their secret, shameful, paralyzed burdens start to be lifted with the sometimes-sudden realization that others have the courage and the willingness to talk openly about their situations. They've come to realize that there's another option open to them. Talking about their problems tends to remove some of their guilt and lighten their load.

CLA-East Clutter-Free Day

Spring 2010
Marie M., NY

The CLA leaflet, "Finding Your Life Purpose"[10] says, "The order we seek is not organized clutter, but divine order." Divine Order is also the theme for CLA-East's Clutter-Free Day 2010, which will include a keynote speaker, a guided meditation, nine workshops on different topics relating to decluttering and Clutterers Anonymous. It will be held on Sunday, May 16, at St. Francis College in Brooklyn, New York, from 10 a.m. until 5 p.m.

A subcommittee of CLA-East is planning the yearly event. In addition to attending the workshops and hearing the keynote speaker, participants will have the opportunity to purchase CLA literature and meet more than 100 other CLA members from the East Coast. Guests will hear how others are working the 12 Steps and finding ways to create divine order in homes, apartments, and offices that once were cluttered.

If you want to be a part of the planning—or to volunteer to help at Clutter-Free Day—call (866) 800-3881 or send an email to clarity@claeast.org.

CLA-East's Annual Clutter-Free Day

Fall 2010

The 15th Clutter-Free Day, now an annual event, took place on May 16 at St. Francis College in Brooklyn Heights, NY. We have used this wonderful venue four times. It seems to work well because there are classrooms for workshops, as well as a large auditorium for when everybody needs to be in one room.

Approximately 100 people attended. We had a keynote speaker and nine workshops. All were rated highly by attendees' survey scores, and most sessions were recorded.

The theme for the day was "Divine Order." Workshop titles included: "Steps 1, 2, and 3"; "Spirituality"; "Collaborating with God"; "Beginners' Workshop"; "The Road to Acceptance —Finding Humor in our Cluttering"; "The Road of Life Doesn't Get Easier—We Get Stronger"; "Mourning Clutter"; and "Overcoming Procrastination."

The organizers asked people to (anonymously) evaluate everything that went on. Favorable comments were received on these aspects: good number and choice of workshops; being reminded that others share the same disease; seeing old friends; hearing new ideas; the free packet of literature that we gave to new attendees; nice to see people again and a nice lot of newcomers, too; the keynote speaker was especially good; and thank you for this informative day.

Suggestions and constructive criticism for next time included: provide ample coffee and water; enlist more volunteers to greet and work the tables; return to holding guided meditations; provide an entertainment segment, and print short descriptions of the planned workshops in the program flyers.

To comment, obtain copies of the sessions, volunteer, or attend an upcoming CFD event, email CLA-East at clarity@claeast.org.

Southern California 2010 Clutter-Free Day

Holiday 2010

"How I Work the CLA Program" was the theme of the Southern California Clutter-Free Day. It was held on November 6 at St. Bede's Episcopal Church in Los Angeles. The keynote speaker was Kim. He gave a stirring and humorous address.

There were nine workshops scheduled but presenters for only eight. Workshop topics were: "Car Decluttering" (Laura), "How the Program Works Me" (Alison), "Using Clutter Buddies" (Mori and Sally), "Using the Tools" (Kathy H.), "VAST: Vision, Action, Steps, and Tools" (Katie), "12 Steps" (Kathy A.), "12 Traditions" (Colleen), and a newcomer/beginners' workshop (Rod). The remaining "mystery" workshop was turned over to our Higher Power, and at the last minute Dina stepped up to the plate and presented one on Paper Clutter.

There was also entertainment given by Q, a panel of all Southern California CLA group contacts present, and a presentation by the CLA*rity* team. Lunch was also provided.

The more than 100 people who attended were all treated to a day complete with inspiration, information, and even some time for fellowship. Attendees came from all over Southern California, and even from as far away as New Jersey. It is hoped that an intergroup will be formed to plan an event for next year.

Planning a Clutter-Free Day

Spring 2011

The CLA-East Intergroup was formed in October 2001, originally because, although there was a quarterly face-to-face statewide meeting in New Jersey, we wanted to meet more often and to include surrounding states. We met in a few different locations and immediately elected officers, including chairperson, vice-chairperson, treasurer, secretary, and literature person. At the first meeting there were 15 members representing six meetings.

Since 2002, we have presented 15 Clutter-Free Days in New Jersey and New York City. Although we used to have them twice a year, we now have one annual event. We've learned a lot through trial and error and are in the beginning stages of compiling a guidelines manual to aid others in planning similar events. We are in the process of writing procedures so that even the planning of the event will be clutter-free. It is our hope that eventually there will be Clutter-Free Days all over the country!

In order to plan them successfully, we have recently developed a timeline, setting early deadlines for all tasks involved—from selecting the location and date to printing the program for the day's events. We've found it helpful to have telephone planning meetings every two or three weeks, starting at least five months ahead. Agendas are written and sent out prior to each meeting.

We gather volunteers along the way and form subcommittees to work on the various aspects, such as:

- choosing a theme;
- designing a "save-the-date" flyer accompanied by an outreach letter for prospective volunteers;
- arranging to have the event recorded;
- designing and printing the event flyer, which contains details (date, time, and cost of the Clutter-Free Day), directions, and registration form;
- finding and selecting people to lead the nine different workshops and one person to be the keynote speaker;
- listing workshop titles chosen by each person; and
- ordering supplies of the CLA literature and CLA*rity* newsletter.

On the day itself, additional volunteers set up tables for registration, literature, refreshments, dining, etc. Others greet people at the door, guide them through registration, provide orientation, and direct members to workshop rooms. Optional events may include entertainment and guided meditation if volunteers are willing to initiate these.

All our events have been successful, with attendance of more than 100 people for the last several years. It's a great way to meet other clutterers and reunite with old friends!

Spring 2011 Clutter-Free Day Report

Summer 2011

Betsey K., NJ

CLA-East's latest Clutter-Free Day was held on Saturday, April 16, in Metuchen, NJ. Although attendance was down from the last few years, the 70 or so people who attended heard inspirational speakers, gained valuable information on a variety of topics, and had the opportunity to meet and reconnect with other clutterers. It was a great opportunity for fellowship. Attendees came from New York, New Jersey, Pennsylvania, and Massachusetts. Our keynote speaker, Susie, came all the way from California.

The theme of the event was "Cleaning up My Corner of the World." There were nine workshops on various topics related to cluttering. Although we had lined up all the workshop leaders ahead of time, the one who was to lead the newcomers' workshop was not able to attend; but we were able to find a substitute leader on that day.

Highlights of the day included Susie's presentation as keynote speaker and Bobbie's PowerPoint presentation. The meditation session toward the end of the day also drew rave reviews.

We look forward to our next Clutter-Free Day, which is expected to be held next spring.

Spring 2011 Clutter-Free Day—My Experience

Summer 2011

Ruthe S., PA

I love attending Clutter-Free Day (CFD). It always feels like I've come home. Clutterers are loving people, and CFDs are very supportive and affirming. This CFD was no exception. Despite the pouring rain and fewer volunteers than usual, CFD 2011 was a success. There were three sets of workshops about different aspects of clutter. These workshops were: "Clutter and Aging"," Letting Go," "Getting Started," "Fear and Procrastination," "Our First Priority Is Our Well-Being," "Phone Meetings," "Higher Power (HP)—Steps 1–3: From Powerless Inside to Power from Outside," and "Weeding Your Wardrobe." There was also a beginner's meeting ("Not Just for Newcomers"). Our keynote speaker flew in from California to be with us, and her message was very hopeful and inspiring. California is, of course, where CLA began.

I attended the workshop on Fear and Procrastination. This workshop talked about how to apply the 12 Steps to deal with procrastination. I also attended the workshop called "Weeding Your Wardrobe." This workshop provided a blueprint for decluttering your clothing. Both were very insightful. I led a workshop called "Getting Started." I talked about how to start slowly and take that first leap of faith. If you attended and had to make choices between workshops or you weren't able to attend at all, you can purchase CDs of any that you missed. The keynote speaker and all of the workshops were recorded and can be purchased. For information, call CLA-East at (866) 800-3881 or send an email to Clarity@CLAEast.org. (CDs from past CFDs are also available.)

Clutter Free Day is an opportunity to be around others who understand the disease of cluttering. It is a day to feel validated and to lessen the shame we feel over this addiction. It is a way to jump-start your recovery and get support for taking the steps to declutter your life. I was reminded that it is progress not perfection and that recovery is not a straight line. I was also reminded that the basis for 12-Step recovery is spiritual. It is not about the clutter but about the emotions that cause us to use clutter as a way to cope.

Most of all, I was reminded how much the 12 Steps have saved my life. I'm not the same person I was almost 11 years ago when I started in recovery in another Fellowship. My life would look nothing like it does now. I have learned how to deal with the negative emotions that used to keep me stuck, which is what most of my recovery has been about. I am now able to deal with life on life's terms. And if I have difficulty, all I need to do is pick up the phone, and there are people who will support me. The 12 Steps have enabled me to deal with unpleasant and upsetting situations and still have a life of serenity. I am grateful to CLA for helping me to declutter enough to uncover who I am and to learn to live my vision. I still have clutter, and maintaining continues to be a challenge, but I understand now that life has both good and bad. I like to say that recovery is how you cope in difficult times and not how you are during good times. I know that I always have CLA to help me navigate through all aspects of my life.

Clutter-Free Day

Fall 2012

CLA members organize events to share, network, and support each other with their experience, strength, and hope. Clutter-Free Day (CFD) is that type of event. Early on, they were held under different names, such as "Birthday Party" and "Share-a-Day."

Regardless of the name, they are great tools for recovery and for members to interact. Their success may serve as a model for others who want to host similar events in their areas.

Questions and Answers

- *Who attends CFD?*
  Any clutterer can participate.
- *Is it for anyone in the Fellowship?*
  Yes.

- *Are newcomers welcome and may I bring a friend?* Yes on both counts.
- *Are outside speakers allowed?* Usually all speakers are members of the Fellowship. However, firemen or mental health professionals have spoken at a few CFDs. This is CLA's version of A.A.'s allowing medical professionals to speak at some conferences.
- *What is the format for CFD? Are there panel discussions, workshops, lectures?* There is usually a keynote speaker, followed by workshops that take place throughout the day. These may be recorded for future use.
- *What types of topics are covered?* Just about anything related to cluttering in the context of the 12 Steps and 12 Traditions and other aspects of our program, such as our Tools[19] and Affirmations.[20] Members generally share from their own experience, strength, and hope.
- *Do people give their full names?* Information (such as full name, address, phone number, and email) is gathered during the registration process. However, this is used only for the purpose of contacting attendees to inform them of future events and to request volunteer help. Members may rest assured that anonymity is not broken. Name badges used on the actual day display only first names and last initials.
- *Are travel expenses ever paid by CLA?* Generally the participant pays for his or her own travel. Sometimes WSO and/or the intergroup may provide a stipend for certain people who are giving a lot of service.
- *Are any items sold at CFD?* We sell CLA literature, the CLA*rity* newsletter, and sometimes recordings of present and past CFD workshops and keynote presentations.
- *Do they take place in different parts of the world?* They may be held anywhere clutterers get together to plan them. They have been in New Jersey, New York, and both Northern and Southern California. Although there are groups in several other countries, CFDs are known to have been held only in the United States.
- *Will there be another CFD this year?* As far as is known, there are none scheduled at this time, although a few individuals would like to do another event in Southern California.
- *If a group wants to host one, how would they start?* The World Service Organization would like to encourage members to form intergroups to facilitate communication between local groups and members. One thing intergroups do is organize Clutter-Free Days, although in the past, some have been planned without the support of an intergroup.

CLA-East Q&A (In October 2001, our only current intergroup, CLA-East, was formed.)

- *When did CLA-East start hosting CFDs?* The first one took place in the spring of 2002 in Plainsboro, New Jersey. The original name was "Share-a-Day," but some members disliked the acronym SAD, so the name was changed to Clutter-Free Day. For the first six years they were held twice yearly. Currently, one per year is scheduled.
- *Are there any recordings or other materials that can be accessed after the event takes place?* Often, audio recordings of the keynote speaker and workshop sessions are available, though this year no recordings took place. Also, individual workshop leaders may make handouts, and people sign up to receive them by email after the event. CLA-East has had six events recorded.
- *How far in advance will the next one be announced in case members want to make plans to attend?* CLA-East usually determines the date and place about six months in advance.
- *When was the most recent Clutter-Free Day?* It was held on May 20, 2012, in Brooklyn, New York.
- *How was it planned?* There was a hardworking committee of about six members, who attended monthly planning meetings and made sure everything was in place down to the last detail. On the day of the event, these people, along with several others who volunteered on the spot, worked tirelessly to make the day a success.

- *If members want to help with planning the next one, who should be contacted?*
Contact CLA-East at clarity@claeast.org, (866) 800-3881, or 184 South Livingston Avenue, Suite 9-203, Livingston, NJ 07039. A Clutter-Free Day planning manual is being written to guide any group.
- *What happened at this year's CFD?*
Once registered, attendees were offered coffee and bagels. People then entered the main hall for a welcome and orientation session. This year's theme was "Time for Serenity." The keynote presenter, a person with many years in the program, shared his experience, strength, and hope. Following a quick break, members headed into their first selected workshops. There were three to choose from in each of three sessions, making a total of nine. After a long lunch, where people either went out to eat or provided their own, the afternoon began with a relaxing meditation session. From there, it was on to the other two workshop sessions and an official closing, where people voiced their views on the day. About 100 people attended, and the day went very smoothly.

Clutter-Free Day

Fall 2013
Eleainor, PA

Editor's Note: Most Clutter-Free Day sessions were recorded; for information on obtaining the CDs, contact CLA-East at Clarity@CLAEast.org.

Clutter-Free Day (CFD) was recently held on May 4, 2013, in Metuchen, New Jersey. I was very excited to attend, and a group of us were fortunate to receive a ride from James and excitedly headed to CFD from Philadelphia.

Upon arrival I met members from New Jersey, and we made ourselves available in preparing brunch and, later, lunch. They were organized and made quality decisions on the selections offered.

Keynote Speaker

The keynote presenter began by introducing the sloth named Sammy. Her theme was "Simplicity, not Procrastination." I enjoyed her sense of humor. She showed pictures of her home before and after her decluttering. She said that clutter troubled her husband and damaged their marriage.

The speaker spoke of the importance of a clarity diary, 10-minute phone calls with clutter buddies, affirmations, and commitment time. Her strongest statement was that her first priority is, and continues to be, her well-being. She had the help of a therapist to reach her goal.

Making Progress: Stop Acquiring and Start Discarding

The presenters of this session use teamwork to work their programs. They have garage sales and take items to consignment shops. If items did not sell at either location, an agreement was made that they were to be given to a favorite charity. They opened a second group so there would be two meetings a week for those in their area to attend.

They suggested we be aware of emotional and physical clutter and seek small, attainable decluttering goals. For example, start by decluttering a square-foot area.

A question was raised: Is your time more important than your clutter? To avoid impulse buying, leave cash and credit cards at home.

Releasing My Clutter Comes from Releasing Myself

This speaker presented the last workshop I attended. I felt she really exposed herself by revealing unbelievable circumstances as a child that continued into her adult life until five years ago.

She was well-prepared and gave her audience opportunities to read her written material out loud. While attending CLA, she utilized a professional counselor.

Her closing was a most profound poem. At the end of the session, she received a standing ovation.

In Closing

What I gathered from all the talks is that there comes a time or circumstance where one says, "This is it. It is time to unload!" It is not worth the heaviness, pain, and rejection of family and friends. For some, a professional adds to the positive equation.

I believe that the Philadelphia group was the largest in attendance. We want to thank James, who made it possible for so many of us to attend.

The New Jersey group that sponsored CFD made an outstanding effort, and it showed. The food and drinks chosen for snacks and lunch were gobbled up. The way the tables were arranged made it easy to reach out to members of other groups through conversation and made it possible to exchange phone numbers.

I believe the sunshine that was visible from the outside made its way inside each of us.

Clutter-Free Day 2014

Fall 2014

Carol N., CA

I had the great fortune to attend Clutter-Free Day on May 18. For me, it began as people started coming in, and I really began to feel the excitement of the day. Up to then, my emotions had been kept in check by my attention to the tasks at hand—but here was Alison! And Mary! And Peter!

Other people who looked familiar came into view, and I was glad to see them, too. Dody W. from Pennsylvania introduced herself, and for the first time I met others I had come in contact with through phone conversations. I realized then that this was why I had driven three thousand miles and braved deserts, mountains, and a few storms (not to mention road work). I needed this! I needed to gather with people I knew and who knew me.

The keynote speaker was Betsey K., and (oh, dear!) she was coming down with laryngitis. Coincidentally, the college had neglected to provide us with a microphone. Betsey soldiered on, though, and her speech about the history of CLA and of her own progress in recovery came off without a hitch and was well received.

In the first round of sessions, I gave a workshop on "How to Find a Sponsor, How to Be an Effective Sponsor, and What to Look for in a Sponsor." I think that one of the reasons our Fellowship is shy of sponsors is that members won't step up because they believe they aren't recovered enough to qualify for the job. My personal belief is that anyone can sponsor someone newer than themselves, providing they are willing to grow in the program themselves.

At the same time, Bonnie W. of New York was giving a session on resistance, why we resist decluttering and some ways out of that resistance. Ted S. of New York was also presenting on meditation.

After lunch, Ted led a meditation session for all participants.

I attended the workshop led by Alison B. of New Jersey called "My Struggle with Abstinence." There was a lot of personal sharing on that subject at the end. At the same time, Mary P. of New York presented on being "Powerless Over Paper" and included strategies on dealing with paper clutter, and Peter L. of Georgia also presented on the "Fourth Tradition and Clutter," reminding us that "we should not take ourselves too seriously."

The third round of workshops presented me with a dilemma—I wanted to attend all three. Kathy H. of California talked about "My Sacred Place—A Journey in Progress," and her experience in using the Steps and Tools[19] of the CLA program to aid in decluttering. At the same time, James C. of New York was presenting about how "Mourning the Old Leads to Mornings New!" I wanted to hear James speak about how "mourning our clutter" would "regenerate itself into new mornings of peace, order, and space."

I ultimately decided on Ted's workshop on putting an end to the cycles of procrastination surrounding our planned projects. All the sessions looked so intriguing and inviting that I wished I could have split myself three ways, but I figured I needed the one on procrastination the most.

From the opening sentences, I could really relate to everything he said—from the initial enthusiasm and resolve ("I'm really gonna do it this time") to "It would really be better to start fresh on Monday." How Ted described the mental manipulations he used to avoid action during the rest of the week was so hilariously close to my own way of convoluted thinking that I was roaring with laughter along with the rest of the group. Then he talked seriously about using the Steps to get out of that trap.

Then we all met again for recognition of the various groups, CLA announcements, and sharing about what we as individuals had gotten out of the day. The general sharing was uplifting in itself, a good ending to the day. On the way home, memories of workshops and fellowship moments danced in my head.

I am already looking forward to next year. I don't want to miss out on the opportunity to meet new kindred spirits and become closer to the people I love and who love me.

A True Opportunity to Gain Insight & Willingness to Change

Holiday 2014

Sheila L., NY

He was "meant to be," as the Yiddish expression goes.

At 8:30 a.m. on Sunday, May 18, 2014, I took the train from the Upper West Side of Manhattan to the tony enclave of Brooklyn Heights, where approximately 70 self-described chronic clutterers gathered at St. Francis College to share their experience, strength, and hope. God truly looks out for me; and I met Ted, who cut through my resistance and taught me how to meditate and release it. I became willing to develop the key skill to begin to heal as an addict of money, food, space, and debting, using the 12 Steps. Now I am trying to organize a much-needed Upper West Side CLA group meeting and hoping to attend the 25th Anniversary Convention of CLA in California on October 11-12, 2014. Hope to meet you there. Best to all. We are worth it.

Clutter-Free Day

Fall 2015

Ted S., NY

A Day of Service, Sponsorship, and Steps. It seemed far off in the future when the CLA-East Intergroup started officially planning their Clutter-Free Day (CFD). But typically, the usual mindset for a clutterer is, "There's plenty of time and it will all work out." Such readily acceptable optimism often leads to late-night, Herculean efforts to complete the necessary details and plans.

I have to say, the keystone keeping the committee on track and focused was dependable Betsey, a longtime member who has been on just about every committee the CLA World Service Organization or CLA-East has ever had. I, as chairperson, and Betsey K., as vice-chairperson, guided an eager and innovative committee for 2015. Betsey—with her soft voice ever mentioning the schedule, how behind we were, and always speaking as an observer and never as an accuser—gave the CFD Committee a steady course to follow. Ron M. and James C. made various efforts to have the workshops recorded, making phone calls to several organizations and researching ways in which we could do our own recordings. Mary P., a former CFD chairperson who served for many years, gave valuable insight and encouragement as per her practical knowledge. Dody W. was a voice of reason as well.

Experienced workshop leaders volunteered as the planning moved forward and word spread that CFD 2015 had a date. Some leaders, who were gently persuaded that they were capable of offering workshops, were surprised at how well they did according to the evaluations. Many thanks to workshop leaders Bonnie W., Martha H., Mary P., Melanie T., Elaine E., Gladys H., and Carol N.

Help also came in the form of people offering service the day of CFD. Eileen M. worked tirelessly in the kitchen, along with two other women. At the end of the day they helped by putting chairs and tables away and removing trash. I remember their helpful manner in seeing what needed to be done and taking care of it—the food tables, the kitchen, and all around the workshop areas. Peter L., a long-time member of CLA, made several trips to secure the all-important key to open the church door and to purchase and deliver the food. Many thanks for his patience and persistence in offering help with whatever was needed. If I failed to mention any names, I apologize.

My personal feelings about the day are:

1. The schedule was adhered to without continual announcements or a necessity to remind people that the workshops were starting.
2. There was a general feeling of "we are here to get better" and a willingness to work together.
3. In retrospect, I would have wanted to spend more time with the workshop leaders to make sure they had everything they needed as far as room set-up and to offer support.

Comments from participants included: "I felt I was not alone," "renewed sense of hope and inspiration," and "it's always encouraging to be in the company of people who understand the problem."

Other comments were: "Many people helped doing service during the day" and "Wonderful day. Thank you all who gave service—this is sacred work. Well-organized and well-run; very impressive, helpful; spiritual focus, most appreciated."

Participants gave the following suggestions: "possibly a face-to-face meeting—short qualifier and open sharing," "a morning CLA meeting... chaired by some of the early arrivals during bagels and coffee," and "a beginners meeting for newcomers to go over the basics."

Twelve people signed up to help with CFD 2016. Hope to see you there!

Impressions of Clutter-Free Day

Fall 2016

Alison B., NJ

I was highly thrilled with Clutter-Free Day this year, and I think CLA-East did an outstanding job. They whittled the number of presentations down to six workshops, a keynote speaker, a session on meditation, and another on problems and solutions. There were two workshops at a time to choose from. It worked for the most part, except for the fact that the workshops were then overcrowded. The theme was "Letting Go: Releasing Fears, Attachments, and Clutter."

First I went to a workshop called "Letting Go and Finding Myself." Here are some highlights: Resentments can take away from constructive energy. I need to set better boundaries. I need to do Step Four. Working an inventory can be uncomfortable, but it can also free me. I forgive so I can heal. Put photographs online. How do I deal with perfectionism? The key is in working the program. CLA gives me boundaries, structure, and separation.

From the next workshop, "Releasing Shame for Your Own Serenity," I learned the following: If you don't like your Higher Power, find a replacement and write a new job description (I love that!). The shopping process gives greater satisfaction than buying. I have to surrender repeatedly to avoid shame. I need to use the CLA Tools of Recovery.[19] My mind is a bad neighborhood to go in alone. It is my choice whether or not to stay in the negative feeling. I am certain that God never uses shame against me, and I choose to accept my Higher Power's love and guidance. I learned a lot here.

During the lunch break, it was fun meeting new people and saying hello to those I knew. I met somebody whom I had known only on the phone—that was wonderful!

Meditation was next for me. The speaker said that for a beginner, it is important to do one minute of meditation per day and to have a clear space to do it in. He said that you can stare at something or close your eyes—it doesn't matter—but you must concentrate on one thing; and, if your mind wanders, bring your thoughts back to that one thing. We practiced in increasing time increments. I left the room feeling very peaceful.

Then I went to "Time Management and Procrastination," thinking that would be a good one for me. Ironically, I was late and had to sit on the floor at the back. Not an ideal place to take notes—and I didn't take many, but there were two handouts. One had 12 questions about procrastination; it was like an inventory on procrastination. What are the five most important things you procrastinate about? The other suggested I do a week-long self-assessment of my time by using a blank schedule that is marked off in 15-minute increments. I am supposed to evaluate the time spent in different areas of my life, like sleeping, food preparation, eating, cleaning, decluttering, working, time-wasters, etc. Of course, I haven't gotten around to working on these!

The keynote speaker shared her experience, strength, and hope about letting go of resentments, clutter, and fear. She said that she had lost her husband recently, and if it weren't for CLA, she wouldn't have been able to hold a rather large memorial service in her house. It seems that because of CLA, along with the help of others, she had been able to completely clear up her clutter. I came away from that session with a little more hope and knowing that I have to work a lot harder at cultivating local friendships and working the Steps yet again.

There was a closing session with entertainment by a CLA member who sang a couple of song parodies about clutter. She was pretty funny. They made me realize that I could do that, too. There was also recognition of groups and sharing on the day's events. We ended with the Keep and Release Serenity Prayer, which was a lovely way to end this beautiful day.

Conventions

CLA 25th Anniversary Convention

Summer 2014

To mark the occasion of CLA's 25th anniversary, the CLA World Service Organization is holding our first-ever national convention. It will be filled with recovery, program, and fellowship with other clutterers.

The event will be held at the Hacienda Hotel in El Segundo, California (near Los Angeles International Airport) on Saturday and Sunday, October 11 and 12, 2014. There will be an informal meetup on Friday, October 10.

The hotel has free 24-hour shuttle service to and from the airport, and the 25th Anniversary Committee can reserve rooms for those members not in the Los Angeles area. Also, for those out-of-town guests wishing to do sight-seeing, tours can be arranged before and after the event.

Flyers have been sent via email or postal mail to all group contacts, as well as to other email addresses on the WSO mailing list. For more information, send an email to CLA25thDay@gmail.com or use one of the contact methods listed in the frontiespiece.

Also, check www.clutterersanonymous.org for more information as it becomes available.

CLA 25th Anniversity Convention

Fall 2014

CLA will hold its 25th Anniversary Convention on Saturday and Sunday, October 11–12, preceded by an optional, informal meetup starting in the afternoon of Friday, October 10. The convention will be held at the Hacienda Hotel located at 525 North Sepulveda Boulevard in El Segundo, California. All members are welcome to preregister and attend.

The convention will include a keynote speaker, workshop sessions, an old-timers panel, and other activities. This event will be an opportunity to enjoy fellowship with others from across the country and elsewhere. For out-of-town attendees, sightseeing tours can be arranged on the days before and after the event.

There is free shuttle service between the hotel and Los Angeles International Airport. There is also free hotel shuttle service for guests to go shopping and sightseeing within the nearby area. For those who will be driving, the onsite hotel parking costs $4 a day for event attendees or $8 for overnight parking.

Advance registration for the convention is required, and October 3 is the last day to register. The cost for attending the convention's all-day activities is $80 for the full weekend and $45 for a single day; cost includes breakfast and lunch daily. Early registration discount levels apply. (September 12 is the last tier cut-off for a reduced rate at $70 for both days and $40 for a single day.)

The Saturday dinner banquet requires a separate $35 ticket. The Friday hospitality meetup is complimentary.

You may book hotel accommodations directly with the property. Call early for discount room rates, starting at $79–$89 per night + taxes. When making reservations, state that you are attending the Clutterers Anonymous 25th Anniversary Convention. There are also several other options for accommodations in the nearby LAX area.

Refer to the CLA website at Clutterers Anonymous.org for current event information and updates.

Won't you join us for this exciting, first-ever CLA convention? We would love to see you there!

CLA 25th Anniversary Convention

Holiday 2014

Our first-ever CLA convention was held on October 11 and 12, 2014, marking the 25th anniversary of our Fellowship. About 75 people came from 15 states—Arizona, California, Florida, Georgia, Illinois, Kentucky, Maryland, Missouri, Nevada, New York, New Jersey, Oregon, Pennsylvania, Utah, and Virginia—and even from Australia, making it a truly international affair!

Sessions included featured presenters, workshops, a Q&A panel with old-timers (members with ten years or more in CLA), and opportunities for fellowship and sharing. The subjects of the ten workshops included working the Steps, physical decluttering, understanding sponsorship, and focusing on spiritual aspects of the program. On Saturday night there was a banquet followed by a speaker and magical, musical entertainment. At the business meeting on Sunday, we made a group decision to hold our second annual convention in northern New Jersey in October 2015.

The sessions were recorded and are available for purchase either as individual CDs or as a set of 14, which includes all sessions. For pricing and ordering, go to the News page on the CLA website, or contact us by one of the methods listed in the frontispiece.

Attendees were asked to give written evaluations and offer suggestions for the next convention.

When asked to comment about the convention, one attendee replied, "Glad that we had one," and another said, "Wonderful gathering of the Fellowship."

Many stated that what they liked best was networking and having fellowship with other clutterers. One added, "Now I don't feel alone."

Others also were delighted to hear about CLA meetings in other parts of the country and also about telephone meetings. One commented on "the power of such a large group of us coming together," and another said, "I so enjoyed fellowshipping with other CLA members. This was a great practice of our first Tradition—unity."

Some attendees commented that the convention gave them a place to find sponsors, while others enjoyed the workshop on sponsorship and hearing stories about clutterers finding success through working the Steps with a sponsor.

Most of the comments about workshops and presentations were favorable, although one complimentary complaint was, "It's sooooo difficult to decide which [workshops] to attend—all were great!" One person commented on hearing "solutions that have worked" and another liked "the variety of topics and activities [that] were presented."

Some liked the handouts, and others enjoyed the before-and-after decluttering photos that were shared. The Old Timers Panel also received mostly favorable comments. One attendee particularly liked "when they share more intimately...what they believe now and how it was then."

One clutterer liked the "folder [provided to attendees] with the schedule, evaluation form, and especially blank lined paper to write notes."

While there were a few complaints about the venue and the food, most who mentioned it gave favorable reviews, with one stating, "The hotel was old but clean and the service was good. The food was great." And most said they enjoyed the banquet entertainment.

Some members' favorite things about the convention included: "the laughter," "hearing the recovery stories," "the loving kindness of all the other people," and the "inspiration." Some said they "loved everything."

One attendee summarized the event this way: "This was incredibly well organized. I'm so happy that I came. ...the friendliness and openness of the members, everybody's tips on leading clutter-free lives—both speakers and from individual shares..." And one said the convention weekend "will set my next week off to a motivating start!"

Suggestions for changes at the next convention included: more signs and communication, more workshops, more entertainment, a message board to note schedule changes, more interactive workshops, sponsorship networking, information on how to strengthen local meetings, more panels, better communication to members who do not use email, and allowing more time for open sharing.

There were suggestions for certain workshop topics for next year: "grief and loss," "cluttering because of poor memory," and "abstinence." It was also suggested that in the general meeting, there should be a request that those open to being sponsors identify themselves.

Overall, the comments were very positive. One member said, "It was a powerful weekend of spiritual growth and fellowship. Energy and enthusiasm levels were uniformly high," while another stated, "The convention was excellent in all respects—welcoming, friendly, informative, and inspiring."

CLA Second Annual Convention

Spring 2015

The Second Annual CLA Convention is expected to be held in northern New Jersey in the fall of 2015.

A scholarship fund is being set up to help defray costs for those CLA members with financial difficulties who wish to attend.

For up-to-date information on the convention—including details on scholarships and registration—do one of the following: check the Events web page at ClutterersAnonymous.org, send an email to CLAConvention2015@yahoo.com, or call the CLA phone number, (866) 402-6685.

CLA 2015 Convention

Summer 2015

CLA will be holding its Second Annual Convention on October 3 and 4, 2015, at the Embassy Suites Hotel, 455 Plaza Drive, Secaucus, New Jersey (in the Harmon Meadows area). There is a direct train from the Newark Airport to the Secaucus Junction, with free hotel shuttle from the junction to the hotel. There is easy bus transportation from the hotel area to New York City for those wishing to do sightseeing.

The "Save the Date" flyer can be downloaded from the Events Page at ClutterersAnonymous.org. Lunch will be included in the registration price. Further information will be available when the primary convention flyer is published, including information on reserving suites at the hotel.

This beautiful site includes spacious two-room suites, a nine-story atrium, a fitness room, and a swimming pool. Each suite has a bedroom with either two double beds or a king bed, as well as a separate living room with a desk and workspace area. A free hot breakfast will be available for each registered guest, as well as a Manager's Reception each evening, which includes hors d'oeuvres and beverages.

"Making New Connections: Sharing Our Experience, Strength, and Hope" is theme of the convention.

It will include speakers, workshops, fellowship, and entertainment.

Most attendees agreed that last year's convention was uplifting and fulfilling, with lots of good fellowship and fun entertainment. For comments on last year's convention, refer to the Holiday 2014 issue of CLA*rity*. This year's convention promises to be just as rewarding. So why not consider a wonderful weekend full of recovery, fellowship, and fun?!

A Scholarship Fund is in place to allay costs for those who are unable to fully pay for their convention attendance. Members can donate any amount to the Scholarship Fund. Send a check or money order payable to CLA WSO. Mail to CLA 2015 Convention, PO Box 91413, Los Angeles, CA 90009. Online donation options information will be coming soon.

Be sure to check the Events page on Clutterers Anonymous.org for updated information, or contact the Convention Committee via one of the methods listed in the frontispiece.

CLA 2015 Annual Convention

Fall 2015

Excitement is building toward CLA's 2015 Annual Convention, which promises to be a wonderful, interesting event, filled with lots of recovery and fellowship.

There will be many activities aimed toward bringing clutterers together, especially since the theme of the convention is "Making New Connections: Sharing Our Experience, Strength, and Hope." Besides the usual workshops, the 2015 Convention Committee is planning more activities that will include all attendees, such as panels on various topics, icebreakers, and a session on sponsorship. The convention will include various small recovery group sessions to be held in a separate room throughout the day. Evening entertainment promises to be a lot of fun, with karaoke, as well as other activities.

The convention will be held at the beautiful Embassy Suites Meadowlands Hotel in Secaucus, New Jersey, on Saturday and Sunday, October 3 and 4, 2015. The price of attendance for both days is $95, which includes lunch each day; the price for attending one day only, with lunch, is $55. There will be no registrations taken at the door, so if you want to attend, you must register by September 18. Space is limited, so register early.

The flyer and the registration form for the convention have been finished, along with an "Accommodations Fact Sheet," with information about the hotel, and a "Transportation Fact Sheet" with directions and maps. All of these documents are posted on ClutterersAnonymous.org on the Events page. They are also available via any of the contact methods in the box on the frontispiece.

Registration fees can be paid online at Clutterers Anonymous.org. Donations to the convention Scholarship Fund may also be made online.

For more information, send an email to Info2015@CLAconvention.org.

Second Annual Convention

Holiday 2015

The Second Annual Convention of CLA was held on October 3 and 4 at the Embassy Suites Meadowlands Hotel in Secaucus, New Jersey. Recordings from the convention are available for sale at ClutterersAnonymous.org.

It included two panels, one on sponsorship and one on the "Measuring Progress on Our Journey in Recovery"[13] leaflet. There was a writing session and several workshops: "Getting Unstuck," "Decluttering Resentment," "CLA Tools of Recovery," and "Step 4 and Group Inventory." There was a meditation workshop, a face-to-face recovery meeting, and an interactive session on "Handling Stress in the Holiday Season."

There was also a session entitled "Problems and Solutions," in which the attendees broke into small groups. Members were able to share about their problems and recovery from clutter, while others offered feedback based on their experience, strength, and hope.

More than 70 clutterers attended from ten states and from Australia.

Based on the evaluations and spoken comments, the convention was a resounding success. Some comments from the Evaluation Form are included below.

One member wrote, "The atmosphere was electric, healing, loving, and giving."

Many attendees remarked on enjoying the fellowship and meeting other members. One comment was, "Useful to connect with people from my state, meeting people whose voices I recognized from phone meetings (putting a face to the voice)." Another comment was "Great theme, 'Making New Connections,' and many new connections were made…enabling me to share my experience, strength, and hope." And yet another said, "…but to see clutterers from throughout the U.S. and the world!"

One was pleased with the level of recovery evident in the session leaders, and several said that they had found sponsors at the convention.

Paul K., who acted as master of ceremonies, was complimented, with one person writing "Paul did great! Tried to keep time [program] on schedule." Several attendees applauded Frederick W.'s dynamic speech filled with program recovery, with one calling him "phenomenal."

Many liked the sessions in which there was sharing and audience participation One said, "...helpful in knowing what others do to help themselves." Several attendees shared that they were pleased with the various sessions on the 12 Steps.

There was a recovery meeting, and—for the first time—there was a phone meeting held and shared in real time with convention attendees participating. One attendee commented that it "was quite a technical achievement."

Another one said "We are growing and recovering as a Fellowship."

Other comments about the convention were: "Great! I am so happy that I came. I got so much more than I expected," "Very professional—well planned and carried out," "Spectacular!" and "This was the best ever. I learned a great deal. I loved the workshops. They were different and unique. Keep up the uniqueness!"

"This was a wonderful experience. We are a remarkable group of people who are united in our efforts to solve our common problem, which is clutter."

The CLA*rity* team would like to encourage all CLA members to consider attending the next convention. Some scholarships may be available to help members with registration expenses. Keep reading CLA*rity* or check the CLA website for more information as it becomes available.

CLA 2016 Convention

Spring 2016

The CLA Convention Committee is busy planning the 2016 convention, which will be held in the San Francisco Bay Area of California in late September or early October. The theme for the convention is "Building Bridges: Keeping the Connections."

It is anticipated that final information on the location and date of the convention will be available by the end of March.

If you have ideas for sessions or know anyone who would like to be a presenter, send an email to Info@ClutterersAnonymous.org by the end of April.

The committee is seeking members to help before, during, and after the convention. As the old adage states, "many hands make light work," so if you are interested, send an email to Info@ClutterersAnonymous.org.

We've created a scholarship fund to help allay costs for those who are unable to fully pay for their convention attendance. Members can donate any amount to the Scholarship Fund via Clutterers Anonymous.org or by postal mail. Send a check or money order, payable to CLA WSO, to CLA 2016 Convention, PO Box 91413, Los Angeles, CA 90009. Scholarship information and request forms will be available at a later date.

Keep an eye on this column for further information on the convention, or check our website for updates.

Summer 2016

On March 27, 2016, the CLA World Service Organization (WSO) voted to separate the Convention Committee from WSO. The committee will still be a CLA entity but have its own structure, independent of WSO, much as an intergroup does.

That means it will set up its own financial structure and have separate accounting—although it may borrow funds from WSO, which it will pay back from monies received from convention registrations. Since the Convention Committee is still a functioning part of CLA, any member may elect to join it or help in various ways.

At a recent meeting of the Convention Committee, there was discussion about the ramifications of trying to totally redo the structure for it. It was pointed out that it would be extremely difficult to get everything in place in time to hold a convention this year.

Because of this, the committee reluctantly decided not to have a convention in 2016 but, instead, to work on the structure for the committee. This will give time to gain a good head start for the next convention, to be held in 2017.

As further decisions are made, they will be posted on the CLA website and printed in CLA*rity*.

Holiday 2016

After a vote at the March 26, 2016, meeting of the CLA World Service Organization (WSO), the Convention Committee was unclear about its status and decided not to hold a convention in 2016.

During the last few months, the committee has been working on a "Convention Planning Manual." A "Financial Policy" has been adopted to help keep the committee within its budget. The Convention Finance Subcommittee has met to discuss structure and has begun a 2017 committee budget.

At the October 22, 2016, meeting, WSO passed Motion 2016-04, which stated: "To change the status of the CLA Convention Committee to one that is semi-autonomous from WSO, with its own bank account and funding."

This clarified the status of the committee. It will be able to open an umbrella bank account under WSO and use WSO's nonprofit status. The committee will set its own budget and manage its own finances. It may borrow money from WSO for certain initial expenses, which it will then pay back from proceeds of convention registration fees. CDs will once again be available for purchase, either through ClutterersAnonymous.org or by sending a check via postal mail.

The committee is anticipating holding next year's convention in Oakland, California, in September or October. Final negotiations should be completed by January. Once negotiations are completed, a "Save the Date" flyer will be sent to all meeting contacts and other interested CLA members. The final convention flyer should be disseminated later in the spring, along with a registration form and other pertinent documents.

As was done for the previous two conventions, a Scholarship Fund will be set up to help defray costs of convention attendance for those in need. Once the fund is set up, any member can contribute to it either via ClutterersAnonymous.org or by sending a check to CLA Convention at 184 South Livingston Avenue, Suite 9-203, Livingston, NJ 07039. It is requested that donors indicate that the check is for the Convention Scholarship Fund.

As they become available, flyers, forms, and further information will be posted on the CLA Convention page at ClutterersAnonymous.org—or, to learn more, use any of the contact methods listed in the frontispiece.

Declutterthons

CLA's New Year's Marathon

Summer 2009
Marie M., NY

Wow!

What a wonderful way to end the old year and begin the new. Aside from the meetings where I got to share and to serve, I was also grateful to "ring in" 2009 in several different time zones as I joined meetings from Eastern to Pacific times. Usually I don't pay attention to this part of the annual celebration, but it was fun to share this experience with CLA friends and CLA strangers.

Unlike making New Year's resolutions, participating in the Marathon was living my resolution with regard to my decluttering goals. And so far this year, I am keeping my resolution to strengthen the spiritual and mental parts of the program.

For me, the Marathon was an unforgettable experience, giving me strength to continue taking the actions I need to take and more hope for a clutter-free 2009.

CLA's New Year's Marathon

Summer 2009
Lisa M., CA

My friend Delores lives on the other side of the country, and I would never have had the privilege of meeting her if it had not been for the phone meetings. She and I would talk about anything and everything. I had heard about another marathon that I really did not want to attend so much, mainly because CLA is where I most identify.

I thought, wouldn't it be great if CLA did a marathon? Then I thought in a negative kind of way that I would not be supported, and I didn't want to get rejected. To my surprise, Delores read my mind and spoke up about it. She was thinking what I was thinking and put the first step into action. She said, "I will ask at the WSO meeting." I thought that was very bold of her. We asked Alison; she said, "yes,"* and the door of my thoughts opened up. So there we were with three days to do this, so we jumped on it.

One of the things I love about CLA phone meetings is that announcements are made exceptionally well. They are so informational—about being of service and getting the message out to people like me who are hurting. So many people were so willing to participate. We were blessed that we were not going to have to be alone over this holiday. Leaders' spots were filling, and evening meetings were a great help in having so many people attending and hearing of the marathon. I've been in CLA for over six months and have received so much love from everybody that it was with gratitude for the program that I reached out to our group. By the time the marathon started, we lacked leaders for about 5 of the 24 one-hour slots. The service we received that night left no vacant slots. I came on the line ringing in the New Year with the east coast and heard a lot of appreciation for CLA and the marathon.

I always hear a lot of inspiration and such kind words, but this time it was a 24-hour dose. One person, whose New Year's resolution was to keep a particular area clean, was extremely amazed about the decluttering in that area done that night. I am still hearing about it today. It was a holiday that helped me and others share our sorrows and joys.

Thank you so very much for *everyone's* interest, participation, love, and service. You're the best!

**All decisions are made by group conscience—Ed.*

Declutterthon Summary

Summer 2013

Wendy L., IL

Periodically, the CLA Focused Action Session phone group organizes sessions of eight hours or longer on the telephone. The exciting and well-attended CLA phone Spring Cleaning Declutterthon was held on March 22 and 23. Organizers Susan M. of North Carolina and Wendy L. of Illinois would like to thank every volunteer who gave service by moderating one (or more) of the 45-minute sessions that made up the event. Thanks also go out to all Declutterthon participants who shared about their decluttering actions. Without each and every participating clutterer, this event would not have been the success it was.

Modeled after the daily phone CLA Focused Action Sessions, the Declutterthon allowed participants to share their focused actions at the top of the hour. At the bottom of the hour, the moderators asked participants to check in to share progress reports. Newcomers to the phone lines were welcome.

During most sessions, a volunteer moderator read from a written format and was invited to read out loud from CLA or A.A. literature. If a moderator was not available, participants shared using a round-robin format, where each participant asked for the next clutterer's share. At times, more than 25 CLA members were on the call at the same time.

Members enthusiastically shared stories of their decluttering accomplishments and expressed gratitude for the literature readings. Many stayed on the Declutterthon for hours and participated on both days.

In the weeks that followed, some participants joined the Focused Action Sessions (FAS) that occur daily from 1:00 to 1:45 p.m. ET. These sessions give clutterers a chance to put their recoveries into practice by sharing with other clutterers and by living the Twelve Steps and Twelve Traditions. Often, participants stay on the phone line for hours, so if clutterers can't get on the line until after 1:45 p.m. ET, they should still call in. The FAS phone number is (218) 339-2500, access code 185487#.

Declutterthon co-organizer Susan shared that "trusting in a Power greater than myself is always helpful, as is having a service attitude to be of help whenever possible." She relies on our literature to motivate and guide her.

More thanks go out to Lorraine of California for her assistance with the written format and to Jane D. of California and all other clutterers for publicizing the Declutterthon during phone sessions and meeting announcements.

For information about the Declutterthon or the Focused Action Sessions, please send an email to Clarity@ClutterersAnonymous.org.

CLArity Box

The CLA*rity* Box column in CLA*rity* includes various topics. It consists of questions by clutterers and answers to those questions.

Summer 2009

Dear CLArity Box: I sometimes want to go to a meeting, but there's no meeting in my area until the weekend. I often feel isolated and a bit crazy. Can you suggest something that I can do? (Are there other options I haven't thought of?) *A Fellow Clutterer*

Dear Fellow Clutterer:

People from all over the country, and sometimes other countries, call in to telephone meetings seven days of the week. It is easy do so: Simply dial the telephone number; and, when prompted, dial the access code, followed by the # key. Once you enter the meeting, it runs similarly to a face-to-face meeting.

For a listing of phone meetings, their topics, numbers, and access codes, refer to the printed CLA Meeting Directory or the Phone Meetings portion of the CLA website (ClutterersAnonymous.org) or call (866) 402-6685 and leave a message.

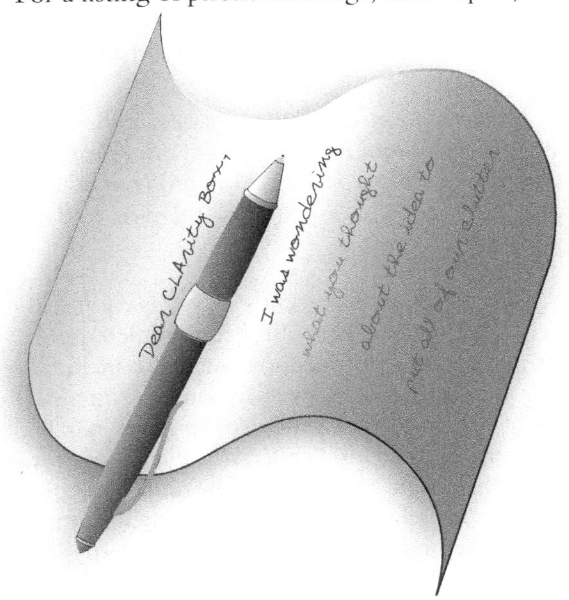

What else can I do during the week if I can't go to a meeting? I might read CLA literature, call my sponsor or other members of my group to talk about decluttering problems or whatever is on my mind at the time, or do writing.

If you are really ambitious, start another meeting in your area during the week on a day more convenient for you. Meeting Starter Kits[7] sell for $15 and can be ordered via the CLA website or by sending a check to CLA WSO, PO Box 91413, Los Angeles, CA 90009.

Good luck.

Holiday 2009

Dear CLArity Box:

I like several books that are not CLA-approved. Is it okay to use them in my CLA meeting?
A Book Lover

Dear Book Lover:

We never use outside literature in meetings. Once the meeting has closed, it's fine. Two of CLA's 12 Traditions cover this topic. Tradition 6 states: "A CLA group ought never endorse, finance, or lend the Clutterers Anonymous name to any related facility or outside enterprise, lest problems of money, property, or prestige divert us from our primary purpose." Tradition 10 says, "CLA has no opinion on outside issues, hence the Clutterers

Anonymous name ought never be drawn into public controversy."

For even more information on this topic, see "CLA Literature and the Traditions" in the Fall 2009 issue of CLA*rity*.

Spring 2010

Dear CLArity Box:

Someone at my meeting insists that a Higher Power has to be God. How can I convince her that it can be someone other than God? *Concerned, CA*

Dear Concerned:

None of us can convince someone else of anything, nor are we here to convert anybody. Part of recovery is learning tolerance for others' struggles and beliefs, and that includes their choice of Higher Power.

Step 3 states: "Made a decision to turn our will and our lives over to the care of God, as we understood God." CLA membership is open to any clutterer. Not all those who come to CLA have a religious faith. Those who do would, of course, use their own concept of God as their Higher Power. But others must be free to rely on any Higher Power which would help them to recover because recovery must be an option for everyone who desires to stop cluttering.

Summer 2010

Dear CLArity Box:

A member of our CLA group paid for some folding chairs to use in our meeting space. We never voted to approve this purchase, but now he wants to be reimbursed. Our group's treasury is very small, and it will take several months to collect enough money to pay him for the chairs. Should we tell him we can't afford the furniture and let him take it back or should we try to take up a special collection to raise the money? *People Pleaser*

Dear People Pleaser:

In the "12 Concepts"[17] of Alcoholics Anonymous, Concept 12 states: "...that it reach all important decisions by discussion, vote, and, whenever possible, by substantial unanimity." You might tell the member who bought the chairs that, in future, before taking any action that affects the group and/or its finances, he should bring the matter to the group at its regular business meeting. It is better for the health of the group if decisions of this nature are made by group conscience before any action is taken.

Since the chairs have already been purchased, we would suggest taking up the matter in a business meeting to decide whether to ask the member to take the chairs back. The group needs to make plain that it does not condone any unauthorized actions. While we understand the fear of being paralyzed by the idea of hurting someone or the fear of recriminations from the hurt person, we must remember that there is strength in numbers. It helps to remember not only about how we may hurt the person, but how the person may be hurting the group. It must be done without blame or finger pointing and with as little recrimination as possible. Our program teaches "principles before personalities." Whatever the group decides is up to group conscience.

Editor's Note: All questions are answered by two or more people. If readers have comments, we will welcome their input.

Fall 2010

Dear CLArity Box:

My home group is planning to start a meeting where we read and discuss the A.A. "Big Book."[4] Is there any literature we can use to guide us in our study? *Trying to Recover*

Dear Trying to Recover,

CLA's literature currently includes eight leaflets and a soon-to-be-published complete guide for newcomers, but meetings may also include A.A. literature as a recovery resource. You also might find an A.A. 12-Step study guide in a recovery book store. While *Alcoholics Anonymous* (the "Big Book") was written by and for alcoholics, it does include much information about recovery through the 12 Steps, which are applicable to any 12-Step program. There are some other A.A. resources which may be helpful: "Questions and Answers on Sponsorship," *Twelve Steps and Twelve Traditions,*[16] *Came to Believe,*[6] and *A.A. Comes of Age.*[1]

One last item: When you read from the A.A. literature in a meeting, read the words as written (A.A. and alcoholic).

Trying to Recover, Too

Spring 2011

Mary P., NY
Public Information Officer

Dear CLArity Box:

I am aware of a documentary that is looking for hoarders to appear. Can we advertise it in CLA, and can I be on the show? *Lazy Susan*

Dear Lazy,

Regarding a documentary on hoarding—no, we really can't advertise it in CLA because CLA as a Fellowship can't "endorse, finance, or lend the Clutterers Anonymous name to any…outside enterprise" That's Tradition 6. We don't take any position on "outside issues," such as other approaches to cluttering—therapy, professional organizers, books on clutter, etc. As for being a part of a documentary, that's an individual choice. However, according to our guidelines, if you choose to participate, you cannot identify yourself as a CLA member. This is because of Traditions 11 (anonymity at the level of press, films, etc.) and 12 (anonymity is the spiritual foundation of all our Traditions…). Good luck with your decluttering, whatever you decide about the documentary. Just try to keep the Traditions in mind.

For other questions like this, you can send an email to the public information link on the website, www.clutterersanonymous.org.

Fall 2011

What do we mean when we say that we use only CLA-approved literature in our meetings?

Confused CLA Member

Dear Confused,

In keeping with our Traditions, we use only CLA Fellowship-approved literature, which has been submitted to the Fellowship for feedback and approved by the CLA World Service Organization (WSO). Literature from A.A. is also acceptable; but, in accordance with a request from A.A., we do not change any of their wording (such as substituting "clutter" and "clutterers" for "alcohol" and "alcoholics") when reading it in meetings. Also, we do not mention outside literature by name or author.

Why is this included in the Traditions? First, bringing in outside literature can lead to controversy if members take differing opinions on what to use—and this could weaken or even break groups apart. Also, if we focus on other items, it takes away emphasis from our own program, thereby watering it down. If we try to do everything, we end up with nothing but clutter.

Of course, CLA members are free to use whatever materials they wish in their own personal lives, but we do not bring unapproved materials to meetings for discussion.

Holiday 2011

Why do the meeting pages on the CLA website not include the contact information for CLA meetings?

Desiring Contact

Dear Desiring,

Since CLA is a 12-Step Fellowship, with a strong tradition of anonymity, we are wary of putting members' names and phone numbers on our website. However, our printed Meeting Directory does list names and telephone numbers of meeting contacts. To obtain a Meeting Directory or to get contact information for a particular meeting, do one of the following: (1) On the web, go to www.ClutterersAnonymous.org, click on the "contact" menu, and send an email by selecting "Meetings" in the drop-down box and filling in the appropriate information.; (2) Send a postal letter to CLA WSO, PO Box 91413, Los Angeles, CA 90009; or (3) Call (866) 402-6685 and leave a message.

Spring 2012

Dear CLArity Box:

What is crosstalk, and why don't we allow it in our meetings? Scared to Share

Dear Scared,

Crosstalk includes: interrupting another person while he or she is sharing, dominating, commenting on someone else's sharing, using "you" and "we" statements, giving unsolicited feedback, arguing with each other, giving advice, making personal comments while reading meeting format, and talking directly to one person during the share.

We don't crosstalk in meetings for these reasons:

- As children, many of us felt we weren't listened to, or we may have been told that our feelings were wrong.
- We come to CLA to heal from our broken past. We need to think our own thoughts and feel our own feelings. Any comment, good or bad, could touch an emotionally sensitive nerve and be painful.
- Those with sensitive feelings may be loathe to share if they feel ridiculed. For many, this may be the whole crux of their addiction.
- As adults, we may often focus on taking care of other people rather than taking responsibility for our own lives.
- This is a formal meeting designed to help us with learning discipline in the rest of our lives.

So, in our meetings, we speak only about our own experience, strength, and hope; and we suspend judgment on what others say because it is true for them.

Summer 2012

Dear CLArity Box:

What is meant by "closed meeting" and how does it get that way? Confused About Terminology

Dear Confused:

Clutterers Anonymous handles this subject the same way most 12-Step programs do. In CLA, meetings are designated either closed or open—which refers to who may come to the meeting. Anyone may attend an open meeting (but only those who identify as clutterers are allowed to share). If the meeting is closed, only clutterers may attend.

The group itself decides to designate their meeting as closed. If there is someone in the group who wishes to have the meeting become closed, a group conscience is called at the next business meeting. Once the majority votes to have a closed meeting, then the World Service Organization is informed and asked to designate the meeting as closed on the CLA Meeting Directory.

Fall 2012

Dear CLArity Box,

Some members have talked about attending one or more CLA phone meetings, as well as their face-to-face meetings. Should I consider calling in to phone meetings in addition to attending my regular in-person meeting? Scared of Phone Calls

Dear Scared,

Members (newcomers included) may visit any local CLA meeting or call in to any phone meeting, which is held as a group conference call—or do both. It is not uncommon for members to go to their local group meetings and also attend phone group meetings. It is a matter of personal choice and, sometimes, circumstances.

Some members have no face-to-face meeting close to their home towns; therefore, phone meeting groups offer a viable alternative for many of them. Thus, some members refer to a phone group commonly as their home meeting.

CLA phone meetings take place at least once per day, in conference-style groups with varying numbers of callers. For some members, phone meetings provide a seven-day-a-week opportunity to share with and receive experience, strength, and hope from other members. There are other reasons why members attend phone meetings exclusively or in addition to face-to-face meetings.

Some members choose certain phone meetings because of the focused discussions and topics, such as writing goals, envisioning, qualification speakers, or sharing on select CLA leaflet topics—for example, "Home: Our Sacred Place"[11] or "Decluttering Resentment: Steps 4–10."[8]

Furthermore, those who attend face-to-face meetings regularly may still find the phone group meetings to be a helpful addition for other reasons. For instance, phone meetings are accessible when members are traveling outside their local area for business, vacation, or family matters.

Members may attend phone meetings whenever transportation to their regular meetings becomes challenging due to bad weather or car troubles, for example. When a member is physically unable to leave home for medical or other reasons, phone meetings are a way to participate in the Fellowship and get support from others. Phone meetings are also forums for members to do service as meeting leaders, spiritual timekeepers for speakers, and newcomer greeters, among other forms of service.

For more details and phone meeting schedules, refer to the CLA website or send an email inquiry (see the CLA Contacts in the frontispiece).

Holiday 2012

Dear CLArity Box:

What is the meaning of the CLA logo (a triangle, circle, and square)? *Curious Cat*

Dear Curious:

The current CLA logo (shown at right) is based on the triangle-in-a-circle symbol originally used by Alcoholics Anonymous.

In its early years, A.A. chose the triangle and circle because those were considered the strongest shapes. Other than strength, the circle had no particular meaning; however, the three legs of the triangle were said to stand for Unity, Service, and Recovery.

In 1993, A.A. decided to discontinue its official use of the logo and holds no copyright claim. Their decision allowed any of its groups the freedom to use it at will, as many do, but A.A. no longer uses any logo.

In 2007, several logo designs were disseminated to members in the CLA Fellowship for input. The graphic chosen is the one shown on the newer CLA leaflets: the triangle and circle with an added square. CLA*rity* uses a similar logo theme on the cover page.

Not at the time of adoption nor since has any official meaning been assigned to CLA's logo. Unofficially, some members still refer to the original 12-Step program's triad of Unity, Service, and Recovery.

Spring 2013

What is an intergroup and what does it do? *Wondering*

Dear Wondering:

An intergroup is usually comprised of a number of CLA groups within a specific geographical area. Intergoups can strengthen CLA groups and lend support to the members of the CLA 12-Step program.

CLA currently has only one intergroup, CLA-East. It is made up of about 30 face-to-face CLA groups, mostly in the northeastern part of the United States. The main focus of this intergroup is to host in-person Clutter-Free Days. These events provide a full day of activities that include workshops, a keynote speaker (and occasionally a second speaker), and fellowship with other clutterers. In the 11-year existence of this group, CLA-East has held 17 Clutter-Free Days; the 18th is scheduled for Saturday, May 4, 2013.

Initially, when intergroup meetings were face-to-face, the intergroup provided free CLA literature to the member groups; this service was discontinued when the meetings began to be conducted by phone, as additional postage costs were involved. CLA-East does provide meeting lists and has a toll-free telephone number, a mailbox, and a website, all of which can provide ways for clutterers to make contact. CLA-East attempts to reach out to its member groups to support them.

Clutterers Anonymous encourages the formation of intergroups in other parts of the country. CLA-East has been working on a manual and would be pleased to share it with any groups interested in planning Clutter-Free Days.

Summer 2013

What is meant by the term "Group Conscience?"
Ann O'Nymous in Arizona

Dear Ann,

Group conscience refers to how decisions are made in CLA groups and business meetings. It is different from methods of election used by most other organizations and political systems.

Making a group conscience decision involves more than just taking a vote. When we make our decisions, everyone in the group has a chance to say his or her piece. If there is a great division between members, we have further discussion to try to find some equitable solution.

Most organizations have a discussion (or often, an argument) and then vote, with the majority vote winning. But, as it says in A.A.'s "12 Concepts of Service,"[17] we are admonished to pay particular attention to the minority opinion. Since no one person sees every angle of an issue, it is important to listen to all. Often, those who are in the minority can demonstrate enough good reasons for their decision that the majority changes its mind.

Whichever way the vote turns out, a good-faith effort must be made to consider the opinion of everyone in the group. Our groups are stronger and happier when each member is involved in the process of decision-making.

Fall 2013

How do CLA groups find affordable meeting space?
Frustrated About Locations

Dear Frustrated,

There are several types of organizations that commonly offer meeting space to 12-Step groups. While some locations may be too expensive for our (usually) small groups, others are very inexpensive or even free.

Begin by asking people you know about locations they may be aware of. Ask members of other groups (12-Step or otherwise) if they know of possible meeting rooms. Search the phone book or online phone books for likely organizations, and call them with your request for meeting space.

Most commonly, meeting space is found in places of worship, libraries, Alano clubs, and community centers; but other venues should not be left out of the search. For instance, one CLA meeting is held in a rented room at the back of a self-help and recovery store. There is a cafe in Los Angeles that provides a meeting room (for free!) to 12-Step groups, including a CLA group.

The key to finding meeting space is persistence; don't give up. But don't be afraid to be creative in designing the parameters of your search. You never know where that perfect spot may be found.

Holiday 2013

Does CLA have a relationship with A.A., and if so, how does it work?
A Program Fan

Dear Fan,

While CLA's 12 Steps and 12 Traditions are based upon those of Alcoholics Anonymous (A.A.), there is no formal tie between the two. CLA does have permission from A.A. to adapt the Steps and Traditions for its use; however, A.A. has requested that CLA not make any substitutions when reading directly from A.A. literature in meetings.

What CLA has done is adapted the principles of the A.A. program. Not only do we use (the adapted version of) the Steps and Traditions, we also refer to other A.A. literature when dealing with program issues. CLA members have benefitted by studying the A.A. books *Alcoholics Anonymous*[4] (the "Big Book") and *Twelve Steps and Twelve Traditions*,[16] which deal extensively with how to work a 12-Step program. Anyone in a service position is encouraged to become familiar with A.A.'s "12 Concepts of Service"[17] to gain knowledge on the successful functioning of groups and service bodies.

As you can see, while there is no formal tie between the two programs, CLA remains very connected to the program principles set forth by A.A., the progenitor of all 12-Step programs. It is a fact that without A.A., there would be no CLA.

Spring 2014

I came to CLA expecting to get organizing tips, but I'm mostly hearing about how people feel about cluttering. Are they ever going to give me tips and how can CLA help me anyway?

Searching for Organization

Dear Searching,

While organizing tips do have their place, that is not what CLA is about. It is easy to find organizing tips in magazine articles, books, and on the Internet; feel free to use them if they help you. Most clutterers have found that tips by themselves do not help them to maintain clutter-free environments.

CLA is focused on helping us solve our clutter problems by tackling the inner causes of our cluttering, rather than the symptoms. We do this by working the 12 Steps, which are based on those of Alcoholics Anonymous, and are the basis of the CLA program of recovery. (See the "Twelve & Twelve FAQs" article on pages 20–21 and articles in back issues of CLA*rity* for more information.)

The CLA Tools of Recovery,[19] like earmarking and streamlining, have helped many clutterers. They are printed in both the leaflet, "A Brief Guide"[5] and the booklet, "Is CLA for You? A Newcomer's Guide to Recovery."[12] CLA*rity* back issues contain articles on all of the Tools.

By attending CLA meetings, we find that we are not alone in this disease. When we share our experience, strength, and hope, not only do we help ourselves come to grips with our clutter problems, but also other clutterers may find insights into their own problems by listening to our shares.

So you see, there is a lot of help for the clutterer in CLA, but there is no magic button; it takes some effort to work a successful program. As they say in A.A., "It works if you work it!"

Summer 2014

I am told that I should have a sponsor. How do I get a sponsor?

Wannabee Sponsee

Dear Wannabee Sponsee,

"Action is the magic word!" The short answer is to ask a fellow CLA member to sponsor you.

There are no formalities or rules that govern who sponsors whom, although it is suggested that a sponsor has previously worked at least one Step higher than the sponsee—or, for someone doing the Steps the first time, has at least completed Step 4.

However, there are a few things to consider when you decide whom to ask. Look for someone in the program who shows evidence of having had some recovery from working the Steps and from whom you can take direction without any personality conflicts. It is usually suggested that a sponsor not be a close friend or of the opposite sex.

Then, once you have decided whom to ask, simply approach the person and ask him or her to sponsor you. The answer may be yes, but if the person either doesn't feel he or she has enough time or recovery, you may be told no. In that case, look for another member. But the first step to gaining a sponsor is up to you—keep asking.

Fall 2014

What does the CLA Cyber Committee do?

Signed, Internet Inquirer

Dear Inquirer,

Well to start, if you've ever wondered whether CLA's web site is professionally managed, the answer may surprise you. It's actually run by our industrious CLA Cyber Committee, which consists of three busy CLA member volunteers who meet weekly (for now). Together, they manage ClutterersAnonymous.org (formerly Clutterers Anonymous.net).

By manage, we mean that our committee makes sure the web site is functional and provides members and potential members with vital information about CLA, including meeting lists and access to literature, among other things. We do pay a webmaster to fix anything that breaks and to make minor changes that we can't make ourselves, and we pay a hosting company to host our web site.

Looking forward, we are in the process of streamlining our site with the goal of being able to make more of our own changes, thereby lowering our costs. The look and feel of the web site will be updated and modernized, and to meet this goal we have contracted with an affordable web designer to help us do the redesign within our budget.

We have several enhancements in the works, including allowing recovery meeting group contacts to register their meetings online with CLA, as well as allowing group delegates to register themselves. If the price is within our budget, we hope to allow subscribers to view the CLA newsletter, CLA*rity*, electronically. In addition, we'll be including more information about WSO elected positions and service committees. Our wish list includes allowing purchasers to view CLA literature electronically as well, and we will be researching the possible use of social media to better reach clutterers.

Your feedback and suggestions are very important to us, and we would love to hear from you. Feel free to contact the Cyber Committee using any of the CLA*rity* contact methods in the the frontispiece or by choosing the webmaster as the subject in the "Contact" feature on Clutterers Anonymous.org.

So sit back and stay tuned for the much-anticipated launch of our redesigned web site. Coming soon to a computer near you.

Holiday 2014

Why is anonymity so important in CLA?

Outgoing in Omaha

Dear Outgoing,

The principle of anonymity is so important that two of the CLA Traditions (11 and 12) deal with it. Maintaining anonymity protects both the individual and the Fellowship as a whole. Of course, members may, if they wish, tell family, friends, coworkers, etc. of their membership in CLA.

Recovery in CLA requires a certain amount of trust, especially for newcomers. If members learn that what they share is being repeated, they may cease to speak at meetings—or even leave the Fellowship altogether. Therefore, CLA members should never relate what others have shared at meetings without their permission.

But there is another aspect to the Traditions on anonymity, and that is protection of the CLA Fellowship. As with all our Traditions, those regarding anonymity were based on early Alcoholics Anonymous experience. After A.A. had grown quite a bit and was beginning to be accepted in many places, some members went very public about their membership and how A.A. had helped them to remain sober. Unfortunately, some of these began drinking again. The resulting negative publicity hurt the A.A. Fellowship and prevented it from reaching some alcoholics who still suffered. Because of this, all 12-Step Fellowships, including CLA, insist on anonymity at the public level.

Also, if a few individuals are seen as representing CLA, the media may begin to consider these individuals as speaking for CLA—which can result in resentment by others in the Fellowship. The resulting dissension could ruin CLA. In addition, it could negatively impact the recovery of the well-known individuals, since working the 12 Steps successfully requires a degree of humility, which is hard to maintain when the public considers someone an expert.

All of these reasons explain why the 12th Tradition ends with "...principles before personalities."

Spring 2015

During discussions about getting CLA's message out, it has been stated that CLA does not promote itself. Why not?

A Clutterer Wanting to Spread the Word

Dear Clutterer,

Tradition 11 states that "Our public relations policy is based on attraction rather than promotion..."

It is understood in 12-Step programs that there is a fine line between attraction and promotion. But what is the difference? Mainly, it means that in our interaction with the media—whether it is via news articles or reports or advertising—we state what CLA is, what its principles are, and how to find meetings. We may share personal stories if we keep our anonymity.

What we don't do—that most non-12-Step

organizations do—is give endorsements from well-known people and make promises that if you follow our path, recovery is guaranteed. We don't act like messiahs with a cure-all. We let clutterers make up their own minds about whether the program is for them rather than trying to influence them with a dazzling display.

But why is it so important? The benefits of this method were found in the early Alcoholics Anonymous program. They found that the Fellowship reached many more people by giving the facts of the Fellowship rather than giving glowing before-and-after stories of members. In fact, members of the news media were so enchanted by an organization that didn't toot its own horn that they were much more supportive than they would have been otherwise. And since we are stating facts rather than shining a spotlight on individuals, we avoid controversy which could tear apart the Fellowship.

Summer 2015

What are we allowed to do to attract new clutterers?
Seeking New Members

Dear Seeking,

CLA's Tradition 11 states: "Our public relations policy is based on attraction, rather than promotion…" But how can we attract clutterers to the Fellowship without promoting it?

Many groups put up flyers in various locations, such as stores, laundromats, libraries, community bulletin boards, etc. Basically, any place that allows you to post notices will do, provided that CLA is not required to advertise or show affiliation with the owners of the space.

Other groups have found it helpful to announce their meetings in local newspapers or online lists, at little to no cost. This is a good way to interest newcomers. Either method is perfectly acceptable, as long as we do not break members' anonymity, make claims for the program, or use personal testimonials.

If a group wishes to put up flyers but doesn't want to design their own, they can use the flyer included in the "CLA Meeting Starter Kit."[7] There is a sample flyer, with dummy information filled in, and one with blanks for the group to fill in. If the group does not have a starter kit, it can request the flyer by using any of the contact methods in the frontispiece.

Sometimes newspaper articles which are wholly or partly about CLA may be helpful. If you are talking to the news media about an article, radio show, or television program, make sure they are aware that we must maintain personal anonymity by not using last names or pictures of our members. If you have questions about how to proceed in dealing with the news media, feel free to talk to CLA's public information officer. She can be reached by using any of the contact methods in the frontispiece.

CLA recommends that you be prepared to welcome potential large numbers of participants should your group receive media coverage.

Fall 2015

There are no meetings in my area. What shall I do?
Seeking Support and Serenity

Dear Seeking,

You have three options: (1) you could begin attending phone meetings, (2) you could start a meeting in your area, or (3) you could do both.

There are CLA phone meetings held every day of the week. To view a list of phone meetings, go to the "Phone Meetings" link at ClutterersAnonymous.org. Or to request a printed list, use one of the contact methods listed in the frontispiece.

If you wish to start a face-to-face meeting in your area, we suggest that you order the "CLA Meeting Starter Kit."It can be ordered online by going to the Order Literature link at Clutterers Anonymous.org or by downloading and mailing the "CLA Literature Order Form" along with a check or money order to: CLA WSO, PO Box 91413, Los Angeles, CA 90009. You can also obtain a copy of the order form by using any of the contact methods listed in the frontispiece.

If you are not already a member of a 12-Step Fellowship, it is suggested that you attend several 12-Step face-to-face meetings (such as those of Alcoholics Anonymous) before starting a CLA meeting. You may also benefit from attending CLA phone meetings. This will help you to understand how the Steps and Traditions work and how 12-Step programs in general work. Although clutter is a different problem from those covered by other 12-Step Fellowships, the principle of spiritual recovery through the Steps (which is the basis for recovery in CLA) is the same for all.

Holiday 2015

Where does new CLA literature come from?
Literature Lover in Louisiana

Dear Literature Lover,

The origins of Clutterers Anonymous literature have been varied, although each piece has been approved by CLA World Service Organization (WSO).

The first seven leaflets to be published were written by Varda, one of CLA's co-founders. CLA's leaflet, "A Brief Guide,"[5] was put together by other CLA members using pre-existing CLA literature. The "Measuring Progress on Our Journey in Recovery"[13] leaflet, the booklet "Is CLA for You? A Newcomer's Guide to Recovery,"[12] and the "CLA Meeting Starter Kit"[7] were written by the CLA Literature Committee—although some parts of these had been started by other CLA members and rewritten by the Literature Committee.

All of the literature was submitted to the Fellowship for review. Often, based on Fellowship feedback, it was rewritten, resubmitted and eventually approved by WSO before publication.

But who decides which literature to write? Occasionally, WSO directs the committee to write a particular piece. Other times, the Literature Committee decides what to work on next. It takes into account suggestions from CLA members and makes decisions based upon what is perceived to be the greater needs of the Fellowship.

This process can be very lengthy. Often, it takes one to two years or more for a publication to make it from the first draft to the final document. But taking the time to get Fellowship feedback has strengthened and enhanced the final products.

Are there any topics you would like to see written about? If so, let the Literature Committee know, and they may consider them. You can reach this committee by using any of the contact methods in the frontispiece.

Spring 2016

How can CLA help me to better organize?
Hopelessly Disorganized

Dear Hopelessly,

CLA is a spiritual program of recovery, with the 12 Steps and 12 Traditions as its foundation. We believe we must fix the underlying causes in order to maintain any decluttering success.

As it says in the CLA Tools of Recovery,[19] "Action is the magic word." In fact, Daily Action is one of the keys to maintaining any organizing you do.

Buddies and sponsors can help by giving you a listening ear and helping you to formulate a plan of action. By attending meetings, you can hear how other clutterers have tackled similar problems, which may help you to figure out how to solve your own.

In fact, all of the Tools can be helpful in your efforts to organize. When we are Focusing (doing one thing at a time) we are concentrating only on the problem and ruling out distractions. Streamlining (setting limits on our possessions) is also important because if we have too much stuff, it is difficult to find a place to put it. Earmarking (providing places for our possessions and returning them there) is helpful for maintaining the organizing we have done.

Also, you may wish to look at the leaflet, "Measuring Progress on Our Journey in Recovery," which can help you recognize what choices and behaviors may lead to failure or success in your attempts to organize.

Whatever you do, remember to listen to your sponsor and your Higher Power. If you search with an open mind, the answers should come.

Summer 2016

Can I talk about non-CLA literature in CLA meetings? *Wondering in Washington*

Dear Wondering,

While it is tempting during CLA meetings to discuss various books and articles that have caught your attention, that is in conflict with our Traditions. The CLA newcomer's guide, called "Is CLA for You? A Newcomer's Guide to Recovery,"[12] states that "We use CLA literature and that of Alcoholics Anonymous." In addition, our preamble states that, "CLA is not affiliated with any public or private organization." Thus, we do not discuss literature that is not from CLA or A.A. in our meetings.

There are reasons for this. Were we to focus on all the books and methods written on the subject of decluttering and organizing, we would leave little time to focus on our own spiritual program of recovery. We might also miss the opportunity for the growth offered by CLA. In fact, doing so might generate conflict, as members might argue for the non-CLA systems that work for each of themselves.

That doesn't mean you can't speak about non-CLA literature at CLA meetings. If you want to discuss this literature, you may want to describe it as "something I read that helped me."

But does that mean that you can't use the methods outlined in books or on the Internet to help with your decluttering efforts while working the CLA program? Not at all. What you do outside the meeting is your own business. If a method helps you, go for it.

There is no conflict to working the 12 Steps and following some author's system of organization. You can even discuss it with other members of the Fellowship outside CLA meetings and events. If you mention it during sharing, it's best to use general terms, such as "...an organizing method that I use..." We suggest you focus on the CLA program in your shares.

Fall 2016

What should I tell the non-clutterer in my life who pressures me? *At My Wit's End in Wisconsin*

Dear Wit's End,

If you are a clutterer, you have likely had complaints from the non-clutterers in your life. Many people do not understand clutter; they think it's just a matter of cleaning up. In reality, clutter is a physical manifestation of an inner spiritual turmoil.

You may wish to remind the non-clutterer that it took a long time to get to the point you are at now, and it probably will take some time to find recovery. If you are working the CLA program, it may help to remind them that you are doing so; and, as we say, "progress not perfection." You may also wish to invite them to attend an open CLA meeting with you or to read our CLA literature so they can learn more about how the program works.

It is not unusual that non-clutterers are unable to understand, but you can still work your program—work the Steps, pray and meditate, and ask your Higher Power for guidance. As you make progress with your decluttering efforts, you can share your victories with the non-clutterers so they understand that you are progressing.

No matter what, remember to be gentle with yourself, reach out to your Higher Power, and get support from your fellow clutterers when you need it.

Holiday 2016

What does it mean to place principles before personalities? *Confused in Connecticut*

Dear Confused,

What happens when 12-Step members place personalities before principles? This contradicts Tradition 12. Some examples of this would be:

- decisions that are based on personal likes, dislikes, and grudges;
- taking an action without consulting, or getting approval from, the rest of the group; and

- arguing or cutting someone off if a member does not agree with what is being said.

Tradition 12 reminds us to put "...principles before personalities." That means we vote, so everyone gets input into how things are done.

If Traditions are not followed, it may engender controversy and upheaval among members. Some people will stop participating in meetings or leave CLA altogether.

Tradition 5 tells us that our primary purpose is to help other still-suffering clutterers. If the group is not there to carry the message, there will be no recovery for anyone. So all decisions are made with that in mind.

When we follow Tradition 12, the group becomes a place of more serenity, recovery, and cooperation—and newcomers feel more welcome.

The bottom line is, as Tradition 1 states, "personal recovery depends upon CLA unity." And that's why principles come first.

Letter from the Chair

Articles in this section appeared in the "Letter from the Chair" column and were written by chairpersons of the CLA World Service Organization. They include both information about CLA and sharing on personal recovery.

Spring 2008

Alison B., NJ

My name is Alison. I am a recovering clutterer, originally from London, England. I have been in this country about 22 years and in Clutterers Anonymous about five years. I have approximately 24 years of 12-Step experience. I have recently become the chairperson for the CLA World Service Organization. I regard myself simply as a facilitator of a somewhat larger meeting.

Clutterers Anonymous is about 19 years old and is a fairly young Fellowship compared to many 12-Step programs. Because of this (and because of our inherent, disorganized clutterers' traits), there are still gaps in our collective education. Perhaps I can rephrase that and say that we have the knowledge, but there is still much information to be disseminated into written form.

We will do our best to support CLA groups and help them grow. However, we may not be able to answer all your questions readily because we are still going through some stages of growing pains ourselves. What we are attempting to do is draw from the experience, strength, and hope of other well-established 12-Step programs; and we especially welcome people who have experience in different arenas.

We know the theories; we know what is supposed to work—but it appears that many of us are extremely stubborn when it comes to commitments and follow-through. It is my personal belief that cluttering is the overflow of many compulsions/addictions, largely based on the need for instant gratification. ("Wait, I've got something to do over there; let me just drop this item here for now!")

We can talk about our clutter forever—and, believe me, we do—but actions are needed on a daily basis. I am learning this more and more as I do service behind the scenes and need to be more organized for that alone.

A.A. will tell you that service is the way to recovery; I truly believe this. I encourage people to try a little bit of service, only to the degree that they feel comfortable. If each person in the group is responsible for one thing, much will get done. From doing service, I have been learning commitment, work ethics, teamwork, trust, discipline (a dirty word for many of us!), routine, structure... the list is endless. It can have its negative side, too. In order to be able to live in a balanced way, I must rest when I need to, laugh when I want to, and follow the CLA Steps, Traditions, Tools of Recovery,[19] and the Affirmations[20] in the program to the best of my ability. This is not easy for me, and I am always working on it!

We are planning many changes in the next year, and this is a very exciting time to be more involved with CLA; we are still laying the groundwork, and there are many learning opportunities for those who listen, observe, and keep an open mind. We are working hard to make the World Service Organization business meetings more functional and friendly.

May Higher Power bless you with love and abundance (and not clutter!) in all areas of your life.

Summer 2008

Alison B., NJ

Dear CLA Friends,

This is Alison. I'm not only the chairperson, I am also a member. I volunteer my time for CLA. Although I have been a member since the end of 2002, it wasn't until the end of 2006 that I began to realize how much my complacency was ruining my plans and dreams for a successful life. A woman in her mid forties isn't at her best when she is spending most of her time at home in her pajamas watching soap operas.

A local CLA member thought I might be interested in helping with an editing project, and I was contacted because a member wanted to start a CLA newsletter. I used to be fairly good at writing. I didn't know what I could do to help, but I had heard the theory that service equals recovery. I also realized I might be able to help "carry the message to those who still suffer" in a much larger way, and that appealed to my altruistic side.

So I started going to organizational meetings held on the phone. I was fascinated. Here was a group of people who obviously had trouble communicating because of their own cluttered thinking; some, including myself, were rather impatient, yet they seemed to have a certain kind of efficiency. They had a drive to get things done, even when they weren't too sure of their direction.

Suddenly, I realized that with my many years of experience in different 12-Step programs, and all the self-seeking I have done in my life, I had information to offer from my experience, strength, and hope. My self-esteem began to flourish as I found that people were paying attention to me and liking my views—they didn't have any preconceived notions about me, and they were not judging me for past mistakes or for my clutter. That felt wonderful.

I tell this story because, although my road to recovery has not been smooth, I'm traveling much faster these days. I subsequently volunteered for as many committees as I could because I was bored with my life.

Then came the time when I was inundated with CLA volunteer work. I wasn't sure how to ask for help, but I knew that if I didn't come right out and say I needed it, I would not be able to fulfill my commitments.

That was a turning point for me. I became aware that I was not making enough commitments in my own life, but that was okay. I had semiconsciously planned it that way: I had been previously wasting the years away without making a significant contribution to the world around me.

I began following more of the program to the best of my ability. I love the Tools[19] and Affirmations.[20] I have been pushing myself to do more decluttering. I always need to remember that my recovery comes first; and if I fall behind in my CLA commitments, I turn it over to HP, prioritize, ask for help, and do the best I can.

I tend to see everything in black and white; so I need to seek balance, and I learn best when I let the pendulum of responsibility swing, first one way and then the other.

If any of you can relate to the emptiness I felt in my life, come and volunteer with us. You will find contact information in the frontispiece. Just start with one project (it can be time limited), and see how you feel. There is a lot of love and acceptance here, and I am so thankful for that energizing support.

Thanks, CLA. Thanks, HP. I am forever grateful for having my eyes opened to all kinds of possibilities. Now I have hope that I can help myself. I'm doing it—and as I help myself, so I help CLA.

Fall 2008

Alison B., NJ

Dear CLA Members,

As I said in the last issue, I am working my program more seriously these days. I think much more clearly when I put my current decluttering and my own recovery before service projects.

Now I am being forced, yet again, to look at the addictive side of myself, and relationships seem to be the order of the day. I have been told that service brings out people's worst character defects so they can work on them. Is this true? I can speak only for myself, through my own experiences.

We conduct all of our committee meetings by phone and email. We have become like a family—and as in any family, there are varied interactions, depending on what each of us has to bring to the table, our different styles of communication, and whether or not we are able to check our egos at the door.

We all probably have trust issues and personality conflicts from our past that "push buttons" and cause misplaced anger in the present. Sometimes, though, we plainly just annoy each other, and tempers flare.

Despite it all, we know that we are here for one purpose only: to carry the message that there is relief from this addiction. And a handful of people work incredibly hard to do just that.

Part of the program speaks to humility, so you will never hear how many hours are poured into keeping it all together. And we have a tendency to allow individual clutter problems to slow our progress, so maybe we take a bit longer to produce results than we originally intended. But we have learned to persist to the best of our collective abilities, and we do produce tangible results, even if the membership cannot see much in the way of progress.

We are intently building overall structure at present, and there are many gaps in the communication chain, which we are eager to fill. We have learned to make time schedules when necessary and to build in early deadlines whenever we can. We put the best parts of ourselves into cleaning up our little corner of the world, so to speak, and we are happy to serve you.

Holiday 2008

Alison B., NJ

Dear CLA Members,

Since I reside in New Jersey, I was thrilled when I was invited to visit Los Angeles for their recent Clutter-Free Day. It was my first trip to California—a precious opportunity to see friends, meet those I know from phone meetings, and make new connections—what could be more exciting?

Oh, believe me, during the planning I tried to complicate matters with job-seeking ideas... fantasizing about a "geographical cure," with the mistaken belief that if I change my surroundings, my life will drastically improve. The problem with that kind of thinking is that I have to take myself with me! I have learned from personal experience that I need to change my insides before I can change my outside, or else I am doomed to repeat clutter patterns in my home, relationships, and life. Still, I can't help but think that miles of palm trees, mountains, constant sun, and endless coastline must make the transition just that bit more pleasant. I voiced one such thought to a resident clutterer, who replied that "paradise gets old." I commented about "being spoiled." But I get the point.

Have you heard the saying, "The other man's grass is always greener"? Well, so it is with my clutter. I know because I transplanted myself from England looking for big flashing neon lights and "streets paved with gold." But I always had a feeling of automatic entitlement, and I didn't understand the hard work ethic. I am making myself work for myself much more than I used to. It is often difficult for me to believe that I am really worth the effort, and I still want to reward myself with things rather than push myself to develop a better quality of life. My cluttered thinking makes almost everything difficult for me, and I am scared of my own shadow, though now I talk my fears out so I can face them, or I "act as if" I am confident—and suddenly I become so, even if only temporarily.

I was the keynote speaker at Clutter-Free Day. I

wrote a list of key words, I asked my Higher Power to help me, took my turn, and apparently was well received...only my friends knew that I broke down afterwards because I was overtired and disoriented. I have to take care of myself with plenty of sleep, good food, and exercise. My clutter has not manifested itself so much in the realm of hoarding, maybe because my opportunities have been limited. But I did notice all over again—from living in close quarters with a fellow clutterer—how cluttered my thinking is and how hard I have to work to think in a linear fashion. This is the big thing that we clutterers and hoarders seem to have in common.

Now is the winter of my discontent. I should be ending my term as chairperson; instead, the World Service voted to extend the service period of the officers until March so that we can work on the job descriptions that were never finalized. I enjoy "carrying the message" in this fashion, but we do need many more hands to make lighter workloads so that we don't get burned out and so that others may benefit from doing service that is so vital to recovery. It is certainly helping me—it gives me a sense of responsibility that I never enjoyed in the past. And, yes, I am enjoying it—as long I remember the idea of balance, another thing that doesn't come easily to me. Just so you know, it is less than a week since I returned from the West Coast. I am already unpacked, and my clothes are washed and put away. I'm proud of myself for that; last time I returned from a trip, I stared at my open suitcase for months—and this time I emptied it in about 15 minutes and was able to put it in the closet. Yippee!

Spring 2009

Alison B., NJ

For me, my own procrastination is like being part of a 50-car pileup with myself, as well as with others. When I suddenly stop doing something in my routine that's essential for my well-being—such as going to sleep on time—I start to suffer, and then all the other parts of my life suffer, too. At the moment, parts of my life are inexorably linked with CLA business—and it seems that others' actions are often based on my decision to organize a meeting; talk about a group problem; write an agenda; or answer an email by imparting some of my experience, strength, hope, and ideas pertaining to the Twelve Steps and Twelve Traditions. If I fail to do my part in a timely fashion, I stop others from doing the parts to which they have committed. Part of the problem in WSO is that each person is already wearing far too many hats, which means that there are so many things going on for each of us that we are scattergunning.

In addition to facilitating WSO and Executive Committee meetings, I am supposed to oversee all the committees and help sort out communication problems. I do that to the best of my ability; and, as an added bonus, I am also highly involved in all the committees. I thoroughly enjoy helping to write literature and editing articles for the newsletter you are now reading. Aside from those responsibilities, there are technical issues—such as the transition of our toll-free information line (which has not been toll-free up 'til now) and the business of updating website information and various technological faculties. I know very little about these things and don't have time enough to study, not if I want to have my own life too. Because we are invested in group decision making and action taking—to teach us various aspects of recovery, such as tolerance, for example—the completion of every project depends on the timely actions of every single person in the group who has committed to do something to move that project towards completion. Here's the problem: every single person in the group procrastinates to a greater or lesser degree, and all the delays can be justified in one way or another.

At some point there are no more excuses. It's up to each and every one of us to prioritize, get better organized, clear our heads enough to make rational decisions, and back out responsibly if we've taken on more than we can handle at any given time. What constitutes responsibly? Well, if I commit to showing up every week for a business meeting and then something else comes up, how do I handle it? If I just fail to appear, do people understand that they are to move the meeting along without me, or are they wasting valuable time waiting for me, wondering what happened, or trying to call me? In other words, have I made my position clear? I have been raised to expect people to call if they can't show up. I would certainly do that, and I am constantly hurt by others who don't show the same consideration, and so I often feel the need to talk about it, wasting valuable group time. To go one step further, I have been raised to commit to something only if I fully intend to follow through, whatever it takes. It may be why I have so much trouble making commitments, but at this stage in my life, I have resolved to work much harder on the follow-through. I'm not sure how much expectations come into play here—mine versus others'—but I do know the program suggestion that we learn to lower our expectations, and this is a tough lesson, especially for someone who wants to raise her own standards at the same time.

Please understand: I am not assigning blame in any way, shape, or form. We are clutterers—we are in this program because we are working through our inadequacies, and on the whole, we are winning the wars that we seem to be fighting with ourselves, though it often takes many years before the "clutter fog" really lifts. I urge that everybody, please, take this program more seriously. I didn't know what kind of fog I had been in all these years 'til I started to pull out of it, and that happens with continual working on myself, the 12-Step way. I know that I have to help myself first before I can be of real help to anybody else—and as I recover, so the group recovers.

Summer 2009

Alison B., NJ

As the outgoing chairperson, I would like to say that I feel so privileged to have served this wonderful Fellowship in this manner. Not only that, an old friend, who is also a member, visited my apartment the other day and was amazed at how much I have cleaned up! The funny part is, I am not always aware of the progress, and I was a bit worried about letting her in, but she was genuine and profuse in her compliments. If you're anything like me, even compliments are uncomfortable, but I have learned to smile, say "thank you," and to practice gratitude in my mind.

I attribute my new positive attitude towards having a comfortable home to the fact that last year, after I became chairperson, I decided I truly needed to "walk the walk" so that I would have more experience, strength, and hope to pass along to others. I decided to learn to let go of an underlying addiction that wants to suck me in and stop me from dealing with my life. The addiction itself is not as important as the fact that I joined another 12-Step program and took a temporary sponsor. I was instructed to call her every day, and she asked me to read Step One in that Fellowship's literature. I'd been in CLA for six years and have been in other programs in years prior; but now, from a deep and personal point of view, I began, once more, to see how important it was to admit my powerlessness over "people, places, and things." I have heard that phrase so many times over the 25 years I have been in different Fellowships, but the sad truth is that I had not officially sat down and written my story or how I felt about all the different aspects of my character. I have been told over and over again how freeing it is. However, we cannot pass along our own feelings. There are some things we all have to experience for ourselves, from deep inside.

Every clutterer/hoarder/addict, without exception, does this self-destructive behaviour because there is an empty hole inside, which never seems to get filled. I've often heard that this hole was spiritual in nature. Now I have a new perspective: I believe the answer is practicing self-love—doing things that are important for my overall being in the long run. That means eating properly, sleeping restfully, taking time to relax, meditating, or just quieting the mind daily for at least half an hour. I'm also learning to do for others, but only after I've taken care of myself. These new habits take practice. They begin with little rituals like dropping the grocery bags in the kitchen instead of just inside my front door, taking a short rest, and then making sure all the items are put away. I take my cues from the CLA program and the other one, and I work hard to remember that love is also a verb.

My favorite saying from this program is: "Action is the magic word." To give you an example, I did not want to sit down and write this letter. I have procrastinated 'til past the deadline actually, but this morning I made myself sit down at the computer with this specific action in mind, knowing that once I started writing, the words would likely start to flow as they always do. Do I want to take the action? No. What's my payoff? Well, I know I will feel a tremendous release and satisfaction after it's done, especially since I made a commitment to do it. I told myself many years ago that I make commitments only if I am prepared to see them through. Do I want to take on more tasks that seem overwhelming? No—I want to be selfish; I want to tell the world to leave me alone, and yet I want to let people in too. I don't want to make decisions, yet I know I must. It's such a quandary, isn't it? That's why I seek opinions from lots of different people about the same subject, and then I make my own decisions. In effect, I take my own personal "group conscience" all the time.

Oh, by the way, the WSO group conscience saw fit to rotate the chairperson position to the vice-chairperson, Kathy—so congratulations to her—and it was decided that I will be the new Communications coordinator. It is a job I will relish, though I do have clutter to clean up from being chairperson, in the form of replying to overdue emails. I used to think that "discipline" was a dirty word. I have learned in the rooms that "discipline is remembering what we want." True words indeed!

Fall 2009

Kathy H., CA

As I sat down to write this article, I started to reflect on my journey in 12-Step programs.

I began my recovery in another program many years ago. I loved that program and still think very highly of it and those I met there, from whom I learned many good life lessons. But, somehow, I drifted away. First it was transportation; someone would have given me rides, but I never asked. Then it was just habit not to go, though I kept telling myself I would return. I have never forgotten lessons I learned there.

Then, about seven years ago, I found CLA and realized that this is the place I really need to be. Yet I have been without a CLA sponsor and have felt the lack, the hole in my life. It has been many years since I consistently worked the Steps, although I have tried to apply them in my life. However, I have now started to work the Steps with a sponsor.

Why did it take so long? Unfortunately, we have few sponsors in CLA—especially in face-to-face meetings, which are often small. However, the difficulty in finding a sponsor and my habit of procrastination, combined with a fear of getting deep into the Steps (even though I want the freeing of self-bondage that results) led me to put it off again and again. When I realized that I had actually committed to working the Steps again, I felt an amazing sense of relief.

I consider the dearth of sponsors in CLA to be one of the more pressing problems we face, but the Literature Committee and others are working on solutions.

So, my term as WSO chairperson began in April of this year. There are many things happening now, some of which began while Alison B. was chairperson. The Communications Committee is now functioning; the new website redesign has been completed, including online ordering; and we have set up a Service Committee.

One of the thorny problems facing us at this time is what WSO should do when groups are not adhering to the Traditions. This has been talked about occasionally for many years, but we have never had a policy on how to handle it. So, when it happens, we talk again and flounder.

Currently, there is quite a bit of controversy about this. The Executive Committee is researching what other Fellowships do, and we will eventually formulate a proposal to be put before our Fellowship and voted on in the WSO. I strongly believe that we need to address this so when it comes up again, we will have clear-cut guidelines of what we should do.

The importance of Traditions is shown in the common saying that "the Steps are to keep us from killing ourselves and the Traditions are to keep us from killing each other." We have also set up a committee to educate the Fellowship about Traditions; it is planning a series of phone seminars as a part of this endeavor. Won't you please join us?

During my term as chairperson, I hope to make progress on these two issues—service and adherence to Traditions.

Holiday 2009

Kathy H., CA

At this time, nearing the end of CLA's 20th Anniversary year, I have been thinking about the many changes that have happened in my years in the Fellowship.

My first CLA meeting was the Altadena, California, Tuesday meeting, which I still attend occasionally. In those days there were about 20 meetings—none outside the United States. Now there are many more face-to-face groups, meetings in three other countries, and daily telephone meetings, as well as telephone activities, including the Commitment Line.

When I first started attending the World Service Organization (WSO) business meetings, they were held in a physical location in Los Angeles, California, rather than via conference calls as they are now. Also, there were no real functioning WSO committees at that time, but we now have several up and running (including CLA*rity*). While we have made great strides on the service level, we still struggle with not having enough hands to do the jobs.

As well as being able to celebrate much achievement, the Fellowship has also had to deal with controversy from time to time. But, as we are taught in program, we manage to put principles before personalities and learn to rise above our problems eventually. Hopefully, we grow from our mistakes.

However, as important as the service structure is, the vital part—the backbone—of the Fellowship remains the local group, whether it is a face-to-face or a telephone group. That is where recovery happens. I am very pleased with the progress of my home group this year. You might say we are having a renaissance. Not only have our numbers grown a little, but there seems to be a new focus on recovery for most of us. The new dynamic has been very heartening. Having a few newcomers join us has helped to revitalize our group.

A 12-Step group is a like a living, breathing organism. Feed it properly and give it the right atmosphere, and it will thrive. Ignore its needs and it begins to die. I think "food" for a group is a focus on recovery—on trying to work the Steps in order to find solutions to our vexing problems. If the group is caring and fosters an atmosphere of spiritual growth, great things can happen. When the group members share in a dishonest or shallow way or when the focus is on something other than the program, recovery begins to dwindle and the group begins to wilt. The success of the group depends on all its members—newcomers as well as old timers.

Truly, it is by helping each other—by sharing our experience, strength, and hope—that we grow as individuals and as a group. That was brought home to me recently, as I helped a CLA member with her 5th Step. Listening to her inventory led me to realize many things about my own disease. It all really brings home to me the fact that, ultimately, if we don't work Step 12, our progress will begin to dwindle, regardless of what else we do. It is the group and other members that help me to keep the focus on my own recovery.

So, Happy Birthday, CLA. I hope all our members have had a wonderful year of discovery and of recovery.

Spring 2010

Kathy H., CA

Lately I have had difficulty in releasing resentments. I recently read a quote from a famous person about how forgiveness liberates the soul and makes us strong. This is something I truly believe; I have known this for a long time.

Then, it also occurs to me to read our own CLA "Decluttering Resentments"[8] leaflet. There is a lot of meat packed into that one piece of paper. There has been a good deal of controversy in CLA in the past months. I think many of us could stand to read and reread that leaflet—not only read it but learn from what we are reading. Only when we learn to let go of resentments can we begin to grow.

Yes, CLA has had a few bumps along the road lately. But that is often a part of growing pains—and CLA has grown tremendously in the last several years. Think of it—in 2000, CLA consisted of 22 face-to-face meetings in the United States, with no meetings in other countries and no telephone meetings. Now there are about 70 meetings (including those in three other countries), as well as phone meetings every day of the week.

But numbers are not the whole story. We have periodically been reporting in CLA*rity* about new happenings in CLA: Clutter-Free Days, CLA website doings, our new Traditions seminars, to name just a few. The first of the Traditions seminars, covering Traditions 1–3, was held on November 27, 2009. About 35 members attended this seminar, which was widely judged a success. I hope more of you can join us for the next seminar, which will be held on Saturday, March 6, 2010.

One other thing that has me excited these days is the new booklet, "Is CLA for You? A Newcomer's Guide to Recovery."[12] This was sent to the Fellowship for feedback and approval in 2008. The response was generally favorable, with some minor changes requested. The Literature Committee has been hard at work during the past year implementing those changes.

On January 23, 2010, it was presented to WSO and was approved for publication. The Literature Committee will format the document as a booklet, and it will be printed and available for purchase soon. Check www.ClutterersAnonymous.org for ordering information.

All in all, I am happy that we have been making progress in the Fellowship. There is still much to be done, however. We all grow when we become a part of the larger whole, and CLA definitely needs the help of its members to finish the tasks. Won't you join us in giving service during this wonderful time of exciting changes in the Fellowship?

Summer 2010

Kathy H., CA

As my term as CLA WSO chairperson comes to a close, I have been thinking about the past year. It has been an eventful one, both in my personal life and in CLA.

This year has brought some new things to CLA. Our website, ClutterersAnonymous.org, has been totally revamped and made more user friendly. If you haven't done so, check it out. It is a good source for knowledge about current events, meeting details, and other information on CLA.

The World Service Organization has begun holding telephone seminars on the CLA Traditions, discussing three Traditions at each seminar. There are two objectives in holding these seminars: (1) to educate the Fellowship about the Traditions and (2) to gather material for possible inclusion in a Twelve Steps and Twelve Traditions book to be written sometime in the future.

And speaking of literature, the new booklet, "Is CLA for You? A Newcomer's Guide to Recovery," should soon be available for purchase. This one is exciting; it is the first piece of new CLA literature in a long time, as well as being the first-ever multipage publication by the Fellowship.

Personally, this has also been a year filled with many occurrences. I have been working with a new CLA sponsor, and finally worked through all my Steps in CLA. (I had previously worked them with a sponsor in another program.) I attended the Clutter-Free Day in Berkeley, California, in November 2009 and that of CLA-East in Brooklyn, New York, on May 16. There have been a lot of family matters to take my time, most notably a special celebration for my mother's 90th birthday.

In spite of all the things to take my attention away from my program, I also managed to focus on decluttering. In the past, I would never have put attention on taking care of my clutter with so many other things happening. And yet, in spite of so much going on, I have made bigger strides in decluttering and maintaining my home than ever before. And it's all because of CLA.

My sewing room was the first to get tackled. A shelf had fallen and dumped books on top of other furniture. Then a moderate earthquake had dumped other things around the room. I took the opportunity not only to clean up but to also reorganize the entire room. And I was able to fill serveral large boxes and take them to the thrift shop.

Then I started on the kitchen. It had been years since I had really gotten into all the cupboards completely. Now my counters are clean and free, my cupboards are all organized (and not overstuffed), and I took five large boxes of items to the thrift shop. It's wonderful to look at the kitchen and see clean, decluttered counters and to easily be able to retrieve items and put them away. Thank you, CLA!

Although I am leaving as WSO chairperson, I will still be involved in CLA and WSO, and I look forward to another great year in the program and in my personal life.

Fall 2010

Alison B., NJ

Hello dear CLA friends—this is Alison. I started my second term as the chairperson of the World Service back in April. However, those of us working on CLA*rity* agreed when we created this column that the outgoing chairperson deserves to send a parting message, and so readers were treated, once again, to the fine written stylings of Kathy H.

I want to take this opportunity to thank Kathy as she continues to work hard for us after many years. You may not know this, but she has long been providing the layout for all our CLA leaflets, as well as this newsletter you are now reading. She's also responsible for the idea and most of the planning for the series of Traditions workshops we are now holding by telephone conference call, four times a year, in order to help members learn about the foundation on which the 12-Step Fellowships are built. Traditions are central to the integrity we practice. There are also endless other ways in which Kathy helps out where needed, and she will probably never even mention them. Thank you, Kathy, for your seemingly boundless energy and your commitment to helping make CLA a stronger Fellowship. Thank you, too, for being my dear friend.

It is said that service is its own reward and that doing what we can to rise above our own problems by helping others not only bolsters self-esteem, but also increases self-reliance and teaches self-discipline and self-awareness. It is desirable, too, that we remain humble and teachable—that is the part that helps each of us to grow.

I know that most of us are overwhelmed with all the activities we tend to pack into any one day, and so many members feel that they have too much going on and cannot dedicate time to any kind of service. If you are like me, you are afraid that if you take on one more thing, it is just something else that you might forget to do.

I practice service precisely because I know I forget and sometimes tend to let others down. I want to be reliable—somebody others can count on—and frankly, I have to work at it very deliberately. I do make mistakes and fall short, but as time goes on, I'm learning how to prioritize, write all appointments into my calendar (and consult it daily!)—and, most importantly, I'm learning how to slow down and not take on as much in any one day. It is often tough, but necessary, to let go of that feeling of urgency and make time for friends or precious hobbies.

The interesting paradox has been that I achieve more on average, and because I take time to assign days and time-limits to my activities, my concentration is better for the allotted time and I am less stressed; and therefore, the quality of my work also improves. I often use a timer to declutter, too, and this is a great tool. I'm always amazed by how much more I get done when I know my task is temporary and I can rest afterwards. This has been even more evident since I have had physical problems and lately have needed to rest more frequently.

I'm still learning to admit my weaknesses, to apologize when I'm wrong, and to ask for help where I really need it. I've found that in requesting help, I need to be careful and not take anyone for granted. I try to be sensitive to others' needs, yet not put them above my own. This is a difficult balance and something I will be learning every day for the rest of my life.

Oops, I just remembered—I promised to make some phone calls this week, but I forgot because I didn't write that chore into my schedule. Now I have some apologies to make. I'd better write myself a note...

Thank you, CLA, for teaching me a new maturity level and for letting me continue to serve you. In doing so, I am truly serving me!

Holiday 2010

Alison B., NJ

Dear Readers,

Since the theme for this issue is giving thanks, I want to express my gratitude for being involved with this wonderful newsletter and the team that puts it together.

We have created a regimented schedule with built-in deadlines for all our procedures. There have been times in my own life when my mood has been lifted, and I've been inspired by the formal weekly meetings (even when there are only three of us!) and specially prepared charts and flow lists which help keep us organized. Truthfully, in the beginning our regimen was cluttered, and it has taken much trial and error to teach us to make the best use of our time. I am truly glad for the experiences and all our time-management mistakes. Initially, there were times when some of us would stay up until dawn just proofreading. This seemed like fun at first, but soon we realized it was tedious and impractical. All in all, staying with the team has helped me become a team player, helped raise my self-esteem, helped me realize that it is OK to make a long-term commitment, and taught me several worthy recovery lessons. So with that in mind, I'd like to describe our practices, which are repeated for each issue.

First, we agree on a deadline for asking potential contributors to write. Oftentimes I think it should be easier to find writers—after all, don't many of us do writings as part of our program? If you're reading this and you realize you already have writings, please consider adapting a piece of your work for publication—and please don't worry if your composition isn't the best. It's our job to make sure that all articles make grammatical sense and also adhere to the Traditions.

The next vital date is when articles are due. If you write for us, we send article guidelines with word counts. We encourage timely submission so that we can start the next stage: the first round of editing. Did you know that we carefully edit each article twice with different people? Two team members are assigned, or they volunteer as necessary. A time is picked when the two can meet by telephone. One reads as the other corrects the copy. We try hard to keep the essence of the story intact, which means that usually we change very little. Sometimes we split longer pieces into two parts, or we shorten the article if we think that's a viable solution.

Once we've completed second-round editing (yes, we need more editors!), our layout person produces the first draft. Now comes the exacting work—the proofreading. I especially enjoy this process, and I must admit that I do get a kick out of finding mistakes! We go through proofing at least three times, often more. Every time a change is made, the final copy has to be sifted through again. This is important because one or two extra letters could cause several lines to move out of place. Personally, I derive tremendous satisfaction in making sure we do the best job we possibly can. When the issue is complete, one person is responsible for having it printed and sending it out. Of course, there are more intricacies than I can describe here, but I hope I've given you a descriptive overview of our methods.

I'm most appreciative of the wonderful CLA*rity* team. These people have been steadfast in their dedication and loyalty. Sometimes it's tough to keep the enthusiasm high, so we gently coax each other to keep the job moving along. We believe the results are worth the effort—what do you think?

Spring 2011

Alison B., NJ

Happy New Year to all my CLA Friends...those I know and those I've yet to discover!

In the realm of service work, I've come to believe that recovering clutterers are amongst the most genuine, well-meaning people I could ever wish to meet. I've realized that oftentimes I've had to find a way to get past the tough facades or imaginary walls that clutterers tend to build for their own protection. But having negotiated outside friendships where it's hard to know whom to trust, I would rather put my faith in my recovering clutterer friends, even when they've sometimes failed to deliver. Practicing forgiveness is good for me, and it's the program way.

I'm learning to delegate. I try hard to keep the faith, let go of negative judgment along the way, and if all else fails, to keep my big mouth shut! It is perfectly fine to respectfully remind someone when a commitment is due or overdue, but it's up to the other person to speak up if he or she requires assistance or can't do the work. It bothers me when people don't communicate, and I have to watch my reaction to that.

I feel that it is critical not to judge anybody's recovery and to be patient with other people's relationships to time (yes, we can change our relationships to time). I've figured out all of this solely because of my own horrible reactions to being judged and my ultimate wish to be treated with respect, both of which just so happen to coincide with this program!

When I was growing up, I perceived my parents as being so judgmental that I lost my self-esteem and my intuitive senses. I've carried that burden with me all through adulthood. I've believed negative opinions about myself to the point where I've been stuck and unable to work on the simplest chores for years at a time—unable to make decisions, big or small. This program has worked wonders for me, but I have to push myself.

There is the logical and self-educated side of me which knows that feelings are not facts. It takes constant practice to positively transform my negative thinking, feelings, attitudes, and habits, especially when I'm tired and my emotional side takes over. I have to make a commitment every week at my home meeting to "stay plugged into HP, and turn negative thinking into positive [thinking]." I've discovered that restorative sleep is the most important gift I can give myself, and I'm working on changing my attitude about wanting to stay up as late as possible—another childhood whim I've carried all my life that has caused me to sabotage my own sleeping patterns.

My recovery from this cluttering addiction is a life-long work in progress, and I believe the best way I can continue to overcome my own character defects is to allow others the space to overcome theirs and to be gentle with my own progress. I'm learning my life lessons here, and, tedious as it can be at times, on the whole, I'm thoroughly enjoying the process!

Summer 2011

Alison B., NJ

Hello CLA Friends,

Lately I've been receiving phone calls and emails about personalities on the phone lines using their so-called authority to make demands of some people and to negatively judge others. In fact, a recent Communications Committee meeting was devoted to this topic.

And it's not just what's being said—it's the way people are yelling and talking over one another. I'm exceedingly troubled, and I feel horrible about this because I'm hearing that several people who have been in CLA for years no longer feel safe about going to phone meetings.

If that's true, then I'll bet we're scaring off new people, too—people who desperately need our help. It is our duty to extend our help to everybody who needs it. And all who come to us obviously need our help.

A huge part of the reason I go to any 12-Step program is that people are taught not to judge one another—not out loud, at least—and, ideally, not at all. We don't compare ourselves to others either—we learn to keep the focus on ourselves and just keep trying to do the next morally right thing.

If I have a problem with a particular personality, I have learned in the rooms that I don't point fingers—in other words, I don't say: "This is what you did." Believe it or not, we can learn preferred ways of conducting ourselves in meetings so as not to humiliate ourselves or hurt others.

The very first thing I learned was to speak in the first person. This is how I react/feel. I try to remember that nobody can make me react or feel a certain way—that is my responsibility.

Also, I learned to practice speaking in a low, even-toned voice and to come from a place of love. My voice is naturally loud and high-pitched, and I admit to having unresolved anger, so this is a constant effort for me. However, I know that what I put out is what I will get back, so I try to make myself sound calm even when I don't feel it.

Actually, when I have to lead a meeting, I don't answer the phone for one hour before. I spend at least 15 minutes meditating, or at least sitting quietly, and I try to give myself enough time to be prepared. Often that means reading over minutes or some of our wonderful literature.

It is very uncomfortable for me when people interrupt one another. When I was growing up, I was never allowed to finish what I was saying. The chairperson of any particular meeting is the only one who is allowed to interrupt, and that's only if someone else is hogging the time, being impolite, or not following protocol. We all need to be respectful of the chairperson if any given meeting is to run smoothly.

My experience tells me that, having gone to face-to-face meetings for many years, people often learn to take cues visually...a look, a nod, a shake of the head...there are so many ways to let people know how to behave without even speaking.

I believe that one reason we're having so much trouble on the phones is that we don't even realize how much we miss these visual cues. The Communications Committee wants protocols to be written for business meetings, but I think it begins with how we conduct ourselves in every meeting.

So, as it says somewhere in the literature: "Let there be no gossip or criticism of one another, but let the love, understanding, and peace of the program grow in you one day at a time."

Thanks for allowing me to be your trusted servant.

Fall 2011

Alison B., NJ

Dear CLA Friends,

We had our most recent WSO meeting on the fourth Saturday in June, and it was well attended. Much more than that, I was gratified to find that everybody was paying complete attention to the protocols, which made my job as facilitator much easier. It was actually the smoothest meeting I had ever led, and I left with a euphoric feeling that lasted all day. There was a very real spiritual bond and a strong willingness to cooperate, a sentiment which somebody expressed that day. It's truly a miracle when the Higher Power within the group is so obviously greater than the sum of its parts.

I've felt a spiritual camaraderie when I've been on telephone recovery meetings and often in face-to-face meetings. I would like to experience that more often when it comes to business meetings. I believe it happens when people care about what they're doing and take the time to prepare. In my own quest for togetherness in this area, I make it a point to try not to take any phone calls one hour prior to the meeting, preferring instead to spend the time in prayer and meditation, as well as going over minutes and protocols.

If you enjoy attending recovery meetings, please consider that there would not be meetings without a central organization that keeps the literature and information flowing. People are always needed to give service at that level. We would like the group delegates to consider joining a committee so that they can experience service at the WSO level, especially since these meetings are monthly and WSO is now quarterly (except for elections). Please look at www.ClutterersAnonymous.org for information about helping us on one of our committees.

Holiday 2011

Alison B., NJ

Dear CLA Friends,

This year has been particularly overwhelming in my personal life and in the lives of some of those closest to me. Without going into detail, let me just say that the hospital has been a featured accommodation on several occasions. As a result, I had no choice but to slow down in the realm of CLA service work. This stemmed from the fact that my email inbox became way too cluttered while I was in the hospital, recovering, or taking care of someone else; and since we do a lot of work by email (and on the phones) I naturally fell behind.

Although my health is, thankfully, much improved, the lingering effects of my service reduction are noticed and felt by certain parties, since I have considerably lessened the number of emails to which I reply and certainly to which I respond in any great depth. As time is unfolding, I have been assessing those emails which I feel the need to answer and trying harder to use my self-allotted email time more sensibly—especially since, try as I might, I have still not caught up with all my email traffic.

In the process, I have been criticized for not doing my job. Admittedly, like a lot of clutterers, I am a procrastinator to begin with. But I have to laugh at the criticism when I consider that, generally, the job of a chairperson is just to chair meetings and be involved with writing the agenda. That same critic wanted me to resign, and a close friend thinks I should leave to look after myself. However, I feel I am taking care of myself and the group best by choosing to stay and to whittle down what are, apparently, my expected duties, in preparation for the next person who is elected to the position of chairperson.

According to the guidelines for my duties, I am also supposed to oversee all the WSO committees, and it is into this murky pool that I have, in the past, dipped my toes too deeply, way too many times. It wasn't entirely my fault—this was the legacy I inherited. However, it is up to me to be protective of my own space, time, and brain power; and this is a lesson that I am slow in learning, although it is easier for me to fight for my rights here than in the "real world," so to speak.

It's my belief that it is fine for service people to work with each other by email, as long as no more than basic expectations are placed as to the culpability of sender and recipient alike. It may be that we need established, written, common protocols or ground rules in these emotionally vulnerable areas—but I don't think so. Rather, it is up to individuals to firmly state and restate their needs, as and when necessary, and to firmly stick with their own boundaries—after all, these are voluntary positions!

Happy holidays.

Spring 2012

Alison B, NJ

Dear Readers,

My mind has been so cluttered lately that I've been arguing with myself for several weeks about the content of this article—so much so that I passed the deadline for submittal. This is an infraction I take very seriously. Worse yet, it's the second time I've been at fault in this manner. Procrastination rears its ugly head yet again.

According to my mother, it started at my birth, beginning with my tardy arrival into this world, two days later than my predicted due date. According to me, my nuclear family permanently perpetuated this predicament—in other words, we were more often late than not.

As I laugh at myself and make jokes about my well-meaning Mum—who still tries so hard for her family and always did the very best she could—I've realized what's really bothering me: the fact that after my serving two more years in the chairperson's seat following an earlier term a few years ago, it's time for me to let go, once again.

I know that we need rotation of leadership in this program; therefore, it's the right thing to do—but it's going to hurt.

In the meantime, we in the Executive Committee (WSO officers and committee chairs) have been putting our heads together and trying to make sure we're all on the same page as far as the WSO meeting goes, especially the elections. As you are reading this, the nominations will have already been made, and I do not predict a big change, but I am hoping and praying that others will step up this year to fill the chairperson and vice-chairperson seats. By the way, if it encourages anyone and helps in the decision, as my own experience proves, leadership can be learned. Generally speaking, the Executive Committee is made up of people who truly enjoy their service positions, and WSO would, in fact, be lost without them. (I have just realized how excruciatingly painful it would be for me if I were no longer serving on the Executive Committee.)

During my five years of service in WSO, I've been slowly but surely learning that we have to start documenting projects, such as those for the elections process, several months ahead of their deadlines. I slowly began to get the message to apply that approach to my own life, to help me with my time clutter.

I dared to write down one big project I have to complete and then began to break it down into smaller sections. I've started showing it to people and am receiving the affirmations I seem to need so badly in order to run my own life. I now need to break it down into doable tasks. Unfortunately, now I've stopped—terrified, as usual, unable to move forward.

I began writing weekly lists because I had committee meetings to attend and I had to fit other things in between. (I really didn't have much of a life before I started doing service. I had been watching a huge amount of television.) Then I started making daily lists. Have I been making any lists lately? Nope. And then I wonder why I get stuck.

I think I will try adding minute-by-minute lists next because I have such trouble getting myself out the front door early enough to be, well, early enough. And I really need a proper timetable.

I must also commit to getting my full complement of sleep and daily meditation—disciplines I find to be highly effective, but not always habitual for me. And it's not just remembering. I have to confess that there are times when I deliberately sabotage myself, which definitely explains why my mind has been so cluttered lately.

I've read the CLA green leaflet, "Declutter Your Mind,"[9] many, many times. I will also get to proofread it with the Literature Committee before it gets reprinted. Interestingly, I was just writing about time clutter, yet I referred to the leaflet on mind clutter. It seems that the two are inexorably intertwined. Presumably, then, if I declutter my mind—by writing down every goal, challenge, event—my mind will then be clear enough so that I may concentrate on getting out the front door in a timely fashion!

That reminds me of a suggestion I heard: to spend 15 to 20 minutes listing every major goal I ever had. I commit to doing that here and now, along with focusing on my New Year's resolutions, which someone in my home group had us writing.

It's customary for the chairperson to write a "swan song" column, so in the next issue, I'll report my progress.

Summer 2012

Alison B., NJ

I'm a stubborn clutterer—I really don't like change—which is why I waited 'til the very last minute to write this, my final article as chairperson. It's not as if waiting would delay the inevitable—that I have to step down, whether I want to or not. I'm just feeling uneasy about hanging up my hat at this time. There is so much more work to be done. The best I can do now is to make the transition easier for the new chairperson.

The thing I do feel good about is that we worked so hard on the protocols for the nominations and the elections, and I think it went a whole lot more smoothly than last year. For that I am truly thankful.

I want to thank the entire Executive Committee team. They have really stood together with me, and we have supported each other through thick and thin. We have solved many problems together, working by phone and email, through more hours than I care to admit. I really hope that the new chairperson can streamline her job as I streamlined it down from the person before me. I also hope that people step up to fill any vacancies that may remain on the Executive Committee. I would have run for vice-chairperson, but I was not allowed to because we passed a motion this time saying that we had to have true rotation of leadership. Therefore, that position is currently unfilled, and so are several others. If you've been attending WSO meetings and you're a delegate, please consider serving in one of the vacant positions.

I haven't been able to hold down a job in the "real world" due to personal issues. Because of that, I've been able to spend multiple hours each month trying to help fill the holes in CLA by doing committee work. I know others don't always have the luxury of that kind of time, but we need all the help we can get, even if it's only an hour of your time here and there at a meeting of a committee that you feel drawn toward. And any commitment you could make would be exceedingly appreciated. Committee meetings are usually only once a month. Please come and help us; we could really use your help, especially if you have experience from other 12-Step programs. In my vision for the Literature Committee, we'd have so many people that we'd have different projects going at the same time!

Anyway, I've been so glad to be of service. I've made many mistakes along the way and I've certainly learned many life lessons. And I will continue to do what I can to help the growth of this wonderful Fellowship.

By the way, I remembered as I was writing this that in the last article I said I was going to write down every goal I ever had. I didn't do it. I'm a stubborn clutterer—I really don't like change....

Finally, I'd like to extend a hearty welcome to the new chairperson and to thank you all for letting me serve.

Holiday 2012

Each year, CLA members nominate and elect a chairperson. He or she accepts the responsibility to lead World Service Organization meetings, which are held at least ten times throughout the year. In addition, the chairperson works on the Executive Committee with other WSO elected officers and works with the various committees that meet regularly to do the work necessary to support the Fellowship. The term for a chairperson is one year, from April 1 to March 31. Several members have served more than one term.

In past issues of CLA*rity*, presiding chairpersons have shared their viewpoints with readers. Earlier this year, members elected a first-time chairperson, Stephanie A. from Minnesota. CLA*rity* welcomes her to this column, where she will contribute her "Letter from the Chair" during her inaugural term.

One common theme expressed by past chairpersons is the importance of doing service, a message Stephanie A. echoes.

Perhaps a bigger question than why anyone would want to take on the position of being chairperson of CLA is the question of what the person gains from service and how it may support recovery. CLA*rity* spoke with Stephanie A. to get her experience and insights.

Q: How does service help with your recovery?

A: I have been in other Fellowships and taken part in service, and I find that taking on service roles moves me to another level in recovery....That is one of the joys of taking on service at different levels.

I came to this position after [several years] in the Fellowship. I [was doing service] as the WSO delegate for my face-to-face group, and I had some service in other programs where I had chaired phone meetings and done other service.

So, when the call for service in [WSO as an officer] came, I shifted some service in other areas. I wanted to help take the burden off so many people who had been doing so much service [especially as WSO officers] in our Fellowship. Stepping up is very important to me.

Q: In what other way(s) has service as chairperson been of benefit to you?

A: It makes me more aware of my time issues and how I deal with [them]. I am taking care of things as they come. I was doing this before I took on this service, but I am doing that more now....I am taking time with my home, with my sponsor and foundational things.

Q: Can you share more about how you manage time and doing this service?

A: It requires a little bit more than I might have expected....Sometimes the meetings go a little longer, and sometimes [they go] in the other direction. ...The biggest block is that I don't know what to ask for until it's up to the wire. I don't expect anyone to be a mind reader.... That's been the most difficult thing for me.... In a perfect world, you would have a chairperson who had already been on the board and knew [the process]....My first recollection is putting together the agenda for the next month's WSO meeting—with help from the previous chairperson. Everyone I've had contact with is so supportive and understanding and willing to help....The more often you do something, the less time it takes, and the better you can do it.

Spring 2013

Stephanie A., MN

I believe that doing service is critical to my recovery. When I see others with great recovery, I see that they do service. The first service is getting a sponsor, working the Steps, and being abstinent. In CLA, for me, that means I make my bed every morning, I do the dishes before I go to bed, I declutter at least one item, and I do the completion cycle to the best of my ability (I'm a work in progress). The next service is sponsoring others, helping others to experience the freedom and joy of being disciplined in recovery. It still amazes me that discipline leads to freedom. Doing service at the local meeting and at WSO are the next levels in Clutterers Anonymous.

I believe that part of a group being self-supporting in the spirit of Tradition 7 means the group sends a delegate to the monthly WSO meeting. For WSO to grow and to be able to give more service to the Fellowship means that we need more people to add their voices to the decisions made, as well as to do service at the WSO level. It has been disappointing to have 10 or fewer groups represented at recent WSO meetings. And all of the committees doing service could make more progress in less time if there were more people on those committees helping to do the work.

The "Recovery Affirmations"[20] and other literature created for CLA by those doing service on the Literature Committee are special to me. This is the result of people doing service at the WSO level. So many of the affirmations hit home for me: I try to use "Before I accept any new commitments, I release one that demands equivalent time and energy" when considering taking on new commitments of any sort.

The idea that I should release an activity when I take on a new one was a concept that CLA introduced to me, and it was completely foreign. I still get a week here or there that gets a bit too full, but it's no longer normal. I'm so grateful for that! I was fortunate that my term of service for a previous commitment was ending as I was nominated to be chair of WSO.

It has been an honor to serve as your chair, and—echoing my experience with doing other service— it has given me so much. It has allowed me to work on a lot of my character defects, especially the defects of perfectionism and procrastination. One day at a time, I'm growing up and growing into the person I'm meant to be.

Please consider joining us at the next WSO meeting on the fourth Saturday of the month from noon–1:50 p.m. Central Time. Everyone is welcome to attend, but only meeting delegates and WSO officers may vote at the meetings.

Holiday 2013

Deborah, G., AZ

From Isolation to Service: Our Invitation to You

From childhood on, my cluttering and hoarding were unmanageable and elicited strong negative effects on my relationship with others. For much time, I was in denial or minimizing, telling myself I was simply neither hung up nor rigid like others! I rationalized that I was doing more "important" activities in my life and, although I would have denied this, I judged more organized people mercilessly.

Eventually, as this disease of rampant, unmanageable clutter tends to do, I felt the "incomprehensible demoralization" that the A.A. "Big Book"[4] describes as happening with addiction.

People did not want to share my living space and pointed out to me that I was impossible to live with due to my clutter. I could not invite others over to socialize and ended up living a life of isolation.

My world became narrower and narrower as I felt more and more shame. What was wrong with me? Why couldn't I get a handle on this? Why was I the only one in the world who ever accumulated so much stuff? Why could paperwork throw my life into utter disaster? I felt alone, terminally unique.

Out of desperation, I searched the internet one night and found CLA.

I started attending phone meetings. What a flood of relief to discover others in the world who also struggled! Better yet, these people on the other end of the phone had real solutions to offer. Instead of facing my cluttering and hoarding all by myself, fellowship existed and phone activity sessions began to spur me to action.

Half a year later, I mentioned to some friends in another 12-Step Fellowship that at last I was finding relief and actually making progress with clutter for the first time in my life. Immediately, Susan C., Mary H., and Cindy K., said, "Let's form a face-to-face meeting. We know we could use this!" Thus were the beginnings of CLA in Tucson, Arizona.

Suddenly, I experienced fellowship not only on the phone but also in person. I found others, locally and in lands far away, who experienced not only the same suffering I did but also solutions that led to serenity. Through CLA, my life slowly began expanding.

Service calls me out of isolation and invites me to a life of fellowship. Through service, I meet incredible people on the phone from all over the world. Through service, I develop new ways of thinking and acting. Through service, I no longer have to hide in shame in my house. In fact, if I miss just one physical CLA meeting for any reason, I will receive emails and at least one phone call asking me what is going on and encouraging me to attend the following week. I'll get lovingly called on my isolation right away so that I can return to the path of recovery. Plus, with encouragement to participate in WSO, my life has become incredibly enriched in even deeper ways. I learn about all the service that some of our long-timers have offered for so long. I am reminded of the importance of CLA as I meet newcomers. All in all, rather than feeling as if no one else in the world has my problem, I now live a life of companionship along my journey of recovery.

I invite you all to share in the joys of service. I wish for you to have some of the same wonderful benefits of service that I have experienced. There are many areas to serve. We particularly can use help on the Finance and Cyber Committees. We will be celebrating our 25th year of CLA next year and will need help with local events, a phone marathon, and a national observance. I encourage you to ask your Higher Power how you can serve; attend local meetings, as well as some WSO meetings, to see what sparks your interest, passion, and imagination. And doing so can help you lead a life beyond your wildest dreams!

Spring 2014
Deborah G., AZ

Spring Cleaning, Spring Decluttering: A Fresh, New Self Emerges Through CLA Participation

Spring cleaning, spring decluttering. Visions of freshness and newness abound.

Or so I had heard.

Before CLA, spring cleaning and decluttering were not activities I practiced in any season: spring, summer, fall, or winter. It is not because I never heard of such behaviors. Indeed, I often heard others talk about getting their houses in order for the spring. However, I was too preoccupied with more "important" things to do and think about. So, instead of a fresh living place with clean, empty spaces—a place renewed by attention to details that nourished and supported inhabitants—the place I called home was filled to the brim.

I had flung leftover winter holiday items here and there and had smashed winter and spring clothes together until closet poles broke. Second-semester paperwork vied with first-semester paperwork to see just how high piles could be stacked. Spring cleaning? I couldn't find a broom, let alone use one (although, of course, I did have multiple brooms bought at different times that I could not see due to the piles). Since I kept forgetting I owned brooms, I kept buying more. Home, my sacred place? Try home, my scary space.

Yet it was indeed at last that I found CLA in the spring one year. In the winter of my soul, I searched for some light to shed upon my situation. Why couldn't I get organized, ever? Why did this look awful, always? Why was I so unique, utterly? Through the flickering rays of computer lights, I searched for answers. Through what I believe was my Higher Power's help and to my complete amazement, eventually I found that I was not alone. Indeed, an actual 12-Step group called CLA existed for those like me. And with this discovery and the phone Fellowship, I could begin behaviors that would lead to my own cleaning and decluttering. During this springtime, a fresh, new self began to emerge from the clutter.

In a manner similar to my personal recovery, CLA as a Fellowship also is experiencing new growth this season. As this article goes to press, the wonderful CLA WSO Literature Committee's work on an abstinence model has helped spring forth exciting discussions about abstinence in our program. The great work of the CLA Registration Committee is helping us declutter our lists, ensuring that CLA recovery meetings are actually current and active. Plus, plans continue to grow regarding celebration of our CLA 25th Anniversary. Thus, CLA as a Fellowship continues to emerge, bringing forth new growth and developments.

In this time of new ideas cropping up and new behaviors emanating, I plan to try out new developments in my own CLA recovery and encourage others to do so as well. Moreover, this is a great time to make new efforts, explore new possibilities, and seek out new horizons in service to CLA as a whole. Start a new CLA meeting? Hold a local CLA office? Serve on a CLA committee? Our WSO committees are always looking for new members and would love to have your participation. In other words, opportunities are always present to enrich our lives with service to the Fellowship.

This spring, we can challenge ourselves. We can renew our commitment to our own recovery. We can encourage others to cultivate new sprouting of participation in CLA. Additionally, we can expand our possibilities within CLA and support others to do so as well. Through all these means, we can watch our growth, as well as that of others, proliferate.

And through working our program and decluttering the wreckage of our past, our present will emerge and a space will be uncovered for our future.

Happy spring cleaning and decluttering!

Saving. Planning. Budgeting. Preparing. Washing. Drying. Ironing. Packing. Unpacking. Splurging.

Summer 2014
Deborah G., AZ

No wonder, "There ain't no cure for the summertime blues!"

We clutterers have a special relationship to summer. Or at least I did. Here's the opportunity for more time clutter, physical clutter, and mental clutter on a scale larger than I ever dreamed possible.

Summer was less a vacation and more a frustration when it came to clutter. Time clutter was the first type to appear, as I tried to wrap up school administration responsibilities. One time my anniversary occurred during spring graduation and several times during the first day of summer school—resulting in chaotically wishing my husband the best while lurching from one event to another. Simultaneously appearing with my time clutter, of course, was my physical clutter. I had competing piles of student-related matter. Every week I had to update these piles; and, of course, I just started new stacks without touching the old piles.

I had good reasons as well as lame excuses for this. Or so I told myself. After all, I was fearful a computer glitch would lose all the records: a legitimate fear based on reality. However, I also have to admit that I lived by my own adage, "Never throw anything out anytime because someday, sometime, somewhere, somehow, I might need this." Of course, I would not admit to myself the plain and simple fact that when I did need something, I could never find it because of all the other things I was saving, in case I needed them someday, too!

You may be wondering about my mental clutter. Or maybe not, by now. I was constantly trying to keep mental track of lists of things I needed to remember. I understand that others in life actually wrote things down—things they wanted to remember—but this method was not helpful to me because later I could never find what I had written down. Other well-meaning coworkers would see me inevitably forget something and buy me an organizer in hopes of helping me, but I would lose those, too, in my piles of clutter. In fact, when I joined CLA, I found at least four old organizers people had given me, not counting the organizers coworkers had bought me recently. Indeed, some of them I could not use because a decade had passed between the time they were given to me and when I finally found them.

All these types of clutter made for a frenetic summer for me and a frantic summer for my husband.

So what does recovery from cluttering look like in the summer?

Summers can now actually be particularly productive seasons of physical decluttering for me. I find this rather strange, considering that the area where I live experiences many summer days in 100-degree-plus temperatures. Believe me, that is not the get-up-and-go type of atmosphere conducive for accomplishing activities. The key for me is looking at my time clutter. Am I not allotting the amount of time certain activities require? Am I trying to cram in too many activities in a given time period? Am I dashing hither and yon, or am I allowing breathing room between events? Am I factoring in my family time in my planning?

I cannot answer these questions alone. This is why the first Step of CLA states that we, rather than I, admitted we were powerless over clutter and that our lives had become unmanageable. Left to my own devices, I will inevitably underestimate the time activities take while overestimating the number of activities that can be accomplished in a given time period. Consulting only with myself, I will stuff my schedule too full of activities while not allowing enough time for my family. Discussing my situation only with myself certainly has resulted in even more dashing around, as is evident by my inevitable accumulation of summer speeding tickets.

However, when I discuss these matters with others, an entirely new perspective occurs. Reality. There really is only so much that can be done at any one time. Inevitably things take longer than I think. Life happens in between events, and breathing room needs to be scheduled so that others are not waiting while I arrive late once again. And when someone in CLA offers this perspective, someday, sometime, somewhere, somehow, I hear this. And as my poor, long-suffering husband says, "I didn't even have to pay someone else to agree with me!"

This is why recovering together in a Fellowship is so critical for me. I simply cannot do it alone. I cannot see these things on my own. I cannot think my way out of this. I cannot figure these things out. But you can see my dilemmas and offer me solutions. With your experience, strength, and hope, new steps can be taken in my life. And this can happen for all of us. We can all support each other in recovery. We can all learn from one another. We can all grow together. As we begin the summer season, we can do our life differently in recovery. When we travel, we can find other CLA meetings and attend them. And wherever we go, we can always attend CLA phone meetings. Even in the sweltering hot summer sun and dog days of summer, by building meetings and support into our schedules, CLA helps us recover. See you as we travel the great summer highway of decluttering. And in my case, without any more speeding tickets!

Fall 2014

Deborah G, AZ

Let's Celebrate 25 Years of CLA!!!

We invite you to help us celebrate 25 years of CLA! Be there at our first convention, which will be held in El Segundo, California, the weekend of October 11-12, 2014. By attending, we can strengthen our program as well as cherish those who have gone before us and laid the foundation for our recovery.

There, we can talk about how—one day at a time, one piece of clutter at a time—we can clear our homes of the goat paths that have plagued us. There, we can listen to how others created space for eyes to rest on, rather than being bombarded with visions of ever-increasing large piles. There, we can find out how others, with the help of their Higher Power, have created structure in their lives to declutter.

There, we can meet up face to face with others who have struggled with the cunning, baffling, and powerful disease of cluttering and yet are walking a path of recovery with others, using the CLA Steps, Traditions, and Tools[19] of our program. In other words, we can enhance our recovery by attending the CLA 25th Anniversary Convention.

One of the benefits I'm looking forward to is finding out from others at the convention how they develop practices of decluttering. From attending meetings, I have learned about actions others take that are helpful. I've learned to take some sort of action each day in between commercials if I watch TV. I've learned that even one action per day is better than no action.

Another wonderful thing I learned from other members pertains to time clutter and making the decision to create a schedule that realistically addresses the amount of time each task takes. That way, enough time is allocated for doing the tasks and having breathing space between them. I especially enjoy hearing weekly reports of how many donations are being made to local charities after members declutter.

By attending meetings and embracing fellowship with members, I have learned new approaches to decluttering. Just imagine how much more can be learned at the convention!

With that in mind, I hope to see you at our celebration. There, we can strengthen our own programs, support others, learn much, and enjoy our CLA Fellowship. We can personally thank those we know who give so much each month so that CLA can continue to operate and grow. We can give service at the convention, as well as enjoy hearing about the journeys of others. With all that experience, strength, and hope, I know the convention will offer new ways to enhance our program. And I look forward to meeting you soon!

Holiday 2014

Deborah G., AZ

**Spiritual Decluttering:
Finding Our Vision and Purpose**

At this time, in which the northern hemisphere experiences the longest night of the year, I find darkness symbolic of the long nights I experienced before CLA. My long nights were filled with a spiritual void, a deep emptiness inside that I tried to compulsively "fill by clinging to useless objects, nonproductive ideas, meaningless activities, and unsatisfying relationships," as is stated in the Invitation to Recovery document in the CLA Meeting Starter Kit.[7] Like my life before recovery, at this time of year the earth is filled with peoples having traditions that describe a spiritual darkness.

My own Irish culture has a strong Celtic tradition in which the coldest, longest nights of the year are marked by cultural traditions that connect people through song and dance to the dark death of the old year and our journey toward the light of the birth of a new year. Other cultures and traditions celebrate the miracle of light found during this time of discovery and journey. Various cultures refer to a miracle of light which sustains a people, or the loving light of the world coming to humanity, or the light involved when observing the winter solstice and journey toward light, or the lighting of holiday candles that for me symbolize the lighting of spiritual virtues celebrating our community.

All of these traditions speak to me of facing the dark void in my life and letting the light of my Higher Power fill it. Our Higher Power wants to fill our void and is described in "Home: Our Sacred Place,"[11] as a Power "who is beauty, joy, peace, love and divine order," who "knows our needs better than we do" and "wants our good even more than we do." As we experience the journey from this dark spiritual place toward light, I celebrate how our souls are filled with the light of our Higher Power. This light illuminates our true path and purpose in life, and as "Finding Your Life Purpose"[10] states, "to bring more truth, beauty, divine order, and love into the world" through using our spiritual gifts of vision, peacefulness, resourcefulness, consensus building, listening, humor, and simplicity.

These are truly the divine gifts of this program available to us. During this time of year when many fill the void with physical clutter, instead, I invite us all to make space in our lives to receive these spiritual benefits available to us through working the beautiful Clutterers Anonymous program. May we all find deeper levels of the wonderful gifts available to us in this incredible spiritual program of recovery.

Spring 2015

Deborah G., AZ

Spring cleaning, a popular activity at this time of year, often includes washing windows. Decluttering the dust away from the window so that light can shine through is a good metaphor for the process of decluttering in CLA. We think we see what is dirty, but when we get up close, we find out how much real grime is there. Maybe there are areas no one sees that need cleaning.

Firstly, we see and know things about our clutter and ourselves that others also see and know. For example, everyone, including myself, can clearly see in plain view all the paper stacks on my desk. Secondly, we see and know things about our clutter and ourselves that others do not see or know. People don't see I have a hidden drawer that I shoved some of my clutter into, but I know it was there—out of sight, out of other people's minds. Thirdly, I am blind to certain clutter that others see. In other words, I've tuned out the awareness of the cups on my desk that need removing, but they are in plain sight of others. I am no longer noticing them at all, but they are glaringly visible to others as out of place on my desk.

Fourthly, some information about my clutter is hidden from everyone, including myself. For example, a long time ago, I shoved my clutter into desk drawers that I hadn't opened in months, so now I forget about the clutter—and no one else sees it either because they aren't opening my drawers. The knowledge of clutter hidden in desk drawers is hidden now from both myself and others.

This self-awareness helps me emphasize what I know is clutter but can tell myself, "That's not so bad" until others notice it, too. It can help me to see what others see about my clutter that I don't if I ask them for their perspective. I can't broaden my own perspective on my disease by myself. I need the input of others and to value others enough to ask for input, even if I don't like what they say, or if what they say involves additional work on my part—or any other problem I see with their input.

This occurs on the group level as well. We are all responsible for our own recovery, and our personal recovery depends on CLA unity. This means that if we want to recover personally, we cannot just show up for recovery meetings, expect others to give service so that meetings are run, perhaps gripe about what others are doing in the meeting or how "they" are running things, or what WSO is doing, while doing nothing ourselves to serve and be part of the solution. We just won't grow that way.

So please consider serving. It will deepen your recovery immensely. I started serving as CLA WSO chairperson in September of 2013 simply because no one else would serve, and CLA had given me back so much. I had felt sad that only a handful of people did all the enormous work and had done so for decades. I originally thought I would just serve as vice-chairperson because I had been involved in CLA for only a few years, felt I didn't know what I was doing, my personal recovery wasn't yet where I wanted it to be, and I thought vice-chairperson wouldn't be much work!

I never "wanted" to serve as chair but I did want to give back. I share this only because, while this is not exactly an attitude of recovery, it is how I felt.

Yet I have grown immensely, particularly after our CLA convention last year when, as a result of a casual conversation while going to the airport, I realized that I did have one character asset that I could actually offer. This was during a time in my life that I did not see any character assets at all in myself, so it was a real gift from God that someone else saw something. And why did this occur? This was only because another clutterer shared her perspective with me at the conference, where we both offered service!

Now I am keenly aware of some of my character defects that negatively impact how I have done my job as chair of CLA because others have pointed them out. These are some of the same character defects that have plagued my life professionally and personally, yet CLA has given me a place to admit them to myself, not deny or minimize them, and to ask God to replace these character defects with His character assets so that CLA WSO meetings can be chaired more effectively. And who knows? This is beginning to positively impact my work performance, as I learn the importance of preplanning, time organization, decluttering, and pacing.

So, if you care about your own recovery, please consider service. You will grow spiritually. Also, your group will benefit. This is particularly important if you want to see your group's views represented at the WSO level by having delegates from all meetings—both face-to-face and phone meetings. It would be helpful to increase the number of face-to-face delegates representing their individual group meetings at WSO. Thanks to some dedicated wonderful delegates, we have seen the number of phone meeting delegates increase.

However, at the actual WSO Executive Committee level, which is composed of committee chairs and WSO officers, there are only three people, including one officer (myself) and two committee chairs, who regularly attend phone meetings. If phone meetings want to feel represented, then we need delegates from phone meetings at the WSO level. So please do yourself and your group a favor by growing spiritually through service to your group and to WSO!

Summer 2015

Deborah G., AZ

As we collectively move forward in our next step along the journey of recovery under the exciting WSO co-chairpersons, Parker and Judy, I wish to thank all of you who have so enriched the blessings I have had of chairing WSO.

During my time, we planned our 25th Anniversary Convention—a great celebration of recovery where we could finally start to put faces to the wonderful voices we had come to love. It was simply awe inspiring to see the tireless and almost endless work of Kathy and Carol, working so valiantly behind the scenes to make the convention idea a reality. It was a remarkable labor of love that resulted in an incredible gift for those of us fortunate enough to be able to meet and embrace each other!

We became much more professional looking in terms of our website. Since I originally came to CLA by finding the website on the Internet, it has been incredibly meaningful for me to see all the work that has been done in this endeavor. We hired a consultant who has been so great to work with, and we continue to work on upgrading our website to appeal to all. Kudos to the Cyber Committee and wonderful Wendy, the chairperson!

We gained much practice during the process of writing and revising our new leaflet, "Measuring Progress on Our Journey in Recovery,"[13] as we sought to incorporate the processes of truly seeking a group conscience that reached out to all types of meetings. The co-chairpersons, the steadfast Mary and the stout-hearted Kathy, led us along this path.

During that process, we made an initial leaflet available to all meetings and then incorporated the feedback. Even though this meant that the leaflet took about two years from its initial inception to its ultimate form, the time was well worth the great effort involved. It became a much stronger and more effective document, but perhaps even more important was that we asked for and incorporated feedback from everyone. And who knew we have so many experienced proofreaders in CLA?

We started an All Phone Groups Committee to coordinate group conscience on matters related to the phone meetings under the auspicious leadership of Audrey. This group continues to move forward in addressing many pertinent concerns. They have developed guidelines for conducting meetings.

I hope all the various phone groups will incorporate these guidelines into their meetings. I am so happy that WSO protocols were already posted on our website. By developing boundaries regarding ways to treat one another with respect, we can establish an environment in which people can be heard, honored, and supported.

Many other developments occurred during the one-and-a-half years that I chaired CLA WSO. I have greatly enjoyed seeing the increased number of people offering service, and I appreciate all the old-timers who have offered and continue to offer service year after year. Without them, we would not be where we are today. To those new to CLA service, welcome! You are in for the ride of your life. I could never have anticipated all the joy and deepened relationships I have discovered along the path of service.

To all who received the CLA WSO agendas late every month, I apologize. I obviously still have far to go in my own recovery regarding deadlines and procrastination, and my living amends is to address this issue and change my behavior. Being queen of the last minute serves neither CLA nor my own recovery anymore!

I wish to thank all who have supported me as chairperson. Thank you, committees, for all you have done and are doing, and for letting me listen and be a part of your groups. Thank you to all those, too numerous to mention, who have reached out to me and supported me personally as we tackled different issues. You know who you are! And for all they have done for me and for CLA, a special shout out to the wonderful Kathy and Betsey.

As we move forward under the remarkable combination of the incredibly organized and insightful Parker and Judy, I look forward to this new leadership team taking us even further along our journey. I particularly love thinking about ways we can expand our outreach internationally

I also anticipate the joy we will have in incorporating even more CLA services through technology. My wish for the future is to have a Facebook page and for CLA to host online meetings. As we expand our knowledge of the world and, indeed of the universe, who knows where CLA will be headed next?

Fall 2016

James C., NY

Give Every Thing a Home

As a clutterer struggling to recover with, and only with, the help of my Higher Power, I have been facing many challenges and not having as many victories as I would wish.

However, I have gained a few successes in terms of not losing as many "critical use" objects (for example, keys, wallet, cell phone, etc.) as I used to. I attribute these successes to living in divine order. It's as in the phrase I heard from a CLA veteran, "Give Every Thing a Home."

It means taking each and every object/thing in my cluttered quarters into my hands and thinking through a place for it (whether trash bag, donation box, or specific site in a room).

Then I announce to myself and my HP and my buddy or sponsor, "Such and such, this here is your new home," and then I place the thing in that spot.

I find this helpful because, while I might not always place the thing there due to tiredness, laziness, or thoughtlessness, I know the object is supposed to be in its "home." If I misplace it, as soon as it is found again, I say, "You really belong here." By saying that and setting the thing in its proper place, I therefore reinforce its chances of remaining in its true "home" over the near future. It will then be of easiest access for me in my everyday life.

I hope what I have just written will be of benefit to you, my fellow clutterers, as we continue our journeys towards discovering the sacred space truly present in our homes and lives.

Officers' Corner

This column includes articles from officers and committee chairpersons of the Clutterers Anonymous World Service Organization (WSO) and CLA intergroups. Some of the articles deal with the officers' service positions, some with their personal recovery from cluttering, and some with both.

Summer 2007

Jan G., CA

Hello Friends,

I'm nervous sharing about my personal life and recovery. Briefly, I have served two terms as the WSO chairperson from 2005 through 2006, and this third term expires December 2007. There will be no fourth term for me, and HP will provide a reliable replacement to our Fellowship starting in 2008.

I came to CLA as 2001 started and haven't been able to leave it, much as I've tried to do so! I have since been able to stop some of my old unconscious cluttering behaviors for all of 2006 by not going to any garage sales or thrift shops and avoiding alley shopping of discarded furniture items. I have also been able to withstand the several phone calls from well-meaning friends telling me of free stuff outside of thrift stores. This has been my firm resolve to keep, and I've managed to do so for over 475 days (other than two thrift shop visits in January and May 2006, for $16, in weaker moments).

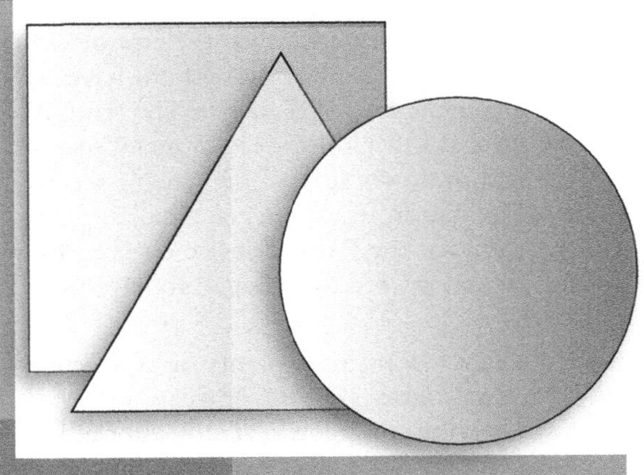

Behind the Scenes

I am pleased to let you know about some of the behind-the-scenes matters going on with CLA.

- Phone groups meet all seven days of the week at the same phone and time, 8-9 PM Eastern.
- Saturday's new phone group will be focused upon the purple CLA leaflet, "Home: Our Sacred Place."[11]
- CLA has a check-in and commitment line, with many people sharing their goals for reducing clutter. People share about their decluttering plans and bookend with each other. These brief calls begin at the top of every hour. If you are alone on the line, wait a few minutes or call back later. Most activity is between 7 and 11 p.m. Eastern Time. Commitment calls are short, about two minutes per caller.
- CLA will be taking orders online using PayPal services for all literature, starter kits,[7] and audio orders soon.
- CLA online meetings may become another source of recovery for computer users around the world. This is being researched, and details will be revealed later.
- Every CLA member is welcome to attend a WSO or Intergroup (IG) meeting. You don't have to be a delegate of your local group to attend. Many groups are not represented; we would like to have more delegates supporting CLA. It is at these business meetings of the CLA WSO and IG where people come to learn about another side of being of service. They become willing to give back to the Fellowship some of what they've gotten from CLA. It is in this way

that they are able to gain experience toward becoming officers for either WSO or IG.

Thank you for letting me serve you as your CLA WSO chairperson. It has been a distinct pleasure sharing with you. Keep coming back, it works; whether or not you work the program, it works you!

Fall 2007

Mary P., NY

My Clutter Odyssey—So Far

I came to CLA by way of, as we say, another Fellowship (or as I call it, the Mother Ship). After several years of recovery, my life had changed for the better in many ways. Yet I still had problems to cope with. My "wreckage of the past" included an apartment that was a cluttered mess, giving me a lot of shame and regret.

In my other program, I had finally learned to ask for help; so I started mentioning my clutter in those meetings. Someone introduced me to a woman who agreed to work with me, and for the next five years I paid her to declutter with me once a week for five hours at a time. She was not an organizer or CLA member, but she had decluttered her own space, and we shared a belief in the 12 Steps as a solution to most problems.

Shortly after I started working with my declutterer, I heard about CLA. I started going to one or two meetings a week (we're lucky in New York). My program experience tells me that "meeting makers make it," so I've continued with a weekly meeting religiously (you'll pardon the expression) for over five years. Since I really believe in the service side of the recovery triangle, I took positions as chairperson, secretary, and intergroup representative for my home group at various times (not treasurer, though; I'm not that recovered). I try to do service in my own meeting, in WSO, and in CLA-East (our intergroup, which I'm currently chairing). I started attending the CLA-East Share-A-Day events (now called Clutter-Free Day, which I prefer, because I didn't like the acronym SAD). I've given a workshop at each of the last half dozen or so. One way that I've shared is by showing my collection of photos, which I take to document my decluttering journey. People are always especially interested in my "before" pictures. I don't know why I ever took those, but I'm glad I did. Showing these "atrocity shots" helps dispel shame—mine and yours. There are also photos of two-foot stacks of newspapers going out, treasures I'm releasing at yard sales, bundles of books and bags of clothes being donated to various organizations, and pictures of new furniture, new appliances, and actual guests that I'm finally able to have in my home.

One recovery milestone was hosting a meeting, with a buffet dinner for 12, for a women's organization I belong to; I had been a member for 13 years before I was able to play hostess. I had always had to co-host with someone else in her lovely home. You can bet I proudly reported this progress in my CLA meeting.

The past couple of years I have also participated in the phone meetings, and I sometimes use the commitment/check-in line, especially when faced with a daunting task, such as having to change a light bulb. I also have a number of clutter buddies whom I talk with on the phone. Clutterers Anonymous has been very helpful to me. As one of our affirmations[20] says, "I accept my progress as proceeding in God's time. I know that patience, tolerance, and taking my time aid me in my recovery."

Winter 2007

Alison B., NJ

The road to recovery has often been a bumpy one for me. I'm bipolar, mostly on the depressed side. If someone had asked me at the end of last year to even write an article, I could not have consented with any degree of certainty. The truth is, I hadn't written a substantial piece in many years—I had all but shut down; it was only when I received a personal invitation to experience a meeting behind the scenes at the World Service Organization that my life and my recovery began to have new purpose.

It's not that I don't have plenty of experience with 12-Step programs. I do—23 years at least—but this cluttering thing has certainly knocked me for a loop in more ways than I can describe here.

It's different—it requires constant vigilance, for me more than any other addiction. I have found that by passing on my "experience, strength, and hope" gained from other Fellowships at a personal level, that *my* little voice really counts, and I—yes, unimportant Alison—am making a difference at a national (and even international) level, simply because during my lifetime I have made a practice of following the 12 Steps and 12 Traditions to the best of my ability. During those times when I want to just sit around and remain lethargic, I now make a practice of pushing myself to strengthen my ability—I will take an action and put away something that I have left out–especially when I don't feel like it.

My turning point was when I realized that, despite all my knowledge and experience, I had not really practiced the 12th Step in any depth. Any recovering alcoholic knows that he has to help a fellow sufferer in order to stay away from alcohol, and the more he helps, the better chance he has. Why? Because if I want you to follow me, I need to show you the way, right? And if I'm going to do that, I have to become somewhat responsible!

It was with this plan in mind, that I became, first, an alternate representative for my group at both the intergroup and world service levels; then at my local group, I was naturally elected group representative for both. (Besides, I'm extremely curious; I just love to know what's going on!) Now I am recording secretary at the CLA-East intergroup, which means I take down meeting minutes monthly, and—to my own surprise—I stepped in to become the vice-chairperson of WSO when the position suddenly became vacant.

There is one personal rule I have (well, there are many, but this one in particular). I make sure I speak up at least once at every meeting I attend. It pushes me over my shyness. But the opposite side of this same rule is that I work very hard to listen, and in doing so, I exercise a lot of patience. I have learned that a little love can go a long way, and if I need help, I ask. I am an imperfect human being who has tried to become perfect and failed. I'm not trying anymore—I'm just doing the best I can!

Spring 2008

Jan G., CA

Seeking Service Supporters

Dear CLA Friends,

I have served as either chairperson or vice-chairperson for seven of the last five years. How did I manage that? For the CLA World Service Organization, I was vice chairperson from 2003–05 and chairperson from 2005–08; for CLA-East, one year each as chairperson and vice chairperson, 2004–06.

Five regional events, now called Clutter-Free Days, were produced in California and New Jersey for WSO and CLA-East. I've officially retired to the old chair's home that is nicely decorated with clean, orderly, and tidy furnishings!

Someone saw my enthusiasm for service in my third CLA month, recommending me to attend a WSO meeting. Whilst being a trusted servant and attending these business meetings, I learned how valuable service is. People said that my writing and organizational skills improved. I began to realize that I was amongst friends. Consistent attendance has maintained my sanity. I felt encouraged to reduce both my home and car clutter. Giving service also provided me the opportunity to help contain my ego, although others may disagree! I became involved with many issues (phone calls, discussions, emails, and meetings) and helped put out fires. It was a wonderful time, indeed, behind and in front of the scenes, watching the Fellowship grow stronger.

In What Ways Can You Be of Service to CLA?

Rotation of service and officers' positions is the lifeblood that keeps those involved behind the scenes fresher. Service is needed in all areas; for example, in making periodic contact with groups to update them on happenings in CLA and in being involved with monthly WSO and intergroup business meetings. You can help bring people to them. If you recognize the potential of someone at a meeting, take an action and suggest that he or she attend a business meeting. This would provide great service to our program.

In the past few years, CLA has experienced some incredible growth and a spectacular worldwide presence. CLA has finally become international, having successfully established groups in the UK and Germany. We are proud of our Fellowship's glowingly successful newsletter, CL*Arity*, now presenting its fifth quarterly issue. CLA is making some amazing strides to gain more credibility, polish, substance, and stability into the future. We are seeking members who are consistently working the program and gaining some clarity to come forward. When you provide service to the Fellowship, chances are, you will experience more in-depth recovery.

These are some of our WSO committees: CL*Arity* newsletter, literature, finance, bylaws, cyber (website and info technology), and phone groups. Several dedicated and committed people share their collective experience, strength, and hope, and we need others, too. Steady, consistent progress is being made as CLA matures into adulthood—our program was born in 1989!

In my time of service, I have handled the printing of the CLA literature, materials for regional events, and CL*Arity*. Other services included organizing three dozen business meetings, helping on the various committees, answering the CLA phones and emails, satisfying the literature requests, stocking the materials, and buying postage.

Life would have been less stressful had I served just one term as chair of WSO; three terms were taxing. By seeking feedback through emails and phone calls, when support didn't meet my timeline, I got frustrated. Surely, it took a toll upon me; I had some resistance in trusting job delegation, so I often did tasks myself. In taking on so many functions, I am sure that I alienated many supportive people with my stubbornness. At some point, I hope that my plethora of amends are honestly written, sent, and equally received by all.

Thanks for permitting me to witness so much upward growth in the CLA fellowship during these years!

Summer 2008

Carol N., CA

Hi, my name is Carol, and I'm a clutterer—I'm also one of two WSO corresponding secretaries. A corresponding secretary gives service to the CLA program by keeping an open channel to you, the members, through the mail, by which you can: (a) order literature—either in single packets or in bulk, (b) subscribe to our quarterly newsletter, CL*Arity*, (c) send in 7th Tradition donations, (d) order a starter kit,[7] and (e) send any CLA-related correspondence from you or your group.

My history with 12-Step groups started many years ago in our parent organization. I was slow to get into action and was about six years sober before I found out how enjoyable doing service was. After that, I jumped in with both feet. For five years, it was a whirlwind of first being a panel speaker for hospitals and institutions—taking the message to those who couldn't get out to a meeting—then being a leader, responsible for taking a panel once a month on a regular basis. Eventually, I was encouraged to become chairperson. I coordinated a particular panel venue each week, which meant covering anyone who didn't show up—sometimes this was many times a month—in addition to doing my own panels; and I had a different one for every week of the month. Whew! But it helped me grow.

Little by little, I've become interested in what was, and what is, necessary to keep a 12-Step program going, taking on commitments as I felt I had the strength and time to do so. Now to me, it means being responsible, along with my co-secretary and friend, Kathy H., for picking up the mail from CLA's post office box. We have been able to go at least once a week, and with two of us doing it, the tasks aren't so overwhelming. We record who is making the request, what the request is for, and any form and amount of payment received. We determine who can best handle requests and pass them on when necessary.

Just recently, CLA WSO received two sizeable 7th Tradition group donations, and it just warmed my heart to see such support for our program. It is inspiring. The process of recovery can't be undertaken alone—and when I see others giving, it reminds me of the blessings I've been given and that I need to give back. I am also inspired by the messages that are included with some donations, thanking the program (and us specifically). Such gratitude brings tears to my eyes.

I feel so blessed to be doing this job and don't think of it as work or effort; it is actually fun (I really enjoy taking care of the mail and making the CLA bank deposits).

Fall 2008

Ruthe S., PA, and Andrew S., MD

Where Are We Now and Where Are We Going?

Both of us have been talking about CLA and how we can be part of it since we met at a Clutter-Free Day, a CLA-East event, held in Brooklyn in 2006. Here we are now, newly-elected co-chairs of CLA-East, with our Fellowship on the verge of its 20th birthday.

Each of us wanted to be more involved in the CLA recovery program, but we weren't sure how to fit service into our busy lives. We each felt a lack of confidence about taking on a responsible position. We continued talking and planning, but the time just didn't seem right.

In Spring 2008, we finally resolved to do the best we could by jointly taking on the chairperson and vice-chairperson positions of CLA-East, as coequal participants. Our shared vision is to help enhance the health and vitality of our groups overall, especially at the level of the individual group.

The next challenge was simple: When would we talk? It took a little while to work that out. Now we've set up a routine schedule of weekly conferences and monthly business meetings. Our business meetings are held midday, usually the second Saturday of the month. All are welcome to attend. However, you need to be chosen by your group to be able to vote.

Next Steps: Taking Action

Now, we'll need your help in finding where we are and where we, as a Fellowship, want to go. The power base of a 12-Step program is democratic in a radical way. You, the members of the CLA Fellowship, lead. Officers are "trusted servants," coordinating the communications between our members and following their group conscience.

How does one take a group conscience of folks who may have never met or talked to each other? We're putting together a survey to try to take the pulse of our membership. Will you please give us your opinion? Is there something about our program or your group that has been trying to get your attention? We need to hear from you. Watch for our survey, look it over, and send it back or request a call back. Can't wait? Send us your input now! You can email CLA-East at clarity@claeast.org

We know you can find a way to get involved in the exciting process of CLA's coming of age. Make a connection, and see what recovery will come to you.

Yours in Service.

(Editor's Note: CLA-East is a regional partnership of 26 CLA groups, most of which are located in the northeastern part of the United States. CLA-East has held meetings and been involved in CLA activities for approximately seven years.)

Holiday 2008

Kathy H., CA

Six-and-a-half years ago, a friend convinced me that Clutterers Anonymous was for me. Since I had had several years' experience with 12-Step programs, she didn't have to convince me that the 12-Step approach works, only that I belonged in this Fellowship. I have since come to believe that CLA addresses my primary problems of procrastination and lack of motivation better than any other program.

A few years ago I retired. I thought that, having more time on my hands, my decluttering would proceed at a rapid rate, leaving me with a neat, orderly house to maintain. Not so! It was only after getting more involved in doing service in CLA that I was able to make significant gains in my decluttering.

There is a saying in 12-Step programs that "Service equals freedom from bondage of self." It wasn't time that kept me from my chores but, rather, motivation and inspiration. I am now usually less "stuck in my head," allowing me to deal with my physical clutter in a clearer frame of mind.

So where am I now? I still have quite a lot of physical decluttering remaining to be done, and I still struggle with my daily maintenance—just not as badly as I did before. However, as I tackle my mind clutter, I am also able to work on the physical aspects more easily. Lately I have found that when I just let go and trust my Higher Power, each plan feels inspired, new, and wonderful. Trusting my Higher Power more is something I always struggle with, which reminds me that I need to do more Step work. Always we come back to the Steps as the key to recovery. Working the Steps is especially critical to controlling our mind clutter. As our literature says, "Physical clutter is only the outward manifestation of our inner emotional problem."

As for the service in CLA, although I love doing most of it, right now I am wearing too many hats, which is true of all of the few of us heavily involved in WSO. (I am currently WSO vice-chairperson, co-corresponding secretary, and CLA*rity* editor-in-chief and am on the following committees: Bylaws, Executive, Finance, Cyber, and Literature.) This leads me to forget or goof up tasks.

Someone gave me a good analogy the other day: Think of it as juggling balls. What makes the juggling difficult is not the size of the balls so much as how many balls are being juggled. So, if those of us in WSO seem to make an occasional mistake, please remember that we are working as hard as we can at many jobs. If any of you feel inclined to lend a hand, we will welcome you. Remember that service is a large part of Step 12 and that you can't fully recover through the Steps without doing some kind of service at your local group, at an intergroup, or at WSO.

I envision a CLA with a revamped, smoothly running website; helpful literature on sponsorship, abstinence, and other needed subjects; occasional nationwide conferences; several functioning intergroups; and a World Service Organization represented by every meeting in the Fellowship. Won't you help make my dream come true?

Yours in recovery.

Spring 2009

Betsey K., NJ

My first CLA meeting was on April 7, 1997, in East Orange, New Jersey. Although the leader of the meeting told me that there were other members, she and I were the only ones there that night. The following week was the same—only the two of us attended. The leader, now somewhat embarrassed, once again assured me that there were others, but she did not know why they weren't there. I thought for a moment and said, "Last week we read about clutterers' traits, one of which was procrastination. Perhaps they're all home preparing their income tax returns, which are due tomorrow." Whatever the reason, more people did show up the following week.

After five years (by which time it had moved to Bloomfield), I left that meeting and began attending one in Boonton, which has since moved to Wayne and finally Garfield. At this time I am trying to find a location for a new CLA meeting closer to my West Orange home.

I have been a part of CLA-East from its inception in October 2001, serving as secretary for the first six months and literature person for the next year and a half. At that point, I was expecting to step down from service, but I was drafted to become treasurer, a position I have held ever since.

In August 2005, when CLA WSO changed from face-to-face business meetings in Los Angeles to telephone meetings, I began attending them also and was immediately elected treasurer of WSO. I have since become active on many of the committees in CLA—CLA*rity*, Cyber, Finance, and Literature, to name a few. I'm also treasurer of CLA*rity*.

I have attended all 13 of CLA-East's Clutter-Free Days (formerly known as Share-A-Days) and a CLA Birthday Party in Southern California, as well as the Clutter Free Day held there this past October.

Through the years, I've made some progress with decluttering, but it's been a slow process. I have also found that my service in CLA has added some challenges. I have more papers coming into my house—bank statements for four CLA-related accounts, for instance—and I have to maintain records of financial transactions. I also receive many emails relating to CLA committees and feel a need to print out many of the documents. Now, as I print out a new version, I try to discard older ones. That at least reduces some of the piles.

Sometimes the job of treasurer can be frustrating and irritating, but then when the numbers come together it is very satisfying. I enjoy working with numbers and compiling meaningful and accurate reports. There is also a joy in being of help to the Fellowship.

Summer 2009

Jane M., CA

As I began to work the CLA program, I noticed a pattern that I had been in denial about, oblivious to, and unconsciously doing: I was not completing tasks in almost every area of my life.

For example, tools were scattered around rooms and not in the toolbox; the front yard edging was only three-fourths completed; and a sprinkler hole was waiting to be filled with dirt. It was the first time I *really saw my distracted thinking in action.*

The tools were put down wherever and whenever I was distracted by another thought. For the most part, I could not complete a single task. For example, I could not get the hammer from the toolbox, hang the picture, wipe the tool down, and put it back in the toolbox.

But it wasn't because I just found "it easier to drop something instead of putting it away, or to wedge it into an overcrowded drawer or closet rather than finding space for it."[23] I was just not following through with the action needed.

Then I realized that most daily tasks or activities have a process, a completion cycle: get it, use it, clean it, and put it away. I was always leaving out a step or two in the cycle, and normally it was the clean-it and put-it-away steps.

When I tried to put the completion cycle into practice, I had to keep my attention or focus on a CLA Tool of recovery[19]—specifically, the tool that advises, "Our goal is to do one thing at a time." This thought helped me to let go of the distracting thoughts while I was on the mission to complete a task.

By doing the small tasks, the big tasks get done. Completing a lot of the little parts of the bigger job makes the whole thing easier to finish. When something is completed, it doesn't stay in mind clutter.

Many times I was unable to complete the cycle; therefore, I could see myself not being able to complete the task. So I just had to ask HP for help at these times and laugh at myself. Other times I would tell myself, "What a great idea; let me do it after I complete the cycle."

I never worried that I was not using the completion cycle process on every task. That type of thinking was demanding my perfection. I needed to focus on progress, not perfection. If I completed one or two tasks in a day, that was exciting!

Realizing the importance of completion has helped me. I think I used to look to the outside to fulfill me. CLA is teaching me to go from inside to out. There is an inside satisfaction that comes with completion, knowing something is accomplished successfully.

It is gratifying when I manage to complete the cycle.

When you look at a big project, you can't get your mind around everything. By breaking it into small, manageable parts and action items or making a series of smaller decisions, it helps any individual or group project get completed.

I have been in recovery for many years, and I have done service all along. In the first five years, I focused on my own recovery; doing service is an adjunct to my recovery. I started one of the meetings in Northern California and served as secretary. In addition, I have been a WSO delegate. Currently I am the chair of the CLA Literature Committee and work on several other committees as well. Using all of what I've learned in CLA is helpful in all areas of my work and service positions.

Often I find myself moving forward one or two steps and going back three or four steps. I still get a sense of accomplishment when completing the cycle and avoiding distraction, not jumping from one thought to another. With the help of my HP, I'm breaking my unconscious pattern of not completing the cycle. It is a miracle to me. I am forever grateful, and I give thanks to the CLA program.

Fall 2009

Marie M., NY

I first attended a CLA telephone meeting on September 17, 2007. For me, decluttering was not just a matter of getting rid of a "tchotchke" on a shelf, an outgrown dress, or a few tattered books. I was in serious trouble and in the midst of eviction proceedings in housing court.

By the time I came to CLA, I had already taken significant physical actions. With the help of two friends, I had spent a Saturday five months earlier cleaning up and throwing away bags full of items.

Joining CLA began a dynamic journey, which has led me to a destination that is healthier and saner than the cluttered apartment I used to live in. After that day in May, I was pretty much on my own. But thanks to my friends' initial encouragement, I continued to take actions that have evolved as my time in CLA has increased.

The smallest task I undertook after joining CLA was to clean out a pottery jar that held pens and pencils, many of which were dried out and broken. So I tested every pen. Then I washed out the jar and put back the usable implements. Now I could write with all of them.

The largest task I undertook was cleaning out my closet, throwing away every dress, skirt, and jacket hanging there, as well as two bags of clothes I had packed away after a previous attempt to create space. This time, I could face the fact that the items in my closet were old, didn't fit, or hadn't been worn in several years. Then I created room for the clothes I currently wear. Clothes didn't hang on chairs and doors or lie on the floor. I could open and close the closet doors.

My most lucrative action occurred a few months after I had joined CLA. While cleaning out a dresser drawer of scarves, belts, and purses, I discovered $250 lying on top of the discard pile! It paid for several visits to the hairdresser.

When I first came to CLA, I went to a meeting nearly every night and also used the morning check-in line and the hourly commitment line. Eventually I facilitated one of the evening meetings and then one of the morning check-ins. Later I became a delegate to CLA-East, where I now serve as recording secretary, and I helped plan this spring's Clutter-Free Day.

I became a delegate to the WSO and last spring was elected to serve as telephone correspondent. I have also served on several committees, including the Cyber Committee, which recently updated the CLA website. I am also a delegate to the telephone intergroup.

Doing service has been a tremendous help in my recovery but is a supplement to meetings, prayer, meditation, and reading the A.A. *Twelve and Twelve*[16] and the "Big Book."[4] Service is a link to the CLA program and strengthens my commitment and connects me to other people and to my Higher Power.

Holiday 2009

Peter L., NJ

I attended my first CLA meeting in River Edge (now in Teaneck) about 11 years ago. This was after I hit my "low," losing my keys in all the clutter in my apartment in Hackettstown, New Jersey.

At that time there were no phone meetings. I tried to go to my first CLA meeting in East Orange, New Jersey, but the CLA website showed the wrong address and time of the meeting.

After failing to find the meeting in East Orange, I found that the River Edge meeting was at a Jewish temple. I telephoned the rabbi of the temple and asked him whether he had any 12-Step meetings. "We have only one," he replied to my query. When I asked which 12-Step group meets at the temple, he said, "Clutterers Anonymous."

I found that with the help of my Higher Power and the members of CLA, I was able to move toward being clutter free. In addition to having little physical clutter, most of the time I am able to reduce nonphysical clutter, including emotional clutter such as resentment.

Eventually, I made the then-new Boonton

(now Garfield) meeting my home group. Since that first meeting, we have added three other meeting locations in New Jersey.

I also attend telephone meetings, which are held every day of the week at 5 p.m. Pacific Time (8 p.m. Eastern).

We also now have a regional group, CLA-East, which meets over the phone the second Saturday of the month. The World Service Organization (WSO) meeting is the fourth Saturday of each month, also on the telephone. Last year we started the Telephone Intergroup, with representation from all the telephone groups. I have recently been elected as its chairperson.

Anyone who wishes current information about all our meetings may visit our website, ClutterersAnonymous.org.

Spring 2010

Alison B., NJ

Before I joined CLA, I had plenty of 12-Step learning and experience, but I was not a leader of any kind. I believed I was not capable of leading a meeting, that a person needed to be really special and gifted to do that. I found out I was wrong. All it took was a willingness to step outside my comfort zone and follow the format. I've always enjoyed reading aloud, so it was easy. It made me nervous, but almost everything does, and I've learned that the the only way to face my fears is head-on.

I'm wearing many hats in the World Service Organization at the moment—amongst them, I'm chairperson of the Cyber (website) Committee. Although I was elected to this position, I will openly admit that I was reluctant and scared to take it on, but now it feels gratifying when I look at the wonderful results our group has achieved. All I really had to do was pick a meeting date and time, open a virtual conference room online, and get people to make a list of the issues. I've learned how to make a businesslike agenda from others who went before me, so all it takes is a sample agenda (template), and I just type on top of it. Then we meet, decide on small actions, go away and do them, report back the following month, and the magic begins to happen. As reticent as I am to take *any* kind of action, I have to say I do enjoy the results. Of course this is also true of mundane chores I do at home, like washing the dishes, for example!

Please go and take a complete tour of our totally revamped website at www.ClutterersAnonymous.org. It has been up and running for almost a year, and although we hired a talented person to put it together, there has been a core group of service volunteers which has been involved with every part of the decision-making process, from the design of the website to all the different pages. Once a month we meet for updating purposes, and when we decide to add more text, we hand over our ideas to a special subcommittee which pores over the fine details and carefully makes sure that all information meets the requirements of our program and effectively communicates the contents.

You may have been wondering why we don't have more literature. Although we do have a very active and enthusiastic Literature Committee, there are only a few of us, and we can't produce publications fast enough because there are many facets to this organization, and all group actions require larger group approval. All of this takes an extraordinary amount of time, but we could speed it up if you will help.

We welcome suggestions, new ideas, and fresh voices on Cyber and all our other committees. Also, in my other official position as Communications Coordinator, I welcome any and all ideas about how to spread the word to the entire Fellowship that WSO needs help. Please see the frontispiece for contact information, or write to us at the website.

Summer 2010

Mary P., NY

How does an organization built on the ideal of anonymity handle the necessity to provide information and education to those who are looking for solutions to a complex personal problem?

As the Public Information Officer of CLA, I see my responsibility as working to provide helpful, consistent, and accurate information about the Fellowship to the public. Through a link on the Clutterers Anonymous website, as well as by phone and mail contacts, we receive inquiries from outside print, broadcast, and electronic media outlets. For instance, we hear from book and magazine writers who want to write about CLA and want to speak to members. We remind them not to use members' full names. Often, they request permission to quote CLA's 12 Steps or 25 "Am I a Clutterer?"[23] questions. CLA has copyrighted these items. It's nice when an author fact-checks his or her piece with us for accuracy, but we cannot control or edit what is written about CLA. We just hope for "good press," but must never be "publicity hungry."

What makes CLA's public relations stance different from that of many other organizations is that we must always observe and uphold the 12 Traditions,especially numbers 6, 10, 11, and 12. Our policy depends on "attraction, rather than promotion." We keep a low profile and do not aggressively trumpet what we have to offer. We "maintain personal anonymity at the level of press, radio, films, television, and all other media." We "never endorse, finance, or lend the Clutterers Anonymous name to any related facility or outside enterprise..."

We will cooperate, but not affiliate, with social service agencies, hoarding task forces, etc.

CLA has a Public Information Committee, which recently created an informational leaflet geared to professionals, such as those in law enforcement, health and hospital groups, human resource and senior citizen agencies, and others.

This committee is open to any interested CLA member and would welcome participation by more people. The committee can help local groups develop effective meeting announcements, appropriate press coverage, and public service announcements.

Sometimes the job of the public information officer is to—politely—"just say no."

Cluttering has become a hot topic recently, and CLA has been approached by a number of television producers, who typically want people to "go public" with their cluttered surroundings, which the show will then film and "fix," usually with the help of a cleanup team, a professional organizer, or a psychologist. However well-intentioned, shows like this are not consistent with CLA's Traditions, particularly those that address anonymity.

Recently, some CLA members did participate in a nationally syndicated radio show which focuses on 12-Step recovery. Without visuals and without surnames, the committee considered this was an acceptable way to present the CLA message to, we hope, a large and interested audience.

Yours for better public information.

Fall 2010

Kathy H., CA

In the eight years I have been involved in the CLA World Service Organization, I have held a variety of different positions, and I am currently the chairperson of CLA*rity* and also chairperson of the Traditions Committee.

Throughout my time in CLA, I have gone through many different phases in my decluttering efforts.

One member in my group has started using a system of picking up ten things each day and putting them where they belong (putting them away, throwing them away, or taking them for recycling or to the thrift shop). I decided to try doing the same last week, and I am excited about the results. An item can be small, such as a pen, and still count. Of course, some days I take care of many more than ten items, but ten is the minimum. Now I just need to keep doing it.

One thing that seems to be helpful, time and again, is the CLA Tools of Recovery.[19] Although I don't always consciously think of doing things because they can be considered Tools, I find that all this time of listening to the CLA Tools read in meetings has helped me internalize and use them.

Lately, I have been thinking about how helpful it can be to bookend when you are stuck. I have a telephone buddy with whom I often bookend. Actually, he usually calls me more than I call him, but it does work both ways. The other evening I was stuck. I was running into a great deal of resistance trying to finish a time-critical task. It would have been smart of me to pick up the phone and bookend, but I guess I was resisting doing that also.

Then, just as I really needed it, the phone rang, and it was my bookending buddy, wanting to do an every-thirty-minutes call, since he was also stuck. And that was just what I needed! The task still proceeded in fits and starts, but I finished it that night. Then I was able to continue with other things. The CLA Tools[19] really do work, if you make the effort to use them.

Holiday 2010

Ruthe S., PA

CLA*rity*: What is the purpose of CLA-East?

Ruthe: It is the intergroup for the northeastern part of the country and spans a lot of people because there are no other intergroups at present. The purpose, in my opinion, is to facilitate and support these meetings and to help facilitate events, primarily Clutter-Free Day.

C: Who attends meetings?

R: The officers (chairperson, vice-chairperson, secretary, treasurer, list keeper, and WSO delegate) and representatives from meetings in CLA-East. Every CLA member from the area is invited to attend.

C: How does it benefit CLA members?

R: We produce a Clutter-Free Day, which members have said is a wonderful thing. Also, we have a toll-free number where people can get their questions answered. We troubleshoot problems if meetings have them.

C: How long have you been chairperson of CLA-East?

R: Two terms. At the moment there is no one to take my place. I also serve as co-chairperson of the Monday night phone meeting.

C: What led to your becoming chairperson?

R: So many things that have happened to me in a good way I credit to CLA. I had been involved with CLA for years but hadn't held any position yet, and I felt that it was an opportunity to help grow our small program. Also, I believe that leadership should rotate, and I was the only one who hadn't served.

C: In what way has giving service supported your recovery?

R: Part of the 12-Step approach is that you have to give it away to keep it. Everything we do deals with helping people deal with clutter.

Being involved with CLA-East has helped me learn to declutter myself—by waiting until someone else finishes talking, working together, and taking votes. Sometimes you get your way; sometimes you don't. That's how 12-Step works. You're with clutterers while doing service, so it's like going to meetings. I know some of these people outside the meeting now. It's more people to talk to who are not judging me for my clutter.

C: What have been some of the highlights for CLA-East during the past two years?

R: Always the Clutter-Free Day. I think we do a pretty good job of putting on the East Coast Clutter-Free Day, especially with our limited resources. We have some very dedicated people.

The highlight is being able to help build something. I'm part of a group that's trying to make this into a true intergroup. We developed a meeting protocol, which has helped the meetings to run more smoothly.

C: Looking ahead, what do you see for the group?

R: CLA as a whole is a program in its infancy, and we've had a lot of growing pains. Some new things we have been working toward are organizing a retreat, producing a Clutter-Free Day manual, and holding a 12-Step workshop. All these things will benefit CLA, and it's very exciting.

I hope we will eventually visit, support, and guide the eastern meetings and encourage people to have their own events. I would like to see groups putting on workshops and having more speakers at meetings. But we need more people involved in order to do what we want to do.

C: Is there anything else you would like to discuss?

R: I found CLA several years ago because of

proximity to a different group's meeting. But I couldn't do it all, so I stopped going to CLA. A year or so later (about seven years ago) I was reading the leaflet "Spiritual Timing"[15] and burst into tears because it felt as if it was written to me.

What happened to me through CLA is pretty amazing. I had to do nonphysical decluttering before I could do the physical. I had a lot of things I was afraid to throw out and TV shows I was afraid to miss.

I couldn't deal with anxiety and disappointment. I was afraid to stop going to places and doing things. Very slowly, I learned that I didn't die if I didn't do these things. Now I have been working more on my physical clutter. I feel as if this program has really changed my life. I am no longer beholden to certain books, magazines, or TV shows. Doing mental decluttering gave me freedom and flexibility in my life. In one of the leaflets, it talks about having God provide what you need when you need it; that's one thing that helps me. Living in fear exacerbates this whole thing. I'm not perfect, but if I tend to see a title of something and I am afraid I'll forget it, I say, "if it's meant for me, it'll come back to me." I've been able to stop focusing on things that were leading to physical clutter.

I find we clutterers are really wonderful people struggling with a very difficult disease. How wonderful for us to realize that we're not alone!

Summer 2011

Betsey K., NJ

To paraphrase a statement by a fellow officer and apply it to my own situation, I have been treasurer of CLA for 15 of the last 7 years—a seemingly impossible situation. The explanation is simple—I have been treasurer of CLA-East for the past seven years, treasurer of Clutterers Anonymous World Service Organization (WSO) for five years, and treasurer of CLA*rity* for three years. That doesn't even count the four-and-a-half years I had previously served as treasurer for my local CLA meeting!

In CLA-East, because of my position, I have handled the registrations and preregistrations for 12 of our 16 Clutter Free Days. (See the section on Events for reports on Clutter-Free Days.) For CLA*rity*, I maintain the subscriber list, and I am heavily involved in editing and proofreading.

As treasurer of WSO, I also serve on the Finance Committee, of which I am currently chair. This committee is responsible for establishing a budget for WSO. It also develops, implements, and oversees policies and procedures in all matters concerning the finances of CLA WSO. The committee also works with WSO to help increase financial support from individuals, groups, and Intergroups within the guidelines of the 12 Traditions of CLA. We are seeking more volunteers to aid us in these tasks.

Since I became active in WSO almost six years ago, I have also served on many of its committees, including Literature, Cyber, and Communications. Most of the committees in CLA welcome new members. The Literature Committee, for example, has compiled a long list of worthwhile projects, but at the current rate of participation, it will take several lifetimes to complete them.

We are proud of our CLA*rity* newsletter, now in its fifth year. It takes many volunteers to produce it four times a year, including writers, editors, and proofreaders. Not all of these positions require attendance at our weekly planning meetings.

We have had little rotation of service in CLA—not because the current officers insist on keeping their positions, but because nobody steps up to fill them. There are about a half-dozen volunteers who serve on most committees, and while they enjoy doing such service, some are getting burned out. Remember the adage, "many hands make light work," and consider aiding your own recovery by running for office in WSO when the current terms are up early next year. In the meantime, consider joining a committee and getting involved.

Fall 2011

Jan G., CA

As a CLA World Service Organization officer, I have been privileged to witness many changes within our Fellowship. One of the most rewarding aspects of my recovery within program has come while providing service. In giving, I am also receiving benefits on a continual basis, which in turn bolsters my desire to continue giving back to the Fellowship. This is one gift that keeps on giving to me!

It has been a pleasure meeting members throughout the world who have come to me due to this service. In advance, thanks for bringing what you have into our Fellowship, and please consider giving back to us with service!

The CLA*rity* newsletter still represents the jewel in our crown for bringing the message of recovery to the Fellowship. It can use more of your support, whether by subscribing (hint, hint!) or by contributing articles of your recovery to be shared with other members.

Regional Clutter-Free Days were held in New Jersey in spring 2011 (with about 75 participants from six states) and in Los Angeles in fall 2010, drawing over 100 people from all parts of Southern California. As these events require much preplanning and a large amount of effort, they are usually done once a year. Other areas have expressed interest in producing similar events, and details will be posted at www.Clutterers Anonymous.org, when available.

The CLA Literature Committee has been editing the lengthy Meeting Starter Kit[7]; and when the task is completed, each existing CLA group will receive the updated and revised version for its use.

The CLA Registration Committee is preparing a new worldwide form that each group, for better representation purposes, will complete annually to keep its meeting listed in the CLA Meeting List (Fellowship Directory).

Many of our groups have experienced growth within their ranks. Since July 2010, we are pleased to have added 12 new meetings in: California (West Los Angeles, Santa Cruz, Seal Beach), Massachusetts (Amherst), Michigan (Muskegon), Minnesota (St. Paul), New Jersey (Stone Harbor), Ohio (Maumee), Oregon (Beaverton and Portland), Pennsylvania (Philadelphia), Virginia (Virginia Beach), and UK (London).

New CLA groups have started up and continue. There are now 79 CLA groups, 74 of which are in the United States. We have groups in Arizona, California, Connecticut, District of Columbia, Florida, Hawaii, Illinois, Massachusetts, Maryland, Michigan, Minnesota, New Jersey, Nevada, New York, Ohio, Oregon, South Carolina, Texas, and Washington. We also have international groups in England, Germany, and Iceland.

In California there are 25 CLA meetings, with about two-thirds in the southern part of the state and one-third in the northern part. In New York State, there are six meetings, with three in Manhattan. New Jersey has five. The numerous phone meetings—at least one on each day of the week—have experienced an increase in membership.

My duties include gathering the mail sent to the Post Office box, processing it, and then sending out the various CLA orders to individuals wanting literature packs, beginner's booklets,[12] Meeting Starter Kits,[7] and group bulk literature purchases. I also fill orders that were placed online.

During the past year, 64 Meeting Starter Kits were sent to 25 states and 4 countries, including eight states and four countries where no CLA meetings exist thus far. This is a practical demonstration of how widespread our cluttering problem is.

Starter kits were sent to the following areas that don't already have meetings: Alaska, Alabama, Colorado, Georgia, Louisiana, Missouri, Tennessee, Wisconsin, Australia, Canada, France, and New Zealand.

**Editor's Note: CLA-East is in the process of preparing a manual on how to plan a Clutter-Free Day. They could use your help if you have prior experience. When completed, they will be glad to share the manual with any group interested in holding a similar event. You may contact CLA-East at its website, Clarity@claeast.org.*

Spring 2012

Bobbi H., NJ

Bobbi H. was elected in October to be the new chairperson of CLA-East for the next year. When asked about her story in CLA, this is what she had to say:

Looking back, I can see now that cluttering was a problem in small ways throughout my life. And of course, it had gotten worse; the older I got, the more I accumulated, and the more belongings I put into storage. It reached critical proportions, though, when I married in 2002 and moved from my home in Wilmington, Delaware, to Medford, New Jersey. Now we were combining two households' worth of "stuff," so I discovered that I had a huge problem on my hands! Also, I had even less time to deal with it, because I had married into a very large family—we have six kids, plus their spouses, and 14 grandchildren in our lives! I was feeling really desperate, that I might never dig out from under the mess.

I saw a meeting notice in a local free magazine for "Clutterers Anonymous," and the name and concept intrigued me. I was just beginning an awareness of my own problem with clutter. I thought this organization might help me to solve my problem, so I attended my first meeting. That was over six years ago; little did I know that CLA had just come to southern New Jersey only a short time before that. I was about to embark along with them on a journey of growth that has led me thus far. (Keep putting those notices in your local publications—you never know who might show up!)

Over the years, room by room, most of my home has become reclaimed. I still have two rooms that I struggle with in the upstairs of my home, but they are usable. I'm pleased with my accomplishment: that, now, anyone can come into my home at any time and I would not be embarrassed. I even have a clean guest room, in case an overnight guest might arrive. I have stopped my acquiring behaviors, and that has helped a lot. This program requires a lot of work, with conscious thought daily, but it can be done. If ever I have achieved some serenity in my life, I would say it is now.

About four years ago, I was asked to chair our local meeting. We have developed such a strong and supportive Fellowship here in Marlton, so I just love my group! I truly believe that CLA has become my passion and my destiny. We are encouraged to attend the monthly business meetings of CLA-East, so I began to do that, as the representative from Marlton. As a result, I found myself volunteering for the Planning Committee for the Clutter-Free Day (CFD).

I attended my first CFD in April 2011 as a member of that leadership team. It was quite an experience—being among the planners "in charge" at the same time that I had so much to learn. But we got through it very well, I think: the CFD 2011 was a fun and informative day for all attending.

I wish everyone could do service by attending business and committee meetings as much as they are able; we learn so much and are so needed. Together, we can do great things, and this CFD was proof of that.

Last fall, I was surprised to discover myself as chairperson of CLA-East. I look forward to the upcoming year of service in this capacity, since I enjoy Clutterers Anonymous very much.

I hope that we will see continued growth and improvement as we move along. We have already achieved a great milestone: a written Mission Statement to guide us as we develop our organization.

Plans for the coming year include visits by attendees of the CLA-East meetings to as many local groups in CLA-East as we possibly can—and, of course, another fun Clutter-Free Day in May 2012. I look forward to seeing you all there!

Summer 2012

The Clutterers Anonymous World Service Organization recently held elections to fill positions that were open due to officers' retiring, though some WSO positions are still open. Many members of the Fellowship choose to do service by holding WSO positions and serving on the Executive Committee. Members who hold positions greatly help WSO to function more efficiently for the Fellowship. Doing service is a significant part of the 12-Step program, and countless members have found that serving in this way is immensely helpful in advancing their recovery. Past and present officeholders have used the words "rewarding" and "fulfilling" to describe their experiences. The opportunities are open or upcoming, and members are invited to learn more.

WSO works well only when members step up to do service in the vital roles of chairperson, vice-chairperson, and corresponding secretary, among others.

Each member is invited to attend WSO phone meetings. WSO needs members working together for the good of the Fellowship.

All WSO positions are important for the proper flow of CLA. When CLA members hold these positions for the designated terms, the necessary work of WSO gets done. For example, the member who serves by performing the duties of recording secretary ensures that WSO agendas and relevant documents are emailed to the Fellowship as needed. The web mail correspondent's duties enable CLA email messages to be answered in an efficient and timely manner.

Won't you please feel free to step up and volunteer for one of these critical positions? Someone would be glad to mentor you. Do you know someone whom you feel would serve the Fellowship well and gain from doing service in this manner? Members may nominate suitable candidates to hold positions. Guidelines for eligibility for each office are available upon request.

There are other ways to do service by helping WSO. Any member can assist an elected officer with fulfilling the position's duties. (Assisting an officer is ideal training for those who may want to run for an upcoming position.) Seeing members assisting WSO's elected officers motivates others to stand as candidates for election. WSO always needs nominees for offices during each election cycle—and sometimes in between to fill unexpected vacancies.

If serving as an officer or assisting one is not possible at this time, another way to help is to share this information and appeal for WSO participation to other members you know. The Fellowship benefits from every positive action each member takes to support CLA.

Holiday 2012

Martha H., MD

My name is Martha, and I'm a recovering clutterer. I love Clutterers Anonymous! I have been a member since 2006, although I don't recall the exact date I joined. (Our group's records were destroyed.)

I am the recording secretary of CLA World Service Organization (WSO), which involves taking minutes at the WSO and Executive Committee meetings and sending meeting notices to the WSO mailing list.

WSO meetings are held once a month. An agenda is prepared by the chairperson, and the treasurer prepares a monthly financial report. I send these reports to all email addresses provided by members of CLA.

Service work is an important part of my recovery. There's nothing like being in the middle of the Fellowship! Trusted servants work tirelessly to manage ways to carry the message of recovery to the still-suffering clutterer. I have a real appreciation for the passion these trusted servants bring to their positions. They actively support the service structure that makes CLA function.

For me, recovery would be flat and two-dimensional without service participation. The program has made a huge difference in my life, and I want to feel that I'm making a difference in the program. Service work allows me the satisfaction of knowing I'm doing what I can to keep things running smoothly.

Service participation also teaches me discipline, a quality I am sorely lacking since I retired from my career. I need a framework of responsibility on which to arrange my daily activities. Service provides that framework.

After attending a WSO meeting and recording the minutes, I feel energized and ready to tackle something on my to-do list!

Service gives me an opportunity to get to know other members of the Fellowship on a day-to-day basis. I get to know the real person behind the name. It's difficult to describe the dedication and devotion to CLA that I've observed in these people.

I am grateful to have a service position that helps me grow in CLA and aids in my recovery. I highly recommend service work to members who want to enhance their recovery experience.

Spring 2013

James C., NY

Dear CLA Members,

I would like to share with you some principles that have helped guide my own life and have given it joy and peace. These principles are:

- My Higher Power (HP) communicates with me in prayer and thought through a clear, objective need.
- I often say "yes" to HP by refusing to say no.
- I declutter effectively when I mourn clutter.

An excellent example of the first two principles working together is the case of my becoming chairperson of CLA-East for this year. The people who have served in various capacities with great sacrifices in past years communicated that they just could not take on the additional burden of being the chairperson at this time. No one else was volunteering for the position. Not having a chairperson could well mean disaster for the entire CLA-East intergroup.

I realized that I could stumble and bumble along just well enough that the entire intergroup would not collapse. Thinking about these clear, objective needs with HP in prayer, I sensed within myself HP saying to me, "If not you, who? Please?" Pondering all the good that HP has brought into my life, I realized I could not say no to HP. I, therefore, decided to trust and accept the post for this year. So far, that decision has resulted in much personal joy and peace. I hope that when future needs in CLA arise (and they surely will!), those who have read this might also trust HP and say, "Yes."

A good example of the third principle has been my struggle with newspapers. While it is true that much information contained in one newspaper is indeed contained in others, this is not entirely true. Fear of losing the valuable, unique information a newspaper might well contain caused me to hoard them for months. However, attending CLA meetings helped me to see that death—including the death of losing helpful information—is a real part of life. Therefore, mourning the loss of possibly valuable information from newspapers helped me to let go of them. Now, every month or so, I pull a chunk of papers from the bottom of my small stack, mourn the fact that I could not glean the desired information from them, and then release them. This is very worthwhile for me. Thank you, CLA.

Spring 2014

Jeannie B., CA

Hi, my name is Jeannie. I am a clutterer and the voice mail correspondent for WSO. When you call (866) 402-6855 and leave a message, an e-mail is sent to me immediately with your voice mail attached. I have always loved working with the public and love the investigative part of this job, especially, where did that meeting go? I took on this position in September 2013.

I come from a family of clutterers—my mother, my father, and three of us five children. The others are perfectionists. I married a perfectionist, too. When I was 8 months pregnant and working full time and taking two college courses, my husband came up with a way to help me streamline washing the dishes. He would smash them on the floor. I started keeping up with the dishes. I started to plan my divorce. Our son and his wife are perfectionists too, and clutter used to keep them from bringing their kids here.

When I lived with someone else—a husband, a child, a roommate—I was less of a clutterer out of not wanting to annoy them. I haven't lived with anyone else for about 17 years. Needless to say, I accumulated a lot of stuff. When I took early retirement, I thought I would catch up and declutter. But I found too many interesting things I would rather do. I became a time clutterer.

I found another 12-Step program and then CLA through them four-and-a-half years ago. Since then, I have found progress not perfection, especially since working the "12 and 12" with a sponsor, which I consider the key to success and abstinence.

I attended the Saturday Newport Beach, California, meeting until we moved to Seal Beach last spring. The group had to go on hiatus, but two of us regulars are left and want to restart the meeting in Seal Beach or Long Beach; so if you know any clutterers who might attend, please let me know as soon as possible. Thank you for letting me be of service.

Fall 2014

Ted S., NY

Ted S. was the vice-chairperson of CLA-East.—Ed.

How to Give Something Away and Keep it at the Same Time

A major factor with cluttering is the difficulty in throwing something away. If someone could use the item, then at least there is the possibility of passing it along. This is far easier than just discarding an object, such as a long-forgotten magazine or another blue bottle that has achieved treasure status. There have been incidents where I gave something away and then asked for it back. The feeling of loss was too great.

Coming into Clutterers Anonymous brought illumination into my cave of deprivation. For the first time, there was an inkling of not being alone. It was as if I had found my tribe. Realizing there were other people who experienced similar anxiety was actually a relief.

Listening to the people with joy in their lives inspired me to do what they suggested: work the 12 Steps of Clutterers Anonymous. Working the Steps illuminated my life with a Higher Power, empowering me to seek recovery in every dark corner of my cave. I felt an excitement of belonging and a desire to be part of Clutterers Anonymous.

The Steps showed me how to find that good feeling inside of me that I tried with such fervor to diffuse from my clutter. That feeling was a "spiritual awakening," and service work helps offer the opportunity to others. The amazing thing is, even though I'm giving it away, I still get to keep it. What is this "it?" The "it" is the grace of recovery. How is this accomplished? Service work is anything that helps to ensure that a suffering clutterer has a meeting to go to seeking help to recover. It can be as simple as going to a meeting and saying hello to someone you haven't seen before.

Service work can start even after the first meeting by setting up the chairs. Meetings have tasks or errands to be done. It could be ordering literature, being a contact person for the group, or making a phone call for a committee. Doing these particular actions helps me as much as it helps the other members. It makes me feel a part of the Fellowship, rather than an individual who attends meetings.

Having a sense of belonging with other people brings about a desire to do better, to show the best side of me while letting them see the worst of me. It feels very freeing to finally be truthful, although I may be comfortable staying with my clutter because people accept me with it. Not being rejected is the best of both worlds. I can have my clutter and be accepted at the same time. My former frame of mind would still keep me in a cave of deprivation without the joy that is possible.

Freely giving away service increases my gratitude for this program. In fact, the more I give away, the more I receive in grace. That grace inspires my desire to declutter. Whenever the question is asked about who will do a certain chore, request, or position for Clutterers Anonymous, there is usually a moment of silence. The members who have been working for years at various levels—group, intergroup or the World Service Organization—might say to themselves, "Oh dear, do I have to do another commitment?" It's not because they aren't committed to service; it's because they have been doing it for years, allowing the rest of us to enjoy the benefits of this program.

The next time a service opportunity comes up at a business meeting, committee, or phone meeting, do not beware of the silence, be aware when the silence comes. Volunteer for that CLA position or commitment. Use it as an opportunity to give thanks for all those who came before us. Use it to ensure that there will be a place for the rest of our tribe to find us.

You don't have to know how to do the job to volunteer for it. The people who have done it will guide you. And they will do it with Grace.

Holiday 2014

Judy K, FL

Experience, Strength, and Hope from the WSO Recording Secretary

With parents who were organized clutterers, I thought that environment was normal. My own home is similar. To console myself after my parents' deaths, my divorces, and serious health challenges, I—unfortunately—participated in some shopping therapy. Perfectionism, procrastination, and fear of being wasteful keep me bogged down with a storage unit and closet full of my deceased parents' belongings.

So, what am I doing about these things? I regularly attend my CLA home meeting in Delray Beach, Florida; bookend; and pray for help, willingness, and a lack of willfulness.

I am whittling my excesses down. I give some items to needy friends. I sell quite a few unwanted items online and some at consignment shops. I take a tax deduction for donating unwanted items to my favorite charities and feel good about helping them and their customers. I help other clutterers and hoarders. I am writing a reference book to help clutterers and hoarders deal with underlying issues. I invite people to my condo; my ego and perfectionism make me tidy up and clean before they arrive.

I have worked hard to eliminate relationship clutter from my life. I divorced my physically abusive second husband. I reduced my involvement with people who didn't appreciate me or took me for granted. This gave me time to invest in people who are true friends, who reciprocate and accept my quirks as I accept theirs. My life is much more rewarding and less stressful now.

My CLA home group is 45 minutes from my condo, and I carpool with one of my clutter buddies. I've attended this meeting for three years. As my group's literature chairperson, I print flyers, order CLA literature, and renew our CLA*rity* subscription. As group delegate, I provide the status of my home group at the WSO business meeting and vice versa. I also vote the group conscience of my home group on issues at WSO meetings. As contact person, I reached out to the other three Florida CLA groups. Our groups were excited that on a Saturday in October, we carpooled to centrally-located St. Petersburg, conducted a closed meeting, enjoyed fellowship, compared meeting formats, and listened to three speakers.

In April 2014, at my second WSO business meeting, voting members unanimously elected me to a one-year term as WSO recording secretary. In that capacity, I type up the minutes for the monthly, open WSO business meeting and closed WSO Executive Committee meeting. Once the voting members approve the minutes, I email them to the WSO archivist.

My hopes are that by the end of the year, I will hire an estate attorney to wrap up my parents' estate and find appraisers and auction houses who will help me empty and make money from the contents of my storage unit. Here's wishing beauty, order, serenity, a balanced life, and harmonious relationships to us all!

Summer 2015

Audrey L., KY

My experience as the All Phone Groups Committee chairperson has been hard work but very rewarding. I love going to the committee meetings on the second Saturday of the month because everyone seems to get along fine. At first, it was a little bit cluttered, and a couple of times the meetings lasted two hours even though I had intended them to last only an hour and a half. So a member suggested creating subcommittees. Ever since that happened, the general meeting has run smoothly.

We organized several successful declutterthons last year. A lot of people came to them for support and to declutter their homes. Sometimes I did the same. From time to time, people have called me at the last minute to chair, and I appreciate others who come and chair. The problem is that sometimes people, without meaning to, have disrupted the group, and boundaries have to be set. However, most of the time, the declutterthons have run smoothly.

At the last two declutterthons, a lot of people stayed to listen to dynamic speakers.

After several declutterthons, we decided to take a break and have fewer of them, which could make them special like they once were.

Holiday 2015

Alison B., NJ

"They" told me it couldn't be done—that I couldn't possibly take over as one of the co-chairs for the convention planning committee. Why? Because I hadn't been to the last convention, and I really didn't know which things were supposed to happen in what order. In the meantime, nobody was stepping up to the plate, so I simply jumped in to fill the gap. After all, we needed to have meetings on a regular basis, and a whole convention needed to be planned over the phone and via email—even if we were making it up as we went along. And I wasn't a complete novice—I did have my experience as chairperson of CLA East's Clutter-Free Day planning committee. Now that I think about it, the members of last year's convention planning committee were novices, too!

There were people on the committee with me who had planned and attended the convention last year. And with them, using our logic, computer skills, and fertile imaginations, and with all the usual procrastination and clutter that sometimes gets in our way, we formed subcommittees. My biggest job at times seemed to be getting most of those committees together to actually hold their meetings. It was really a matter of keeping the enthusiasm high over the latter months when it seemed like little or nothing was really happening.

I do not have much inner drive, and I really had to push myself very hard to get anything achieved. I began to wonder if the subcommittee members had these same problems as well because many times they didn't call in to our meeting conference calls. On several occasions, I found myself asking whoever was on the line to call others and round them up so we could conduct our meetings. Unfortunately, a lot of time was squandered that way.

We began to hold Steering Committee meetings, where representatives from each of the subcommittees would report on their activities.

These meetings weren't very formal. Most of the time, we didn't even have written agendas. We were very proud of the location that we chose for our convention, which was the Embassy Suites in Secaucus, New Jersey. Then we created a written timeline to help us plan the convention program. We wanted a program that would be varied enough to suit everybody. Our next job was to find workshop leaders, the keynote speaker, and someone to record all the sessions. Everything took longer than we expected it to.

Being at the convention itself was, at times, almost like watching a play for me. I found myself looking at it from the outside in, and it was so strange. I met people I had previously known only over the phone. I never expected the tears and feelings of joy from seeing CLA members in person with whom I'd volunteered in various capacities for the last nine years.

I'm so glad I had the experience of being a co-chair for the convention, and it's not over yet. There are evaluations to review to see how we can make it better next time. Also, we want to write down what we did so the next committee doesn't have to make it up quite so much as they go along!

Spring 2016

Martha H., MD

Hello, I'm a recovering clutterer; my name is Martha. I am currently the treasurer and Finance Committee chairperson for CLA WSO.

All those numbers—many people find bookkeeping and accounting unbearably dull. Others are baffled by the whole concept of financial reporting. Personally, I really enjoy preparing spreadsheets and performing financial analysis. The whole process is elegant, and the finished product can be a useful tool—not only for historical purposes, but also for use when preparing projections and budgets.

Each month, I assemble various financial documents that will be needed to prepare my monthly report. Certainly, the bank statement is important, as well as copies of all deposits made. I print out each PayPal document, too. Each document is posted individually to the spreadsheet. The spreadsheet is designed to automatically add and subtract where necessary. When everything is posted, I reconcile the bank account. It's just like balancing your personal checkbook (groan). Once everything is in order, I send the report to the WSO secretary for emailing to the Fellowship prior to the monthly meeting.

In addition to financial reporting, I oversee any transaction that involves money, whether it be paying our bills or receipting 7th Tradition contributions. I make sure we're following IRS rules and other governing laws, and I perform financial analysis when requested. I prepare the annual report that's forwarded to our tax accountant so our tax returns can be filed. I oversee various fiduciary functions, as well, including maintenance of our tax status.

It's a privilege to serve as WSO treasurer. I believe that service is necessary for good recovery, and I'm lucky to be able to serve in a position I enjoy.

Summer 2016

Dody W., PA

Public Information Officer (PIO)...weird title. I have had the privilege of serving in this office for only a year, but as I have learned more, I have become increasingly more excited and grateful to serve. So what is it? The PIO role is focused mainly on the 12th Step, "Having had a spiritual awakening...we tried to carry this message to others..."

Although all Steps and Traditions are important in this work, there are five Traditions that are directly related to it. Tradition 6: "A CLA group ought never endorse, finance, or lend the Clutterers Anonymous name to any related facility or outside enterprise, lest problems...divert us from our primary purpose." Tradition 8: "Clutterers Anonymous should remain forever nonprofessional..." Tradition 10: "CLA has no opinion on outside issues..." Tradition 11: "Our public relations policy is based on attraction rather than promotion; we need always maintain personal anonymity at the level of press, radio, films, television, and all other media." Tradition 12: "Anonymity is the spiritual foundation of all our Traditions..." The following are some examples of how these traditions apply.

Most of us understand the CLA program works best when clutterers want help and attend CLA face-to-face or phone recovery meetings. Clutterers learn about meetings from such places as notices in church bulletins, libraries, and local newspapers and from referrals by landlords, apartment supervisors, hoarding task forces, professional counselors, and clergy.

The PIO can also function as an internal resource to advise and answer questions members have about letting the public know their group exists without actually promoting it. The PIO may function externally by responding to specific inquiries from the media. For example, "No, we cannot supply you with names and addresses of clutterers."

This was an actual call and resulted in a great conversation about what CLA is and why we embrace the principle of anonymity. By the time the conversation closed, the caller was "connecting the dots" about others she knew who might be struggling with clutter. She also left the call having written down resources for help.

In addition, we receive inquiries from professional organizers who are usually looking for partnerships. I've discovered that it is best if I engage them with appreciation about their desire to help people with clutter problems before I explain the 6th and 8th Traditions. If they seem at all open to remaining on the phone, I ask if I can explain the CLA program. If they're still open, I give a short summary, then suggest that they refer their clients to CLA.

I first heard of CLA from a professional organizer I had hired. She interviewed me about my habits, took a tour of my house with me, and said, "You don't need me; you need CLA." Imagine, organizers can be our friends!

So how do "issues" arrive at the PIO's doorstep? Typically, interested parties contact us via our website or leave a voicemail at our toll-free number.

Sometimes members have called me directly with specific questions about their involvement in events and their concerns that they not violate our Traditions.

As we continue to grow, we may develop local public information committees, as well as contact with the professional community committees to actively engage individuals and organizations in local communities.

Holiday 2016

Ron M., PA

Hi, I'm Ron M. and I am a clutterer. My journey started when I said to a psychologist, "It is too bad there is not a program for clutterers." He said, "Let's look" and found a listing for a CLA meeting in Philadelphia with a phone number. I called and received a call back from a member of that meeting, complete with a welcoming voice, some encouragement, and an invitation to a face-to-face meeting in Northeast Philadelphia, which I attended. I received a packet of information and met my first CLA members. Wow! I was welcomed and received much encouragement.

After several meetings, I was told about the Clutter-Free Day coming in May of 2013. At the Clutter-Free Day, I entered into a conversation with a clutterer from Long Island. He explained some things to me and suggested that I call him that following Sunday evening and we could talk more. Even though I was still attending meetings, I procrastinated and waited to call until New Year's Day, seven months after I had met him. He answered, and we spoke for quite a while. I received some wonderful direction, and it was suggested that I keep in touch weekly.

I tried to follow direction, as I am familiar with the 12-Step program, having been a member of another Fellowship for many years. However, it was surprising how little I knew about my well-hidden addiction of cluttering and how much something could control my life in all ways. I thought clutter was only material items; boy, was I surprised! The months rolled by, and I had many complaints to my sponsor of how little progress I was making. He said I was climbing a mountain without any tools. That was true! CLA has the Tools,[19] but I was not using many that would make things go better. My sponsor suggested at a later date that I serve as CLA-East Intergroup Chairperson, as it was different from the types of service I was in and would familiarize me with phone work. It would also help my program, and I will say it has.

I am far from clutter free but am making progress in getting better, not worse, in many of the different cluttered areas of my life—which I never knew existed before CLA. Thanks to my Higher Power, a patient sponsor, and the program of CLA.

Service

Step 12 says, "...we carry this message to others..." Service is embodied in Step 12. There are many ways to do service at all levels of the Fellowship. The CLA Tool of Service says "The CLA program gives us the opportunity to enhance our progress by taking on service responsibilities, from holding offi ce to doing cleanup."

About Service

Summer 2007

Kathy H., CA

Service is one of the cornerstones of any 12-Step Fellowship. The A.A. Service Manual[3] states: "Our Twelfth Step—carrying the message—is the basic service that the A.A. Fellowship gives; this is our principal aim and the main reason for our existence....We must carry the message, else we ourselves can wither and those who haven't been given the truth may die."

Over the more than 70 years that A.A. and other 12-Step groups have been in existence, they have found that those groups who have a strong tradition of service tend to be healthier and stronger. We cannot say that we have worked all 12 Steps unless we have done some form of service, either by helping another clutterer or by doing more formal service in our group, intergroup, or with WSO. I have found that since I have been giving service to CLA, my program has gotten stronger, and I have made more progress on my decluttering.

Giving service is not only an investment in our Fellowship, it is an investment in our own recovery.

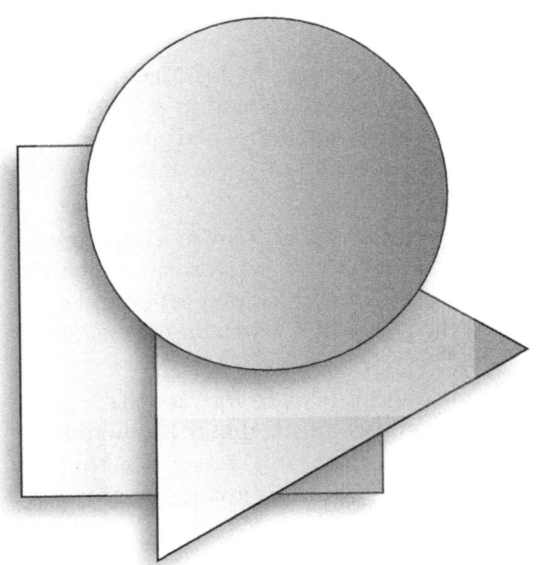

Holiday 2007

Jan G., CA

Elections are held in December for board positions in both the CLA World Service Organization and CLA-East. Those who fill these service positions are usually elected from nominated members who have been attending WSO or CLA-East meetings. There are also many other ways to do service in CLA.

There are various ways to be of service in CLA—at local and phone meetings, regional level, or WSO support. Some service does not require attending business meetings. If you are willing to give back to the CLA Fellowship and want to know how to get started, contact WSO at ClutterersAnonymous.org, or write to PO Box 91413, Los Angeles, CA 90009. If you wish to give service to Intergroup-East, send an e-mail to clarity@claeast.org or call (866) 800-3881.

Fall 2009

Susie S., CA

When initially asked to write this article, I thought it would be focused on the idea of the importance of doing service to "give back what has been so freely given" and the slogan "If you want to keep it (recovery), you need to give it away (do service)." However, after recently working through and completing the 12 Steps of CLA twice, the focus will be on service as a way of life, a way of living our life purpose. I worked first with a CLA buddy in a 12-week process using CLA literature, *Alcoholics Anonymous* (the "Big Book")[4] and A.A. *Twelve and Twelve*,[16] and then with a CLA sponsor in an intensive series of sessions lasting a week and a half using the A.A. Big Book primary purpose process.

Years ago, I was grateful to hear someone share that we can start the program with all the Steps with a "1" in them. This means that we don't have to complete Steps 1 through 9 before we start to work on Step 10, in which we begin doing a daily inventory of feelings and behaviors (looking at resentments, selfishness, fears, and dishonesty). That also includes not waiting to do Step 11, prayer and meditation, where we seek guidance from our Higher Power throughout the day and ask onlyfor knowledge of his will for us and the power to carry it out. And we don't need to wait to get to Step 12 to do the service of "carrying the message" of recovery to others. Anyone can be of service by leading a meeting, speaking at a meeting, sharing information with newcomers, etc.

As it says in the the A.A. "Big Book," "Our real purpose is to fit ourselves to be of maximum service to God and the people about us" and "our very lives, as alcoholics [recovering clutterers], depend on our constant thought of others and how we can meet their needs." After the most recent experience of completing the Steps, I finally see that I now need to be living in Steps 10, 11, and 12 on a daily basis. That means that I'm not here to do my will, I'm to seek guidance continually to do God's will and to be of service.

I cannot say enough about how wonderful it is to work the 12 Steps. It is really life changing to live a life focused on being of service and filtering all decisions through that question: "How can I be of service?" There are so many ways we can be of service when we realize that is our principal purpose in life.

Holiday 2012

Carol N., CA

Of all the service responsibilities I've held over the last 35 years in 12-Step programs (the last 16 of them in CLA), being corresponding secretary ranks near the top. My current volunteer position is something I do in isolation, yet I don't feel isolated. It does keep me busy, but I love every minute of it.

Many duties are involved with this CLA position: picking up mail, keeping records of who orders literature, making bank deposits, processing online order requests and contributions, and accounting for all payments.

It is gratifying to open the post office box and see letters from people I don't even know and will probably never meet but, nevertheless, I feel connected to—people who are reaching out for something.

Perhaps the small act of my response will make a difference in a life, whether it be by mailing leaflets, the booklet, "Is CLA for You: A Newcomer's Guide to Recovery,"12 or the CLA Meeting Directory, or by dropping a short note into the envelope because of some feeling I have about the correspondence.

When someone requests a "CLA Meeting Starter Kit,"[7] I am thrilled to send it; requests for starter kits have increased. Soon, perhaps, I will have the time to follow up on some of those I have previously mailed.

The representatives for any new meetings are asked to send in the "Meeting Information Sheet" as soon as possible in order for that group to be included on the printed CLA Meeting Directory and website.*

It's also my responsibility to forward that information, and that is one of the things I sometimes address in the notes I send out. I may ask about the inquirer's group—how it's going, the group size, or other details—just to get a feel of what's happening around the country.

I have mailed starter kits and literature packets to Australia, England, and Canada. How rewarding it is to do service and experience CLA's global outreach. I often think of how A.A.'s early members must have felt when it expanded from localized, unconnected groups to the worldwide Fellowship A.A. is now.

Service Enhances Recovery

Doing service always rubs off on me in good ways. I feel wanted and needed, and I also want and need my fellow recoverers.

In order for me to go through the 12 Steps thoroughly, I have always found that doing service enhances my recovery; I feel that I am sharing and producing, not just taking and receiving recovery in the Fellowship.

Over my years in 12-Step programs, I began to take on many service roles that I always enjoyed doing but held on to for, perhaps, too long. In the past, I have had some very hard lessons in letting go, even when it was obvious to me that it was way past time to do so.

My practice was to "never say no" to a program request. I have learned, however, that not only do I occasionally need to take a break or balance my time, I also realize something else important: rotating service roles is good for the benefit of the Fellowship.

The program concept of "rotation of leadership" has inspired me to try new things, sometimes in my *dis*-comfort zone. Because someone was willing to mentor me in these new endeavors, I gained more strength and confidence, which helped me to be of greater service — with balance.

It is wonderful to see others enhance their recovery by doing service. Even if it means trying something unfamiliar, just ask someone who is doing it to teach you how to do it, too. Chances are, that person will be grateful to be able to pass on his or her experience and knowledge to another person volunteering to do service in CLA. *

Editor's Note: The CLA World Service Organization (WSO) is currently working on a mechanism for registering meetings and keeping all information current. When the new system is in effect, it will replace the "Meeting Information Sheet" in the "CLA Meeting Starter Kit."

What I Get from Doing Service

Summer 2014

Kathy H., CA

Initially, I got involved in doing service for CLA because our group was without a WSO delegate, and I was the only one able and willing to take it on. Since that time, I have been doing service in one form or another. Currently, I am doing too many jobs—because, once again, the need is there and not enough other members are stepping up to the plate.

But what do I get out of doing service? If nothing else, it gives me a sense of satisfaction. I do believe that, as human beings, we are happiest if we can help others—although we must also take care of our own needs. Also, I tend to isolate less and feel less depressed when I have a task to complete for CLA.

After my retirement eight years ago, I was beginning to get stale. Through doing service, I have once again begun to feel like an accomplished person. I believe that my physical decluttering has also gotten a boost because of my service commitments.

Sometimes the hardest part is just getting started. It is easier to get started when I have a commitment to do a task by a certain date; finishing with a service commitment gets me going so that I am able to do more work on my house and my recovery.

Also, the many telephone conversations I have had with other CLA members through doing service have greatly enriched my life. I have made many friends through my years of service—friendships that I treasure. I got to know my travel partner by serving with her on the same committee, so I no longer need to vacation by myself.

The act of completing my commitments and the joy of contact with other clutterers has led to a fuller and happier life. So I say, thank you, CLA, for allowing me to be of service.

My View on Service

Holiday 2015

Audrey L., KY

I came from other 12-Step Fellowships, and I was raised to give back what was freely given to me. So, I have done service ever since I came to CLA in September 2009.

I have chaired phone meetings, as well as the Shared Activity Line, the Focused Action Line, the Commitment Line, the All Phone Groups Committee, the CLA WSO business meeting, and other business meetings.

I love giving back because people have freely given to me. Read the A.A. *Twelve and Twelve*,[16] page 24, and *Alcoholics Anonymous* (the "Big Book")[4] from the bottom of page 180 to the top of page 181. What is contained in those pages is why I continue to do what I do. I love service.

Fall 2016

Ruthe S., PA

I have always loved editing and proofreading, and I feel that I am good at them. I also have written poetry, but it wasn't until recently that I felt comfortable calling myself a writer. Therefore, when I learned about the CLA*rity* newsletter, it seemed like a no-brainer to join the team. I began working on CLArity in the fall of 2015, after our last convention. I knew the other members, some better than others, and I thought I would enjoy working with them.

I attend weekly meetings where we discuss possible topics for articles, who might be able to write them, and the progress of these articles. I learned what a "flow list" is, about placement of articles, and what are CLA issues and what aren't. I also now have some knowledge about paper and envelope stock.

The first time I edited an article, I was nervous. I didn't know if any grammar rules had changed, and I was worried about looking stupid. In addition, the editing software we use is not optimal, and it hastaken a while for me to learn how to use it. Now, I have written several articles, edited countless others, and have been a part of many proofing sessions. I even had to quickly rewrite an article, and I was impressed with myself because I was able to do it overnight. I also took a turn at mailing out the newsletter, and they all made it out!

I love working on CLA*rity*. I enjoy talking to my comrades weekly and editing and writing articles. It is the best 12-Step service I have ever done. Where else could I serve CLA members, spend time with people I like, and get experience writing? It is definitely a win-win situation.

Spotlight on Service

Holiday 2016

Giving service can be very rewarding and satisfying. The CLA Tool19 of Service states: "The CLA program gives us the opportunity to enhance our own progress by taking on various service responsibilities.... As we serve, we risk moving out of isolation...."

It is very common for clutterers to isolate from others. Often, this is because we are embarrasse about allowing anyone into our cluttered homes. Some of us clutter in order to isolate. This isolation can lead to loneliness, fear, and depression.

Attending CLA meetings can help toward moving out of isolation. But giving service can put us even more in touch with others, since most service positions require some communication with other members. Also, it is often easier to keep a commitment to a group or other person than to ourselves; that helps us to start being more accountable to ourselves. And knowing that we are actually completing tasks while helping the Fellowship can lead to an enormous sense of satisfaction, which can energize us to tackle the problems in our lives.

But there can be a danger if we seek that satisfaction without adhering to the principles of the Steps and Traditions. The Steps lead us to seek self-knowledge and to maintain good relationships with others. Some of our Traditions tell us that our common welfare should come first, our leaders are but trusted servants, and that we should place principles before personalities.

See the Clutterers Anonymous Program section, pages 63 and 67, for more articles on service

Facilitating or Leading Meetings

Leading Meetings at Local Groups

Summer 2009
Kathy H., CA

Every CLA meeting has a leader, although different terms are used in different places. The leader is the one who facilitates the meeting; in some cases leadership is rotated each week.

Some in the Fellowship seem to think that only "oldtimers," or those with years of recovery, may lead meetings. Also, many members—even though they may have attended CLA meetings for quite some time—fear to lead a meeting. I can definitely understand this, since I also have difficulty in speaking before a group. It was even very hard to share when I first started attending 12-Step meetings; it is still not always 100% comfortable for me to do so, although it is much easier than it used to be. However, I have made myself do so, because I know that my recovery will not progress if I do not speak with others about my problems and successes.

But leading a meeting was easier for me than simply sharing. Usually, a leader is accomplishing three tasks: reading from a printed or typed format, asking other members to read certain CLA-approved literature (which varies from group to group), and recognizing those who wish to share. In some meetings, the leader also qualifies (shares what it was like before, how it changed, and what it is like now).

So you see, leading a meeting is nothing to worry about; any CLA member can lead the meeting. It is just one more way of giving back to the Fellowship. And remember, giving service is embodied in the 12-Step way of life and tends to aid us in our recovery.

Facilitating a Phone Meeting

Fall 2012
Wendy L., IL

There are no CLA face-to-face meetings in my area, so phone meetings are all I know. One benefit of phone meetings is that participants get to "meet" CLA members from around the country, and even from around the world sometimes. Phone meetings take place in all kinds of weather, so there's no worry about driving. I am grateful for the phone meetings.

To be of service is to help out both oneself and others, but it can be a little nerve-wracking leading a phone meeting the first time. By following the written meeting format, which I received from a member via email, it became easy and very doable. And, odds are that there will be at least one CLA member on the call who has phone meeting experience and can help you out in a pinch.

I facilitated my first literature phone meeting at 2:00 p.m. Central Time on a sunny Wednesday afternoon. If you haven't participated in this call, you will find that the weekly literature meeting is a wonderful experience. We read aloud through an entire CLA leaflet and share on the contents. I love our literature and jumped at the chance to facilitate this meeting for one day.

It was show time, and I dialed in with the leader's code and heard many bells as CLA members joined the call. I had the printed meeting format in front of me and began to read from it. I had chosen the "Declutter Your Mind"[9] leaflet to read. When I first read this leaflet, I found myself highlighting quite a lot of it. Bits of it stood out, like "we prioritize our goals" and "I trust that when I need a fact or an item, it will be available to me."

This leaflet is still very relevant to me today, as I still have unorganized and too-long to-do lists for an upcoming vacation. Well, if I forget to pack it, I'll find a way to get it at my destination.

Per the meeting format, I asked for volunteers to read sections of the leaflet, and five members quickly volunteered. After each section was read, members jumped in and shared. The call was flowing well, and my nerves were calming down. I concluded the meeting and was thrilled to have facilitated a meaningful literature meeting call. I even received a few compliments!

My fears—that no one would volunteer to read from the leaflet, that no one would share, or that someone would ask questions I couldn't answer—were laid to rest. Even questions about sending literature outside the U.S. were answered by members. (Yes, the CLA World Service Organization does mail our literature out of the country!)

Based on my great experience, I highly recommend that you volunteer to facilitate a phone meeting, if phone meetings appeal to you. It felt good to be of service, and maybe to have made a difference in members' lives. You can make a difference, too.

Managing a Shared Position

Fall 2015

Sometimes a CLA service position can seem to be too overwhelming. Or, perhaps, the potential candidates are already overburdened with service work. At such times, it may be possible for two (or more) persons to share the duties of the position.

This has been done at times when potential World Service Organization (WSO) delegates feel that they are unable to make a once-a-month commitment to attend WSO meetings. In those cases, it has been helpful to elect co-delegates, or a delegate and an alternate. This has workedfine when the two delegates have come to a clear understanding of which one will represent their group at any given WSO meeting. The delegates themselves decide, either soon after their election to the position or on a month-to-month basis—but the decision must be understood and agreed upon by both.

Sharing the load has also occurred in the chairpersonship of WSO, as well as at the committee level. Although all were well-intentioned from the outset, some shared service positions have been more effective than others.

The shared path is smoother when the personalities are more compatible and strive for group conscience. It may be less productive when the service partners have extremely different methods of working, though sometimes this has a benefit of giving balance. As Tradition 12 states, "...principles before personalities."

In order to be successful in such an undertaking, all parties must agree on what the position entails and have a plan for dissolution. It is also important that they communicate with each other on a regular basis about what has been happening and what is coming up in the future. Ultimately, all should agree on the direction to take for given issues.

Currently, there are committees which have co-chairpersons, including the Literature and Convention Committees. Service partnerships tend to work well when service partners keep the lines of communication open and keep spiritual principals uppermost in their thoughts and decisions.

Sharing positions can work when communication is frequent and all parties keep the ideals of the CLA program firmly in mind, remembering that we are but trusted servants of our Higher Power—we do not govern.

Business Meetings and Group Conscience

Fall 2008

The business meeting of a group is where all decisions about the group are made—changes in format, elections of officers, and other decisions affecting the group as a whole.

Most groups have a short, separate business meeting, usually held once a month either before or after the regular group meeting. Some groups have a separate business meeting only for unusual occasions, such as elections. If anything else occurs, these groups usually hold very short business meetings (lasting five to ten minutes) at some point during the regular meeting.

In either case, no major vote should occur without an announcement to group members before the meeting.

In 12-Step programs, all decisions of importance should be decided by group conscience whether at the local group level or another segment of the service structure.

Group conscience entails more than just asking for a majority vote. Through group conscience, the members should strive to reach substantially unanimous decisions on important matters. This is arrived at through discussion by all members of the group.

Pains should be taken to allow those with minority opinions to present their views more than once. Trusted servants should pay special attention to the minority view. It is even the duty of those with diverging opinions to present their views to the group. There have been many times when the majority has reversed itself because of compelling reasons given by those holding minority views. Thus, all members have a right to be heard—which often also leads to better decisions.

The A.A. "12 Concepts of Service,"17 Concept XII, states:

> ***Warranty Four:*** *"That all important decisions should be reached by discussion, vote, and wherever possible, by substantial unanimity." This Warranty is, on the one hand, "a safeguard against any hasty or overbearing authority of a simple majority; and, on the other hand, it takes notice of the rights and the frequent wisdom of minorities, however small. This principle guarantees that all matters of importance, time permitting, will be extensively debated, and that such debates will continue until a really heavy majority can support every critical decision."*

About People

Spring 2007

The CLA*rity* editors would like to introduce you to Betsey K. of New Jersey.

In April, 1997, Betsey began attending the East Orange (now Bloomfield), New Jersey, CLA Meeting. In 2002 she moved to the Boonton group, which now meets in Wayne, New Jersey. Her long period of service in CLA began with her group's representative to CLA-East Intergroup after it was formed in 2001. She has also served as its secretary, literature person, and treasurer.

Currently she is treasurer of both the CLA East Intergroup and CLA World Service Organization. She also coordinates registration for the Clutter-Free Days.

Fall 2007

Kathy H, WSO Recording Secretary, 2003–2007. Kathy H. came to CLA in 2002 and has fulfilled her commitment to providing exemplary service in the WSO business meetings for nearly four years as recording secretary. Her role has been quite important to the behind-the-scenes work that has kept CLA WSO running smoothly from the beginning.

She is a tireless worker, volunteering her time to take minutes during the face-to-face WSO business meetings in Los Angeles, California, from 2003–2005, and then transitioning to the WSO phone meetings ever since. Her note-taking skills are extensive, often including direct quotes. Having accurate records of meetings has often avoided confusion about what a speaker did or did not say and what agree-ments the group reached. Kathy acts as a virtual recorder, capturing all that was said!

Her service committee work has extended to taking subcommittee meeting notes and putting the bylaws into their important final form. She has also been instrumental in the preparation and designing of the CLA*rity* newsletter. She has diligently presented the various drafts and layouts for committee members' discussion and approval and made changes up to the final version.

Kathy is due for a large gold star of appreciation. She often says she enjoys doing service for CLA, which aids her own recovery.

Holiday 2008

Q, CA

I would like to commend the people who gave service to make the Southern California Clutter Free Day such a success. Kathy and Carol and

Rita did a great job of behind-the-scenes work. I came along just as a "go-fer," filling in where my strengths took me. Then there was a crew who volunteered to man the tables for registration and literature. But, unfortunately, not enough people received the blessing of helping. Please be aware of this at future events. Even volunteering for the most mundane tasks helps things go smoothly.

Service is freedom from bondage of self. The more we do to help our meetings along by volunteering to read, be a speaker, or take on other duties, the stronger we make ourselves. The more we give of ourselves, the more we have to give. It is an odd phenomenon, but very true.

Editor's Note: We would like to give this person credit for the volunteering she did. Because of her skills as announcer and moderator, things stayed on time and on track. She practices what she preaches.

World Service Organization (WSO)

Summer 2008

CLArity provides the following Q&A about WSO, its benefits to members, and the abundant opportunities for doing service. Those who serve at WSO level as officers, committee members, delegates, or meeting attendees say that service aids recovery. This is the first part in a series.

What does 'WSO' stand for?

WSO stands for the World Service Organization *of Clutterers Anonymous. It is referred to as CLA WSO.*

What is the World Service Organization (WSO)?

WSO is a group of trusted servants who meet on matters that affect the fellowship as a whole. WSO handles the functions through its various committees and subcommittees. When required, the Executive Board of CLA WSO meets to handle matters of greater urgency. WSO is not a governing body; it can share experience, strength, and hope with the groups, who then make their own decisions through group conscience.

What does WSO do to benefit CLA members?

WSO benefits the fellowship by producing and selling CLA literature; maintaining the CLA website, post office box, and message phone; compiling and disseminating meeting lists and other information; providing a forum for discussion and advice on matters that affect CLA as a whole, especially in matters involving the Traditions; and providing starter kits and help, as requested, to groups. WSO administers the 7th Tradition contributions to pay expenses for mailing, website, telephone, printing, incorporation fees, and so forth.

How does WSO conduct its meetings and when are they held?

Initially, as CLA developed, meetings were held in person but now are accessible through phone teleconferencing. This allows members in all areas to attend. Meetings are usually held once a month. At present, the scheduled meetings are the fourth Saturday of every month, with exceptional changes for holidays and some months in the summer.

Who may attend the WSO meetings?

Any CLA member may attend. Only delegates, officers, and chairpersons of standing committees may vote.

Who are delegates and what do they do?

Local meetings and phone meetings may elect delegates to WSO. Delegates represent their groups at WSO meetings and vote on all motions. They keep their groups apprised of CLA news, information, and decisions of WSO. It is important for all groups to have a delegate to keep the flow of information between WSO and the groups.

What are the elected positions in WSO?

The annually elected offices on the WSO Board are: chairperson, vice-chairperson; treasurer, recording secretary, corresponding secretary, public relations, and Wwebmail, along with chairpersons of the standing committees: Communications, Literature, CLA*rity,* Cyber (website), Bylaws, and Finance.

How do members get service positions in WSO?

All positions on the board are elected—officers, as well as chairs of standing committees. Any member may volunteer to participate on any committee or subcommittee.

For more information or questions, email CLArity at claritynwsltr@yahoo.com or WSO at ClutterersAnonymous.net, or write to CLA WSO, PO Box 91413, Los Angeles, CA 90009.

Fall 2008

CLA*rity* provides the following Q&A about the CLA World Service Organization (WSO), its benefits to members, and the abundant opportunities for doing service. Those who serve at WSO level as officers, committee members, delegates, or meeting attendees say that service aids recovery. This is the second part in a series.

Who can be a WSO trusted servant?

In general, any member of CLA may serve, provided he or she meets the prerequisites for the position. Our definitions of positions are growing and changing as the program grows and changes. If you feel you have enough experience, please contact WSO. We really relish experience from other 12-Step programs.

What are the WSO officer positions?

Currently, WSO officers include chairperson, vice-chairperson, treasurer, recording secretary, corresponding secretary, webmail, communications coordinator, and public information chairperson.

When are WSO officer elections held, and how long are the terms?

Nominations are now held in January and February each year, with elections in March. Positions are for one year. Officers may run for reelection for one more term.

Why does CLA have a WSO-type structure?

In CLA there have to be committed, trusted servants who administer the functions of maintaining the treasury records and overseeing expenses, such as the WSO telephone, PO Box, website, printing, and other needs. Also, meetings for the general fellowship must be conducted, so a WSO chairperson is elected to undertake conducting the meetings and other related duties. This is in keeping with Tradition 9: "CLA, as such, ought never be organized, but we may create service boards or committees directly responsible to those they serve."

Is this WSO-type structure common in 12-Step programs?

Yes. Alcoholics Anonymous, the program after which CLA and most other 12-Step programs are patterned, has a similar structure. In AA, the board is larger and the service structure is more complex, because the AA Fellowship is larger than newer programs, such as CLA.

How does the fellowship find out about WSO meetings?

Emails are sent and delegates' make announcements at local and phone meetings to make members aware of the upcoming WSO meeting.

Do members have any input about what WSO discusses or puts to a vote?

Yes. The agenda for every meeting is open to input from any member attending the WSO meetings. In advance of the upcoming meeting, the WSO chairperson will send an agenda for members and officers to review. Motions for items to be voted upon should be submitted in writing at least two weeks prior to the WSO meeting.

Does WSO have an office?

WSO does not have a physical office. We have a permanent mailing address where literature orders and contributions are mailed. Except for the monthly WSO business meetings, most business is conducted through committees and subcommittees by use of telephone conferences and the internet.

If you have any further questions or would like additional information, please email CLA*rity* at ClarityNwsltr@yahoo.com or write to CLA WSO, PO Box 91413, Los Angeles, CA 90009.

About WSO: Service Equals Recovey

Holiday 2008

CLA WSO elections are being held in March, with nominations at the January and February meetings. Listed below is information about officer positions. All terms are for one year; duties may be shared. Do you want to help? We suggest you attend at least two WSO meetings and become familiar with how it works. You can join a committee or run for office. You can put as much or as little time into service as you wish. Meetings are held the fourth Saturday of most months.

Basic Requirements for Nominees

- Working the Twelve Steps of CLA with a sponsor or other mentor
- Being familiar with the CLA Twelve Traditions and the AA Twelve Concepts of Service
- Regularly attending a group for at least one year, having given service for at least six months, and having attended at least two consecutive WSO meetings prior to the elections
- Having the determination to complete projects
- Willing to be a team player
- Having email access and the ability to communicate via the Web

Once elected, officers are expected to attend monthly telephone business meetings of the World Service Organization and the Executive Committee.

Specific Requirements for Various Positions

- Chairperson: Must have excellent communication and interpersonal skills
- Treasurer: Must be clear in his or her personal money issues
- Recording secretary: Excellent writing skills and the ability to transmit minutes to multiple email addresses
- Webmail: Excellent writing skills and enthusiasm for "carrying the message"
- Public Information Officer: Excellent writing skills and a good grounding in the 12 Steps and 12 Traditions

Positions Open for Election

- Chairperson: Establishes all WSO agendas and presides over WSO meetings, maintaining order. He or she oversees all WSO committees and may appoint special ad hoc committees.
- Vice-chairperson: Assists the chairperson whenever needed and serves in the absence of the chairperson. Makes recordings of WSO meetings. He or she may attend all committee meetings.
- Treasurer: Maintains bank accounts for WSO funds. He or she maintains financial records, files taxes, and makes reports at WSO and Finance Committee meetings, as well as securing and publishing an audit of financial records before a newly installed treasurer assumes the responsibilities.
- Corresponding Secretary: Collects mail from the post office box and assumes responsibility for maintaining and sending correspondence, literature, and other items; forwarding letters to other officers as appropriate; and responding to all meeting inquiries. He or she forwards money received to the treasurer or deposits it into the WSO bank account and informs the treasurer of the details. The corresponding secretary needs to pick up the mail near Los Angeles International Airport.
- Recording Secretary: Writes minutes of all WSO meetings, distributing them by email. If absent, he or she is responsible for finding a substitute who is not an officer.
- Web Mail Correspondent: Replies to inquiries sent via email, maintaining careful records. He or she consults with other officers on all emails prior to replying.
- Telephone Correspondent: This person responds to messages left on the WSO voice mail, maintaining careful records and reporting the results. He or she consults with other officers prior to replying.
- Public Information Officer: Makes contact with the media upon request, as well as providing media guideline sheets (yet to be finalized) and also has a strong hand in completing them.
- Archivist: Maintains copies of legal documents, as well as WSO meeting minutes and agendas. (This is a new position. The archives are currently being maintained on someone's personal computer, and we need to have them on a central location online.)

Additional service opportunities are available on the following committees: Bylaws, CLA*rity*,

Communications, Cyber (website), Finance, Literature, and Public Information. Watch the CLA website (ClutterersAnonymous.org) for further details.

WSO and Intergroups: What's the Difference

Spring 2009

This article attempts to enlighten those in Clutterers Anonymous who are confused about the functions of the World Service Organization (WSO) and intergroups.

What is the difference between an intergroup and WSO? Intergroups are established to deal with matters concerning individual CLA groups, while the WSO deals primarily with the entire Fellowship. There may be many intergroups, but there is only one WSO in CLA.

WSO is responsible for producing, printing, and disseminating our literature; helping with problems of groups, upon request; dealing with professionals and the public; making decisions that affect the membership as a whole (while not interfering with group autonomy); and maintaining a mechanism to disseminate information to and answer questions about CLA (via our website, message telephone, post office box, email, and CLA*rity*). WSO is composed of delegates from groups, as well as elected WSO officers.

Some of the functions of an intergroup overlap partially with those of WSO, but the intergroup is concerned with issues in its area. For instance, an intergroup may print a meeting list that shows the groups in its area, while WSO will print a list covering all of CLA. Also, an intergroup may set up a telephone and website to deal with local matters, while those of WSO cover the entire Fellowship. And, while WSO may someday hold a national conference or convention, intergroups do hold local conferences and seminars (although any CLA member may participate). Any group which has joined an intergroup may send representatives to its meetings.

Why this duplication of effort? Since we know our own areas best, it is often helpful that questions from members and groups be answered by someone who resides in that area, especially when it concerns a local matter. Therefore, the intergroup's telephone and website make a great deal of sense. It may be easier to find a meeting on a shorter list printed for a local area, rather than having to look through the entire CLA Meeting List. Also, many members will attend conferences and seminars only in their own areas, so regional events are important. Furthermore, intergroups may, from time to time, cooperate with WSO to disseminate information to area members and to help maintain the flow of communication between the groups and WSO.

Intergroup Representatives and World Service Organization (WSO) Delegates

Spring 2010

What is the difference between a representative and a delegate? If I attend a local meeting or a phone meeting and then attend an intergroup or WSO meeting, does that make me a delegate? How do I get to be a representative or a delegate, and what are the duties and responsibilities?

These are some of the questions that have lately been asked in WSO. We will attempt to answer some of them here in CLArity. For the purposes of this article, we will use the term "group" to mean a CLA group, either a local face-to-face group or a phone group.

There has been a lot of confusion about the difference between a representative and a delegate. Both are elected by group conscience, but delegates represent their groups at WSO, while representatives do so at intergroups. For more information on how group conscience works, see article on on group conscience on page 246.

So just what is a delegate or representative? Any CLA member may attend intergroup sessions or meetings of WSO. Any member can speak, subject to terms of the meeting protocols. However, only those who have been elected by their group as representative or delegate are entitled to vote. Those who have been elected officers for an intergroup usually can also vote in meetings of that intergroup. Additionally, WSO officers and committee chairpersons can vote at WSO meetings.

Every CLA group can elect one delegate to WSO. Also, each participating group of an intergroup can elect a representative to that intergroup. What are the duties of delegates and representatives? The delegates and representatives should attend WSO or intergroup business meetings. They should bring their group's conscience to this body and vote according to that.

They have the further duty of informing their groups of the decisions of WSO or intergroup and of occurrences in CLA. This is usually done during the announcements section of the weekly group meeting. Many groups have elected an alternate in case the delegate or representative is unable to attend a meeting, or so that two people can share the responsibilities. This is up to the group itself to decide. As you can see, these duties are not onerous. WSO meets ten times a year; most intergroups meet once a month. Thus, the duties consist of attending a one- to two-hour telephone meeting once a month (or less) and reporting on it during the local group time.

So, if your group wants a say in matters that affect a wider arena in CLA, we suggest election of a delegate to WSO or a representative to an intergroup or both. We also suggest getting a mail slot at your group's location—or electing a separate group contact who is willing to give his or her address—to make it easier to receive mailed information from WSO and/or your intergroup.

Why I am Grateful for WSO

Holiday 2010

Since this holiday issue has the theme of "gratitude," we decided to include an article on why we are grateful for WSO. Below are comments from three members of the WSO Executive Committee.—Editor

Jan G., CA

I am grateful to CLA WSO because it:

1. reminds me that I am not the only one who clutters,
2. instructs me on the best tools for me to use for my recovery,
3. brings order to the chaos of meetings that get out of hand,
4. provides the balance between what I think and what is correct,
5. is always there to help me achieve sobriety and maintain abstinence,
6. gives me the opportunity to help others,
7. has brought so many opportunities for me to hear from other clutterers, and
8. teaches me how to work the program.

Mary P., NY

My gratitude for WSO is that we have a central "place," even though it's not a physical space, for providing service to the Fellowship. In monthly meetings, our small but hardy band of officers and delegates deals with questions and concerns of our far-flung groups. Various committees (established by WSO) work tirelessly (well, sometimes tiredly) on the finances, the website, producing literature, and, of course, answering mail, email, and phone calls from individuals who've just learned of CLA. I'm grateful for the technology that makes this possible—conference calls, email, voicemail, and group online editing, for example—but mostly for the democratic and service-oriented spirit of the people who participate. WSO does very well, for a bunch of recovering clutterers.

Kathy H., CA

I am grateful to WSO for providing a framework to bring the Fellowship together. Because of WSO, we have literature and the means to disseminate it; we have a telephone, a website, and places to receive both snail mail and email. It gives us the means to connect clutterers from anywhere in the world, to answer their questions, and direct them to both face-to-face and telephone meetings. I am grateful for the people I have met through WSO and for what I have learned about working with others. I am grateful for my responsibilities in WSO, which inspire me to resist sinking back into my cluttering ways.

World Service Organization—Information and Delegate Duties

Spring 2011

The CLA World Service Organization (WSO) is the body that writes, publishes, and sells CLA literature; maintains the telephone lines, website, and postal box; and answers general inquiries from the public and the media. It may set suggested policy guidelines and mediate between CLA groups and individuals. It is managed by six executive officers, who dedicate much of their spare time and energy making sure that CLA as a whole continues to follow the ideals and principles set down by Alcoholics Anonymous.

At WSO meetings, delegates and officers vote on matters affecting the operation of WSO and other issues which may affect the entire CLA Fellowship. A typical meeting also has time for the WSO treasurer's report, reports from the various WSO committees, intergroup reports, CLA news and events, and news from local and telephone groups. The day after the WSO meeting, the executive officers meet to discuss matters affecting WSO and its committees. (Any CLA member who wishes to give service may join most committees; details of various committees are on the website.)

Any CLA member may attend and speak at WSO meetings, but only delegates and officers vote. Each group may elect, by group conscience, a delegate who will represent that group at WSO meetings.

All WSO meetings are held via conference call on the fourth Saturday of most months. When there is a holiday weekend, there will be an alternate meeting date. If making a long-distance call entails financial hardship, the group may wish to purchase a calling card for the delegate(s). If they are unable to do so, WSO may be able to help.

Delegate duties consist of:

- staying informed of WSO matters by reading agendas, minutes, and other materials sent by WSO;
- seeking group conscience on items to be voted on before the WSO meeting;
- attending WSO meetings or, if unable to, arranging for a substitute to attend in place of the delegate;
- representing the group at the WSO meetings and voting as decided by group conscience;
- reporting to the group on items discussed and the results of votes taken at WSO meetings; and
- bringing matters of group concern to the WSO meeting.

WSO rules state that all matters to be voted upon must be introduced either at a prior meeting or by email at least two weeks prior to the meeting. To find the schedule of meetings and to request that the delegate be added to the email list for WSO agendas, minutes, and other materials, write to CLA WSO at PO Box 91413, Los Angeles, CA 90009 or telephone (866) 402-6685. Emails may be sent to the CLA website, ClutterersAnonymous.org, via the contact page. Certain information about WSO is also available on the website.

We urge your group to elect a delegate because it's so important to share information among groups. If attending a meeting held once a month seems to be too much, two or more delegates may share the position, each attending alternate WSO meetings.

CLA WSO Officers Guidelines

Holiday 2011

Nominees shall:

1. be committed to working the 12 Steps of CLA, preferably with a sponsor;
2. have a clear understanding of the CLA 12 Traditions and the A.A. 12 Concepts of Service;
3. be in the Fellowship for at least three years, having regularly attended recovery meetings for at least one year, having given service for at least six months at the local level;
4. be willing to serve on or work with committees to accomplish specific tasks or projects;
5. be willing to be a team player;
6. be willing to devote time and energy to the duties and responsibilities of the position;
7. have a working computer at home and the ability to communicate via the Internet; and
8. have demonstrated leadership in service work at the local level.

Once elected, officers are expected to attend all telephone business meetings of the World Service Organization and the Executive Committee.

Specific Requirements for Various Positions

- Chairperson and Vice-Chairperson: Excellent communication and interpersonal skills. Must have attended WSO meetings for at least one year.

- Treasurer: Clarity in his or her personal money issues. The treasurer shall have experience and some demonstrated expertise in the handling of, and accountability for, money and assets. Must have attended WSO meetings for at least six months.
- Recording secretary: Excellent writing skills and the ability to transmit minutes to multiple email addresses. Must have attended WSO meetings for at least six months.
- Webmail and Voicemail Correspondents: Excellent writing skills, knowledge of 12-Step program, and enthusiasm for carrying the message. Must have attended WSO meetings for at least six months.
- Public Information Officer: Excellent writing skills and a good grounding in the 12 Steps and 12 Traditions. Must have attended WSO meetings for at least six months.
- Corresponding Secretary: Ability to pick up mail weekly from the Post Office near LAX Airport. Must have attended WSO meetings for at least six months.
- Archivist: Ability to organize and maintain large database of documents online. Must have attended WSO meetings for at least six months.

Positions and Duties

- Chairperson: Presides over WSO and Executive Committee business meetings and maintains order, using Robert's Rules of Order. Establishes all WSO and Executive Committee agendas in collaboration with the recording secretary. He or she oversees all WSO committees and may appoint special ad hoc committees.
- Vice-chairperson: Assists the chairperson whenever needed and serves in the absence of the chairperson. Makes recordings of WSO meetings. He or she may attend all committee meetings.
- Treasurer: Maintains bank accounts for WSO funds. He or she maintains financial records, files taxes, and makes reports at WSO and Finance Committee meetings, as well as securing and publishing an audit of financial records before a newly-elected treasurer assumes the responsibilities.
- Corresponding Secretary: Collects mail from the Post Office and obtains orders placed through the CLA website; maintains and sends correspondence, literature, and other items. He or she forwards money received to the treasurer or deposits it into the WSO bank account and informs the treasurer of the details.
- Recording Secretary: Writes minutes of all WSO meetings and distributes them by email. If absent, he or she is responsible for finding a substitute.
- Webmail Correspondent: Replies to inquiries sent via email and maintains careful records. He or she may consult with other officers where necessary prior to sending replies.
- Telephone Correspondent: Responds to messages left on the WSO voice mail, maintains careful records, and reports the results. He or she may consult with other officers where necessary prior to replying.
- Public Information Officer: Makes contact with the media upon request and provides media guideline sheets (yet to be finalized) and has a strong hand in completing them.
- Archivist: Maintains copies of certain CLA documents in a central location online.

What Is WSO and Why Should I Care?

Fall 2012

Mary P., NY

WSO is the World Service Organization, a relatively small group of trusted servants (fewer than a dozen), the purpose of which is to serve the Fellowship as a whole. It is a pointedly minimalist group, not a top-heavy bureaucracy, in keeping with Tradition 9. (Clutterers Anonymous, as such, ought never be organized, but we may create service boards or committees directly responsible to those they serve.)

It handles only matters that affect the Fellowship as a whole; it does not govern or decree every detail of how a CLA group should run. There are committees and subcommittees, to be sure, but these are channels of shared experience, strength, and hope, not rule-making bodies. There is also an Executive Committee, which handles administrative matters.

Through the committees and subcommittees, WSO produces and distributes CLA literature and CLA Meeting Starter Kits. It maintains a website, which is usually the newcomer's first point of contact with CLA. With minimal organization, it oversees a number of conference call phone lines. It also keeps track of the face-to-face meetings in the U.S. and abroad. A registration project is underway, which will facilitate communication between the individual groups and WSO. In addition, WSO has sponsored phone meetings on the CLA Steps and Traditions. The emphasis is always on service, helping those who suffer from cluttering and its effects.

WSO is made up of trusted servants, including officers who are elected by delegates from the far-flung groups of our Fellowship. That's where the individual CLA member comes in—volunteering to serve on WSO and its committees, probably after having done service such as chairing a meeting or acting as secretary or treasurer of a local group. This benefits the group, as well as building satisfaction and self-esteem in the individual member. It's a pleasure to see someone grow from a timid, tentative, uninvolved person into a helpful, confident leader/trusted servant.

WSO runs on a shoestring budget, which is supported by the 7th Tradition, including donations from member groups and individuals. The organization doesn't do fund-raising in the usual sense, but rather depends on this well-established Tradition. So an individual or group is gently encouraged to contribute to keep WSO flourishing.

So that's what WSO does for you, and what you can do for WSO.

Here's how service in WSO helps us:

- We've made extraordinary friendships.
- We isolate less often because we interact with others.
- We become more focused, which spills over into other areas of our lives.
- We learn better time management.
- We become team players, learning how to work with others.
- We practice building relationships.
- We are obliged to study Traditions, and we realize how integral they are to recovery.
- We learn to do the "next right thing."
- We have an opportunity to share what we've learned with others in the Fellowship.
- We learn to give without expectations of receiving.
- We can deal with resentments by working through the Steps.
- We learn to ask for help or support, although many of us may still have difficulty.
- We feel more needed.
- We are able to validate ourselves and each other.
- We teach each other different ways of commnicating.
- We learn to do things in a timely fashion, to keep our commitments to others.
- We learn how to use computers and digital technology more efficiently.
- We meet people with diverse talents and learn from them.
- We exercise our own talents.
- We learn to practice more tolerance and patience.
- We find more direction in our lives.
- We become better listeners.

Spring 2013

Alison B., NJ; Betsey K., NJ; and Kathy H., CA

As CLA members, we are encouraged to give back to the Fellowship what has so freely been given to us. Many of us feel overwhelmed, and the thought of doing service can make us feel more overwhelmed. But if it is done properly, service can help us deal with our problems of procrastination in all areas of our lives.

Holiday 2013

My name is Betsey K., and I have been a member of CLA for 16 years. I am currently the treasurer of CLA WSO and have served in that position for the past eight years. It is an elected position which requires experience and some demonstrated expertise in the handling of, and accountability for, money and assets. A candidate for the position must have clarity in his or her personal money issues and must have attended WSO meetings for at least six months.

The treasurer does not need to have an accounting background, but it does help to like working with numbers and to have an understanding of the basics of financial recordkeeping. The treasurer maintains bank accounts for WSO funds, maintains financial records, files taxes, and makes reports at WSO and Finance Committee meetings. The treasurer also secures and publishes an audit of financial records before a newly-elected treasurer assumes the responsibilities.

Seventh Tradition contributions, as well as payments for CLA literature and Meeting Starter Kits,7 are received via the post office box in Los Angeles and online. The corresponding secretary deposits the money she receives and sends me the details. The information about the Internet transactions comes directly to me. I record the details of all the transactions and use them to balance our bank accounts. I also transfer funds from our Pay Pal account to the appropriate CLA bank accounts.

Although only the treasurer has access to our accounts, there are opportunities for others to give service in this area. Our Finance Committee currently needs more members and a new chairperson. This committee has prepared a budget for WSO and is working on such things as setting new prices for our CLA literature, separating the postage cost from the literature price, and preparing to secure a California tax resale permit, which will require us to charge California sales tax on items shipped to residents of that state.

In addition to serving as treasurer of WSO, I was treasurer of CLA-East from 2003 to 2012 and have just been elected to serve in the same position for the coming year. I have also been treasurer of CLArity since its beginning in 2007. That adds up to 24 years of serving as treasurer in CLA in the last 10 years!

Giving service as treasurer of your local CLA group is relatively easy. Most groups do not have checking accounts or the expenses which can be associated with them—so the treasurer receives the 7th Tradition money collected, pays expenses (rent, literature, etc.), sends the group's donations to WSO and/or the intergroup, and maintains records of all the transactions. I served as treasurer for my local meeting for most of the first five years I was in CLA.

I have always enjoyed working with numbers and take pride in keeping accurate records and producing meaningful reports for the Fellowship. A lot of my clutter issues deal with paper clutter, and I have a tendency to print a lot of records; this presents a challenge to me, as I try to balance keeping appropriate documents on the one hand and reducing paper clutter on the other.

WSO Committees

Literature Committee Survey

Spring 2008

"CLA literature is amazing. It is kind, compassionate, and gentle. It restored me to myself and myself to my home. I love my home now."

This is a sample of the replies CLA members wrote in response to a recent survey about existing literature. The Literature Committee recently asked a number of questions about how and when the literature is used and how satisfied folks are with it.

The respondents were thoughtful and thorough.They were generally very positive about the current pastel-colored set of leaflets CLA publishes. The one-page survey was emailed to all known contacts of about 70 CLA groups, along with a request that it be copied and passed out at their meetings. The committee received feedback from several groups, with 30 individual replies. The responses were informative and enthusiastic.

Most of those who replied to a question about sharing the literature said they had given copies to others outside CLA. Literature is considered one of our Tools of Recovery.19

How and when do people use it?

"I read it when I am discouraged," said one. Another reads it "for inspiration," and someone else said, "I read it in the a.m. as meditation."

In face-to-face meetings, the CLA literature is used, varying in frequency from weekly to monthly to occasionally. Several groups alternate long and short readings. One group reads aloud and then writes on what's been read.

Formats vary, as well. Many of the survey respondents include a Step study in their groups; others use affirmations, which are often read towards the end of the meeting as an important part of their format. Most phone-based meetings use CLA literature regularly.

Other reading material used in the phone groups and face-to-face meetings include: *Alcoholics Anonymous*, the "Big Book";[4] *Twelve Steps and Twelve Traditions*;[16] and other literature from A.A.

When asked if they had any favorites, several survey respondents mentioned "Home: Our Sacred Place"[11] and "Declutter Your Mind."[9]

The survey asked if more literature was needed, and here the responses varied. What kind of literature is needed? Here, too, the responses varied. CLA members like the idea of "success stories," "stories of recovery describing the process," or "various stories from people sharing experience, strength, and hope."

A book on working the Steps in CLA was suggested by several, as was a "4th Step workbook." A number of people expressed a desire for a CLA book comparable to the basic texts of other Fellowships, such as Twelve Steps and Twelve Traditions; literature for newcomers; and information about the Fellowship and service structure, as well as "descriptions of different types and styles of clutter."

People also requested literature on practical techniques, such as on "where and how to begin a daily routine and goal setting, broken down into manageable steps."

CLA members did come up with good ideas and astute observations. Respondents identified some challenges in the process of recovery that affect many CLA members.

One member's input suggests, "We really need to hear more from people who are able to get any real 'clean' time. From what I have read, this disease one of the hardest to put into remission, because it's so hard to see any progress. People just give up or decide that it's not that bad of a problem."

Someone asks, "How [do we] overcome resistance, reluctance to decluttering, and resentment about having to declutter," adding, "Also, I don't know how to go about decluttering... Also, how do you keep clutter from returning after you have decluttered successfully?" Good questions, with no easy, standardized answers.

So, that's an overview of what emerged from our 2007 CLA Literature Survey, which is part of an ongoing process.

Feedback, good ideas, suggestions, and even "partially baked ideas" continue to be welcome. You're encouraged to share them with the Literature Committee and CLA*rity*.

CLA literature is "inspirational. I believe it is inspired, thought provoking, and spiritual." As the saying goes, "More will be revealed."

CLA Literature (Literature Production)

Spring 2009

Using literature is one of the keys to recovery in any 12-Step program; in fact, it is one of the CLA Tools of Recovery.19 But how do we get from the initial idea to the final publication you can hold in your hands? The following is an overview of the process:

A. First, the concept is discussed, then written and developed:
   1. Ideas are submitted to the Literature Committee—from a CLA member, from WSO, or from a Literature Committee member.
   2. A subcommittee writes the initial draft of the document.
   3. The Literature Committee edits and proofreads the proposed document and sends a final draft to the CLA Fellowship.
   4. CLA groups send input on the proposed document to the Literature Committee.
   5. The Literature Committee makes changes to the document based on group input.

6. The document is submitted to WSO for initial approval; the Literature Committee makes necessary changes and sends the refined document to WSO for final approval.
7. Upon WSO approval, the final graphical layout is determined, and typesetting and proofing are completed.

B. When the document is ready for initial printing (or when supplies run low) it must be reproduced:
   1. The Printing Subcommittee specifies the paper, obtains bids from print shops, and sends the finished document to the selected vendor.
   2. The finished copies are delivered to the corresponding secretary, who maintains the literature inventory.

C. Once the literature is reproduced, groups and individuals can purchase copies from WSO:
   1. Copies are ordered, either by individuals or by designated members on behalf of groups.
   2. The corresponding secretary collects literature orders.
   3. The corresponding secretary sends the literature ordered to groups and individuals in the U.S. and abroad.
   4. A person designated by the group disseminates the literature at face-to-face meetings.

As you can see, much effort is put into getting these information-filled pages into your hands. If you are looking for a way to give back to the Fellowship and aid in your recovery, helping at some point in our literature chain—including ordering literature—is an excellent place to start!

CLArity Committee Report

Summer 2009

The CLA*rity* Team

CLA*rity* is now in its third year. We think this is a good time to reflect back on our journey of producing CLArity and to share some of our experiences with our readers.

The CLA Newsletter Committee became "official" when empowered by a motion in the November, 2006, business meeting of WSO.

But the story started somewhere else altogether, somewhere "behind the scenes," months or years earlier, planted and nurtured in telephone and email conversations. In fact, aside from the earlier newsletters produced by the Fellowship in bygone years, there were individuals saving gems of recovery, so they would not go to waste.

A small group of people volunteered to plan the launch of our new CLA newsletter.

But what about the name? Another decision to make—and best to do it in a hurry, so the design of the masthead could go forward. Then someone noticed that one of the names we had from someone's collection had the CLA initials in it—CLA*rity* went to the front and became the natural choice.

The team prepared a budget proposal for the December business meeting, and we were off and running when WSO gave a startup grant to the CLA*rity* team. Then we started up the production process. Not really knowing what we were doing, we slowly started moving toward the Spring issue—Number 1! We created a flyer announcing the new publication, started collecting articles, and sold our first few subscriptions.

The first issue was mailed in February 2007. It was one 11"x17" sheet folded book style to make four 8½"x11" pages. It was mailed to several hundred people in the Fellowship. How many meetings did we have before we could put Volume 1, Number 1, "to bed"? It must have been 15 or more, and hundreds of emails and phone calls. How much time? Hundreds of hours.

Now, more than two years later, we're producing the tenth quarterly issue of CLArity, Summer '09. It is now eight pages, with about 200 subscribers.

It took a lot of time and teamwork to get from the original vision to where we are now. And there has been some turnover on the committee, but not much. The committee developed into a team, as we traveled the rollercoaster road of production. There were debates, endless meetings, confusion, and more than a few late nights to challenge us.

How do a bunch of clutterers (and nitpickers) get from the idea to actually producing four newsletters a year on schedule? Would you believe one day at a time? Would you believe only with the help of a Higher Power and the strengthening motive found in Tradition 5: "...to carry its message to the clutterer who still suffers"? You had better believe it, because our plans were changed a thousand times, and nothing stood still. We devised some procedures to guide us through the process and maintained the discipline to stick with it. We plan every detail of each issue in a skeleton form first. It is the structure that has kept us on schedule.

We got stressed out by deadlines, personalities, procrastination, money, perfectionism, fatigue—you name it. But somehow we kept trying, in the 12-Step program way, to maintain a working situation where the committee members felt they could express themselves freely and contribute, no matter whether the process was rough or smooth.

Another piece of the story links us to the CLAEast intergroup. Their financial gift gave us great validation of our efforts and helped us not only toreduce the subscription rate until August '08 (later extended through December 31, '08) but also encouraged us to double our subscription base.

We may not have known what we were committing to when we volunteered for this duty, but what came unexpectedly was a wonderful recovery experience. We are grateful for the support of all who inspired and sustained this opportunity to do service in the CLA Fellowship.

Spring 2010

WSO has several committees in need of volunteers.Below is a list of areas which need help from members of the Fellowship at this time. If you cannot commit to a set block of time each month, there are many tasks which need only occasional help. So why not take a step toward helping your own recovery while helping our Fellowship?

Finance Committee

This important committee currently needs members to begin functioning again. You do not need any special skills in working with budgetary matters to join the Finance Committee. It meets periodically to set a budget and to deal with decisions about any unusual budget requests. The Finance Committee does not keep books or write checks; those are functions of the WSO Treasurer.

Service Opportunities Committee

This committee is currently nonfunctioning and needs reconstituting. Its purpose is to coordinate efforts of those wishing to do service in CLA and to find mechanisms to reach members willing to help. It also defines areas of CLA that need help and breaks them up into manageable projects.

Literature Committee

The Literature Committee needs members to help write, edit, and proofread new CLA literature. It can also use input from those members who believe they have knowledge and experience about the program to share but who are uncomfortable about their language skills. In other words, you do not have to be a writer to have your voice heard. The Literature Committee can also use help occasionally in conducting surveys for the Fellowship.

CLA*rity* Committee

CLA*rity* is always in need of those willing to share their experience, strength, and hope. For those uncomfortable with writing, there are several mechanisms in place, including being interviewed by a CLA*rity* staff member for an article. CLA*rity* also needs members who will help plan issues, edit content, and proofread the newsletter.

Public Information Committee

CLA's Public Information Officer is looking for members willing to work on this committee. The PI Committee has grown in importance with all the publicity about hoarding and cluttering. It also deals with general inquiries from the public about CLA.

Volunteers are needed to help disseminate information. A working knowledge of the 12 Steps and 12 Traditions is required.

Communications Committee

The Communications Coordinator is currently working on several aspects of communication among service volunteers. Although the committee has met a few times and includes those holding certain officer positions, it is seeking additional members from the Fellowship at large and exploring many areas of communication.

Fall 2010

Editor's Note: The CLA WSO Executive Committee recently approved purpose statements for each of the WSO Committees. Following is an excerpt from the approved document, which will be posted on the CLA website.

The purpose of the World Service Organization (WSO) is to provide the business services that are necessary for the Fellowship to function.

The standing committees of WSO include, but are not limited to:

Bylaws Committee

The Bylaws Committee formulates and reviews the regulations by which the World Service Organization operates. The bylaws are a legal document.

CLA*rity* Committee

CLA*rity* is an eight-page quarterly newsletter produced by CLA members, written by both committee members and others in the Fellowship. It is supported by subscriptions and 7th Tradition contributions.

The purpose of CLA*rity* is to educate and inform readers about CLA and act as a forum where members may share experience, strength, and hope.

Communications Committee

The purpose of the Communications Committee is to set procedures guided by the 12 Traditions to encourage the free flow of information among WSO, the intergroups, the face-to-face and telephone groups, and to present a unified message at all levels of public information, literature, and correspondence.

Cyber Committee

The Cyber Committee is responsible for working with CLA WSO, its committees, and the Fellowship at large to establish, develop, maintain, and oversee CLA's presence on the Internet. It provides current information about CLA to the public, to our members, and to those who might need CLA. The committee reviews content to assure that it follows the guidelines of the 12 Steps and 12 Traditions.

The website is maintained by a webmaster under the direction of the Cyber Committee.

Executive Committee

The Executive Committee consists of WSO officers, committee chairpersons, and intergroup liaisons. The purpose of the Executive Committee is to make WSO run more effectively. It deals with current concerns of WSO and the Fellowship itself.

Finance Committee

The Finance Committee is responsible for establishing a budget for CLA's World Service Organization. The committee also develops, implements, and oversees policies and procedures in all matters concerning the finances of CLA WSO. It allocates funds to the various committees based on their requests and the available funds of WSO. It works with WSO to help increase financial support from individuals, groups, and intergroups, within the guidelines of the 12 Traditions of CLA. The Committee prepares an annual financial report.

Literature Committee

The Literature Committee is responsible for creating, reviewing, and editing literature that is submitted for Fellowship approval. Its function is to facilitate the expression of our Fellowship's experience, strength, and hope through the writing of material for distribution. The Literature Committee oversees the approval and publication processes and works with WSO and its committees to prepare Fellowship-approved literature for final publication.

Public Information Committee

The Public Information (PI) Committee provides helpful, accurate, and consistent information about CLA to interested organizations; broadcast, print, and electronic media; and the general public. It is guided by the 12 Steps and 12 Traditions, emphasizing the principles of anonymity and attraction rather than promotion. The committee also assists local groups with public information needs.

Service Opportunities Committee

The Service Opportunities Committee identifies and describes service opportunities within CLA. It coordinates efforts to communicate this information to the Fellowship.

Structuralization Committee

The purpose of the Structuralization Committee is to develop, define, describe, and clarify the service infrastructure of the CLA Fellowship.

Traditions Committee

The purpose of the Traditions Committee is to educate and inform the Fellowship about the 12 Traditions. It provides public forums for information and discussion.

Five Years of CLA*rity*

Holiday 2011

This issue marks five full years of CLA*rity*, and we are amazed at how quickly the time has gone by.

CLA*rity* has about 200 subscribers from 34 states and the District of Columbia in the United States and from five other countries—Canada, Iceland, Italy, New Zealand, and the United Kingdom.

As CLA*rity* has grown in size and readership and evolved in the scope of articles, so has the CLA*rity* team grown. Some of us never thought we would be able to make such a long-term commitment, but here we are. We are a very close-knit team and enjoy our committee meetings, which are usually held every week. This enables us to plan issues way ahead and pay attention to all the details—a necessity for producing a quality publication. As we write this article, it's August—and you won't be reading this until November or early December.

Working with CLA*rity* is teaching us lots of lessons: to think ahead, to work as a team, to keep promises, to show up for ourselves and each other, to give each other slack (although we try really hard to start meetings on time and to keep each other on track gently). It also teaches us how to write articles—such as this one, on which three of us are collaborating.

How did we start?

WSO gave us seed money to begin; and in early 2008 we received additional funds from CLA-East and WSO, which allowed us to continue at the time. Since then, we have been totally self-supporting. The first issue had four pages, and we were so careful about picking out paper and fonts and doing the design layout. We edited with attention to detail, proofed it lovingly, and chose our print shop with extreme care—and, lo and behold, it was printed back to front!

At the end of the first year, we had six pages, and at the beginning of the next year, we had eight pages. By this time, one of us worried that it was getting a bit cluttered and wondered how the CLA community would react. We needn't have fretted. Since 2008, we have nearly doubled the number of subscribers, and the feedback we have received is mainly positive.

We work really hard to keep the Traditions intact and get to practice them in the process. We often refer to the literature when necessary. As with other WSO committees, the CLA*rity* Committee is open to new members.

CLArity FAQs

Summer 2012

Readers often ask us about the production, distribution, costs, and source of the content associated with CLA*rity* newsletter. Here are some answers to frequently asked questions:

- *How often is CLArity published?*
  It is published four times a year, one issue per quarter.
- *How do I subscribe to CLArity?*
  You can order and pay for subscriptions online with several convenient payment options at ClutterersAnonymous.org. If you do not have

Internet access, mail your subscription order with a check or money order (US dollars) to the address in the front of this book. CLArity subscriptions may be ordered at some CLA events. We do not take telephone orders.

- *Is CLArity available online to download?* No. At this time, CLArity is available in hard copy only via postal mail. But CLArity can be ordered online, and the order forms can be downloaded.*
- *How can I order CLArity?* CLA*rity* can be ordered with or without an order form. Print out order forms or place your order directly on the ClutterersAnonymous.org website. You may also request a "CLA*rity* Order Form" by email, phone, or postal mail. Please use the most current version. Since prices and ordering details are subject to change, the "CLA*rity* Order Form" is updated as needed.
- *Can I combine CLArity and CLA literature together in one order?* Yes, if you are placing your orders online. In fact, we encourage you to combine your Internet orders for CLA*rity* in a single transaction with any CLA Literature you wish to order. However, when ordering by mail, there are separate forms because CLA*rity* and CLA literature requests go to different postal mailing addresses.
- *Can I order a single issue of CLArity?* Yes. Order single copies of the current or bac issues and pay online at ClutterersAnonymous.org, or mail your request with a check or money order (US dollars) to the address in the frontispiece. CLA*rity* can also be purchased by the single copy at some CLA events.
- *Are three-year subscriptions still available?* No, we offer only one- and two-year subscriptions.
- *How does CLArity use the money it receives?* All subscriptions and 7th Tradition contributions to CLA*rity* go fully to cover the expenses for printing, mailing, payment processing, and banking, and for necessary minor incidentals.
- *Where do articles in CLArity come from?* All content in CLA*rity* is written by CLA members. We welcome members to send articles in accordance with the CLA*rity* "Article Guidelines for Authors," available upon request. We accept only original work, authored by the member submitting it. All submissions are subject to editing by the CLA*rity* team before publication. Any material published outside CLA or not in accordance with CLA Traditions is not acceptable. For guidelines or information, use one of the contact methods in the frontispiece.
- *Can I reprint any article from CLArity?* No part of CLA*rity* may be reproduced without expressed permission. CLA*rity* is a copyrighted publication of Clutterers Anonymous; all rights reserved. Please contact CLA*rity* if you have any questions, requests for reprints, or need bulk quantities.
- *How is the newsletter designed and created?* The CLA*rity* team selects and edits articles and other content during the weeks leading up to each issue. A CLA*rity* team member with a graphic design background does the layout, typesetting and images using an advanced page layout software. Finally, the team comes together to proofread the entire document. Team members live in various parts of the United States and communicate by phone and Internet to complete each issue.
- *How does CLArity get printed and distributed?* CLA*rity* is professionally reproduced by a print shop. Printing and mailing is coordinated by a CLA*rity* team member with a background in print production. Each issue is processed for sending and mailed to subscribers by CLA*rity* team members only. Some issues are offered directly to members at CLA events, such as Clutter-Free Day.
- *Does anyone get paid for working on CLArity?* No. CLA*rity* is produced entirely by members volunteering service and published solely for the benefit of the CLA Fellowship.

*CLA*rity* is now available in electronic form distributed via email—although it is not available as a download.

About WSO–The Executive Committee

Summer 2012

The Executive Committee consists of the WSO officers and committee chairpersons.

What does the Executive Committee do?

- Collaborates with the WSO chairperson in developing agendas and negotiating problems that arise
- Develops ways to make the WSO business meetings run more smoothly (encouraging the use of protocols, Roberts Rules of Order, motion forms, etc.)
- Oversees office matters (post office, emails, and voicemails), distribution of literature, maintenance of the CLA archives, and recordings and minutes of WSO and Executive Committee meetings
- Maintains the structure of and recordings for the toll-free number
- Works with the public information officer in dealing with the media
- Oversees WSO financial matters, in conjunction with the Finance Committee and the WSO treasurer
- Works with the Literature Committee on the development and printing of CLA leaflets, booklets, and "CLA Meeting Starter Kits."7
- Works with the following committees to set goals and help solve problems:
  - Registration Committee, which has been developing a procedure for registration of CLA meetings and WSO delegates
  - Structuralization Committee (currently not meeting), which was working toward setting a service structure for the whole Fellowship
  - Cyber Committee, which works with a we master to maintain the CLA website
  - Communications Committee, which was created to facilitate communications among WSO, phone groups, and face-to-face groups
  - Bylaws Committee (currently not meeting), which develops and changes the WSO bylaws
  - CLA*rity* Committee, which produces and disseminates the CLArity newsletter
- Discusses ramifications of the 12 Traditions20 and the A.A. "12 Concepts of Service"17
- Develops and implements WSO election procedures
- Maintains a log of WSO motions

CLArity for the Soul

Fall 2013

Wendy L., IL

Language is constantly evolving. The addition of new vocabulary words is the most obvious change; but, surprisingly, the use of spaces and commas has changed as well. These aren't exactly conversation starters, but to the members of the CLA*rity* Committee, including myself, the creative and proper use of language is our heart and soul.

Besides honing our writing and editing skills for CLA*rity*, our members give service to CLA while enjoying each others' companionship across the miles. We even get to occasionally meet each other, as I did when I had lunch with one member who was traveling through Chicago.

Writing about my experience, strength, and hope regarding clutter has led me to explore uncomfortable topics like procrastination and stress. Thinking through difficult issues like these can actually stir up painful emotions that I've needed to process, sometimes with other clutterers. Now that I think about it, writing about my clutter issues can be therapeutic. Now that's quite a bonus for being on a CLA committee.

Even the process of writing has become anenjoyable activity that I look forward to every couple of months. A skinny peppermint mocha goes great with a pad of ruled blue paper and my favorite pen. I start by jotting down bullet points of information and ideas about my article topic. Call it free associating about clutter. Then I take off a few days to let my ideas percolate before I write out the first version of my article.

I'm a proud mama when I complete and submit my articles. Often I get compliments from other CLA*rity* members and clutter buddies on my submissions, which definitely enhances my self-confidence. I haven't received feedback from any CLArity subscribers at large, but I can only-hope that my articles help other clutterers, or at the very least entertain them a little.

It's funny, but I didn't subscribe to CL*Arity* until I joined the CL*Arity* team because I didn't want the additional paper clutter in my life. (The good news is that the CL*Arity* team has a wish list to produce an electronic version of our newsletter.) So I missed out on some very heartfelt and thoughtful reflections about being a clutterer. Talk about a turnaround, now I write for CL*Arity*.

I hope CL*Arity* enhances your recovery from clutter as much as it does mine. If there are any subjects regarding clutter that you'd like us to cover in CL*Arity*, please don't hesitate to contact us at Clarity@ClutterersAnonymous.org. Stay tuned for more informative and entertaining articles!

Not Your Grandmother's Committees!

Spring 2014

Is volunteering on your bucket list? Ever wanted to do service? How about from the comfort of your own home?

It's as easy as joining a CLA committee, or assisting a committee. It takes less time than you might think, depending on the committee.

Here's your opportunity to enhance your own recovery while doing valuable service.

Additional benefits include:

- Practicing Teamwork: Provide input and offer feedback as you work through the committee's agenda. In some committees, you may collaborate with other team members on specific action items.
- Practicing Accountability: You take on the responsibility of attending meetings and participating in them. As clutterers, it sometimes helps us to follow through when we know others are counting on us.
- Practicing Time Management: You plan time to attend meetings. In some committees, you help determine the date and time of the next meeting.
- Using Your Creativity: Brainstorm ideas, offer suggestions, and develop solutions. Opportunities are open to create content for CLA publications.
- Experiencing Pride: Take pride in knowing you're contributing to an organization that helps clutterers around the world.

The committee meeting frequencies and volunteer responsibilities are listed below. To volunteer, all that is needed is a willingness to execute the responsibilities of the committee.

To join any committee, please use one of the contact methods listed in the frontispiece.

CLA Committees

- **Cyber:** meets one hour every 1-3 weeks. Help to determine the content, design, and operation of the CLA website, www.ClutterersAnonymous.org. No programming experience is needed, but familiarity with the Internet is recommended.
- **Finance:** meets once a month. Help to establish the CLA World Service Organization (WSO) budget and allocate funds to CLA committees. Also develop, implement, and oversee policies and procedures in all matters concerning the finances of WSO. No accounting background is required.
- **CL*Arity* (CLA's quarterly newsletter)**: meets one hour every week. Help to determine the content of each issue, write and/or edit articles, proof the final copies, and assist with the operation of CLArity. Assist the committee: edit or write articles, up to four times a year. CLArity members are happy to provide guidance. For all editors: no experience required, but a good basic understanding of English language, spelling, and grammar is recommended. All writers are welcome; no experience is necessary.
- **Communications** (currently not meeting due to lack of members): meets once a month. Help to facilitate a forum where individuals of any committee or group may present ideas, suggestions, or grievances for discussion. Prospective chairpersons should work good personal programs so they don't get personally involved with the problems presented.
- **All Phone Groups (Committee):** Facilitate liaison between the phone groups and WSO.

Any CLA member who attends phone groups is welcome.

- **Literature:** meets once a month. Help to plan, write, and edit new CLA literature, and occasionally help to revise current literature. Several exciting new literature projects are in the planning stages.
- **25th Anniversary:** meets once a month. Help to plan celebrations to mark the 25th anniversary of CLA. The focus is the planning of our first-ever convention, which is expected to be in the Los Angeles area in the fall of 2014.
- **Registration:** meets once a month. Help to create, prepare, and send out registration materials to every CLA recovery meeting contact and assist with obtaining them. Registrations include the meeting location name and address and other pertinent information. Also, help to make sure this information is kept current.
- **Bylaws**: meets once a month. Help to formulate and review the regulations by which WSO operates. The bylaws are a legal document, and experience with bylaws would be a plus.

Join a committee today!

Finance Committee

Holiday 2014

Martha H., MD

The Finance Committee is responsible for establishing a budget for CLA's World Service Organization (WSO). The committee also develops, implements, and oversees policies and procedures in all matters concerning WSO finances. Responsibilities also include allocating funds to the various CLA committees based on their requests and the available funds of WSO. In addition, the committee works with WSO to help increase financial support from individuals, groups, and intergroups, within the guidelines of the 12 Traditions of CLA.

Most people think finance is either too boring or too complicated to comprehend. They shy away from anything that has to do with numbers, accounting, or business. Some people are just plain scared of math!

Fortunately, participation in the Finance Committee requires only a desire to serve CLA. There is no math involved.

The biggest job of the Finance Committee is preparation of the annual budget. This is a simple process. Someone, usually the treasurer or the committee chairperson, prepares a spreadsheet or chart showing the income and expenses for the most current year. Then, the Finance Committee decides what a realistic goal is for each type of income and expense. These are added to the spreadsheet. This proposed budget is then presented to CLA's memership for review and discussion at the December WSO business meeting. After any changes are made to the budget, it is voted on and approved by the membership present at the meeting.

If something in the daily operation of WSO is causing a problem and it has to do with money or finance, the problem is brought to the Finance Committee. The committee discusses the situation and develops a plan or change in procedure to address the problem.

Certain committees, such as the Cyber Committee, need money to help carry the message of recovery to clutterers who still suffer. The Cyber Committee needs money for the upkeep and development of CLA's website. The Finance Committee would, within the limits of the WSO budget, allocate funds to cover this important 12th-Step activity.

During the year, the Finance Committee monitors CLA's financial progress. The committee compares actual income and spending with the budget and looks for potential problems. When a situation arises where CLA is overspending or there is not enough income to cover expenses, the Finance Committee examines the records and offers recommendations to WSO.

The Finance Committee welcomes participation at every level. Your ideas, opinions, and input are what make the committee thrive in order to grow and serve CLA. We meet once a month via a phone conference. The Finance Committee line is (712) 775-7100, and the access code is 458865. We meet the third Wednesday of each month at 9:00 p.m. Eastern Time.

Please, won't you share your experience, strength, and hope with us?

Ten Years of CLArity

Holiday 2016

At the November 18, 2006, meeting of the CLA World Service Organization (WSO), a committee was formed to produce a newsletter.

The committee's first task was to decide on a name for the newsletter. Several ideas were presented. However, since one of them was the word "clarity," a committee member noticed that the first three letters spelled CLA—and that became the unanimous favorite and was adopted. Thus,- CLA*rity* was born.

The first three issues contained four pages each. With the Holiday 2007 issue, we upgraded tosix pages, and since then each issue has included eight pages. In every issue, the team has focused on printing recovery articles, along with some informational items and an occasional artistic or humorous piece.

Below is a listing of the various types of articles as they have evolved throughout the years.

- Most issues have included the following articles: "Officers' Corner," "Letter from the Chair," and either "About WSO" or "Spotlight on Service."
- For the first few years, every issue included an article on a Step or Tradition. These were printed in order, for Steps 1 through 12, followed by the Traditions. Between the Spring 2013 and Summer 2014 issues, a series of questions\ and answers regarding Steps and Traditions was printed. Since then, various issues have contained articles on Steps and/or Traditions, but in no particular order.
- Originally, every issue included a "Recovery Moments" article, but the past several years, fewer of these articles have been submitted.
- CLArity has included Clutter-Free Day articles in many issues since the summer of 2007. Also, since the summer of 2014, most issues have included an article about CLA conventions.

Group-Level Service

Summer 2008

While the duties of service positions at the local level are entirely up to group conscience to determine, many groups use the service structure listed below. The length of service is also decided by group conscience and can be from one week to a year. Rotation of service is recommended.

Chairperson/Leader/Secretary: Often the primarytrusted servant for a meeting. Some groups make this one position, while others use two different positions.

- Usually opens the meeting place and maintains the group's format and other materials.
- Leads the meeting by following the printed format.

Treasurer: Collects 7th Tradition donations at meetings. Pays any moneys due by the group (rent, literature purchases, refreshments, etc.). Sends 7th Tradition donations to CLA World Service Organization (WSO) and Intergroup, as decided by group conscience

Literature Person: Orders and maintains a supply of literature.

Newcomer Contact: Welcomes newcomers and keeps in touch with them between meetings.

Contact Person: A group member whose name, address, telephone and email are listed with Intergroup and/or WSO.

Intergroup Representative (if the group is an IG member): Elected by group conscience to represent the group and vote the group conscience at the Intergroup meetings. Reports back to the group any information from Intergroup.

WSO Delegate: Elected to represent a group and vote at WSO meetings and report information back to the group.

Small groups often combine several functions into one, or drop some duties altogether.

Doing Service at the Group Level

Fall 2011

CLA*rity* has often discussed various service opportunities found at the CLA World Service (WSO) level. But there are many ways to get involved at your local group—and that is often the best place to begin.

Why would a member want to take time out of a busy schedule to do service in CLA? For one thing, our Fellowship—especially at the group level—is built on volunteer participation. If no one is willing to take on the simple chores, the group ceases to run. At least, it ceases to run well. Another reason is to further one's own recovery. Service is embodied in Step 12, which says "...to carry the message to others...." This means not only talking to other members, but also includes doing service. Then we find that when we give back what we have been given, it aids our own recovery.

So what is entailed? Large CLA groups may have many service positions available, while smaller ones may either combine positions or do without some altogether. Listed below are some common service opportunities at the group level. Be aware that CLA groups in different areas may give various titles to some positions; therefore, some of them include a second designation in parentheses. Except for setup and for cleanup and refreshments, all service positions should be filled by someone with at least six months of recovery in the program, if possible.

- Secretary (leader): Responsible for the smooth functioning of the group. The secretary (or leader) should be someone who is well versed in the Traditions and in how 12-Step programs work. It is often the responsibility of this person to speak up in a meeting if a Tradition is being violated or if there is crosstalk or a problem with a disruptive member. Often the secretary may be consulted if a member is unable to fulfill a service commitment or for any other problem. Sometimes this position may include keeping meeting materials and keys.
- Leader (chairperson): Responsible for reading the meeting format and leading the recovery meeting. Sometimes leading the meeting will include qualifying—sharing what it was like, what changed, and what it is like now. Often, the leader will be the one to pass out literature for reading at the meeting.
- Treasurer: Responsible for keeping 7th Tradition monies, making reports to the group about its finances, and paying bills, such as rent, literature, and contributions to WSO or intergroups. The treasurer should be reliable in money matters.
- Newcomer Contact: Responsible for keeping in touch with newcomers.
- Meeting Contact: Responsible for having his or her name and phone number listed on printed meeting lists so that both newcomers and other CLA members can find the meeting. Often, this position and that of newcomer contact are combined.
- Literature Person: Responsible for maintaining the group's literature and bringing it to the meeting. Sometimes responsible for purchasing literature.
- Setup and Cleanup Person: Responsible for the physical setup before the meeting and the cleanup afterwards. Often, especially in smaller groups, all the members of the group take part.
- Refreshments Person: Responsible for purchasing, storing, and bringing refreshments to the group (if the group has decided to offer refresments; many do not, but some have water or coffee and tea).

As you can see, there are many ways to help your local group function smoothly. None of these positions require spending a great deal of time—but each does require a commitment to come to meetings or to find an alternate if unable to attend. Since many clutterers have had problems in keeping commitments, this is a good way to get ourselves used to being more responsible.

CLA History

CLA was started in February 1989 by two California women who wanted to bring order into their lives.

CLA History: Members Reflect

Summer 2007

Carol N., CA

"Time flies when you're having fun?" The years I've been in CLA have sure flown by. I believe I first heard about CLA around 1996. I met Alice C. (who I think started the same year) at a meeting, and the two of us planned a get-together to help each other. I don't know which of us was at the other's home first, but when she came to my house we just talked; she later said she felt bad that she didn't help me because we didn't do anything. That wasn't true in my mind because it did a lot for me just to have her there. The fact that someone would actually come into my house (and that I would let them) and do it without criticizing and judging me was so precious that I couldn't have explained it. That was the beginning of my understanding of CLA's buddy concept, although we didn't think of it as that at the time.

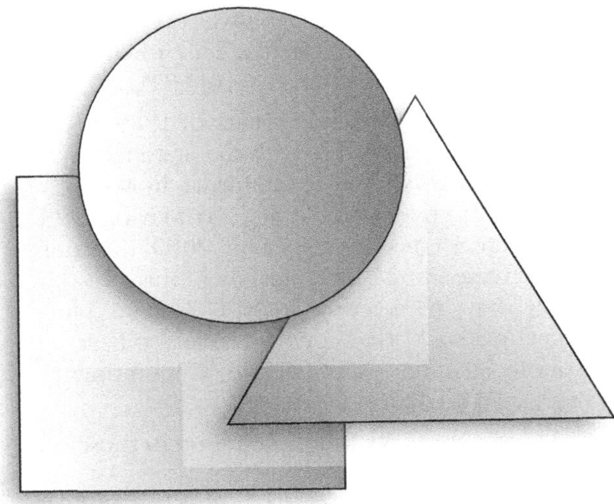

In those days I think there were only 13 meetings in the whole country. There was not even a meeting every day of the week, and sometimes I would really need a meeting that day. I had been very active in giving service in A.A. above group level, but it took me a while to go to my very first intergroup meeting. Then, as now, it was hard to get people to attend; and at my first meeting there were just Varda (our co-founder), Marylyn (secretary of my first CLA group, which became my home group), myself, and possibly one other person.

That was my one and only intergroup meeting; later intergroup was disbanded, and the World Service Organization was subsequently formed. I think Alice was in her second term as chair when I started coming to WSO on a regular basis. When I realized that it was my friend from years ago, it gave me a good feeling to know that she was still around, even though I hadn't seen her for years. For some reason, the time was right for me to begin giving service above group level, and I began to attend WSO on a regular basis.

History of CLA-East Intergroup

Fall 2007

Betsey K., NJ

For a number of years, we held so-called state meetings on a quarterly basis in a diner in Northern New Jersey. Members of all the CLA groups (3 or 4) in New Jersey were invited to gather for a time of sharing and fellowship.

Some members who wanted to meet more frequently (and also join with groups from New York and Philadelphia) started the CLA-East intergroup in October of 2001. Since then, we have been meeting monthly, first at face-to-face meetings in New Jersey (at a college and then at a library); then, since January, 2004, via telephone meetings.

CLA-East has about 30 regular meetings and holds monthly business meetings. CLA, which has been in New Jersey since 1991, expanded to New York City and Philadelphia in 2001, and then as far as Maine, Virginia, and Pittsburgh. When a group from Cincinnati approached us, we said that any group wishing to join CLA-East might do so. We now have groups in Connecticut, District of Columbia, Delaware, Massachusetts, Maryland, Michigan, New Jersey, New York, Ohio, Pennsylvania, and Virginia.

Twice a year, in spring and fall, we sponsor regional events called Clutter-Free Days. Any clutterer, member or not, is welcome to participate in these events with several dynamic speakers and inspirational workshops. We have had 11 of these events; the first year saw an average attendance of 31 in a half-day-long program. The latest, in the spring of 2007, was a daylong affair with over 100 attendees.

The next event is scheduled for October 14, 2007. Call CLA-East toll-free (866) 800-3881 or email clarity@claeast.org for more information.

CLA-East maintains a toll-free telephone line, where people can call in for information on CLA. We suggest that each group elect a member to represent that group at the monthly telephone meetings. This does not have to be the same person as the contact person who is listed on the meeting list.

The intergroup business meetings are by telephone and usually held during the second weekend of the month, except during the months when we present our Clutter-Free Days, held in the spring and fall of each year.

CLA to Celebrate 20th Birthday

Holiday 2008

In February of 2009, CLA will be 20 years old. Various groups are talking about how they can celebrate this momentous occasion. CLA*rity* plans to focus on this milestone in the Spring 2009 issue.

CLA-East expects to hold a special Clutter-Free Day. Some other suggestions for celebrating at the group level are:

- Throw a CLA 20th Birthday Party.
- Organize a special workshop on the Steps, sponsorship, the "CLA Tools of Recovery,"[19] or any other related topic.
- Find ways to let your community know about CLA.
- Make a special 7th Tradition donation to an intergroup and/or WSO in honor of the occasion.

How would you like to celebrate our birthday? If you or your group has any special ideas, please write a 100-200 word article and email it to Clarity@ClutterersAnonymous.org or send it to CLA*rity* via email or postal mail. You can also share with us by a telephone interview. Send us a message or leave a voice mail, and one of us will call you.

Early CLA History

Spring 2009

Kathy H., CA

Clutterers Anonymous is 20 years old as of February 2009. We hope there are many events to celebrate this milestone, and in this spirit the CLA*rity* team has decided to give you some of the early history of our Fellowship. This article deals with events in the first ten years of CLA.

CLA was founded in February of 1989 by Varda M. and Nicole H., with the first meeting being held in Simi Valley, California, in May of that year. It grew slowly at first. By May of 1995, there were 15 meetings. By early 2000, the count had increased to 22 meetings. As of this writing, we have 64 meetings in 20 U.S. states, plus 5 meetings in 3 other countries. We also have 8 phone meetings, the Check-in/Commitment Line, and the Action Line.

There were many things going on in those early years.

CLA used to maintain a program set up for mail buddies in remote areas. In 1996 and 1997, WSO was planning to write a book of clutterers' recovery stories and asked for shares from the Fellowship. Unfortunately, such a book has not been published to date. And even back in the '90s, WSO had difficulties getting meetings to update their contact information.

During the '90s and early into the new century, WSO produced a quarterly newsletter entitled "Simplicity, Order, Serenity." This newsletter was printed on one two-sided 8½" x 11" sheet of paper, with subscriptions set at $2 per year. It also included a meeting list.

In 1995, it was noted that the Los Angeles City Fire Department was sending CLA literature to each of its stations for posting on their bulletin boards. From that time on, those firemen began referring clutterers to CLA.

In 1996, CLA went online with a bulletin board. The first CLA website, established in the late 1990s, was called "www.visi.com/dsgood."

In November of 1999, WSO met face to face at a location in Los Angeles. Since both WSO and the Los Angeles Intergroup were having trouble finding enough service volunteers, it was decided to dissolve both organizations and form a new WSO, with the remaining funds from both going to support it. This was meant to be a temporary expedient. It is now ten years later, and a new intergroup is finally being formed in California.

As you can see, while CLA has definitely grown, it still remains much the same, with some of the same problems and strengths. We have more meetings, phone meetings, and a few more mechanisms for communication, but the core remains.

CLA 20th Birthday Card

Spring 2009

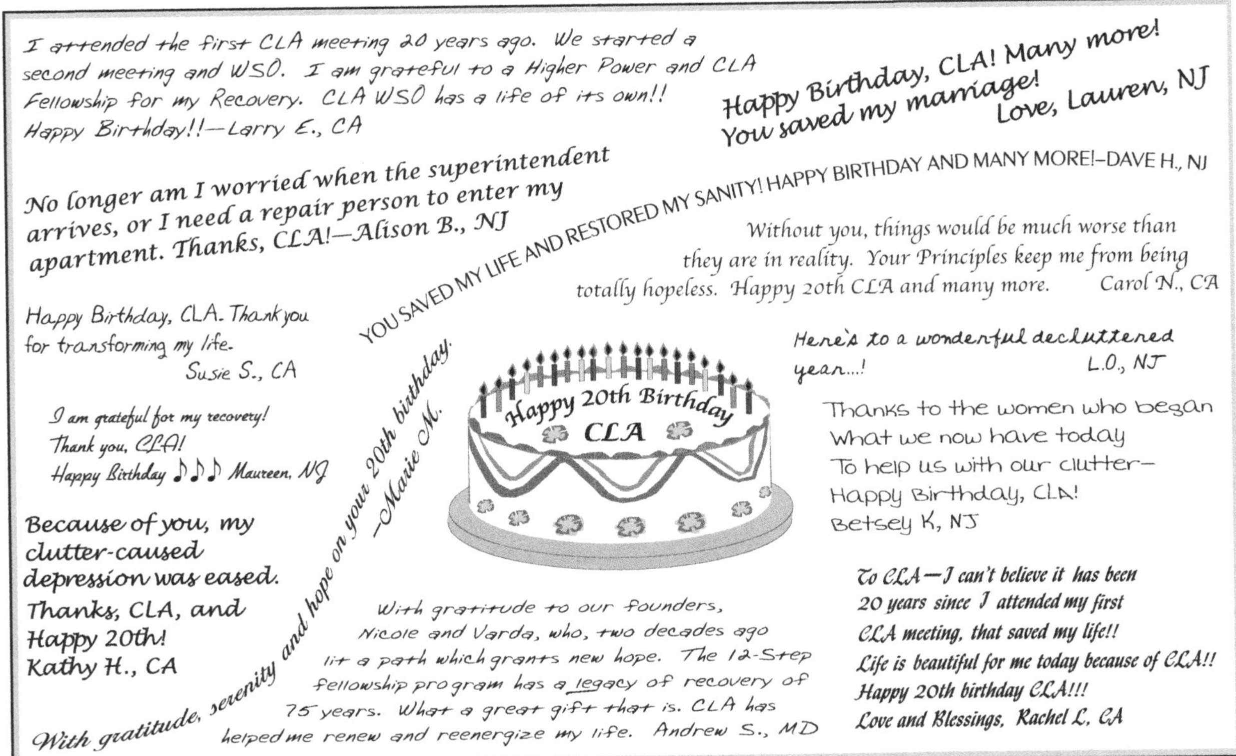

I attended the first CLA meeting 20 years ago. We started a second meeting and WSO. I am grateful to a Higher Power and CLA Fellowship for my Recovery. CLA WSO has a life of its own!! Happy Birthday!!—Larry E., CA
Happy Birthday, CLA! Many more! You saved my marriage! Love, Lauren, NJ
No longer am I worried when the superintendent arrives, or I need a repair person to enter my apartment. Thanks, CLA!—Alison B., NJ
YOU SAVED MY LIFE AND RESTORED MY SANITY! HAPPY BIRTHDAY AND MANY MORE!–DAVE H., NJ
Without you, things would be much worse than they are in reality. Your Principles keep me from being totally hopeless. Happy 20th CLA and many more. Carol N., CA
Happy Birthday, CLA. Thank you for transforming my life. Susie S., CA
Here's to a wonderful decluttered year....! L.O., NJ
Happy 20th Birthday
CLA
I am grateful for my recovery! Thank you, CLA! Happy Birthday ♪♪♪ Maureen, NJ
Thanks to the women who began What we now have today To help us with our clutter— Happy Birthday, CLA! Betsey K, NJ
Because of you, my clutter-caused depression was eased. Thanks, CLA, and Happy 20th! Kathy H., CA
With gratitude, serenity and hope on your 20th birthday. —Marie M.
With gratitude to our founders, Nicole and Varda, who, two decades ago lit a path which grants new hope. The 12-Step fellowship program has a legacy of recovery of 75 years. What a great gift that is. CLA has helped me renew and reenergize my life. Andrew S., MD
To CLA—I can't believe it has been 20 years since I attended my first CLA meeting, that saved my life!! Life is beautiful for me today because of CLA!! Happy 20th birthday CLA!!! Love and Blessings, Rachel L, CA

Holiday 2009 and Summer 2014

Larry E., CA

I am writing this to commemorate CLA's 20th year.

My name is Larry E., a recovering clutterer, and I was privileged to serve as the first CLA WSO chairperson. In conversation with Nicole H., a founder of CLA (along with Varda M.), Nicole shared that she had been praying for relief from the disorganization that prevented her from doing the creative things she wished. At that very time, she learned of a conference the following week (February 1989) that addressed the issue. It was there she met Varda, who was attending in order to help her husband, who had a problem with clutter. (Years later, Varda related to me that she had her own problem with "activity clutter.") The two women were not interested in the commercial nature of the event but did wish to form a group based on the 12 Steps and 12 Traditions of A.A.

Within a month, Nicole had gathered a group and started a meeting based on writings and a format devised with Varda's help. She went on with more writings that provided the basis for CLA literature to follow. Nicole's Simi Valley group grew, especially after some initial articles appeared in the local newspaper.

In 1991, I learned of this group and wished to start a second group in Orange County, California. I drove the 80 miles up the freeway to attend a meeting and was given the format and readings to take back home. I soon started a weekly group in Orange with some of my 12-Step friends.

(From a diary entry I found): On October 20, 1991, Nicole called me saying she had 75 requests for information from a recently syndicated news article, and would the Orange group please help to respond. Later that morning, I received another phone call from Nicole: would I start a WSO as a central office to respond to inquiries (as Nicole and the Simi Valley group were overwhelmed with them)? Nicole asked if I would be the founder of CLA WSO. I said I would be a cofounder along with her and Varda.

On October 25, I received a package from Nicole of 100 letters requesting information—all from Hawaii.

On October 27, Varda phoned and provided guidance and support; for all the answers I needed, my Higher Power would provide what I needed when I needed it.

Later, several members volunteered to serve on a board. In keeping with the 12 Traditions, the group held elections for a WSO board.

I continued to be involved with WSO, working with Varda on the Literature Committee in typesetting the literature pamphlets and other tasks until about 1997, when I left the Fellowship because—unfortunately—I placed personalities before principles.

Two years ago, I was introduced to the Newport Beach CLA meeting, and reconnected with the Fellowship. I learned that CLA WSO has a life of its own and is indeed thriving, now 20 years after the inception of the program.

I'd like to close with the following: I asked Nicole how CLA made a difference in her life. She replied that she now has the beauty, order, and serenity that she first sought. In my own life, the biggest impact is in acquiring the belief that when I need something, it will be made available to me by my Higher Power. This faith displaces the fear of not having enough.

My thanks to Nicole H. and Varda M. (who really was my CLA sponsor) for starting this Fellowship, and to all who continue to carry the message of recovery and ESH—experience, strength, and hope.

Spring 2010

For many years after its inception, Clutterers Anonymous World Service Organization (WSO) held face-to-face business meetings in Los Angeles, California. As CLA grew to nationwide status, most WSO delegates and officers were dissatisfied with the fact that the only representation was from groups in Southern California, so other options were sought.

As modern technology increased, it became possible to hold the meetings via telephone conference calls. In August 2005, the first-ever WSO meeting to be held on the telephone took place. Instead of hearing names of only local groups in the roll call, we also heard from Northern California and from Maine, Maryland, Massachusetts, New Jersey, New York, and Utah. That was exciting!

With the transfer to telephone meetings, there were changes in the mechanisms for running the meetings. One obvious change was in how any printed materials were to be distributed to WSO attendees. During face-to-face meetings, copies of the agenda, minutes, and any other printed materials were brought to the meeting and handed out to members. Obviously, it would be impossible to do this on the telephone, so such items are now emailed to the members ahead of the meeting time.

Another difficulty was the inability of members to raise their hands to be recognized by the chairperson when they wished to speak. The WSO leadership has worked to find other methods to bring order to the meetings and fairness to all attendees.

So will you join us at the WSO meetings as we strive to solve problems and bring good things to CLA? All members are welcome to attend. Perhaps someday we'll get representation from other countries with CLA membership, thereby making it a *true* World Service Organization.

CLA-East Observes Ten Years

Holiday 2011

Mary P., NY

CLA-East, currently the Fellowship's only intergroup, turned 10 years old in October 2011. That intergroup is a loose association of about 25 CLA groups, mostly from the northeastern United States.

The group got its start when 15 members—representing six CLA groups from New Jersey, New York, and Pennsylvania—met at a community college in northern New Jersey for what would become monthly face-to-face get-togethers. The group changed to conference-call meetings in January 2004, as the number of groups grew.

CLA-East's signature event, Clutter-Free Day, started small, as a half-day Share-a-Day held at the Plainsboro, New Jersey, public library in the spring of 2002. About 30 people attended. The event moved to a church in Metuchen, New Jersey in the fall of 2003, scheduling more workshops and drawing more people. In 2006, to get more people from New York City and Long Island, the Clutter-Free Day was held in a city location, St. Francis College in Brooklyn Heights. The event has alternated between New Jersey and New York, with nine having been held in Metuchen and four in Brooklyn. Recent attendance has ranged from about 60 to 125 people. The current format consists of nine workshops, plus a keynote speaker. Some workshop leaders and keynote speakers have come from California for the event.

The next Clutter-Free Day will be in the spring of 2012.

The CLA-East intergroup meets via conference call on the second Saturday of most months. Attendance recently has been disappointing, averaging only six people on the line. The intergroup has its own website, www.claeast.org, and toll-free information number, (866) 800-3881.

Any group in the eastern United States is welcome to send a representative to the second Saturday business meeting, at 1:00 p.m. Eastern Time. For details see the website above.

Editor's Note: In the late 1990s, there was an intergroup in Southern California, which later disbanded; for a couple of years there was a Phone Groups Intergroup; and there have also been some other attempts around the country to start intergroups.

CLA Trivia

Summer 2014

Kathy H., CA

When I began attending CLA World Service Organization meetings in 2002, they were held in a physical location in Los Angeles. When WSO was formed, that may have been acceptable, since there were few, if any, recovery meetings outside

Southern California. But by the time I became a member, there were some groups in other parts of the United States. We began discussing how to include all CLA groups in the WSO meetings.

In 2005, it all changed. I was so excited, when attending that first WSO meeting on the telephone, to know that folks from all over the country (and possibly other countries) could be there, too. I think I speak for most of us who attended those face-to-face WSO meetings when I say that I was relieved to know that at last we had become more inclusive.

Holiday, Seasons, and Travel

These articles discuss how clutter affects the holidays, and how the holidays, seasons, and travel affect clutter.

Holiday Articles

The Holiday Factor: The Season's Effects on CLA Recovery

Holiday 2007
Parker, NV

'Tis the season to declutter...or is it?

CLA*rity* spoke with recovering clutterers from the phone Fellowship to hear how the holiday season—the period from Thanksgiving through New Year's Day—affects clutter and decluttering for CLA members. CLA*rity* composed a list of more than 20 questions on this topic and compiled several responses.

Reactions to questions ranged from deep introspective sighs to Santa-like belly laughter at the realities of "losing an entire set of Christmas decorations" or having to "repurchase" things, like "a bunch of greeting cards" purchased cheaply after last year's holidays but are nowhere to be found to send out this season!

Commonly expressed "frustrations" concern the "extra mail" clutter and "paper assault" from greeting cards and "catalogs" as culprits.

The pressure for hurried housekeeping "perfectionism" in order to host dinners and parties leaves some "frozen." Others are still giving thanks for the Thursday holiday kick-off when there was no work or school, so they "decluttered a child's room" as a family activity.

Although "social pressures" and the urge to add to existing stockpiles is high, presenting "pitfalls" and "boundary issues" for clutterers, the season also offers unique incentives and opportunities for decluttering actions.

In the spirit of giving vs. getting, some have found that charities accepting holiday collections for families in dire need open a chance to "release things" to go to people who have so little. One heartfelt response shows how the season serves as motivation: to "release a lot of clutter, my best things, the things that are more challenging for me to let go of," such as baby clothes collections the now-older child no longer needs, and especially seeing donations "going to real people" via bona fide agencies that have shortages of those items.

Every city has some collection points, like toy drives, homeless and displaced family shelters, pet sanctuaries, and all of them need items, such as old blankets, toiletries, used housewares, and unwanted new gifts; they welcome whatever donors can share —a "great decluttering incentive," CLA members say.

"Out with the old, in with the new," is a holiday theme that plays well with others in CLA who "struggle to find room for new acquisitions" and experience homes that "get out of control." Furthermore, rampant shopping—due to bondage of family traditions, expectations, or even "requirements" to buy new gifts—concerns many who have heightened "indecision" and "panic" as the days count down.

"Lack of time for regular maintenance" because of added demands on schedules is the way clutter increases for many. Family and friends visiting, events and socializing cause "loss of space"—both physical and non-physical—and "time clutter," adding to that old "anxiety" so familiar to recovering clutterers.

Social interaction or even just the opposite—"loneliness" from having too few friends or no "picture-perfect" functional family dynamics—are significant sources of emotional or spiritual clutter and possible resentment during holiday time.

All respondents finding help through the CLA program, meetings, literature, and Tools[19] exemplify the hope of the season.

Telephone work action groups for decluttering get credit for resolving a holiday "clothing and lost shoes" issue. Others say that having newfound CLA support buddies soothes sudden "guess who's coming to dinner?" dilemmas.

To counter some of the "overwhelming feelings," some find the humor in their own responses. Others feel encouraged that "this year will be different," knowing that during this holiday season and beyond, CLA members are not alone in the cluttering and decluttering, the "pain" and the "joy" of the season. ◭

Preparing for a Clutter-less Holiday Season

Fall 2008

As every autumn comes around, another time of year aproaches slowly—or all too quickly for some—because of the end-of-year, holiday-season clutter challenges.

How does the holiday season affect decluttering progress or the accumulation of clutter? Now is a good time to think about how to make this holiday season less cluttered, in terms of time, physical, or emotional clutter. What proactive actions can be taken in advance this year to make the holidays more manageable?

The following is a list of questions that may help clutterers recognize, assess, and prepare better for that time of year. Use it as a personal checklist or as a source of topics for group discussions and member reflections.

Members of the CLA phone groups answered some of these questions and others, which became the basis for *CLArity*'s article "The Holiday Factor: The Season's Effects on CLA Recovery" (Volume I, Number 4, Holiday Issue 2007).

- In what ways does the holiday season tend to cause more clutter in your home?
- In what way does clutter hinder you when you want to host guests for the holidays?
- Do you feel more pressure to have guests come to your home during the holidays?
- How does clutter affect your holiday season outings and social interactions with others?
- Are you frustrated about your home clutter more during the holidays than at other times?
- How does the holiday season affect your level of nonphysical clutter—spiritual and emotional?
- How has home cluttering affected your past holiday seasons?
- Do you become overwhelmed by the need to declutter because of the holidays?
- Do you feel more motivation or less motivation to declutter during the holiday season?

- How does the holiday season affect your time clutter?
- Are you always unprepared for the holidays because of your clutter?
- Does the holiday season tend to interfere with or encourage your recovery process?
- Do you find it easier or harder to declutter because of the holiday season?
- What types of clutter do you reduce or eliminate because of the holiday season?
- In what ways does your cluttering change before, during, and after the holiday season?
- Do you have to buy replacement gifts because you cannot find the ones you already purchased?
- Can you find your wrapping supplies and decorations from last year?
- Does clutter keep you from having room to wrap gifts comfortably?
- Do you feel concern that gifts you receive make your clutter worse?
- Is there room to put up the favorite decorations or symbols that you would like to display?
- Do you have fear during the holidays about being able to clean up and put everything away after the holidays?
- In what ways does the holiday affect the spiritual aspects of your cluttering?

Spirituality and the Holidays

Holiday 2008

Alison B., NJ

There are many religious holidays from September to December. It is at this time of year when many of us start to place more emphasis on giving. Even those who don't usually think much about a power greater than themselves find they are engulfed in the so-called "spirit" of the holidays. This is a precarious time for clutterers. There are so many decisions to be made. Many have expressed a desire to decorate their homes according to the season: "...if only I had the space." Many suddenly find themselves wanting to receive guests and then wishing they were recovered enough not to throw themselves into a frenzy of last-minute cleaning activity each time they wish to hold a gathering in their homes. Then there are those who buy mountains of gifts, which may or may not get to the intended recipients. And how many of us find ourselves addressing cards at the last possible moment or hurriedly wrapping gifts at the final hour? What happens to those who can't afford to buy presents for everyone or have too much difficulty with the process?

The holidays can be a period of too much mind clutter, activity clutter, spiritual clutter, and physical clutter. Feelings of inadequacy run high. Many clutterers live alone, will not bring guests in, and feel strange about accepting invitations they cannot reciprocate, so the holidays can be very lonely. Addictions can run rampant, especially during parties or when we are alone.

It is up to each of us to stay sober, to seek fellowship, to engage in group prayer if we wish, to meditate, and to give of ourselves. Staying sober in all areas of life enhances our motivation to declutter. It is our responsibility to clean out a little clutter each day—be it physical, emotional, or spiritual—in order to make room for the divine flow of the universe. It makes sense for each person to take care of himself or herself first, so that there is plenty of energy left to give to others. This may be the time to do some volunteer work or some extra service work in CLA. Volunteering through service is a wonderful way to learn cooperation and discipline. There is a saying: "Discipline is remembering what we want."

Doing the next right thing always makes us feel good about ourselves eventually, as long as we do not overcommit and we remember to keep our boundaries intact. Let us remember that being overcommitted means different things to different people. We may have too much mind clutter, and we may need to write lists and prioritize. We need to remember that "we do not add a new activity without eliminating from our schedule one that demands equivalent time and energy." Have you recently read the "CLA Tools of Recovery"[19] and the "Recovery Affirmations,"[20] as well as all the leaflets? Have you made a gratitude list? Have you answered written questions on Steps 1 and

2? Do you attend another 12-Step group, as well as CLA? Do you have an official buddy or sponsor you can call on a daily basis? These are just some of the activities that can help us develop our spirituality—and that has nothing to do with religion, unless that's what you want. We in CLA are not here to judge—only to offer our experience, strength, and hope. Happy Holidays!

Challenges of the Holidays for a Clutterer

Holiday 2009

Peggy A., CA

For years, I struggled through the holiday season, always seeming to add to my clutter. The main reason I would run into trouble was procrastination, which led to over-scheduling.

My biggest problem with clutter during the season was due to gifts and decorations I wished to make. I would plan the projects ahead of time and purchase needed materials but would procrastinate on getting started or continuing with a job. Then, as I began to run out of time, I would purchase gifts in a store instead of making them, leaving unused materials, which substantially added to my clutter.

The second problem was in taking time to attend events without taking into account what else I had meant to do. Instead of saying "No thanks, I'm busy," I would say "I'd love to come," thereby compounding the problem.

There was one other causative factor in all of this. As I would get so busy trying to finish my projects, I would ignore the clutter I would cause. "I'll take care of that later," I would say. Of course, after the holidays were over, I would be confronted with big, out-of-control piles of clutter, caused by not finishing projects and by not putting things away. That situation would be so discouraging that I would keep procrastinating on the cleanup—so, of course, it would get worse.

As you can see, procrastination is my number one problem—as it is for many clutterers. But working a CLA program has helped me to focus on what I need to do. I have made many changes in how I handle the holidays.

At this point, I choose not to make my gifts or decorations, although I have always loved doing it and the recipients loved receiving those gifts. Instead, I purchase everything. In some ways, it is less satisfying but very gratifying when I can look at the house after the holidays without seeing piles of clutter everywhere.

Since I am not making the gifts, I have time to respond to select invitations and to take care of my clutter as it crops up. I still have to work my CLA program hard to motivate myself to keep the clutter at bay at holiday time, but I no longer have the horror of looking at an out-of-control mess afterwards.

Holiday Entertaining

Holiday 2012

Gayle P., NJ

Many of us are afraid to entertain throughout the year, but to attempt it during the holidays seems even more daunting. Some reasons to do it are:

1. It gives me a reason and an incentive to clean up my place.
2. It allows me to create a memory for my guests and me.
3. It's fun!

My neighbor's mantra was "Do what's possible." She was an elegant hostess and believed in keeping things simple. So I either email, mail, or call my guests to give them the date, the time span of the party, and the address. Sometimes I add directions, public transit information, etc. It's nice to include someone new to the group or someone who might not have a place to go for the holidays.

The guest list (and the guests' preferences) help determine what I ultimately serve. I get inspiration from recipe websites. I like to include vegetarian offerings, as well as alcoholic and nonalcoholic beverages. At times I order in, cook, or have a potluck. What I end up serving is based on how much time I have, what I want to eat, and how much I want to cook and spend. I keep my budget in mind when planning my event.

People will offer to bring things—I say yes! I keep in mind what people's capabilities are, and I don't assign something essential to someone who is forgetful. I write down what people offer to bring and summarize it to everyone in an email.

I use lists like crazy. I use a countdown calendar and write down everything that I need to do for the event.

I keep my guest list, menu, and recipes all in a folder. I write a shopping list for everything and group like items together. I shop at off hours and while shopping, I cross things off as I put them in the cart.

I try to get the major house cleaning done the week before (put like things with like, find a home for everything) so I can concentrate on all the other things I need to do. I schedule cleaning help, if possible.

If I'm having 12 people for dinner and I'm planning to use my dining room table, I do a dry run: I put in the table leaves, arrange the chairs, and make sure I have a tablecloth that's clean and fits the table. I get anything repaired that needs fixing for the event. I think of what dishes, platters, and glasses I'll need—and make sure they're clean.

The day before, my husband and I go through, room by room, vacuuming and dusting, and making sure the house is as clean as possible. I clear the clutter! If there's a room I don't want guests to go into, I close and lock the door if possible.

I make sure my bathroom is clean, with plenty of toilet paper, a clean hand towel, nice-smelling soap, and maybe flowers and a sweet-smelling candle, if space permits.

I like decorating with seasonal natural decorations (flowers, clementines, etc.) to make the place look pretty.

I try to clean out my refrigerator by wiping up spills and tossing questionable food items. I make or buy ice (it's important to have enough). I make sure the dishwasher is nearly empty before the party. I plan where to put coats.

When people arrive, I have a pitcher of something to offer and have some nibbles out that they can help themselves to. Having food in several places gives people a reason to circulate and avoids crowding. I make sure to have at least one appetizer out when people arrive. Buying items such as cheese and crackers, salami, hummus, nuts, and grapes gives me one course that's done without cooking.

I try my best to plan food that I can prepare in advance so that when guests arrive, I won't have too much to do. I try to get plenty of sleep leading up to my event and schedule time to relax. Before people arrive, I try to sit down for a few minutes, like my neighbor, and try to imagine everyone having fun! (Stash your perfectionist tendencies, if you have them!)

I dim the lights, light the candles, play some background music—jazz, classical, opera, instrumental. One thing I do is tune into online radio sites or set up my smartphone/tablet.

Be flexible, and have fun!

Handling the Holidays

Holiday 2013

CLA*rity* interviewed several CLA members about their issues with clutter and the holidays.

Most members answered "yes" when asked about their inability to have guests over because of clutter and procrastination, although most said they would like to entertain. One member responded, "That shows why I'm in CLA," and another said that she generally does have one guest over but is reluctant to invite others because she could never get the house ready. One respondent stated that there are public spaces in his shared house that he can use for guests, although there are none in his part of the house. If he knows one person is coming, he can do the preparation but tends to put it off—although it usually ends up being less difficult than he initially thought it would be.

However, when asked if using the CLA program has helped with issues about entertaining for the holidays, he replied that he does intend to invite people in the future. "I have a long-term plan and try to picture how I would like it to be. I try to get rid of something every day. One day at a time."

CLA*rity* asked how indecision and procrastination dealing with gifts add to the stress of the holidays. Some clutterers said that not knowing what to give causes them problems. "I am a terrible gift-giver; I procrastinate because I never know what to give. I would like to make gifts, but I also procrastinate on that." Another said, "I never know what to buy: I am paralyzed. I don't want to buy something that will be clutter, and I don't want to buy something that is thrown away... and then I stress by thinking I should have gotten something." One comment was, "I often have difficulty in figuring out what I should get people, so some get gift cards or subscriptions."

A respondent said, "Before CLA, I was the reason why the post office is open on the 24th [of December]. I have gotten into a rhythm in CLA of getting everything shipped early, so people get their gifts before Christmas."

When asked: "How does it help to use the CLA program to avoid the stress of gift-giving?" one replied, "One of the key components of CLA that has helped me a lot is the whole idea around time clutter. I have learned [to allow] enough time between events and enough time to get to things.... I love the section in the literature where it says 'Action is the magic word.' It really helps me a lot. Instead of thinking about buying gifts, I act."

Another realized that relationships are more important than things, and sometimes it is more important to spend time together.

Several respondents said that they have time and mind clutter because of too many activities, projects, time spent on decorations, and gift buying. One stated that he has decluttered his schedule: "There are a lot of events going on, but I ask myself if it's something I really want to go to. I take stuff out of my calendar all the time to [avoid] overbooking."

Another said, "It is a vicious cycle. I have mind clutter because I have physical clutter, and I have physical clutter because I have mind clutter."

CLA*rity* asked how using the CLA program helps to avoid time and mind clutter. One member said, "Getting back to doing one thing at a time helps when I get swamped. It has been a big help to take something as far as I can, and if I can't go any further, to get onto something else." Another said, "Just doing something, no matter what, if I know I can get this piece done, it gives me some satisfaction and I feel I can do more. Action is the magic word." Other responses were: "learning to simplify and prioritize and let go and let my Higher Power guide me" and "It helps when I make a time plan and use a timer."

When asked how using the CLA program helped with issues about the holidays, one member said it helps to "get out of myself and do something for somebody else. I have learned in CLA to be a little more proactive and not to procrastinate." Another said that when she uses the CLA Tools,[19] particularly that of Bookending, it helps, and another finds praying helpful. Other responses included:

- "It has [helped]—not necessarily with the level of physical clutter—but with my attitude. I recognize that I am not the only one that has this problem but that there is a whole world of people who are not comfortable with the way things are. It's about what's important for me. I try to...[be in touch] with people year-round."
- "We all have difficulties because we put too much pressure on ourselves and value stuff more than the people in our lives. When we focus more on our thoughts and how they create our experience—and learn we can change our thoughts to change our experience—then we can choose more peaceful, joyful, nurturing thoughts."
- "I like it when I can pray and meditate with other people. I am working on a new plan of 15 minutes' decluttering daily."

Handling Stress in the Holiday Season

Holiday 2015

We asked CLA members about their experiences handling stress during the holidays. The responses below came from members of the Teaneck, New Jersey, meeting and attendees at the Second Annual Convention held on October 3 and 4, 2015, in Secaucus, New Jersey.

One of the questions clutterers were asked was what about the winter holiday season bugs them. Some responses were: "The holidays make me stressed because of memories of those whom I loved and have passed." Several members talked about problems dealing with the expectations to spend time with relatives who made them feel uncomfortable or with whom they had deep-seated issues.

Many discussed stresses brought on by the pressure of others regarding gifts or social activities. Others shared on the tendency to overbuy for themselves because of sales and advertising. Some felt the self-induced pressure to return items, which somehow they hardly ever got around to doing.

Some complained about the length of advertising and sales for Christmas; the general feeling was this period is starting earlier than ever. However, one member stated "My favorite holiday is Martin Luther King Day because they haven't figured out how to commercialize it."

Several members shared their dismay at the greed surrounding the holidays, rather than the messages of love, sharing, and humanity. But one said her stress was from the "pressure of trying to recapture the holidays of my childhood."

Members were asked if there was anything about the holidays that was uplifting. Some mentioned they have learned to spend the holidays with those who greet them with joy, rather than greed. One talked about spending time with a group of people who use them to share love. She said, "I will celebrate the excitement of expecting harmony, love, joy, and peace in our lives, and I want that every day." One talked about how giving to others really uplifted her. Another mentioned she has "learned about unconditional love when taking care of elders." Still another clutterer shared that "I often have fun, because I don't put a lot of weight into it."

Clutterers were asked about which techniques they use to diminish stress and maintain serenity during the holidays. Many members shared that beginning their holiday gift-buying or other tasks early, or leaving it until later, helped avoid stress. Others shared that early planning was a key both in gift-giving and eliminating excessive social activities.

Still others said they shopped online, purchased gift cards, or gave cash to avoid stress. Some talked about how reducing their goals or involvement reduced their stress. Another said, "I keep myself stress free by not generally giving or receiving gifts."

Some mentioned it was important to take care of their physical clutter, especially if guests were invited to their homes. One stated that "Holiday stress brings out the need to declutter so that the house looks and feels neater. My mind becomes more organized, which feels like I accomplished something." Yet another member stated that declining unneeded gifts and other items was a help.

Several others shared how they avoided or reduced interaction with family members with whom they were uncomfortable or who had caused them grief. One stated that she and her husband set a time limit on their visit with a family member and after the visit immediately attended a 12-Step meeting.

Some use the same techniques all year long—including prayer, meditation, and reading 12-Step literature—but more so at the holidays. One reduces stress by donating to those less fortunate, and another said, "Try to love people all year long, and that's enough."

Others mentioned the need to practice good self-care in order to deal with the holidays. Several mentioned needing rest and time for quiet and meditation.

Seasons

Summer Challenges and Opportunities

Summer 2009
Tina R., NJ

I love summer, but I have to keep a watchful eye for cockroaches in my kitchen. Some time ago I stopped paying attention and my home became overrun to the point where I had to get rid of a portable wooden closet that they had chosen for their main home. I killed hundreds of them—ugh! Eventually I realized that it was my cluttering—in the form of "street shopping"—that had led to this problem because I had brought in discarded furniture, and I'm sure now that it was already infested. I've had the opportunity to learn that even one roach indicates a potentially serious problem, that roach gel and boric acid are the best deterrents, and that spray poison is not an option because the noxious fumes make me sick. Now I have an incentive to keep my kitchen clean, and I no longer "street shop"!

Summer Challenges and Opportunities

Summer 2009
Peggy A., CA

In the summer, my biggest challenge is related to weather. Normally, it is nice and dry; but with the change in climate these last few years, some days have high humidity. I have trouble breathing when it is humid, and I am tired and lethargic all day. Needless to say, this does not lead to much decluttering.

Another difficulty is my summer travel. While I am not home, I cannot do any physical decluttering.

But it makes sense to turn the challenges into opportunities. Although the hot weather is a problem, longer days and sunshine give me a lift. So I have become a night owl; during summer, I get most of my work done in the cool of the night.

And, although I cannot declutter my home while traveling, I can work on my program and on nonphysical forms of clutter.

In that spirit, I made a special effort to attend a face-to-face CLA meeting recently while in another state. That meeting really jazzed me up and left me eager to tackle my clutter upon my return.

Summer Challenges and Opportunities

Summer 2009
E. T., NJ

As summer approaches, so does a major opportunity to declutter my home. I can donate all sorts of items to a gigantic rummage sale at my church. It is a way of getting rid of clutter and at the same time benefiting those less fortunate than I. In addition, I donate many hours of my time to the sale itself, which is a huge exercise in decluttering.

First, piles of donations are left outside the doors to the building. Next, we bring everything inside, deliver it to the various departments—clothing, linens, housewares, jewelry, toys and games, books, electronics, sporting goods, records, furniture, etc.—and sort it for sale. I am in charge of the women's shoe department, which receives more than a thousand pairs of shoes. I put a rubber band around each pair, mark the size on the bottom of each shoe (to simplify the resorting process), and put them into large boxes, one for each size. After each of the sale days we have to re-sort many unsold items in addition to the new merchandise which arrives on a daily basis.

Even the leftover items are given to charity wherever possible. In the women's clothing department, for example, after the closing bell on the last day of the sale, all the unsold merchandise is removed from the racks and boxes and stuffed into large garbage bags, which are then taken away by waiting trucks sent by various organizations. This process takes slightly more than one hour; by the end of that time, we are setting up tables and serving lunch to all the workers! Leftover books are sent to Africa. For whatever merchandise we are unable to give away, we assemble a team of volunteers to cart the items out to the curb, where they are removed by a garbage truck. The building is returned to its former condition within a day or two!

Through this event, which has taken place every July for the past 75 years, we raise a lot of money (about $60,000 during the seven sale sessions each of the last few years) and donate all of it to many mission projects—local, national, and global.

Travel

How Clutter Affects Summer Travel

Summer 2010

CLA*rity* asked CLA members about problems related to their clutter and travels. While most of the members discussed problems, they also told how CLA has been helping.

Both physical and nonphysical clutter interfere with finding what they want to take and cause the member to run around like crazy. "Yes, I have tons of mental clutter with planning and severe clutter about leaving the house; and then the physical clutter causes me a lot of stress."

Some clutterers have problems in packing because of procrastination. "I am always looking around and panicking." "Recently I finished packing in the car on the way to the airport."

Packing problems also stem from having trouble making decisions, which leads to procrastination and wanting to take too much stuff. "I used to take everything but the kitchen sink because I was so afraid of leaving something behind."

However, some have found that making a list makes packing quicker and prevents forgetting important items. "I don't, but it's a good idea. At night I wake up, wondering if I forgot something."

There were those who bemoaned how not putting things away when packing because of travel anxiety worsens their home clutter.

During a trip, too much stuff causes wasted time and even back pains from handling heavy luggage. For some, the clutter increases as they acquire new things while traveling. "While on a trip, my husband and I took a picture of the mess in the room. It looked like we had been there for a year, the way we had things scattered all over."

But learning to keep it contained and reminding themselves of being in a limited space and the need to keep things to a minimum have kept some from cluttering on their travels.

One problem area discussed was time clutter during a trip, especially from trying to see too many sights. One clutterer gave an extreme example of the problem when she said, "I was late for my own brother's burial because of trying to do too many things. Everyone was about to leave the cemetery as I arrived."

When asked if others traveling in your group ever comment on the clutter, responses ranged from "no, because I try to keep it contained now," to: "Yes, my husband; but he has also admitted he is a clutterer, and we're both frustrated with ourselves in the way we can make a room so cluttered." "Yes, my husband. He tries to keep everything in the drawers very well, but I create a mess."

Most agreed that being away from their clutter gives them a sense of relief and enjoyment of the clean space and not having so much stuff. However, it is often a wrench to come back to the cluttered house. "I had surgery and went away to recover so I wouldn't lie around the house and be frustrated by looking at everything."

Most agreed that cluttering also causes stress while both on a trip and preparing for a trip. They reported of hardly sleeping the night before leaving because of clutter-caused delays. "I could not find things I thought were there. I could not decide what to do, so I left everything out, and I got completely overwhelmed."

But there were also solutions, such as starting early and making a packing list. "I try before leaving to pay all my bills early; it releases cluttering tension."

When asked if using the CLA program has helped alleviate the problem, most answers were positive.

"Yes, because I've made a lot of progress in the past three years. I definitely use the 12 Steps, and on the trips I make a lot of effort to have the room looking nice." "I do better now if I use the Steps and Tools,[19] don't procrastinate, and don't sweat the small stuff!" "Things are getting better. I now don't have a goat path in my bedroom, and my living room has expanded with open spaces, so I can pack easier." "The Serenity Prayer helps me. I'll get frustrated and scared and calm down with the Serenity Prayer. I try to go to meetings before I leave."

Having a Clutter-Free Travel Experience

Fall 2013

Kathy H., CA

Since joining CLA, I have put some effort into avoiding clutter before, during, and after travel—both for vacations and to see family. The key to a stress-free trip is planning, so I don't procrastinate or wait until the last minute.

I often start months before leaving when I plan a vacation-type trip. I access websites for reviews of activities, transportation, and lodging. This helps me to find out what is available, avoids bad experiences on the trip, and allows me to obtain transportation and lodging at the least cost. All this preplanning may seem like a lot of work, but I find, instead, that it's fun. When I am feeling lonely or bored, I go online and research the next vacation site. Actually, I enjoy the planning as much as the trip! If I didn't have internet access, I would use printed books.

Once transportation and lodging reservations are made, I plan activities and reserve tours. Since I already researched online sources, I have an idea of possible activities and tours and how to contact them. I compile and print a list, which contains, for each travel location, both must-see activities and others to visit where time permits. This enables us to have planned goals so we don't waste most of our time trying to decide what to do—but also allows us to be somewhat flexible in our daily plans. By doing the research and planning ahead of time, we avoid stress and mind and time clutter during the trip.

A week or two before leaving, I make to-do and packing lists. I keep generic lists on the computer, which I print out, adding and subtracting items as needed.

I make a conscious effort to pare down items—leaving home what I don't need, layering clothes rather than taking complete sets for different climates, and trying to make items do double duty. Using these lists and not procrastinating on the to-do items helps me to avoid last-minute stress and panic.

I try (although I often don't succeed!) to get to bed early the night before leaving so I am not starting my trip groggy from lack of sleep. I also try to get to the train, plane, or ship early, in case of last-minute transportation glitches.

Then, once I am on my trip, I work on decreasing the clutter, whether I am in a hotel or at a relative's house. It is so easy to spread my items all over—which isn't fair to others, makes it hard to find things, and makes it more difficult to pack up when it is time to leave. So, instead, I try to designate a place for items when I first unpack and put them there during my stay.

I avoid making a lot of purchases to take home. Sometimes it's very tempting to buy that really cute knickknack or T-shirt, but will they fit in the suitcase? Also, I need to keep in mind the Tool of Streamlining: Is there a place for them at home when I return or will they just be more clutter?

After returning home, I unpack my suitcase and put everything away as soon as possible. Once again, a CLA tool comes into play: Earmarking. I have a spot for travel items; they get returned there. Clothes are put away in closets and drawers, and toiletries are put away in the bathroom. With designated places for everything, it is much easier to unpack without leaving a trail of clutter.

Artwork and Poetry

Members share their experience, strength, and hope through artwork and poetry.

Artwork

Summer 2008

Member-created artwork used with permission from "Decluttering 1"

I DON'T KNOW WHY
OR WHEN IT GREW SO
HARD TO LET THINGS
GO OR TO DOCUMENT
WHAT LITTLE PROGRE
SS I WAS MAKING.
WHEN THE OLD HAIR
DRYER QUIT WORKING
. I WAS ABL- TO LE
T THE OLD ONE GO O
NLY AFTER I BOUGHT
THE NEW ONE; BUT
THEN I COULDN'T TH
ROW AWAY THE BOX F
ROM THE NEW ONE FO
R WEEKS. WHEN I F
INALLY GOT RID OF
THE BOX, I SAT LOO
KING AT THE PAPERS
FOR THE NEW ONE F
OR DAYS AND DAYS A
ND DAYS

DECLUTTERING 1

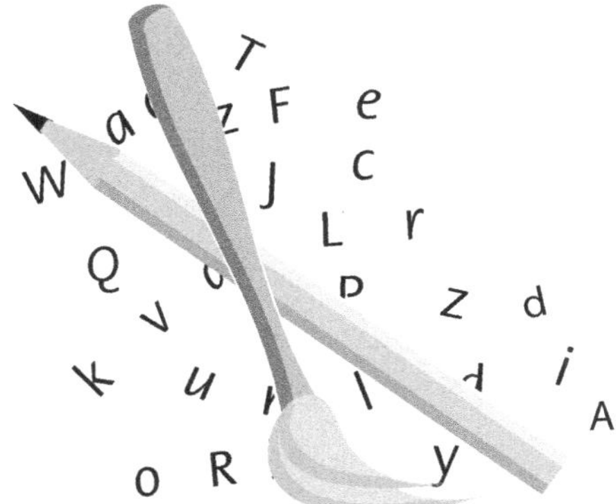

Poetry

The Hoarding Cloud

Fall 2009

Susan B., NY

Underneath the hoarding cloud is rainy and dark.
Cleaning up is certainly no walk in the park

With piles of junk in no certain order—
That is the life of a hoarder.

Logically, I know this doesn't make sense—
But the stuff takes over and it becomes so intense.

Then I joined my CLA 12-Step program and started to listen—
Now my house is slowly starting to glisten.

I am not cured and probably never will be
But I take things step by step and day by day—and I pray.
By trial and error I am learning the way.

How can I go wrong?
With such loving friends, I have become strong.

Now I soon will be able to take a little rest.
I will only keep the best and get rid of the rest.
I will have a beautiful nest.

Happy Birthday, CLA

Holiday 2009

Betsey K., NJ

Back in 1989
Two women met to seek
A way to deal with clutter
That plagued them every week.
They found a program called A.A.
And saw it could apply
To problems with their clutter
And chose to give a try.
They worked the Steps and used the tools.
Recovery was their goal.
Traditions too they focused on
To make the process whole.

One (A Poem)

Spring 2010

Decluttering 1, NY

The blue sheets cascaded over the foot of the bed.
They (the blue sheets) tumbled over the edge
when god climbed out of it (the bed) this morning
(or is it already afternoon...)
They (sheets of sky blue water)
trickled down onto the floor
skirting their way into a pool
flooding the floor
and there they
drifted their way to a beach
of printed matter.
Blue waves splashed against the mountain of yet to be...
discovered materializing there.
Today god would not make the bed
the first thing on this morning
(or is it already afternoon...)
and so it came to pass
that today the bed would just be...
and become...
Even though god was the last to climb out of it
(the sky blue water colored bed),
a giant lumbering over its side,
Today would just be...
and become...
the day.
The day the devil would be in the details.
The devil is always in the details.

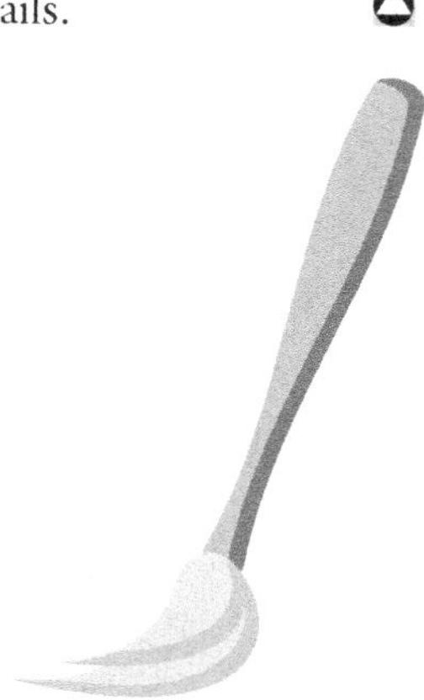

Releasing My Clutter Comes from Releasing Myself

Fall 2013

Risa G., NY

The Journey Towards the Twelve-Step Path

One day sometime in 2002
Something ended and I knew
My life was forever changed, but what would ensue
Was a change of living launching endless snafus.
I used to suffer a lot from the flu.
Then I coped with stress anew.
I discovered shopping could renew
When work piled up and my day was through,
I learned to acquire too.
I saw and suddenly knew
My dreams could come true
If I bought something new.
So in came a purple pair of shoes,
A bright red suitcase for which my husband had no clue
Of the $450 charge on the credit card that was blue
That began a serial mass of what I could accrue.
I had always been true
To tricks of organizing to cover up my growing rue.
I piled and covered stuff when I was through
While I hid, cowered and lied—I ended in a stew.
How to deal with the growing brew
Of stuff that overflowed every room to
The center, the top but still I flew
To anywhere I could get something else new.
The clothes piled up with tags still attached thru
Purple, green, fuchsia, orange, pink and electric blue.
Not just one but every color and hue
In coats, sweaters, shirts, sundries and shoes.
I was never too
Tired to shop and pile my stuff: turtleneck and crew
As I moved from object to object a pattern ensued
I had loyalty to locks, books, fabric and varied strange sorts of goo.
I never admitted the depth of the pain I went through
Nor did I disclose to anyone—certainly not you,
My darling husband whose anger grew
As I was wide-eyed with wonder denying too.
That I couldn't stop and couldn't tell no way—foo!
I began to wonder who
Could save me from this drowning and on this I stewed
Not willing to ask for help though I tried to be through.
I couldn't stop I'd promise and chew
On tons of food for many years too.
I worked on eating better and gyms by the slew,
Lockers in 11 locations with all the same things in them, too.
My compulsion for stuff just kept changing forms—ewww!
I felt shamed and hopeless—I just didn't know what to do.
Thank goodness I found the program—whew! 

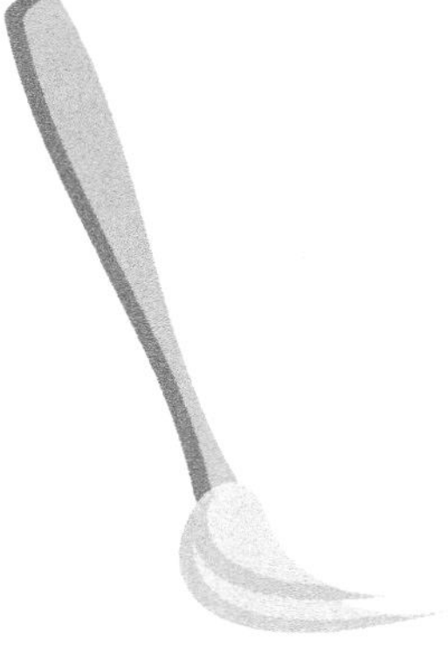

I Hear You

Holiday 2013 and Spring 2014

Lisa P., CT

Here is one way that we move toward healing mind clutter:

A Strong Support System: CLA program, understanding family and friends—whatever gives us the love, strength, and encouragement to tackle this difficult task.

("Declutter Your Mind"[7] leaflet, Clutterers Anonymous, Copyright 1998–2011)

"I Hear You"

When you were struggling in one area,
I heard your recovery in another area.
You were frustrated, overwhelmed, and confused,
but I heard a practice, perseverance, and progress.
Keep going. Keep speaking. Keep sharing.
You may not feel your success,
but I feel your success,
and that success is leading me out of my mess.
I speak my gratitude with one voice,
but thousands in the rooms echo mine.
Take good care of your precious self.
We need a role model.
Don't back up, shut down, or hide.
Your voice is making a difference
to those who themselves will make a difference.
You may still be uncertain on your deathbed, but
from heaven you will see
the importance of your life.

Humor and Cartoons

Scientists have discovered that laughing is not only great for your emotional well-being, it also enhances the immune system. So CLA*rity* has included some humorous articles and cartoons.

Humor

A Bit of Humorous Wording

Fall 2008

Mary Agnes M., MA

We handed out a list of phone numbers, including the CLA phone lines, to members in our Cambridge group. A newcomer, receiving our phone list, asked, "What does it mean, 'You come into the CLA phone meetings unmated'?" We all laughed. It should have said "unmuted."

Could Getting Caught Up on Clutter Be a Downer?

Summer 2015

Wendy L., IL

Someone once asked me what it would be like if I didn't have any clutter. My first thought was, it would be nirvana! Just think, I'd sort the mail daily and get the dishes done every night. My to-do list would always get checked off. Life would be a bowl of cherries. Or would it?

At first glance, it might mean lots of extra time, time that I used to spend dealing with my clutter. You know, obsessing about it, worrying about it, handling it over and over.

But upon further examination, it would leave me with a lot of time to fill. Too much time, actually. And that's not always such a good or desirable thing for me. I love being with my family and friends, but they've got their own lives to lead, too. And for me, being bored is up there with watching grass grow.

Not to worry, as I would now have time to get to my wish lists and to pursue my dreams. But deep down inside, I think I've been avoiding doing these things because I'm afraid of failing at them, afraid of the effort it would take to do them, and afraid of the decisions I would have to make. After all, cherries still have pits.

All this makes me wonder if deep down inside, in some weird subconscious, perverse way, I clutter on purpose. Maybe it's that my clutter has been like a security blanket for me—a binky, if you will. It's given me a legitimate excuse to avoid the things that stress me out the most.

But meanwhile, time is slipping away. And I need to better face my clutter to give myself a chance to seize the moment. Maybe that means throwing something away I might later need. But CLA has taught me that I can deal with that. Maybe it means hanging a couple of pictures in places that I'll later dislike. But I can live with that, or change it, if necessary.

In the end, I want to have too much time on my hands. The fear of the unknown is scary, but facing my spiritual clutter of unfulfilled dreams is even worse. So I need to take it one step at a time, and yes, easy does it.

So it's time to begin letting go of my clutter binky. I don't think I'll ever be without some sort of clutter, but I know I'm capable of creating less of it. Coincidentally, it's spring now, a time of renewal and growth—in fact, I've just spotted my first ladybug, which I'll take as a good sign. Life really can be a bowl of cherries. Sweet and full of possibilities—pits and all.

Holiday 2016

Judith N., CA

Last night my brother, Larry, phoned. When he asked how I was doing, I replied that, since becoming a CLA member, I'd finally reached the point where I was releasing some possessions.

At the end of the call, he said, "Good luck with the 'Possession Reduction Program' or 'PRP.'" That's what comes from a long career working with our military!

Cartoons

Spring 2015

Where I am AT!

Text by Ted S., NY, artwork by Lauren R., NJ

Holiday 2015

The cartoon below was written by members of the CLArity Team and illustrated by Lauren R., NJ.

Spring 2016

The cartoon below was written by the CLArity Team and illustrated by Lauren R., NJ.

Fall 2016

Where I Am At!
7/16
A friend is doing me a favor by coming over today to help declutter.
Great!
She'll be doing me a bigger favor if she doesn't.
?
Ted S., NY
Melanie T., NY

Holiday 2016

BAGELS
Hmmm! Poppy seed My favorite
Sesame is mine
BAGELS
I wonder who invented them?
Don't know, but I know who invented the everything bagel
BAGELS
A clutterer! Couldn't make a decision
Ted S., NY

Community Outreach

Many A.A. intergroups organize Hospital and Institution (H & I) committees. Their purpose is to provide panels of A.A. members to visit hospitals and correctional facilities. They tell their stories to alcoholic patients and inmates.

Hospital & Institution Outreach

Holiday 2007

Jim H., CA

For many years, Alcoholics Anonymous has maintained Hospital and Institution Committees that send panels of A.A. members to speak at hospitals and other facilities. These panels are often not only successful for the residents of the facilities, but are highly regarded by the panel members and staff as helping to further their own recovery.

Many CLA members have discussed establishing H&I Committees in CLA; but, as of yet, this has not been done, nor has there been any procedure established to inform potential panel members of dos and don'ts. If you are interested in participating in the development of such committees, contact WSO or CLA*rity*.

For me, public sharing about clutter began with church organizations and social and business clubs. The positive reactions confirmed just how cluttered we are as a society. Then, recently, I was asked to share our opportunity with a group at a well-known health clinic. The attendees represented people from both individual and group counseling sessions who voluntarily responded to a Clutter Free Workshop flyer.

I felt the presentation went well, and their response seemed to validate those feelings. Arriving back at my office an hour after the meeting, I found the following e-mail from the clinic's case manager waiting for me: "I have done many groups at our facility, but none have matched the interest and number of patients signed up. Not only did the patients show up without a reminder call, but they signed up in advance and were punctual. I have spoken to my colleagues, and they are most interested in learning more about this subject."

We should remember that people are often too ashamed, just as I was, to show up at a CLA meeting. However, once they find themselves in a workshop with others like themselves and discover that they are not alone and that there are solutions, help, and hope, they begin to exhibit a whole new attitude and level of confidence. All of us can speak from our own experiences—where we were before and where we are now with CLA—and often that is all it takes to create a new path for another person's recovery.

But we must also remember that even as we stir up new interest with meaningful outreach workshops at appropriate venues, we have to maintain effective group meetings for these new prospective members.

Nonclutterers

This section contains articles about family and friends: dealing with others, how clutter affects others, and how the family members' actions affect clutterers.

Clutter and Family Ties

Holiday 2007

Liza S., MA

I am thinking back to my first meeting almost one year ago. Yes, I am coming up to my first anniversary in CLA, and it's been an eye-opening year. I am reflecting on my clutter and the family ties that bind. My sister and I attend our home group meeting together; this is not the only family tie I refer to, however.

I remember the shame of growing up in a cluttered house. I did not bring people home much. I think it was in high school that I saw that other people lived "differently." I put it in the back of my mind, though.

I am unsure whether it is learned behavior or genetic or an emotional component that links us all together. I am not sure if cluttering is passed along through the genes or not, but, for me, I see a family tie to this disease.

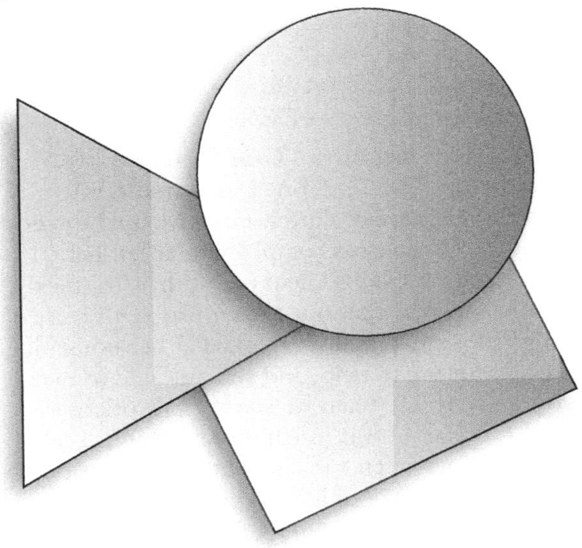

I remember back ten years earlier at Grandma's house; she was going into a nursing home and my dad, mom, brother, sister, and I were cleaning out her house so that it could be put on the market. She had a two-bedroom, relatively small house. I remember thinking how packed it was with stuff for one person, e.g., 55 pocketbooks, 65 coats, and numerous nightgowns still in their wrapping and with the tags!!

I remember thinking that no one person could possibly use all that. I also wondered why Grandma didn't tell us to stop buying stuff; she certainly had too much. What a job it was!!

That experience was a jolt for me. Again, I made note of this but put it on the back burner. After all, my house wasn't as bad as that. I think I thought of things in degrees—and my degree didn't reach that level (but I'm also a lot younger than my 90-year-old grandma).

I'm not sure how it came about, but I went to my first CLA meeting. I remember thinking, "I'm not sure if I should be here," but the group was patient and let me decide for myself. They welcomed me, and I kept coming!!

Just the other day—as I was cleaning out an area of the kitchen (spices and supplies) and clearing out five containers of baking powder (progress not perfection), three of garlic powder, and three of baking soda—yes, I thought back to Granny's house and the ties that bind. It's too bad for Granny and *lucky for me* that I have a program to attend and can recover from the clutter disease!! I have people to talk to, and they are nonjudgmental, understanding people, too. Thank you, CLA.

Notes from a Closet Clutterer

Holiday 2014

Wendy L., IL

When I meet someone new, I am often asked what I do. Because I'm proud of my involvement with the CLA Cyber and CLA*rity* committees, I'd like to be able to share about it. But I don't want to identify myself as a clutterer.

And therein lies the dilemma.

So I say that I help manage a website and write newsletter articles. And cringe. Because, inevitably, about half of the inquirers will ask me, "What website?"

If I tell them it's for Clutterers Anonymous, I've now identified myself as a clutterer. And that, as you may know, garners some, um, interesting reactions. Some say they can totally relate, and others react as though I just grew three heads. In other words, some just don't get it.

It's with the latter group that I find myself backpedaling and explaining, "Oh my gosh, I'm not a hoarder…it's not that bad. I just can't make decisions about what to do with paper and it just piles up."

Or, I totally dismiss the mission of CLA and say things like, "Well, it's all about learning to organize," just to normalize it. But when I say that, it causes an internal struggle that doesn't feel good—spiritual clutter if you will—and I find myself quickly changing the subject.

It also triggers the most uncomfortable of reactions in myself: guilt and shame. So my solution has been to tell a white lie instead. Now, when people ask about the website, I tell them it's for a private, members-only not-for-profit. A what? When they ask what I write about, I tell them about the articles I've written that aren't specific to clutterers, such as those about procrastination and the value of volunteering.

Okay, so what's really going on here? Clearly, I'm embarrassed to identify myself as a clutterer. But why?

Maybe it will make me seem like a defective person who can't handle something as simple as keeping things organized. Which leads to the distorted thinking that everyone else knows what they're doing. Bottom line is, I think people will reject me or make fun of me if they know that I'm a clutterer.

Now this seems quite extreme. But I do wonder if this identity crisis of mine is why Bill W. and other early members decided to make alcoholics be anonymous in Alcoholics Anonymous (A. A.), upon which CLA is based. The anonymity keeps us safe and normal, at least to those who don't know us well. Truth be told, it's really painful to think through this, just as hard as it is for me to write on the 12 Steps—which, incidentally, I've never completed.

Maybe one day I'll come to terms with myself as a clutterer. But for now, I will continue to disguise myself as a manager of a secret, mysterious website. It's definitely awkward but saves me from the stress of admitting to strangers that I'm a clutterer.

Thanks, A.A., you got it right.

Allowing Others to Help Me Declutter

Spring 2016

Ruthe S., PA

(Please note that CLA has no opinion on using professional organizers.—Editor)

I've been a member of CLA for over 12 years. Twice before I was in CLA, I used non-CLA people to help me declutter. First, I joined forces with a friend who was complaining about her clutter, and we tried to help each other. It quickly became apparent that our clutter problems were vastly different. When we worked at her home, it was easy for me to help, and she was able to make progress quickly. When we started to work in mine, however, it was much more difficult. I felt a lot of shame when I realized how different our situations were. We didn't do much in my home because it was overwhelming for both of us, but mostly I really didn't want her there because I was embarrassed.

Later, I hired an acquaintance who advertised herself as a person who helped with decluttering, although I don't think she was formally trained. She helped me clean up, but I started cluttering again after we were finished. I now know this was due to my lack of understanding of my relationship with clutter and that it is an addiction. I used to hold onto things out of fear; I was afraid I would need them someday. It was also a way of trying to feel comforted. I see now the problem is that I have a difficult time making decisions about what I should keep and what I should throw away—and, if I keep it, where it should go. The more stress I'm under, the more difficult it is to make those decisions. One thing that has helped is remembering a line from our leaflet, "Home: Our Sacred Place,"[11] which states that, "God will provide us with what we need when we need it."

Several years ago, I hired a childhood friend to help me. She wasn't trained in organizing, but she had successfully helped others. This turned out to be a disaster. She had a lot of judgments about my clutter, and I felt that her standards were too high. She was also unable to praise me when I did something that worked but criticized me for not doing more. I stopped working with her because I didn't want to subject myself to any more shame.

About a year ago, I decided to use outside help again. I would've preferred it to be another CLA member because I hoped another member wouldn't be judgmental. Unfortunately, there wasn't anyone in my area with whom I could work. I decided to try a professional organizer and chose one who had experience with clutterers. She has been helpful in figuring out where to put things, which I see as more of an organizing issue than a clutter issue. The most important thing I've learned is I have to be the one who makes decisions about what to keep or throw away. I've found that no one can declutter for me; it has to come from within, or I find I start cluttering again. I threw out a lot and found homes for things, and my apartment looked much better. Most importantly, she didn't judge me, and she was often kinder to me than I was to myself, which was much more helpful than my friend's criticism. I have recently learned that—because I have ADHD—it helps if someone is in the room with me while I declutter.

About five months ago, I had to stop working with the organizer because I needed to restructure my spending plan. In that time, things started to get cluttered again. At first, I thought it was because the organizer hadn't helped me. Then I realized I was the problem. I had no mechanism in place to maintain things—which has always been a big issue for me. Also, we originally talked about my decluttering on my own, which I had never made a regular habit. The other problem was I needed to be more stringent about what I kept and what I threw out. (This insight came to me while attending both of the CLA conventions.)

One thing I learned from the organizer is that it helps to sort things, like with like, so it is easier to go through them. I intend to put together plans for continuing my progress and for regular decluttering and maintenance. Another thing I am going to do is to start utilizing our wonderful new leaflet, "Measuring Progress on Our Journey in Recovery."[13] This will help me to understand the behaviors that undermine my progress and to learn what is helping. The most important thing to remember is that what is really guiding me in my decluttering is a power greater than myself and that the 12 Steps are the solution.

Glossary

7th Tradition—There are no dues or fees for membership; we are self-supporting through our own 7th Tradition contributions, neither soliciting nor accepting outside donations.

Clutter-Free Day—Day-long, regional recovery event that consists of CLA speakers, workshops, and fellowship

Convention—Two-day recovery event that consists of CLA speakers, panels, workshops, recovery meetings, fellowship, some meals, and entertainment

Declutterthon—Event that takes place on a Phone Activity Session phone line where clutterers share their decluttering actions. There may also be speakers, goal setting, progress reporting, etc.

Delegate—Elected group member who (1) serves as a liaison between his or her home group and WSO by communicating information between both and (2) represents the group's conscience at WSO

Executive Committee—The Executive Committee consists of WSO officers, committee chairpersons, and intergroup chairpersons. The purpose of the Executive Committee is to address specific concerns critical to the functioning of CLA.

Group Conscience—The group conscience is the collective conscience of the group membership and thus represents substantial unanimity on an issue before definitive action is taken.

Intergroup—Groupings of meetings in a limited geographical area or a group of telephone or special-interest meetings

Representative—Elected group member who (1) serves as a liaison between his or her home group and an intergroup by communicating information between both and (2) represents the group's conscience at the intergroup

WSO—World Service Organization. WSO is the CLA service body responsible for producing and mailing out literature; maintaining the CLA website; answering phone, email, and postal correspondence; support and communication among CLA groups; furthering communication among groups; and making decisions which affect the Fellowship as a whole. All CLA members may attend and participate in WSO General Meetings. Voting members include elected delegates from meetings, WSO officers, WSO committee chairpersons, and intergroup chairpersons.

Guidelines for Submission of Articles

Affirmations

(300-400 words)

Articles discussing a CLA Affirmation

CLA History

(200–400 words)

Articles relating to events in the history and development of CLA regarding any CLA individual or group, including face-to-face meetings and phone conference Fellowships

CLA Toolbox

(400–500 words)

Articles about using CLA-approved Tools, such as Telephone, Buddies, Bookending, etc. (Contact CLA*rity* staff before writing, since we wish to cover all the Tools before we repeat any.)

Event Articles

(150–350 words)

Major news items in CLA, especially conventions, Clutter-Free Days, and declutterthons

General Articles

(400–650 words)

Articles about CLA or cluttering issues not covered in the other sections, especially how the writer personally experienced ESH—experience, strength, and hope

Getting Into Action/Motivation Articles

(400-600 words)

Articles about experiences and methods for motivation toward recovery and on beginning and maintaining the process of decluttering

Group Stories

(400-500 words)

Articles about productive, creative, and successful practices in local groups

My Favorite Saying

(100-200 words)

Articles discussing a CLA slogan, prayer, or the like

News Flash

(Up to 50 words per item)

Brief announcements of CLA news, including upcoming events

Qualification

(500–700 words)

What it was like before, what you did to recover, and what it is like now

Recovery Moments

(200–400 words)

Short articles and anecdotes of personal recovery stories

Spotlight on Service

(200–300 words)

Articles about service opportunities as applied to CLA and profiles of members doing service

Articles on Steps/Traditions

(400–500 words)

Articles sharing personal experience working any of the 12 Steps and 12 Traditions of CLA

Let us know if you wish to be listed as the article's author (with first name, last initial, and state of residence) or whether you wish to be anonymous. We honor program Traditions. Due to our Traditions, and to avoid copyright infringement, we cannot print material collected from the news media—whether newspapers, magazines, television, film, or other sources; we do not publish or reprint material written by any person who is not a member of CLA.

We reserve the right to edit submissions, as well as titles—although we try to keep what the author said. Submissions near deadline may not allow time for communicating with the author. Include a contact number in case we need to speak with you. The submissions deadline for the spring issue is January 4; summer issue, April 4; fall issue, July 4; and holiday issue, October 4. No submissions to CLA*rity* will be returned; do not send original manuscripts, art, photos, etc. Guidelines for each type of article are listed above. We reserve the right to modify or change submission guidelines without notice to meet the needs of the publication.

If you are uneasy about writing an article, contact CLA*rity*; we will interview you and help you with the article.

Contact CLA*rity* for details: CLArity@ClutterersAnonymous.org or visit ClutterersAnonymous.org.

Bibliography

1—*A.A. Comes of Age*, 1957

2—"A.A. Grapevine, Inc." Alcoholics Anonymous, 1948, 1958

3—*A.A. Service Manual*, Alcoholics Anonymous World Services, Inc., 2016

4—*Alcoholics Anonymous,* 4th Edition, Alcoholics Anonymous World Services, Inc., 2001 (also known as "The Big Book")

5—"A Brief Guide," Clutterers Anonymous, 2011

6—*Came to Believe*, Alcoholics Anonymou

7—"CLA Meeting Starter Kit," Clutterers Anonymous, 2016

8—"Decluttering Resentment: Steps 4–10," Clutterers Anonymous, 2009

9— "Declutter Your Mind," Clutterers Anonymous, 2011

10—"Finding Your Life Purpose," Clutterers Anonymous, 2009

11—"Home: Our Sacred Place," Clutterers Anonymous, 2009

12—"Is CLA for You? A Newcomer's Guide to Recovery," Clutterers Anonymous, 2011

13—"Measuring Progress on Out Journey in Recovery," Clutterers Anonymous, 2015

14—"Recovery from Cluttering: The 12 Steps of Clutterers Anonymous," Clutterers Anonymous, 2009

15—"Spiritual Timing," Clutterers Anonymous, 2009

16—*Twelve Stepss and Twelve Traditions* (also known as "Twelve and Twelve"), Alcoholics Anonymous, 1981

17—"Twelve Concepts of Service," Alcoholics Anonymous World Services, Inc.

18—"Welcome," Clutterers Anonymous, 2009

Note:

Some items mentioned in the articles are not individual titles, but they occur in other publications as indicated below.

19—"CLA Tools of Recovery" can be found in the leaflet "A Brief Guide," the booklet, "Is CLA for You? A Newcomer's Guide to Recovery," and the "CLA Meeting Starter Kit."

20—"Recovery Affirmations" can be found in the booklet, "Is CLA for You? A Newcomer's Guide to Recovery," and the "CLA Meeting Starter Kit."

21—"Recovery Slogans" can be found in the booklet, "Is CLA for You? A Newcomer's Guide to Recovery," and the "CLA Meeting Starter Kit."

22— "What Is Clutter?" can be found in the leaflet, "Recovery from Cluttering: The 12 Steps of Clutterers Anonymous" and the "CLA Meeting Starter Kit."

23—"Am I a Clutterer?" can be found in the leaflet "Welcome," the booklet, "Is CLA for You? A Newcomer's Guide to Recovery," and the "CLA Meeting Starter Kit."

Index